EPTW

Educational Programs That Work

The Catalogue of the National Diffusion Network (NDN)

"Linking the Nation
With Excellence"

21ST Edition, 1995

Educational Programs That Work (EPTW) was written largely by the staffs of the programs described, without whose cooperation the program outlines could not have been produced.

Copies can be purchased for $14.95 plus $3.50 shipping/handling (first copy only, $1.50 for each additional copy) from **Sopris West, 1140 Boston Avenue, Longmont, Colorado 80501, (800) 547-6747. An order form for additional copies of** *EPTW* **is included at the back of this volume. Payment or purchase order must accompany order. Nonexempt Colorado residents should add sales tax.**

ISBN #1-57035-038-8

Edited by Gay Lang, Venture Publishing
Cover design by Londerville Design

Published and Distributed by:

Sopris West
1140 Boston Avenue • Longmont, Colorado 80501 • (303) 651-2829

in cooperation with:

NDA
National Dissemination Association
4732 North Oracle Road, Suite 217 • Tucson, Arizona 85705 • (602) 888-2838

national diffusion network

555 New Jersey Avenue, N.W. • Washington, D.C. 20208 • (202) 219-2134

Table of Contents

FOREWORD

The passage of the Goals 2000: Educate America Act in 1994 opened a new frontier of opportunities for states and local education agencies to improve the teaching and learning of all children. Under this landmark legislation, more than 40 states have already applied to the U.S. Department of Education for funding to develop long-range improvement plans with systemic reform strategies promoting change at the local level. Central to this concept of systemic reform of education is coordinated change in the whole education system - particularly with respect to high standards for all students, content-rich curriculum, performance assessment, and professional development for teachers.

This message of change in American education implies a need for innovative education programs that work and for trained assistance in making sure that bright ideas are easily adapted by teachers and students. The U.S. Department of Education's National Diffusion Network (NDN) assists public and private educational institutions in sharing exemplary programs, products, and processes.

Two things distinguish the NDN as a dissemination system: a rigorous procedure for validating the effectiveness of educational programs and a person-to-person support system to assist teachers using NDN programs. The Department's Program Effectiveness Panel judges the evidence of program effectiveness and admits projects to the NDN. What makes the spread of these programs so compelling is NDN's person-to-person dissemination system implemented by state facilitators, program developers, and locally based certified trainers.

There are nineteen new programs in the NDN this year with topics ranging from comprehensive technology planning for schools to a new model for teaching and learning electricity to literacy and more. These new programs along with the other NDN programs described in this directory strive to sustain the imagination required by good ideas, to refresh the research contributing to those ideas, and to deepen the discussion with teachers using NDN programs.

Luna Levinson

Luna Levinson
Acting Director
National Diffusion Network

National Dissemination Association

The National Dissemination Association is a community of educators dedicated to the improvement of American education through the identification, transfer, and implementation of proven educational systems, practices, and products. The NDA works toward this end by promoting educational dissemination, providing networking opportunities among those involved in dissemination, representing the interests of professional disseminators to national educational decision makers and offering professional development seminars and workshops.

The National Diffusion Network is the only national educational dissemination system in the country. It offers the schools of the United States proven programs that have demonstrated their effectiveness in improving student performance, lend themselves to use in a variety of educational settings and are reasonable in cost. The NDN also offers technical assistance to schools in identifying needs, matching programs to needs, and developing effective school improvement strategies using NDN programs and other resources of the United States Department of Education.

The National Dissemination Association recommends the programs of the NDN as resources to the schools and supports the efforts of the Department of Education to broaden its offerings, coordinate Department services, and focus on long-term, comprehensive school improvement efforts. The NDN has a long track record for providing high quality staff development services and curricular materials. It continues to be a most valuable resource to the schools of the nation.

We invite all those interested in educational dissemination as a school improvement strategy to join our professional community. Membership applications can be obtained by writing or calling our office in Tucson.

[signature]

C. Lynwood Erb, Ph.D.
President, Board of Directors
National Dissemination Association

EXECUTIVE DIRECTOR

Max McConkey
4732 North Oracle Road
Suite 217
Tucson, Arizona 85705
602/888-2838
Fax 602/888-2621

Introduction

The National Diffusion Network and Sopris West are pleased to present the twenty-first edition of *Educational Programs That Work*, the annual National Diffusion Network catalogue of exemplary educational programs. The catalogue includes current descriptions of most programs described in previous editions as well as new programs approved for national dissemination since publication of the twentieth edition in 1994.

The National Diffusion Network (NDN) is a dynamic organization designed to improve educational opportunities and achievement for all by promoting the transfer of successful programs from their development sites to other educational institutions. It is based upon the belief that effective programs and practices should be disseminated widely so that they can benefit schools across the country. By identifying effective programs, the NDN provides education agencies with an array of NDN offerings from which to select those that best meet their needs, philosophies, and resources. The NDN also helps them to acquire the materials and assistance needed to install NDN programs.

NDN programs are suited to improve curriculum and instruction, to meet the needs of special student populations, and to foster systemic reforms. The programs address all of the National Goals for Education. The relationship between each program and the National Goals for Education (which are printed on pages 5-7) is identified at the beginning of each section of this catalogue in a grid summarizing program services.

Since its inception in 1974, the NDN has grown from 76 to more than 200 programs that were developed, in large part, by classroom teachers. NDN programs have helped learners with many different needs—preschoolers with disabilities, low-income, inner-city children in primary grades, high-achieving high school students, and out-of-school adults. NDN programs span many fields, ranging from core content areas such as reading, mathematics, and science to health, vocational, and career education. Other programs focus on cognitive skills, classroom management, and school-wide reform. Adopters of NDN programs range from small classrooms in remote rural areas to large metropolitan districts.

The impact of the NDN on American education has been tremendous. The most recent statistics available indicate that in the 1992-93 school year alone, more than 35,500 public and private schools in all 50 states, the District of Columbia, Puerto Rico, Virgin Islands, Guam, American Samoa, Palau, and the Commonwealth of Northern Mariana Islands adopted NDN programs. As a result, over 141,000 persons received inservice training, and an estimated 6.3 million students benefited.

Entry into the NDN occurs only after a program has been approved by the Department of Education's Program Effectiveness Panel (PEP) (formerly the Joint Dissemination Review Panel, or JDRP). Program developers must submit to the Panel evidence of effectiveness in meeting program objectives and evidence that the program will meet the educational needs of others in similar settings. Positive endorsement of a program's claims of effectiveness by a majority of Panel members constitutes approval, and a validation date is assigned.

Once approved by the PEP, programs are eligible to compete for funds under the program category Developer Demonstrators. Developer Demonstrators are exemplary programs that provide training, materials, and technical assistance to those who adopt their programs. In addition, the NDN funds Facilitators (one in every State, D.C., Puerto Rico, and the Trust Territories, as well as a Private School Facilitator) who link NDN exemplary programs with educators who are seeking new programs and practices. Facilitators help to identify suitable NDN programs and assist with training and installation.

For further information about the Program Effectiveness Panel (PEP), contact the National Diffusion Network, 555 New Jersey Avenue, Washington, D.C. 20208-5645. (202) 219-2134.

National Goals for Education

GOAL 1: SCHOOL READINESS

By the year 2000, all children in American will start school ready to learn.

OBJECTIVES:

- All children will have access to high-quality and developmentally appropriate preschool programs that help prepare children for school.
- Every parent in the United States will be a child's first teacher and devote time each day to helping such parent's preschool child learn, and parents will have access to the training and support parents need.
- Children will receive the nutrition, physical activity experiences, and health care needed to arrive at school with healthy minds and bodies, and to maintain the mental alertness necessary to be prepared to learn, and the number of low-birthweight babies will be significantly reduced through enhanced prenatal health systems.

GOAL 2: SCHOOL COMPLETION

By the year 2000, the high school graduation rate will increase to at least 90 percent.

OBJECTIVES:

- The Nation must dramatically reduce its school dropout rate, and 75 percent of the students who drop out will successfully complete a high school degree or its equivalent.
- The gap in high school graduation rates between American students from minority backgrounds and their nonminority counterparts will be eliminated.

GOAL 3: STUDENT ACHIEVEMENT AND CITIZENSHIP

By the year 2000, all students will leave grades 4, 8, and 12 having demonstrated competency in challenging subject matter including English, mathematics, science, foreign languages, civics and government, economics, arts, history, and geography, and every school in America will ensure that all students learn to use their minds well, so they may be prepared for responsible citizenship, further learning, and productive employment in our Nation's modern economy.

OBJECTIVES:

- The academic performance of all students of the elementary and secondary level will increase significantly in every quartile, and the distribution of minority students in each quartile will more closely reflect the student population as a whole.
- The percentage of all students who demonstrate the ability to reason, solve problems, apply knowledge, and write and communicate effectively will increase substantially.
- All students will be involved in activities that promote and demonstrate good citizenship, good health, community service, and personal responsibility.
- All students will have access to physical education and health education to ensure they are healthy and fit.
- The percentage of all students who are competent in more than one language will substantially increase.
- All students will be knowledgeable about the diverse cultural heritage of this Nation and about the world community.

GOAL 4: TEACHER EDUCATION AND PROFESSIONAL DEVELOPMENT

By the year 2000, the Nation's teaching force will have access to programs for the continued improvement of their professional skills and the opportunity to acquire the knowledge and skills needed to instruct and prepare all American students for the next century.

OBJECTIVES:

- All teachers will have access to preservice teacher education and continuing professional development activities that will provide such teachers with the knowledge and skills needed to teach to an increasingly diverse student population with a variety of educational, social, and health needs.

- All teachers will have continuing opportunities to acquire additional knowledge and skills needed to teach challenging subject matter and to use emerging new methods, forms of assessment, and technologies.

- States and school districts will create integrated strategies to attract, recruit, prepare, retrain, and support the continued professional development of teachers, administrators, and other educators, so that there is a highly talented work force of professional educators to teach challenging subject matter.

- Partnerships will be established, whenever possible, among local educational agencies, institutions of higher education, parents, and local labor, business, and professional associations to provide support programs for the professional development of educators.

GOAL 5: MATHEMATICS AND SCIENCE

By the year 2000, United States students will be first in the world in mathematics and science achievement.

OBJECTIVES:

- Mathematics and science education, including the metric system of measurement, will be strengthened throughout the system, especially in the early grades.

- The number of teachers with a substantive background in mathematics and science, including the metric system of measurement, will increase by 50 percent.

- The number of United States undergraduate and graduate students, especially women and minorities, who complete degrees in mathematics, science, and engineering will increase significantly.

GOAL 6: ADULT LITERACY AND LIFELONG LEARNING

By the year 2000, every adult American will be literate and will possess the knowledge and skills necessary to compete in a global economy and exercise the rights and responsibilities of citizenship.

OBJECTIVES:

- Every major American business will be involved in strengthening the connection between education and work.

- All workers will have the opportunity to acquire the knowledge and skills, from basic to highly technical, needed to adapt to emerging new technologies, work methods, and markets through public and private educational, vocational, technical, workplace, or other programs.

- The number of quality programs, including those of libraries, that are designed to serve more effectively the needs of the growing number of part-time and midcareer students will increase substantially.

- The proportion of the qualified students, especially minorities, who enter college, who complete at least two years, and who complete their degree programs will increase substantially.

- The proportion of college graduates who demonstrate an advanced ability to think critically, communicate effectively, and solve problems will increase substantially.

- Schools, in implementing comprehensive parent involvement programs, will offer more adult literacy, parent training, and life-long learning opportunities to improve the ties between home and school, and enhance parents' work and home lives.

GOAL 7: SAFE, DISCIPLINED, AND ALCOHOL- AND DRUG-FREE SCHOOLS

By the year 2000, every school in the United States will be free of drugs, violence, and the unauthorized presence of firearms and alcohol, and will offer a disciplined environment conducive to learning.

OBJECTIVES:

- Every school will implement a firm and fair policy on use, possession, and distribution of drugs and alcohol.
- Parents, businesses, governmental and community organizations will work together to ensure the rights of students to study in a safe and secure environment that is free of drugs and crime, and that schools provide a healthy environment and are a safe haven for all children.
- Every local educational agency will develop and implement a policy to ensure that all schools are free of violence and the unauthorized presence of weapons.
- Every local educational agency will develop a sequential, comprehensive kindergarten through twelfth grade drug and alcohol prevention education program.
- Drug and alcohol curriculum should be taught as an integral part of sequential, comprehensive health education.
- Community-based teams should be organized to provide students and teachers with needed support.
- Every school should work to eliminate sexual harassment.

GOAL 8: PARENTAL PARTICIPATION

By the year 2000, every school will promote partnerships that will increase parental involvement and participation in promoting the social, emotional, and academic growth of children.

OBJECTIVES:

- Every state will develop policies to assist local schools and local educational agencies to establish programs for increasing partnerships that respond to the varying needs of parents and the home, including parents of children who are disadvantaged or bilingual, or parents of children with disabilities.
- Every school will actively engage parents and families in a partnership which supports the academic work of children at home and shared educational decision making at school.
- Parents and families will help to ensure that schools are adequately supported and will hold schools and teachers to high standards of accountability.

Questions and Answers About *EPTW*

The series of questions and answers that follow will help you to become more familiar with this edition of *Educational Programs That Work*. A few minutes spent reviewing these questions and answers will enable you to appreciate its full potential.

Q. **What is the purpose of *Educational Programs That Work*?**

A. *Educational Programs That Work* is an overview of all educational programs approved for national dissemination by the Department of Education (PEP/JDRP). It provides basic information on exemplary products and practices to those who wish to improve their educational programs and services. The catalogue introduces the National Diffusion Network (NDN), its Facilitators, Developer Demonstrators, and Dissemination Processes, and their services to schools, institutions and other agencies that may wish to adopt these programs.

Q. **What is contained in *Educational Programs That Work*?**

A. *Educational Programs That Work* describes programs approved by the PEP/JDRP since its inception in 1974. Programs fall into three categories: active programs, programs with limited activity, and programs with services no longer available. Active programs constitute by far the largest group. A one-page program profile for each active program is included in this edition. A half-page profile is devoted to each limited activity program, while "Approved Programs That Are No Longer Available" can be referenced in list form in Section 16 of the catalogue. Some programs are currently receiving dissemination funds from the NDN to assist them in providing services to schools and colleges across the nation. These programs are identified by an asterisk in the section-divider listings.

Q. **How are these programs approved?**

A. The term "exemplary program" is conferred only after a program has been approved by the Department of Education (either the Joint Dissemination Review Panel [JDRP][1] or the Program Effectiveness Panel [PEP]). Approval by the Panel means that Panel members have examined objective evidence of effectiveness submitted by the developer of the program and are convinced that the program has met its stated objectives at the original development or demonstration site. In addition, the program developer has proved that the program will meet the educational needs of others in similar locations.

---

1 The JDRP underwent reorganization and a name change. The new name of the review panel is the Program Effectiveness Panel (PEP). The titles JDRP and PEP are both used throughout this document. If JDRP is used, it means that the program was approved for dissemination prior to 1987. PEP approval means approval during or after 1987.

Positive endorsement of a program's claims of effectiveness by a majority of the attending Panel members constitutes approval, and a date of validation is assigned. The PEP/JDRP number and approval date for each program can be found at the bottom of each program profile. Programs that continue development and submit additional evidence of effectiveness to the Panel carry two validation dates. In addition, some programs over six years old which have undergone the recertification process are identified at the bottom of the page with a recertification date.

Q. How is *Educational Programs That Work* organized?

A. The active programs are divided into 15 sections, and then arranged alphabetically by program title. Each section groups programs with a common focus. The sections are as follows:

Section 1: Preservice/Inservice Training
Section 2: Organizational Reform
Section 3: Dropout Prevention/Alternative Programs
Section 4: Reading/Writing
Section 5: Humanities
Section 6: Mathematics
Section 7: Science/Technology
Section 8: Social Sciences
Section 9: Health/Physical Education
Section 10: Multidisciplinary/Cognitive Skills
Section 11: Early Childhood/Parent Involvement
Section 12: Special Education
Section 13: Gifted/Talented
Section 14: Special Populations: Adult/Higher/Migrant Education
Section 15: Career/Vocational Education

Q. How can I locate a description for a given program if I know only the name of the program?

A. The alphabetical index (Section 17, Index III) lists all programs by title.

Q. How can I locate programs for a given content or problem area?

A. To help you locate programs for a given area, selected ERIC (Educational Resources Information Center) descriptors have been assigned to all active programs described in the catalogue. These descriptors serve as headings for the alphabetical ERIC descriptors index (Section 17, Index II).

Q. How can I find a description for a given program if I know only the state in which it is located?

A. The index of exemplary programs by state (Section 17, Index I) lists all programs by the state in which they are located.

Q. How can I make a quick preliminary review of the programs in each section?

A. A capsule phrase that summarizes the exemplary program follows each program title. See page 1-1, for example: the first entry, Active Teaching and Learning (ATaL), is described as "A staff development process aimed at improving teachers' classroom management and instructional skills. Active Teaching and Learning also aims to increase the time students spend on academic tasks, and therefore, increase student achievement."

Q. If I have last year's edition of *Educational Programs That Work*, how can I determine what new programs have been added?

A. Programs approved by the PEP since the publication of Edition 20 are listed on pages 13-14.

Q. If I want additional information, such as details on costs of installing an NDN program in my school, how do I obtain it?

A. All entries include the name of a contact person who can answer questions about the program. A mailing address and a telephone number are included in the contact statement. NDN State Facilitators can also provide detailed information.

Q. How can I receive more information about the NDN?

A. Contact your state or regional NDN Facilitator to learn more about the NDN and its programs. A description of the Facilitator's role and a list of Facilitators follow. You may also contact the federal office that administers the National Diffusion Network:

> National Diffusion Network
> Recognition Division
> U.S. Department of Education
> OERI/PIP/Recognition Division
> 555 New Jersey Avenue, N.W.
> Washington, D.C. 20208-5645
> (202) 219-2134

Approved Programs

Since the Publication of Edition 20

Attainment of Algebra I Skills: Cord Applied Mathematics 1 and 2   6-1

A two-year secondary student program providing an alternative classroom experience to traditional Algebra I by offering to the student who learns best in a contextual manner real-life and workplace applications through hands-on activities.

Capacitor-Aided System for Teaching and Learning Electricity (CASTLE)   7-1

An innovative instructional module for use in high schools that can replace the electricity portion of any course for beginning physics students. Its instructional approach is an investigative, model-building mode of learning.

Davis County Indian Homework Centers Program (IHC)   10-7

A tutoring program to increase the achievement scores of Indian students in the Davis County (Utah) School District.

Early Intervention for School Success (EISS)   11-1

A program to provide teachers, support staff, and parents with basic knowledge of child growth and development and basic strategies for application in the kindergarten classroom.

Enriching a Child's Literacy Environment (ECLE)   11-2

A program of classroom and home instruction for teaching parents, teachers, and other care providers to develop oral language, thinking abilities, and motor skills in young children.

Family Intergenerational-Interaction Literacy Model (FILM)   11-3

A family literacy program that works with all family members to increase the educational level of disadvantaged parents and children.

Lab School of Washington, The (LSW)   12-3

A program designed to offer comprehensive educational services that meet the needs of learning disabled individuals preschool through young adult.

Literacy Links (formerly Reading Education Accountability Design: Secondary [READ:S])   10-10

A performance-based reading education model which helps to overcome student reading deficiencies and improve achievement in reading and content subjects.

Maneuvers With Mathematics Project (MWM)   6-6

An innovative, calculator-intensive mathematics program for the middle grades.

Multicultural Literacy Program (MLP) 4-9

A program designed to be integrated with the reading and writing curriculum for students in grades 3-6.

Program for Access to Science Study (PASS) 7-16

A program designed to enable underprepared college students to pass introductory science courses.

Questioning and Understanding to Improve Learning and Thinking (QUILT) 10-13

A program designed to increase and sustain teacher use of classroom questioning techniques and procedures that produce higher levels of student learning and thinking.

SCORE for College (SCORE) 3-5

A comprehensive co-curricular support program that brings together administrators, counselors, teachers, parents, and students to increase student performance and eligibility.

SEED, Project 6-9

A program designed to increase the number of students in grades 4-6 from low-income backgrounds who will graduate from high school with skills required for jobs, careers, further education, and leadership in a technological society.

SPARK: Sports, Play, and Active Recreation for Kids 9-6

A comprehensive physical education program designed to help teachers improve the physical activity, fitness, and movement skills of children in grades 3-6.

Success Understanding Mathematics (SUM) 6-12

A program designed to increase mathematical achievement of elementary school children through improved teaching practices.

Systemic Technology Planning to Support Education Reform (STPSER) 2-5

A program to assist school districts in planning for the comprehensive technology infrastructure needed to implement educational reform programs.

Tech Prep Program 15-5

A program designed to enable secondary students to complete higher-level academic and technical/vocational course sequences.

Webster Groves Even Start Program 11-10

A program that links parenting education, adult basic education, and early childhood education through a single site family learning center and home-based instruction.

Youth Transition Program (YTP) 12-9

An interagency, collaborative service delivery model designed to improve school to work transition outcomes for students with disabilities.

National Diffusion Network (NDN) State Facilitators

To help public and private schools and districts identify suitable National Diffusion Network programs, the U.S. Department of Education, federal sponsor of the NDN, supports Facilitator projects in every state, the District of Columbia, the Virgin Islands, Puerto Rico, Guam, American Samoa, Northern Mariana Islands, and Palau.

Facilitators work with schools and institutions to define their problems, determine which NDN programs hold promise for solving those problems, and help with formal adoption of NDN programs. Facilitators can supply additional information on all of the programs described in this catalogue, and they can arrange for demonstrations. When a school or institution decides to adopt an NDN program, Facilitators can make arrangements for training. Many facilitators also provide follow-up and perform or oversee monitoring and evaluation at adopter sites.

NDN Facilitators are based in local school districts, intermediate service agencies, state education agencies, and private nonprofit organizations. The funds that Facilitators can draw on vary from state to state, and their funding policies vary as well. In some states, schools and districts that adopt NDN programs can be reimbursed by the Facilitator for such start-up costs as instructional materials and teacher training. In other states, the costs of travel to awareness conferences or demonstration sites can be covered by the Facilitator. Readers are encouraged to telephone or visit their NDN Facilitators to learn what services are available.

ALABAMA

Alabama Facilitator Project
Alabama Department of Education
Division of Instructional Services
50 North Ripley
Room 5103, Gordon Persons Building
Montgomery, AL 36104-3833
(205) 242-8176
FAX (205) 242-9708
E-Mail: jautrey@inet.ed.gov

Principal Staff Members

Jacquelyn C. Autrey

Office Hours

8:00 A.M.—5:00 P.M. (M-F)

Host Agency

Alabama State Department of Education

HIGHLIGHTS:

The primary goal of the Alabama Facilitator project is to assist public and private schools in determining the best match with the school's needs and available NDN programs. The State Facilitator (SF) disseminates information and arranges awareness and training sessions that lead to adoptions. The SF also cooperates and collaborates with the 11 regional inservice centers, educational labs and other state agencies to deliver programs in a cost effective manner. Location of the National Diffusion Network in the office of Professional Development allows for sustained, wide-spread, and effective delivery of training and adoptions.

ALASKA

Alaska State Facilitator
Alaska State Department of Education
801 West 10th Street, Suite 200
Juneau, AK 99801-1894
(907) 465-8723
FAX (907) 465-3396
E-Mail: sberry@inet.ed.gov

Principal Staff Members

Sandra Berry

Office Hours

7:00 A.M.—3:30 P.M. (M-F)

Host Agency

Alaska Department of Education

HIGHLIGHTS:

Services of the State Facilitator are provided at no cost to the school district. Technical assistance is made available in identifying exemplary NDN programs which meet a need in schools. Limited funds are available for training. Statewide training is made available at pre-conferences throughout the year.

AMERICAN SAMOA

NDN Facilitator
P.O. Box 1132
Pago Pago, AS 96799
011 (684) 633-1246
D.C. Office (202) 225-8577
FAX 011 (684) 633-5184
E-Mail: sstevens@inet.ed.gov

Principal Staff Members

Sharon Stevenson, NDN
Facilitator

Office Hours

7:30 A.M.—4:00 P.M. (M-F)
• 7 hours behind Eastern Time

Host Agency

American Samoa Department of
Education

HIGHLIGHTS:

First funded in 1989, services at present include for both public and private schools:

- Providing information about all NDN projects;
- *EPTW* to all schools and education divisions in the territory;
- Yearly awareness conference;
- Resource center of D/D materials at DCI and Teachers' Resource Center;
- Summer training conference for selected D/D; and
- Programs to develop certified trainers.

Eventual expansion to include:

- Disseminating ERIC, Regional Laboratory, and R&D research.

If you should need any more information, please feel free to call.

ARIZONA

Arizona State Facilitator
Educational Diffusion Systems, Inc.
161 East First Street
Mesa, AZ 85201
(602) 969-4880
FAX (602) 898-8527
E-Mail: lwebb@inet.ed.gov

Principal Staff Members

L. Leon Webb, Pat Solem,
Bob Webb, Lois Petersen

Office Hours

8:00 A.M.—5:00 P.M. (M-F)

Host Agency

Educational Diffusion Systems,
Inc.
• A nonprofit organization

HIGHLIGHTS:

The Arizona State Facilitator is committed to working in cooperation with educators in order to respond effectively to student needs. Math, reading, early childhood education, language arts/writing, science, and migrant/bilingual education have been determined to be the top six (6) priority areas in which assistance is needed. Linkages with NDN projects throughout the nation will allow the Arizona State Facilitator to provide comprehensive services to potential and actual adopting agencies within the state.

ARKANSAS

Arkansas State Facilitator Project
Arkansas Department of Education
Arch Ford Education Building, Room 203B
#4 State Capitol Mall
Little Rock, AR 72201
(501) 682-4568
FAX (501) 682-5010
E-Mail: jcheek@inet.ed.gov

Principal Staff Members

Jo Cheek, State Facilitator
Glenda Evans, Secretary

Office Hours

8:00 A.M.—4:30 P.M.

Host Agency

State Department of Education

HIGHLIGHTS:

The Arkansas Facilitator Project coordinates awareness information, training, and follow-up assistance to Arkansas public and private schools indicating an interest in exploring and/or adopting NDN programs. Technical assistance is offered in identifying programs appropriate for individual needs. Awareness sessions are coordinated with statewide conferences. Funding assistance for program implementation is available on a limited basis in the form of mini-grants.

CALIFORNIA

California State Facilitator Center
1575 Old Bayshore Highway
Burlingame, CA 94010
(415) 692-2956
In State (800) 672-3494
FAX (415) 692-6858

Principal Staff Members

Lisa Holladay, State Facilitator
Lynda Vaughan, Director

Office Hours

8:30 A.M.—5:00 P.M.

Host Agency

Association of California School Administrators, Foundation for Educational Administration

HIGHLIGHTS:

The California Facilitator Center collaborates with teachers and administrators to determine needs, provides information about available training, helps identify potential funding sources, maintains contact with schools during implementation, and provides follow-up support. The Center publishes a quarterly newsletter, NDN training schedules, and bulletins relating NDN programs to the state's curriculum frameworks. All the services of the Center are free. Training costs can be shared among local schools and districts, the individual participants, and the California Facilitator Center.

COLORADO

Colorado Facilitator Project
The Education Diffusion Group
3607 Martin Luther King Boulevard
Denver, CO 80205
(303) 322-9323
FAX (303) 322-9475
E-Mail: cbeck@inet.ed.gov

Principal Staff Members

Charles D. Beck, Jr., Director
Boyd Dressler, Associate
    Director
Barbara S. Kennedy,
    Assistant to Director
Catherine Felknor, Evaluation
    Consultant
Diana Franks,
    Administrative Assistant

Office Hours

8:00 A.M.—4:30 P.M. (M-F)

Host Agency

The Education Diffusion Group
    • A nonprofit corporation

HIGHLIGHTS:

The Colorado NDN Facilitator links public and private schools in the state with the approximately 300 exemplary, proven programs in the National Diffusion Network. We offer various kinds of awareness activities to apprise our schools of the NDN and its programs and coordinate training to begin the implementation/adoption process. The Facilitator and the NDN actively support America 2000/Colorado 2000. Each program is keyed to at least one of the six Goals.

Facilitator services continue to be free. Every district receives free at least one copy of this catalog. Copies are also available for other schools. Call our office. Sopris West can provide copies for a reasonable price. The facilitator freely cooperates with businesses and a variety of education agencies, such as McREL and the State Education Department.

CONNECTICUT

Connecticut Facilitator Project
RESCUE Education Service Center
355 Goshen Road
P.O. Box 909
Litchfield, CT 06759- 0909
(203) 567-0863
FAX (203) 567-3381
E-Mail: jcosta@inet.ed.gov

Principal Staff Members

Jonathan P. Costa, Director

Office Hours

8:30 A.M.—4:30 P.M. (M-F)

Host Agency

Nonprofit Regional Service
    Center

HIGHLIGHTS:

The Connecticut Facilitator Project is committed to working with schools to provide them with the skills they need to accurately assess their own instructional improvement needs. By using its own Adoption Process Model, the CFP is able to guide school staff through program selection, adoption, and effectiveness evaluation. Our goal is to enable local professionals to make the most of the exemplary programs in the National Diffusion Network.

DELAWARE

State Facilitator Project
Department of Public Instruction
John G. Townsend Building
Lockerman and Federal Streets
P.O. Box 1402
Dover, DE 19903-1402
(302) 739-4670
FAX (302) 739-4483
E-Mail: lwelsh@inet.ed.gov

Principal Staff Members

> Linda Y. Welsh,
>   State Facilitator
> Maria Degnats,
>   Secretary

Office Hours

> 8:00 A.M.—4:30 P.M. (M-F)

Host Agency

> State Department of Public
> Instruction

HIGHLIGHTS:

The Delaware Facilitator Center serves as a resource for information about effective low-cost programs that support the implementation of "New Directions for Education in Delaware." A newsletter, which contains information about National Diffusion Network activities, is distributed quarterly to all schools statewide. A video library is also maintained for use by educational staff. Professional development workshops and limited financial assistance are available through the Project.

DISTRICT OF COLUMBIA

District Facilitator Project
Rabaut Administrative Unit
North Dakota & Kansas Avenues, N.W.
Washington, D.C. 20011
(202) 576-6174
FAX (202) 576-6178
E-Mail: swilliam@inet.ed.gov

Principal Staff Members

> Susan C. Williams,
>   Project Director
> JoAnne Ginsberg, Project Manager
> Christine Curtis, Secretary

Office Hours

> 8:00 A.M.—4:30 P.M. (M-F)

Host Agency

> District of Columbia Public
> Schools

HIGHLIGHTS:

The District Facilitator Project (DFP) provides information on and organizes pre-implementation training and follow-up assistance for National Diffusion Network programs of interest to public and private schools in Washington, D.C. The DFP is particularly active working with public schools undergoing school-wide restructuring efforts through the adoption of validated restructuring programs or by bundling NDN programs to support systemic change. Further, the DFP works closely with the Chapter 1 LEA program to assist with school-wide improvement and program improvement goals that could be met through the adoption of an NDN program. Programs that support instructional improvement for urban learners that tap students' unrecognized intellectual abilities and recognize multiple intelligences of students are priorities for the 1995-96 school year.

FLORIDA

State Facilitator Project
Florida Department of Education
Division of Public Schools
School Improvement Resource Center
325 West Gaines Street, Suite 424
Tallahassee, FL 32399-0400
(904) 487-1078
Voice Mail (24 Hours) (904) 487-6247
FAX (904) 487-0716
E-Mail: jbishop@inet.ed.gov

Principal Staff Members

Judy Bishop, Director
Jan Schaeffler, Research Assistant

Office Hours

8:00 A.M.—5:00 P.M. (M-F)

Host Agency

Florida Department of Education

HIGHLIGHTS:

The State's major education initiative for the 1990s is the implementation of the School Improvement and Accountability Program. This program requires schools to work collaboratively with representatives of the faculty, parents, and community to develop and implement a school improvement plan consistent with national, state, and local goals. Incentive funding is provided for the planning and implementation of the plan.

The Florida State Facilitator Project is housed in the School Improvement Resource Center, Bureau of School Improvement and Instruction, Florida Department of Education, and serves as a source of exemplary programs and practices for schools. The State NDN Facilitator works with the Department's School Improvement Facilitators and with other state networks to target NDN programs to meet specific school needs.

GEORGIA

Georgia State Facilitator Center
124 Aderhold Hall
University of Georgia
Athens, GA 30602
(706) 542-3332 *or* 542-2516
FAX (706) 542-2502
E-Mail: fhensley@moe.coe.uga.edu *or*
            fhensley@inet.ed.gov

Principal Staff Members

Dr. Frances Hensley, Director
Dr. Dale Rogers, Assistant Director

Office Hours

8:00 A.M.—5:00 P.M. (M-F)

Host Agency

The University of Georgia

HIGHLIGHTS:

The Georgia Facilitator Center serves as a source of information and materials on exemplary programs and practices and provides assistance to schools in determining the best match between the school's needs and available NDN programs. The Center collaborates with local and regional educational agencies for the delivery of training, follow-up, and ongoing assistance; works with special program initiatives for school reform at the University of Georgia; and facilitates development of user groups to support implementation.

GUAM

Guam Department of Education
Federal Program Office
P.O. Box DE
Agana, Guam 96910
011 (671) 472-8524 *or* 472-5004 *or*
    472-8901, Ext. 321
D.C. Office (202) 225-1188
FAX 011 (671) 477-4587
E-Mail: mcamacho@inet.ed.gov

Principal Staff Members

Margaret A. Camacho,
    NDN Facilitator

Office Hours

8:00 A.M.—5:00 P.M. (M-F)

Host Agency

Guam Department of Education

HIGHLIGHTS:

The Guam State Facilitator Project disseminates to all public and private school education service providers information about the availability of exemplary education programs in the National Diffusion Network.

HAWAII

State Facilitator
Department of Education
Office of Information and
    Telecommunication Services
637 18th Avenue C-204
Honolulu, HI 96816
(808) 735-3107
FAX (808) 733-9147
E-Mail: mvierra@inet.ed.gov

Principal Staff Members

Dr. Mona Vierra, State Facilitator
Alma Nagao, Information
    Specialist I
Grace Masaki, Secretary

Office Hours

7:45 A.M.—4:30 P.M.

Host Agency

Hawaii State Department of
    Education, Office of
    Information and
    Telecommunication Services

HIGHLIGHTS:

The Hawaii State Department of Education's focus is on literacy, alternative assessment and school community based management. Funds are made available to support these initiatives and those deemed necessary based on a school-wide determination.

IDAHO

State Facilitator
Idaho State Department of Education
Len B. Jordan Office Building
Boise, ID 83720-3650
(208) 334-3561
FAX (208) 334-2228 or 334-2636
E-Mail: lyamamot@inet.ed.gov

Principal Staff Members

Lianne Yamamoto

Office Hours

8:00 A.M.—5:00 P.M. (M-F)

Host Agency

Idaho Department of Education

HIGHLIGHTS:

The Idaho State Facilitator Project (ISFP) is able to help Idaho schools meet restructuring priorities–chiefly the shift to performance-based education through the programs, practices, and products available in the NDN. Technical assistance, awareness materials including videotapes, in-person awareness sessions, and training arrangements are among the services provided free of charge. A partnership with western states facilitators and the Columbia Education Center continues to establish a cadre of local and regional trainers in a variety of programs, which are then available to small-town and rural schools. Forming linkages among other projects, agencies, and teacher education institutions is a strength of the ISFP. We also encourage the use of state-administered funds for implementing exemplary programs and provide assistance in identifying other funding sources.

ILLINOIS

Statewide Facilitator Center
1105 East Fifth Street
Metropolis, IL 62960
(618) 524-2664
FAX (618) 524-2004

Principal Staff Members

Nancy M. Waldrop, Director

Regional Directors

Judith Longfield, Bolingbrook
    (708) 759-5829
William Callahan, Oglesby
    (815) 883-3315
Jessie H. Sanders, Metropolis
    (618) 524-2664

Office Hours

8:00 A.M.—4:00 P.M. (M-F)

Host Agency

Educational Service Region
    • Intermediate agency

Faye J. Hughes, Superintendent
    • Monroe-Randolph Counties

HIGHLIGHTS:

Special initiatives include:

- Collaborating with Educational Service Regions (ESRs) and Educational Service Centers (ESCs) for the delivery of staff development;
- Establishing training in exemplary NDN programs in both urban and rural school districts.
- Providing technical assistance to school districts involved with school-wide reform efforts and;
- Cooperating with the Private-School Facilitator in working with private schools.

INDIANA

Indiana Facilitator Center
Educational Resource Brokers, Inc.
2635 Yeager Road, Suite D
West Lafayette, IN 47906
(317) 497-3269
FAX (317) 497-3461
E-Mail: cerb@inet.ed.gov

Principal Staff Members

C. Lynwood Erb, Director
Joan Kaye,
 Administrative Assistant

Office Hours

8:00 A.M.—4:00 P.M. (M-F)

Host Agency

Educational Resource
Brokers, Inc.

HIGHLIGHTS:

Assistance is provided to Indiana public and private (nonprofit) schools that wish to adopt NDN programs. Such assistance includes consultations to aid in the selection of programs to meet local needs and providing consultants for training workshops.

IOWA

Iowa Department of Education
Bureau of Planning, Research, and
 Evaluation
Grimes Building
East 14th Street and Grand Avenue
Des Moines, IA 50310-0146
(515) 281-3111
FAX (515) 242-5988
E-Mail: jharris@inet.ed.gov

Principal Staff Members

June Harris, State Facilitator
Eileen A. Becker, Secretary
 (half-time)

Office Hours

8:00 A.M.—4:30 P.M. (M-F)

Host Agency

Iowa Department of Education

HIGHLIGHTS:

The State Facilitator at the Iowa Department of Education collaborates with the Area Education Agencies and the local districts to provide staff development opportunities focused on systemic change, supporting curriculum evolvement, increasing instruction in higher order thinking, and enabling students to function in a multicultural environment. The State Facilitator functions as a conduit to bring programs or projects in contact with the Area Education Agencies and appropriate districts with an identified need. The State Facilitator also works collaboratively with other educational associations and organizations in the ongoing school improvement efforts in Iowa. When available, the State Facilitator provides monetary contributions in coordination with Area Education Agency funds, district contributions, and workshop participant fees to implement adoptions of appropriate projects and programs.

KANSAS

Kansas State Facilitator
KEDDS/LINK
Instructional Support Center
412-18 South Main
Wichita, KS 67202
(316) 833-5100
FAX (316) 833-5103
E-Mail: evernon@inet.ed.gov

Principal Staff Members

Ernestine Vernon, Director
Nakita Vance, Facilitator Staff
Patricia Holt, Secretary

Office Hours

8:00 A.M.—4:30 P.M. (M-F)

Host Agency

Wichita Public Schools #259

HIGHLIGHTS:

The Kansas State Facilitator delivers awareness, training, and follow-up three ways—face-to-face traditional method, satellite delivered video NDN broadcasts, and video tapes on a loaner basis—upon request to Kansas Educational Service Providers. The NDN *Educational Programs That Work* and *NDN Satellite Video Broadcasts* catalogues are provided to Kansas Educational Service Providers. Technical assistance is available for staff development inservices on a cost-sharing basis to Kansas Educational Service Providers.

KENTUCKY

Kentucky State Facilitator Project
Kentucky Department of Education
1722 Capitol Plaza Tower
500 Mero Street
Frankfort, KY 40601
(502) 564-2672
FAX (502) 564-6952
E-Mail: jstevens@inet.ed.gov

Principal Staff Members

Janet Stevens, Project Director

Office Hours

7:30 A.M.—4:00 P.M. (M-F)

Host Agency

Kentucky Department of
Education

HIGHLIGHTS:

The primary focus of the Kentucky State Facilitator is to assist public and nonpublic Local Education Agencies throughout the state in selecting, implementing, and maintaining exemplary NDN programs which meet the educational goals and academic expectations specified by the Kentucky Education Reform Act of 1990.

LOUISIANA

State Facilitator Project
State Department of Education
Consolidated Educational Programs
626 North 4th Street, 3rd Floor
P.O. Box 94064
Baton Rouge, LA 70804-9064
(504) 342-3375
FAX (504) 342-7367
E-Mail: bargo@inet.ed.gov

Principal Staff Members

Brenda Argo, Director

Office Hours

7:30 A.M.—4:00 P.M.

Host Agency

Louisiana Department of
Education

HIGHLIGHTS:

This project offers assistance to schools and school districts in identifying exemplary NDN programs to meet established needs. Particular emphasis is placed on the National Goals. Funding assistance for program implementation is available on a limited basis. Awareness sessions are coordinated with statewide conferences.

MAINE

Maine Facilitator Project
Maine Center for Educational Services
223 Main Street
P.O. Box 620
Auburn, ME 04212-0620
(207) 783-0833
FAX (207) 783-9701
E-Mail: sdoughty@inet.ed.gov

Principal Staff Members

Susan Doughty, Project Director
Elaine Roberts, Senior
Project Manager

Office Hours

8:30 A.M.—4:30 P.M.

Host Agency

Maine Center for Educational
Services

HIGHLIGHTS:

The Maine Facilitator Project strives to meet two of the most serious state and national challenges–restructuring and dwindling resources–by framing NDN projects within the larger framework of school reform; by forging strong relationships with existing educational organizations in order to maximize resources; by reformatting NDN activities to accommodate restricted school schedules; and by using distance technology for information-giving, training, and technical assistance.

MARIANA ISLANDS (NORTHERN)

CNMI Public School System
P.O. Box 1370 CK
Saipan, MP 96950
011 (670) 322-6410
D.C. Office (202) 673-5869
FAX 011 (670) 322-4056

Principal Staff Members

Jean B. Olopai, NDN Facilitator

Office Hours

7:30 A.M.—4:30 P.M. (M-F)

Host Agency

A nonprofit, autonomous agency

HIGHLIGHTS:

The Northern Marianas Facilitator Project disseminates information to public and private schools through the distribution of fliers, brochures, and newsletters which are focused subsets of the programs existing in *Educational Programs That Work*. The Project also sponsors awareness and training sessions and advertises these activities through brochures and direct contact with all the school systems. Schools wishing to receive training in specific projects may make recommendations to the Northern Marianas Facilitator for coordination with school principals and district program managers.

MARYLAND

Educational Alternatives, Inc.
P.O. Box 265, Harwood Lane
Port Tobacco, MD 20677
(301) 934-2992
(800) 924-9187 (Maryland only)
FAX (301) 934-2999
E-Mail: rhartjen@inet.ed.gov

Principal Staff Members

Raymond H. Hartjen,
    Executive Director
Helen Springston,
    Administrative Assistant

Office Hours

8:00 A.M.—4:30 P.M. (M-F)

Host Agency

Educational Alternatives, Inc.
    (a nonprofit corporation)

HIGHLIGHTS:

The Maryland Facilitator Project actively supports the restructuring movement in Maryland and the Maryland School Performance Program through the identification of NDN programs that meet the specific objectives of the state's performance testing initiative. These programs are clustered in mini-catalogs that support grade level initiatives, e.g., elementary, middle and high school, as well as the cluster of programs supporting state initiatives in the Dimensions of Learning. Further, special attention is given to those programs that strongly support MSPP objectives through comparison charts that detail the relevance of the NDN program to specific MSPP objectives.

Schools wishing to obtain any of the above resources and/or assistance in selecting programs to meet the needs identified in the state annual School Performance Report need only call the office for assistance.

MASSACHUSETTS

Massachusetts Facilitator Project
The NETWORK, Inc.
300 Brickstone Square, Suite 900
Andover, MA 01810
(508) 470-1080   or   (800) 877-5400
FAX (508) 475-9220
E-Mail: nancyl@neirl.org   or
          llove@inet.ed.gov

Principal Staff Members

Nancy Love, State Facilitator
Mary Poulin

Office Hours

8:30 A.M.—5:00 P.M. (M-F)

Host Agency

The NETWORK
  • A private, nonprofit
    organization

HIGHLIGHTS:

The Massachusetts Facilitator Project coordinates information services, training, and follow-up assistance to Massachusetts schools wishing to explore and/or adopt NDN programs. As local resources for staff development shrink, we are finding creative ways to provide services to schools, such as collaborative ventures with business, The Regional Laboratory for Educational Improvement of the Northeast and Islands, and other state and regional education agencies. We also work with individual schools to adopt multiple NDN programs over time as a vehicle for significant, sustained, school-wide renewal.

MICHIGAN

Michigan State Facilitator Project
Michigan Department of Education
608 West Allegan Street
P.O. Box 30008
Lansing, MI 48909
(517) 373-1807
FAX (517) 373-2537
E-Mail: egordon@inet.ed.gov

Principal Staff Members

Elaine Gordon,
    State Facilitator
Lydia Calderon, Secretary

Office Hours

8:00 A.M.—5:00 P.M.

Host Agency

Michigan Department of
    Education

HIGHLIGHTS:

The Michigan State Facilitator Project promotes the adoption of NDN programs through local, regional, and statewide conference presentations, dissemination of program information to a statewide network of curriculum specialists and professional development directors, and collaboration with instructional specialists and program directors within the Michigan Department of Education. The Project cosponsors an annual summer NDN Institute for the benefit of nonpublic schools. The Project also assists with the cost of trainers when funding is unavailable from other sources, and encourages the collaboration of school districts with corporate and foundation funding sources to support program adoption and development.

MINNESOTA

The EXCHANGE
CAREI-Room #116
2037 University Avenue S.E.
University of Minnesota
Minneapolis, MN 55414-3092
(612) 624-0584
FAX (612) 625-4880
E-Mail: beach001@maroon.tc.umn.edu *or*
dlassman@inet.ed.gov

Principal Staff Members

Diane Lassman, Director
Barbara Knapp, Dissemination
Coordinator
Debra Beach, Secretary

Office Hours

7:45 A.M.—4:30 P.M. (M-F)

Host Agency

University of Minnesota /
Minneapolis Public Schools

A
Linda Olson
Planning and Ed. Srvc.
611 West 5th Street
Willmar, MN 56201
(612) 231-5179
FAX (612) 231-5182

B
Ardyce Pederson/Fred Landis
HCR 3, Box 15
Chicago & Fifth
Staples, MN 56479
(218) 894-1930

C
Barbara Knapp
(612) 624-0584

HIGHLIGHTS:

The EXCHANGE operates the NDN Facilitator Project as part of an LEA-University collaborative center at the University of Minnesota: The Center for Applied Research and Educational Improvement (CAREI). The State Facilitator Project provides planning assistance to schools and districts in the identification, selection, and use of appropriate NDN programs that complement a school or district's overall plan for improvement. Staff coordinate logistics and cost-sharing arrangements for inservice and program implementation. In collaboration with NDN Developer/Demonstrators, staff assist in evaluating program success. Educators interested in learning about an NDN program or arranging inservice may contact the Regional Facilitator that serves their region.

MISSISSIPPI

Mississippi Facilitator Project
Mississippi State Department of Education
P.O. Box 771
550 High, Suite 1604
Jackson, MS 39205-0771
(601) 359-2795 *or* 359-3486
FAX (601) 359-2326
E-Mail: bstacy@inet.ed.gov

Principal Staff Members

Bobby Stacy, State Facilitator

Office Hours

8:00 A.M.—5:00 P.M. (M-F)

Host Agency

Department of Education

HIGHLIGHTS:

The Mississippi Facilitator Project coordinates services, training, and follow-up assistance to local educational agencies (LEAs), higher education, and other educational institutions wishing to explore and/or adopt NDN programs. As revenue continues to shrink for the LEAs, funding for network programs have been available to schools through other federal sources such as grants from Chapter 2 Eisenhower funds and Chapter 1. Collaborative ventures with business have provided additional funds to the LEAs.

MISSOURI

Missouri Facilitator Project
555 Vandiver, Suite A
Columbia, MO 65202
(314) 886-2157 *or* (314) 886-2165
FAX (314) 886-2160
E-Mail: jschulz@inet.ed.gov

Principal Staff Members

Jolene Schulz, Project Director
Patricia Kowalski, Coordinator of
    Federal Programs
Sandy Sapp, Secretary
Gaye Salisbury, Manager
    Business Operations

Office Hours

8:00 A.M.—4:30 P.M. (M-F)
• And by appointment

Housed in an LEA

Host Agency

HIGHLIGHTS:

The Missouri Facilitator Project works closely with the Department of Elementary and Secondary Education to provide staff development opportunities which align themselves with Missouri's current and proposed curriculum frameworks. The project is currently involved in an effort to contact all Professional Development Committee Chairpersons throughout the state to inform them about the NDN and the services provided to them by the Facilitator Project. The Facilitator Project has worked closely with the Eisenhower High Plains Consortium to provide awareness and training in the areas of mathematics and science. The project continues to exhibit NDN programs at numerous statewide conferences. The Facilitator Project is housed within the Missouri Education Center, which also houses the state curriculum dissemination project funded by the Department of Elementary and Secondary Education.

MONTANA

Montana Facilitator Project
Montana Office of Public Instruction
Mail Address: UPS Address:
State Capitol, Room 106   1300 11th Avenue
P.O. Box 202501   Helena, MT 59601
Helena, MT 69620-2501
(406) 444-2736
FAX (406) 444-3924
E-Mail: pjohnso2@inet.ed.gov

Principal Staff Members

Patricia B. Johnson,
    State Facilitator
Sandy Nicholls,
    Program Assistant

Office Hours

8:00 A.M.—5:00 P.M. (M-F)

Host Agency

State Education Agency

HIGHLIGHTS

The Montana Facilitator Project provides information, training, and follow-up technical assistance to over 500 school districts, private schools, and other educational groups seeking ways to improve their programs. Services focus on the areas of curriculum, staff development, and information access. Extensive resources are available in the area of educational technology applications for instruction and management.

NEBRASKA

Nebraska Department of Education
301 Centennial Mall South
P.O. Box 94987
Lincoln, NE 68509-4987
(Voice/TDD) (402) 471-3440
FAX (402) 471-2113
E-Mail: ealfred@inet.ed.gov

Principal Staff Members

Elizabeth Alfred, Director
Pat Morrison, Support Staff

Office Hours

7:30 A.M.—4:30 P.M. (M-F)

Host Agency

Nebraska State Department of Education

HIGHLIGHTS:

The State Facilitator operates through a network of selected **mini-regional NDN centers** housed at Educational Service Units. The mini-regional centers provide for both the public and the nonpublic agencies. The projects coordinate information services, training, and follow-up assistance to the Nebraska schools through projects in the National Diffusion Network that respond to the statewide High Performance Model. The mini-centers and the SF work in tandem to provide creative means of securing services to the Nebraska agencies. Efforts are made to have the mini-centers "specialize" in curriculum areas for affordability.

NEVADA

Nevada Department of Education
Capitol Complex
400 West King Street
Carson City, NV 89710
(702) 687-3187
FAX (702) 687-4499

Principal Staff Members

Roy Casey, State Facilitator

Office Hours

7:00 A.M.—4:00 P.M. (M-F)

Host Agency

Nevada Department of Education

HIGHLIGHTS:

The State Facilitator assists in the implementation of effective programs that support school districts and private schools in reaching their goals. Staff training and limited financial assistance are provided.

NEW HAMPSHIRE

New Hampshire Facilitator Center
80 South Maine Street
Concord, NH 03301
(603) 224-9461
FAX (603) 224-8925
E-Mail: jshady@inet.ed.gov

Principal Staff Members

Jared Shady, Director
Charlotte Moody, Secretary

Office Hours

8:30 A.M.—4:30 P.M. (M-F)
• Saturday and other hours by appointment

Host Agency

School Administration Unit #5

HIGHLIGHTS:

THE Facilitator Center is a full-service resource connecting point with staff linking New Hampshire educators and administrators to NDN projects and funding sources. It serves as a drop-in center for those (teachers, administrators, parents, and others) who wish to review and discuss NDN projects and their materials. Printing and duplicating capacities have been developed to assist NDN projects in disseminating their curricula and training materials to adopters. THE Center supports a comfortable training and conferencing area especially designed with NDN Developer/Demonstrators in mind, and numerous NDN-related training sessions and meetings are conducted therein each year. THE Facilitator Center collaborates with the New Hampshire State Department of Education, the major regional centers, colleges and universities, statewide associations, and other agencies to offer a full range of NDN support services above and beyond awareness, training, and follow-up.

NEW JERSEY

Educational Information and Resource Center
606 Delsea Drive
Sewell, NJ 08080-9199
(609) 582-7000
FAX (609) 582-4206
E-Mail: kwallin@inet.ed.gov *or*

Principal Staff Members

Katherine "Kitty" Wallin, Director
Elizabeth Ann Pagen,
    Dissemination Coordinator

Office Hours

8:30 A.M.—5:00 P.M. (M-F)

Host Agency

Educational Information and
    Resource Center (EIRC)

HIGHLIGHTS:

The New Jersey Facilitator staff offers the following services (which can be initiated merely by a phone call) to all public and private school educators:

- Presentations on NDN projects and/or services of the Facilitator Project at statewide conferences; county curricula sessions, or local district organization meetings;
- Mailing of print/video awareness materials on exemplary projects;
- Maintenance of a library of awareness and training materials available for 10-day loan;
- Arrangement of visitations to NDN in-state adopter sites;
- Coordination of training workshops;
- Suggestions for sources of funding; and
- Follow-up contact to ensure quality implementation.

New Jersey educators, and particularly Chapter I coordinators, responsible for identifying and infusing critical thinking/problem solving into curricula will want to explore specific NDN programs. Additionally, content specialists for science, math, social studies, language arts, violence prevention and holocaust studies will find NDN programs helpful as schools work to meet expanded state requirements and national educational goals. Facilitator staff will work with schools to plan for the implementation of multiple NDN programs that contribute to school-wide renewal.

NEW MEXICO

New Mexico State Facilitator
Department of Educational Foundations
University of New Mexico
College of Education
Onate Hall, Room 223
Albuquerque, NM 87131
(505) 277-5204
FAX (505) 277-7991
E-Mail: aatkins@inet.ed.gov

Principal Staff Members

Amy L. Atkins, State Facilitator
Danica D'Emilio
Francine Stewart

Office Hours

8:30 A.M.—4:30 P.M. (M-F)

Host Agency

University of New Mexico

HIGHLIGHTS:

Located on the campus of the University of New Mexico, Project DEEP is the link between New Mexico educators and National Diffusion Network projects. Project DEEP houses the New Mexico State Facilitator's office, which coordinates NDN trainings and follow-up for all local educational agencies in New Mexico, both public and private. Funding assistance for program implementation is available on a limited basis. Trainings can carry university credit.

NEW YORK

New York Education Department
Washington Avenue, Room 979 EBA
Albany, NY 12234
(518) 473-1388
FAX (518) 473-2860
E-Mail: lrowe@inet.ed.gov

Chuck Weed
Albany BOCES, School Support Services
47 Cornell Road
Latham, NY 12110

Principal Staff Members

Laurie Rowe, State Facilitator

Office Hours

8:00 A.M.—4:30 P.M. (M-F)

Host Agency

New York State Education
Department

HIGHLIGHTS:

The State Facilitator operates through a network of ten Regional Facilitators who maintain communication with local school districts. A satellite nonpublic school regional facilitator site has been established to assist nonpublic schools in the adoption of validated programs. Names and addresses of Regional Facilitators are available upon request. Regional Facilitators assist school districts with awareness, grant writing, and program implementation technical assistance. The New York State Education Department makes competitive grants available to local educational agencies to cover initial training costs for the adoption of new programs. Proposals are due in the spring.

NORTH CAROLINA

North Carolina State Facilitator Project
North Carolina Department of Public
  Instruction
Innovation and Development Services
301 North Wilmington Street
Raleigh, NC 27601-2825
(919) 715-1363
FAX (919) 715-1204
E-Mail: llove@dpi.1.nc.gov *or*
        llove@inet.ed.gov

Principal Staff Members

Linda G. Love, Director
Ruth Baker, Secretary

Office Hours

7:30 A.M.—5:00 P.M. (M-F)

Host Agency

North Carolina Department of
  Public Instruction, Innovation
  and Development Services

HIGHLIGHTS :

The North Carolina State Facilitator Project serves as the model and basis for dissemination of information about proven instructional programs and practices to educators in the state. The project designs and promotes NDN awareness and training activities that use a variety of innovative collaboration models. Technical assistance and follow-up services are provided with special attention given to school change and self-evaluation. Additional services include annual distribution of NDN catalogs (EPTW), arranging site visits to NDN adoption sites, and funding training for certified trainers and development of demonstration sites.

NORTH DAKOTA

Department of Public Instruction
Division of Independent Study
Box 5036 State University Station
Fargo, ND 58105
(701) 239-7287
FAX (701) 239-7288
E-Mail: jrichard@sendit.nodak.edu *or*
        jrichard@inet.ed.gov

Principal Staff Members

Jolene Richardson, State Facilitator
Donna Sell, Secretary

Office Hours

8:00 A.M.—5:00 P.M.

Host Agency

North Dakota Department of
  Public Instruction, Division of
  Independent Study

HIGHLIGHTS:

The State Facilitator works with the North Dakota Teacher Center Network, which consists of ten Teacher Centers across the state, to maintain communication with local school districts. Assistance is provided to schools in identifying exemplary NDN programs to meet their needs. Collaborative efforts with professional organizations are encouraged.

OHIO

Ohio Facilitation Center
Ohio Department of Education
65 South Front Street
Columbus, OH 43215
(614) 466-1317
FAX (614) 752-3956
E-Mail: ae_murray@ode.ohio.gov *or*
        mmurray@inet.ed.gov

Principal Staff Members

Mary Ellen Murray

Office Hours

8:00 A.M.—4:45 P.M. (M-F)

Host Agency

Ohio Department of Education

HIGHLIGHTS:

The Ohio Facilitation Center is located in the Division of Assessment and Evaluation. The Facilitation Center is instrumental in providing assistance to all schools in adopting NDN programs that relate to local and statewide needs. The Facilitation Center also identifies and provides the resources necessary for program implementation.

OKLAHOMA

Oklahoma Facilitator Center
123 East Broadway
Cushing, OK 74023
(918) 225-1882
FAX (918) 225-4711
E-Mail: dmurphy@inet.ed.gov

Principal Staff Members

Deborah A. Murphy, Director
Susan H. Custer, Administrative
    Coordinator
Dixie Bledsoe, Assistant
Jackie Baker, Secretary

Office Hours

8:30 A.M.—5:00 P.M.
  • After-hours answering machine

Host Agency

Cushing Public Schools

HIGHLIGHTS:

The Oklahoma Facilitator Center staff is available to assist schools in accessing all NDN programs and other validated projects. Services include:

- An annual statewide NDN awareness training conference;
- A monthly newsletter, *Educational Excellence*, which provides information on upcoming NDN activities, grant opportunities, and current research;
- Providing information and awareness presentations concerning all NDN programs as well as promising programs, processes, and practices;
- Networking activities with the Oklahoma State Department of Education, the Southwest Educational Development Laboratory (SEDL), and other key educational service providers;
- Coordinating local planning with the efforts of GOALS 2000, Chapter 1, Title II and other federal and state reform initiatives;
- Developing in-state trainers for validated programs;
- Assisting locally developed programs in applying for national validation; and
- Facilitating adoption training workshops.

OREGON

Columbia Education Center
11325 S.E. Lexington
Portland, OR 97266-5927
(503) 760-2346
FAX (503) 760-5592
E-Mail: 76106.3006@compuserve.com *or*
          rnelson@inet.ed.gov

Principal Staff Members

Dr. Ralph Nelsen, Director
John Nelsen, Program Specialist
Arnold Leppert,
     Program Specialist
Barbara Fitzgerald, Admin. Asst.
Sandra West, Bookkeeper

Office Hours

9:00 A.M.—5:00 P.M. (M-F)

Host Agency

Columbia Education Center
   • A nonprofit organization

HIGHLIGHTS:

The Oregon Facilitator has been very active in developing a statewide cadre of leadership teachers (aka certified trainers) for selected D/D programs. Oregon Facilitator staff place special emphasis on services to small-town and rural schools. Other areas of particular interest are gender equity, math/science/technology, environmental education, and social studies. Since 1987, CEC has been the initiating agency for several grant projects featuring selected D/D programs. Over $7,500,000 has been raised for teacher training projects serving Oregon and other western states.

PALAU

Department of Education
P.O. Box 189
Koror, Republic of Palau 96940
011 (680) 488-2570 or 488-1003
FAX 011 (680) 488-2830
E-Mail: memesioc@inet.ed.gov

Principal Staff Members

Masa-Aki Emesiochl, State
   Facilitator

PENNSYLVANIA

Facilitator Project
Research and Information Services for
Education (R.I.S.E.)
200 Anderson Road
King of Prussia, PA 19406
(215) 265-6056
FAX (215) 265-6562
E-Mail: rbrickle@inet.ed.gov

Principal Staff Members

Richard R. Brickley, Director

Office Hours

8:30 A.M.—4:15 P.M. (M-F)

Host Agency

Montgomery County
Intermediate Unit

HIGHLIGHTS:

NDN Services are delivered through collaboration with (1) Curriculum Coordinators in all 29 Pennsylvania Intermediate Units; (2) the Pennsylvania Department of Education through special initiatives such as various conferences of the Division of Federal Programs, Chapter 1 initiatives in Early Childhood and Schoolwide Programs and Science and Math through Title II. Recent revisions in state curriculum regulations emphasizing strategic planning, student learning outcomes-based instruction, service learning, and performance assessment will provide means for significant SEA/NDN cooperation. Nonpublic schools are served through Staff Development Institutes and related systemic assistance.

PUERTO RICO

Puerto Rico Facilitator Project
General Council on Education
P.O. Box 195429
San Juan, PR 00919-5429
(809) 751-5501
FAX (809) 764-0820
E-Mail: m_charneco@upr1.upr.clu.edu *or*
mcharnec@inet.ed.gov

Principal Staff Members

María del Pilar Charneco,
Project Director
Luisa Hernández-Carrasco,
Administrative Assistant

Office Hours

9:00 A.M.—5:30 P.M. (M-F)
Eastern Time

Host Agency

General Council on Education

HIGHLIGHTS:

The Puerto Rico Facilitator Project is ascribed to the General Council on Education (GCE) an agency of the Commonwealth of Puerto Rico created by Law to evaluate, contribute to and systematically follow up on the implementation of process of educational improvement. Through an information center known as REDES Center, we disseminate among educators from public and private schools updated information on research-based exemplary programs and practices. From needs assessment to adoption and adaption the project staff provide sensitive support during change process. In addition, we support the development of local trainers for validated programs and provide the follow up needed to ensure proactive adoptions and program retention. Also, with the support of local resources, we are finding creative ways to translate to Spanish and adapt the materials for their use with hispanic populations.

RHODE ISLAND

Rhode Island State Facilitator Center
Rhode Island Department of Education
Roger Williams Building
22 Hayes Street
Providence, RI 02908
(401) 277-2705
FAX (401) 277-2734
E-Mail: ffogle@inet.ed.gov

Principal Staff Members

Faith Fogle, State Facilitator
Mary Ann Iacobellis, Project Secretary

Office Hours

8:00 A.M.—4:30 P.M.

Host Agency

RI Department of Elementary and Secondary Education

HIGHLIGHTS:

The RI State Facilitator Center provides technical assistance, primarily through inservice training, to school districts seeking to replicate exemplary programs. Assistance is also provided to help districts/schools match needs with programs, identify funding sources, coordinate resources, and plan follow-up activities after training occurs. Awareness presentations are given at local, state, and regional workshops and conferences.

SOUTH CAROLINA

NDN Facilitator Project
South Carolina Department of Education
1429 Senate Street, Room 1114
Columbia, SC 29201
(803) 734-8446
FAX (803) 734-4387
E-Mail: cthomas@inet.ed.gov

Principal Staff Members

Catherine Thomas, State Facilitator

Vicki Rogers, Project Secretary

Office Hours

8:00 A.M.—4:30 P.M. (M-F)

Host Agency

South Carolina Department of Education

HIGHLIGHTS:

The South Carolina Facilitator Project coordinates awareness, training, and follow-up assistance to South Carolina schools wishing to explore and/or adopt NDN programs. Regional trainings are provided in several programs each year at not cost to participants. District and school level support is available upon request.

SOUTH DAKOTA

State Facilitator
South Dakota Curriculum Center
435 South Chapelle
Pierre, SD 57501
(605) 224-6708
FAX (605) 224-8320
E-Mail: wbonaiut@inet.ed.gov

Principal Staff Members

Dr. Wendy A. Bonaiuto, Director
Anita Rau, Materials Specialist

Office Hours

8:00 A.M.—5:00 P.M. (M-F)

Host Agency

South Dakota Curriculum Center
of the Black Hills Special
Services Cooperative

HIGHLIGHTS:

The South Dakota Facilitator Project assists in designing and promoting NDN awareness and training sessions, as well as follow-up assistance with South Dakota schools interested in exploring and/or adopting NDN programs. The Facilitator Project is most interested in promoting programs in mathematics, science, language, and areas supporting K-12 school reform and staff development.

TENNESSEE

Tennessee Statewide Facilitator Project
Tennessee Association for School
    Supervision and Administration
330 10th Avenue, North
Suite C, 4th Floor
Nashville, TN 37203-3401
(615) 963-7211
In State (800) 278-3104
FAX (615) 963-7203
E-Mail: ebentley@inet.ed.gov

Principal Staff Members

Dr. Ernest L. Bentley, Jr.,
    Project Director
Dr. Peggy F. Harris,
    Project Evaluator

Office Hours

8:00 A.M.—5:00 P.M. (M-F)
• Coverage 24 hours

Host Agency

TASSA (TN Association for
    School Supervision and
    Administration)

HIGHLIGHTS:

Normal emphases of adoptions, awareness sessions, dissemination of information on Head Start Models networks (such as ERIC, labs and centers) are achieved through three broad strategies. Expanded in-state networks use influentials from selected target populations to: install a certified NDN representative in all schools and central offices over the four-year grant period; facilitate preparation of a matrix of NDN programs, the national goals, and Tennessee educational reform objectives; and establish a P.E.P.-type review system to determine the exemplary programs in Tennessee.

TEXAS

Texas Facilitator Project - NDN
Education Service Center, Region VI
3332 Montgomery Road
Huntsville, TX 77340-6499
(409) 295-9161
FAX (409) 295-1447
E-Mail: jbramlet@inet.ed.gov

Principal Staff Members

Dr. Judy Bramlett,
   State Facilitator
Judy Preston,
   Education Specialist
Melissa Starnater,
   Program Assistant

Office Hours

8:00 A.M.—4:30 P.M. (M-F)

Host Agency

Regional Service Center

HIGHLIGHTS:

The Texas Facilitator makes grants available to education service centers (ESCs) to assist schools with implementation of NDN programs. Awareness of NDN programs is developed through state and regional conferences and through communication with private school contacts, district contacts as well as ESC contacts. Priority needs statewide are: parent involvement, thinking skills, at-risk students, writing, reading, mathematics, and gifted/talented. NDN programs will be valued as a resource for site-based, shared decision making.

UTAH

Utah State Facilitator Project
Utah State Office of Education
250 East 500 South
Salt Lake City, UT 84111
(801) 538-7823
FAX (801) 538-7769
E-Mail: kmannos@inet.ed.gov

Principal Staff Members

Kathy Mannos, State Facilitator
Marsha Hall, Secretary

Office Hours

8:00 A.M.—5:00 P.M. (M-F)

Host Agency

Utah State Office of Education

HIGHLIGHTS:

The Utah State Facilitator Project coordinates information and technical assistance to public and private schools wishing to explore and/or implement NDN programs in order to meet local needs. Specific services include arranging awareness sessions, making available NDN program informational videos and brochures, arranging visitations to NDN in-state adoption sites, and coordinating training and follow-up to ensure quality implementation. Small assistance grants are available through the project for program adoption and implementation. In addition, we assist districts exploring other potential avenues of funding.

VERMONT

Trinity College
McAuley Hall
208 Colchester Avenue
Burlington, VT 05401
(802) 658-7429
FAX (802) 658-7435
E-Mail: wickedp@aol.com *or*
hverman@inet.ed.gov

Principal Staff Members

Howard Verman,
State Facilitator
Sherry Lemieux, Project Secretary

Office Hours

8:00 A.M.—5:00 P.M.

Host Agency

Institute for Program
Development, Trinity College
of Vermont

HIGHLIGHTS:

The Vermont Facilitator Center provides educators with information, project descriptions, training, and follow-up assistance in the adoption and ongoing use of the programs of the National Diffusion Network. We will also provide consultation and referral for staff, curriculum development, and long range professional development planning using NDN programs to support school and statewide initiatives.

VIRGINIA

The Virginia Facilitator Project
The Education Network of Virginia
3421 Surrey Lane
Falls Church, VA 22042
(703) 698-0487
FAX (703) 698-5106
E-Mail: jmcknigh@pen.va.us *or*
jmcknigh@inet.ed.gov

Principal Staff Members

Judy McKnight
Anita Aldrich

Office Hours

8:00 A.M.—6:00 P.M.

Host Agency

The Virginia Facilitator grant is administered by the Education Network of Virginia, a nonprofit educational firm located in Northern Virginia.

HIGHLIGHTS:

Virginia is currently rewriting its standards of learning. They will be concrete and measurable. Assessment tools will be developed to determine mastery by individual students. School divisions will be held accountable for movement toward mastery.

VIRGIN ISLANDS

Department of Education
Office of the Commissioner
44-46 Kongens Gade
Charlotte Amalie
St. Thomas, VI 00802
(809) 774-0100, Ext. 225
FAX (809) 776-5687

Principal Staff Members

Ellen G. MacClean, State
Facilitator

WASHINGTON

Washington State Facilitator
Educational Service District 101
1025 West Indiana Avenue
Spokane, WA 99205-4400
(509) 456-7086
FAX (509) 456-2999
E-Mail: nmckay@inet.ed.gov

Principal Staff Members

Dr. A. Nancy McKay,
Project Manager
Diane Perry, Secretary

Office Hours

8:00 A.M.—5:00 P.M. (M-F)

Host Agency

Educational Service District 101

HIGHLIGHTS :

The State Facilitator for NDN programs in Washington State helps local educators learn about and adopt proven exemplary programs, products, and practices from across the nation. In addition to traditional methods of dissemination, the Washington State facilitator collaborates with educational service districts in assessing local needs and arranging training, and delivers awareness presentations and training via our premier satellite telecommunications system.

WEST VIRGINIA

West Virginia State Facilitator
West Virginia Department of Education
1900 Kanawha Boulevard East
Building #6, Room B-252
Charleston, WV 25305-0330
(304) 558-2193
FAX (304) 558-0882

Principal Staff Members

Cornelia Calvert

Office Hours

8:00 A.M.—5:00 P.M. (M-F)

Host Agency

West Virginia Department of
Education

HIGHLIGHTS :

The West Virginia Facilitator Project, located within the state's Capitol Complex, operates closely with all state education and related agencies, bureaus, committees, and offices to provide quality NDN dissemination, training, and technical assistance to public/private educators as well as other personnel throughout the year.

All long-range targets of this project align with the six education goals evoked in West Virginia's Policy 2001—especially goals one, two, four, five, and six which speak to school readiness, student performance, school environment, school completion, and adult education.

WISCONSIN

Wisconsin Department of Public Instruction
125 South Webster Street
P.O. Box 7841
Madison, WI 53707-7841
(608) 267-9179
FAX (608) 267-1052
E-Mail: washmore@inet.ed.gov

Principal Staff Members

William Ashmore, State
Facilitator
Amy French, Program Assistant

Office Hours

7:15 A.M.—4:30 P.M.

Host Agency

State Education Agency

HIGHLIGHTS:

The Wisconsin State Facilitator (WSF) provides public and private school educators with information about the network of exemplary program resources available through NDN. In addition, WSF provides consultation about specific NDN programs that support the Wisconsin Learner Goals, federal Goals 2000 initiatives and other activities related state and local systemic improvement efforts. WSF works directly with schools that wish to adapt and implement NDN programs that meet their curriculum and staff development needs; opportunities are provided for local ownership of NDN programs through teacher-leader, or certified trainer professional development institutes. Information on various grant opportunities and external resources are also offered through the project.

WYOMING

Wyoming Innovative Network System
(WINS)
State Department of Education
2300 Capitol Avenue
Hathaway Building, Room 269
Cheyenne, WY 82002-0050
(307) 777-6226
FAX (307) 777-6234
E-Mail: nleinius@inet.ed.gov

Principal Staff Members

Nancy Leinius, State Facilitator

Office Hours

8:00 A.M.—5:00 P.M.

Host Agency

Wyoming Department of
Education

HIGHLIGHTS :

The Wyoming Project, WINS, seeks to respond to schools and districts working on effective schools models, with attempts to restructure schools to meet the needs of a global society. For schools/districts desiring staff training in one of the NDN innovative projects, WINS will fund travel and per diem expenses for training and implementation of a project. The district is asked to purchase supplies and materials for training and implementation, and to pay the consultant fee if the developer of the project does not have funding for that expense. Other arrangements are possible depending upon demonstrated need.

Project emphasis is on thinking skills, creativity, and outcomes-based projects to meet the new state accreditation standards. Awareness sessions are best scheduled the first week in October when all subject areas meet for the Fall Conferences.

PRIVATE SCHOOL FACILITATOR

Council for American Private Education
(CAPE)
1726 M. Street, NW, Suite 703
Washington, D.C. 20036
(202) 659-0177
FAX (202) 659-0018
E-Mail: cape@connectinc.com

Principal Staff Members

Frank X. Delany, Director
Fay O'Brien, Assistant Director

Office Hours

9:00 A.M.—5:00 P.M.

Host Agency

Council for American Private
Education (CAPE)

HIGHLIGHTS:

CAPE's Private School Facilitator Project collaborates with State Facilitators and private school organizations to inform and advise private schools about the NDN and how to best use it as a resource for staff development with maximum classroom impact. The Project actively participates in, and provides practical assistance for, efforts that introduce the NDN to a significant new constituency; or which constitute a model for the use of NDN programs with relevance to a specific segment of the diverse private school community and the range of students they serve. The Project seeks to identify practices and programs in private schools which have potential for NDN validation. Finally, the Project represents the perspective of the private schools and educational pluralism within the NDN.

Section 1

Preservice/Inservice Training

* These programs are currently funded by the NDN.

Summary of Program Services for Section 1

Program	Goal*	Page	AWARENESS — Dissem. Funds Available		AWARENESS — Costs to Potential Adopter			AWARENESS — On Site Visitation Available		AWARENESS — Materials Available				TRAINING — Staff Available		TRAINING — Costs to Adopter			TRAINING — Certified Trainers Available	TRAINING — Training Time Required
			NDN	Other	Hon	Trav	Per Diem	Home Site	Adopt Site	Free Paper	Video	Film Strip	Other	Home Site	Adopt Site	Hon	Trav	Per Diem	State(s)	Day(s)
Active Teaching and Learning (ATaL) (Formerly Effective Use of Time)	3	1-1	✓		✓	✓	✓	✓	✓	✓	✓			✓	✓	✓	✓	✓	AL, AR, AZ, CA, CT, D.C., HI, IA, IL, IN, KY, MA, MD, MI, MN, MS, MO, NC, NJ, NV, OH, OR, TN, TX, VA, VT, WA, WV	3+
IMPACT II	3	1-2	✓			✓		✓	✓	✓	✓			✓		✓	✓		CA, MA, NC, NJ, NY, OH, TX	2
Inservice	3	1-7			✓	✓	✓	✓	✓	✓	✓		✓		✓	✓	✓	✓	AL, ID, IL, KS, LA, SC	2+
Learncycle: Responsive Teaching	3	1-7			✓	✓	✓	✓	✓	✓	✓				✓	✓	✓	✓	CO	2
Learning to Teach … (LTICS)	3	1-3			✓	✓	✓	✓	✓	✓	✓			✓	✓	✓	✓	✓	AL, AZ, CA, CT, D.C., IA, IN, KY, MA, MO, NC, NJ, NV, OR, TN, TX, VA, VT	3+
National Faculty Teaching Project, The	3	1-4		✓				✓	✓	✓	✓				✓				N/A	N/A
Responding to Individual … (Project RIDE)	7	1-5	✓			✓	✓	✓	✓	✓	✓				✓		✓	✓	CO, CT, FL, GA, ID, KY, LA, MO, MT, NY, OK, PA, UT, WA	1
Successful Inservice … (SITE)	5	1-8			✓	✓	✓	✓	✓	✓	✓				✓	✓	✓	✓	GA, HI, MD, VA, WV	3+
Teaching Research … (TRIM)	3	1-6	✓		✓	✓	✓	✓	✓	✓	✓		✓	✓	✓	✓	✓	✓	FL, IA	2

* National Goals for Education—definitions for each goal can be found on pages 5-7.

Active Teaching and Learning (ATaL). (Formerly Effective Use of Time.) A staff development process aimed at improving teachers' classroom management and instructional skills. Active Teaching and Learning also aims to increase the time students spend on academic tasks, and therefore, increase student achievement.

Audience   Approved by PEP for teachers in grades 2-12 in all content areas where reading is required.

Description   The major goal of Active Teaching and Learning (ATaL) is to help teachers improve their classroom instruction with the expectation that student achievement will increase as a result of increased motivation and engagement in academic tasks. This is accomplished by improving teachers' abilities to organize lessons, provide appropriate instruction for the students they serve, and motivate students to succeed. The program works by having trained observers generate an objective observation profile that provides feedback to teachers about their classroom management and instructional behaviors, providing interactive workshops to help teachers develop specific skills, and assessing changes in teacher behavior and student outcomes. The program consists of a series of six two and one-half hour workshops which are evenly spaced across a single semester. Workshops focus on managing classrooms, cooperative learning, planning appropriate lessons, challenging higher-level thinking activities, using positive behavior management techniques, and interactive instruction. Prior to the workshops, each teacher-participant is observed during one classroom period for three consecutive days and a teacher behavior profile is generated. Teachers analyze their profile and set goals for change. Following the workshops, a second profile is generated so teachers can assess their change and progress.

National Goal for Education 3 states that students will demonstrate competency in challenging subject matter after grades 4, 8, and 12. Houston Teaching Academy students have demonstrated competency through their achievement scores, which significantly improved since ATaL was adopted. The students performed better than most other schools in the district and were above average for the state.

Evidence of Effectiveness   Experimental teachers in four states improved on educationally significant teaching behaviors as measured by pre- and posttests using an objective observation instrument. Students in four states whose teachers had been trained in ATaL displayed substantial increases in time on task during the semester their teachers were in training.

Requirements   The school district must commit to hiring and training classroom observers. The school must commit to conducting the series of six workshops; conducting teacher observations at the beginning and the end of the workshop series; and supplying a training room with appropriate audio-visual setup.

Cost   Certified Trainers must have expenses paid to travel to the adopting site, $80 per diem, and a $300 per day consultant fee. Schools must provide a lap-top computer for recording observations. Observation training manuals and workshop training manuals may be reproduced at no charge. Ongoing operation of the program costs only the salary of the ATaL Trainer/Coordinator. Schools or districts may send a staff person to be trained as a Certified Trainer. This training of trainers is conducted each summer in College Station, TX and provided free of charge. Participants are responsible for their travel to College Station, hotel, and food costs for 10 days.

Services   ATaL staff provide staff development activities, such as awareness sessions, training, consultation, and training manuals. ATaL staff also provide interaction with adopters on a regular basis, and monitoring and evaluation of quality at sites.

Contact   **Dr. Jane Stallings or Nancy DeLeon, Educational Research Group, Texas A&M University, Office of the Dean of Education, College Station, TX 77843-4222. (409) 845-8008.**

Developmental Funding: NIE, state, and local.   PEP No. 79-41R2 (3/11/93)

IMPACT II. A model program for disseminating innovative teacher-developed, classroom-based programs for the improvement of instruction.

Audience All teachers in a school system that have adopted the IMPACT II model.

Description With the philosophy that many successful programs start in the classroom, IMPACT II works to improve instruction, facilitate collegiality, and retain good teachers by disseminating exemplary practices from teacher to teacher and across sites.

The IMPACT II model includes two types of financial awards provided directly to teachers. A Disseminator Grant supports creative effective classroom-based programs, and assists teachers in refining and disseminating the programs to other teachers. An Adaptor Grant made to teachers who wish to adapt the programs made available through disseminator teachers. Adaptations are made across grade levels, subject areas, and school and district lines.

In each IMPACT II site, a review committee (primarily consisting of teachers) determines who will receive grant awards, and site staff coordinates dissemination and recognition activities. The staff helps local teachers develop their dissemination and presentation skills.

Evidence of Effectiveness The average participating teacher talked to 43 other teachers about their exemplary program in the course of a year. Also, after a year with IMPACT II, teachers were almost twice as likely to change their teaching approach from large-group presentations to small-group, individualized, independent, interdisciplinary, or student-directed instruction. IMPACT II increased the sense of collegiality among teachers and self-esteem as a teacher based on quantitative and qualitative evaluations of teacher attitudes.

Requirements User school districts, teacher centers, education foundations, states, or consortia of school districts must have a minimum of 2,000 teachers, the critical number for maintaining and expanding a vital network. Superintendents and principals must supply release time for teachers to participate in interschool visits, workshops, and other networking activities. The program should include the basic model of disseminator and adaptor grant awards, the catalog of teacher-developed programs, and activities such as workshops and recognition ceremonies. Local program staff must include a director and a secretary. Existing staff members may be reassigned to these positions.

Services The six-month planning portion of IMPACT II costs about $6,000. Program costs recur from year to year and vary according to size of the teacher population. A typical small-size program costs about $150,000 per year, a large program (such as statewide) $200,000 - $300,000 per year. The total budget includes personnel costs.

Awareness materials are available at no cost. Project staff are available for awareness presentations and training, with all costs negotiable.

Contact Ellen Meyers, Director of Communications, IMPACT II, Inc., 285 West Broadway, New York, NY 10013. (212) 966-5582. E-Mail: elmeyers@aol.com

Developmental Funding: Exxon Education Foundation,
New York City Board of Education, other foundations.

PEP No. 87-15 (4/30/87)

Learning to Teach in Inner-City Schools and With Diverse Populations (LTICS). A program designed to develop teachers who choose to teach in schools with inner-city and/or diverse populations and are effective in teaching these populations.

Audience Approved by PEP for school districts serving low income multicultural families with a teacher-preparation college nearby, school populations that include teachers and students in grades PreK-12, and all subject area teachers, student teachers, and supervisors.

Description Learning to Teach in Inner-City Schools and With Diverse Populations (LTICS) involves the creation of a Teaching Academy that is a collaborative effort of a local inner-city school and a nearby teacher education college. The school/college partnership provides a structure in which a group of supervising teachers, college supervisors, and student teachers develop and learn to implement effective instructional strategies for diverse school populations.

The LTICS program is designed to change how teachers think about instruction in the inner-city schools. Weekly seminars focus on understanding the community and students' culture, working with neighborhood children and their families, managing classrooms, cooperative learning, using positive behavior management techniques, planning appropriate lessons, challenging higher-level thinking skills activities, and linking students background knowledge with school lessons.

Teachers and supervising teachers are observed at the beginning of each semester and set goals for change. At the end of each semester, they are observed again to assess their change in behavior. Time spent on-task is computed for students in the classrooms of the academy student teachers and teachers. Learning materials within the seminars include a Learning to Teach binder, teaching guides, training video tapes, and other current materials.

National Goal for Education 3 states that students will demonstrate competency in challenging subject matter after grades 4, 8, and 12. Houston Teaching Academy students have demonstrated their competency through their achievement scores, which have significantly improved since LTICS was adopted. The students performed better than most other schools in the district and were above average for the state.

Evidence of Effectiveness Experimental student teachers (ESTs) changed their instructional behavior in the desired direction significantly more than control student teachers (CSTs). Students' off-task behavior in ESTs' classrooms decreased significantly more than in CSTs' classrooms. Also, more ESTs are teaching in inner-city schools after completing student teaching than CSTs.

Requirements School district requirements include financial support for one school site, principal's commitment, teacher's union commitment, school faculty willing to have student teachers, observers, or tutors in the classroom, and a commitment to hire and train observers.

College requirements include dean and faculty commitment to partnership, one faculty member committed to serving as college director, student placement office willingness to concentrate a large number of students in the academy, faculty supervisors trained and committed to teach seminars, methods faculty committed to teach their classes at the school site, and commitment to collect and evaluate observation data.

Costs Costs must be considered for teacher incentives, school coordinator, training to develop certified trainers, lap-top computers and observer profiles software, college director and seminar instructor, software for processing evaluation data, materials and supplies, and videotapes.

Services LTICS staff provide staff development activities (awareness sessions, interaction with superintendents and college faculty, updating seminar materials), interaction with adopters on a regular basis, collection of adoption materials, and monitoring and evaluation of quality at sites.

Contact   Jane A. Stallings or Nancy DeLeon, Educational Research Group, Texas A&M University, Office of the Dean of Education, College Station, TX 77843-4222. (409) 845-8008.

Developmental Funding: Houston Independent School District, The University of Houston College of Education.

PEP No. 89-14 (**7/21/89**)

National Faculty Teaching Project, The. The National Faculty. A program to strengthen the quality of instruction for all grades by encouraging professional growth among teachers and increasing their knowledge of their respective disciplines. To accomplish this, scholars from The National Faculty and other scholars from colleges and universities collaborate with local school teachers on site during the school year and on college campuses during the summer.

Audience Approved by JDRP for all elementary and secondary schools.

Description The National Faculty's mission is to improve the teaching of the humanities, arts, and sciences in elementary and secondary schools through a process of staff development by which school teachers and college professors work together on the disciplines they teach. The National Faculty builds an internal school structure to permit the collaboration of teachers with national scholars and with scholars from nearby colleges and universities. Each project gives a school or district the chance to implement a systematic method for improving discipline-based instruction and to utilize the resources of the nation's only national faculty. This faculty—comprised of about 400 scholars and teachers from almost as many colleges and universities throughout the country—is a unique feature of the dissemination process.

Although each project is tailor-made for an individual school setting, a common pattern of activities is developed at each site. These activities include the identification of a core group of teachers that is fashioned into a collegial unit; development of a detailed project plan which is implemented over a period of time, ideally two or three years; a succession of two-day visits on site during the school year from college and university teachers who are members of The National Faculty; participation in summer institutes; sustained attention to the primary texts and concepts of specific disciplines; collaboration with faculty from local colleges; and an emphasis on local ownership of the project by the teachers, with plans for continuing and expanding its impact. By adding to teachers' academic resources in all subject areas, The National Faculty Teaching Project primarily addresses Goals 3, 4, 5, and 7 of the National Education Goals.

The process disseminated by The National Faculty has been selected using criteria developed over the last two decades. Through a process of trial and error, the following criteria have evolved: projects are conducted on site; a project team is formed; a project plan is developed based on an assessment of the school's academic needs; and a project usually lasts at least two years and includes a summer institute between the first and second years of implementation. A typical project framework involves a variety of interconnected components which must be developed and monitored for the duration of the project. These include: initial contact; planning phase; project activities; and monitoring and evaluation.

Evidence of Effectiveness National Faculty projects have been established in almost every educational setting, including rural, urban, suburban, rich and poor, and for members of nearly every ethnic group. Because of the flexibility of the process and the extensive membership of The National Faculty, there is no limit to the number of projects which can be developed. The major accomplishment of the process has been its beneficial effect on teachers, resulting in multiple changes: in teachers' attitudes about teaching; in their understanding of the subjects they teach; in their professional relations with their colleagues; and in the institutional arrangements within which they work. At the heart of this renewal process is a change in what teachers expect of intellectual inquiry and professional esteem, which leads to more effective teaching. These results have been documented in qualitative evaluation studies conducted by the University of Illinois and the University of Colorado.

Costs Project costs are recurring, and vary greatly according to determined needs. A project may begin with several months of planning for as little as $10,000, which can lead to the development of a project of any size. A small project in a school district including 3 or 4 schools may cost $200,000 over two years. A larger project involving many schools may cost $600,000 over three years, with similarly distributed cost categories.

Contact Ms. Andrea C. Fowler, Vice President for Program Coordination and Training, The National Faculty, 57 Forsyth Street, Suite 600, Atlanta, GA 30303. (404) 525-0525.

Funding: National Endowment for the Humanities.

PEP No. 87-19 **(5/15/87)**

Responding to Individual Differences in Education (Project RIDE). A program designed to link behavioral and academic interventions with teachers of at-risk and difficult-to-teach students in regular classrooms.

Audience Approved by PEP for students in grades K-6 with special academic and/or behavioral problems who present themselves as potential special education referrals (prereferral), are returning from special education to the regular classroom, or are simply "difficult-to-teach."

Description The Responding to Individual Differences in Education (RIDE) process involves a series of steps, beginning with a well-articulated description of the behavior, followed by three options: (1) Effective Classroom Practices, which identifies 12 themes from the effective schools research to assist in the modification or refinement of current practices; (2) Computer Tactics Bank and Video Library, which provide over 250 proven successful behavioral and academic tactics, and video demonstrations of how to carry out the tactics; and (3) School-Wide Assistance Team (SWAT), which serves as a building-level resource for generating solutions to problems through a systematic problem-solving process.

Evidence of Effectiveness At-risk students in RIDE schools exhibit significantly greater positive: (1) academic growth on the locally-developed and validated Academic Behavior Scale, and (2) social growth on the Iowa Conners Teacher Rating Scale than equivalent comparison school studies.

Requirements There should be strong administrative support, and three to four teachers should be elected to serve on a building-level team for at least one year. A multiplier-effect training model, whereby the SWAT members are trained and in turn train the remaining members of the building faculty, is recommended. A one-day initial training session (30-40 participants) and a follow-up site visit approximately three months later are strongly recommended. In addition to the RIDE kit, which includes a Computer Tactics Bank, Video Library, SWAT Training Tape, and Program Manual for each participant, the building must have available a VCR with monitor and either an Apple II, IBM, or Macintosh computer with accompanying printer.

Costs Costs are prorated according to the number of buildings in a school district adopting the model. Based on a district adoption including eight buildings with eight teams (32 workshop participants), materials and training costs total $5,880 ($2160 for 8 Computer Tactics Banks; $2360 for 8 Video Libraries; $360 for 24 Program Manuals; $500 for the one-day training; and $500 for the one-day follow-up training). Costs average $735/building, $245/teacher, and $1.21/pupil (600 pupils per building).

Services In addition to training and materials, a follow-up site visit is provided.

Contact **Ray Beck, Project Director, P.O. Box 1809, Longmont, CO 80502-1809. (303) 651-2829.**

Developmental Funding: Local, state, and National Center for Learning Disabilities.   PEP No. 88-14 **(3/92)**

Teaching Research Inservice Model (TRIM). A program to assist educators in designing, delivering, and evaluating staff development activities.

Audience Approved by PEP for educators, inservice trainers, and individuals or agencies with staff development responsibilities.

Description The Teaching Research Inservice Model (TRIM) represents a process for the design, development, and evaluation of inservice training efforts. As a part of recent school improvement and reform efforts school districts are looking at systematic, comprehensive staff development planning as one tool to assist them in meeting their educational goals. This training model provides a school or district with a model for the development of both long and short range staff development goals. Personnel who are primarily trained as educators are provided, through this model, a means for developing training activities that will make a difference in classroom teaching. The Teaching Research Inservice Model will assist the adopter in identifying desired outcomes of training and then designing training strategies to achieve those outcomes. The model provides the trainer with objectives, activities, and evaluation strategies aimed at teaching the trainee new skills and/or procedures that can be implemented in the classroom. Specific content of the training is to be determined by the adopter's needs.

Evidence of Effectiveness The Teaching Research Inservice Model was validated with evidence of impact at three levels: (1) utilizing the components of the TRIM, training could be designed that would teach new skills to teachers; (2) teachers who were trained implemented the major features of the training; and (3) implementation resulted in improved student performance.

Requirements Implementation of the Teaching Research Inservice Model requires attendance at a two-day training session by key staff selected by the adopting district. Training may take place at the home program site or the adopter's site. Follow-up technical assistance is available.

Costs Training costs include $600 plus travel expenses for two presenters and $15-$25 per participant (usually 20 per session) for workshop materials. Costs may be negotiated between the site, the State Facilitator, and Teaching Research.

Services Awareness materials are available at no cost. Visitors are welcome at the program site by appointment. Project staff are available to attend out-of-state awareness meetings (costs to be negotiated). Training is conducted at the program site or the adopter's site. Costs to adopters include a portion of travel, per diem, and materials. Follow-up services are available to adopters (costs to be negotiated).

Contact Torry Piazza Templeman, Teaching Research, Western Oregon State College, 345 North Monmouth Avenue, Monmouth, OR 97361. (503) 838-8766, FAX (503) 838-8150.

JDRP No. 79-34 (11/7/79)
Recertified (4/94)

Developmental Funding: USOE BEH.

Inservice (Promoting Positive Attitudes Toward Learning). An outcomes-based teacher inservice training program designed to help teachers increase the frequency of specific instruction behaviors and strategies which have been proven effective in increasing student growth in grades K-12.

Description The basic Inservice approach is to influence teacher behavior, which, in turn, cause changes in student attitudes and behaviors. The mechanism for effecting teacher change is the use of multimedia, individualized, self-paced, outcome-based learning kits. The kits introduce sixteen specific teaching skills in three complementary areas. Each of the three kits—Classroom Communication and Management, Process of Learning, and Active Involvement—follows the same general format. Teachers are presented a list of four to six outcome-based objectives. For each objective, numerous learning activities are provided, followed by an assessment. Debriefing after peer observation or a microteaching session is a key program aspect of the process. Kits come in notebook form containing all required materials except films and commercially available books.

Data indicate a significant student improvement in each of the following areas as a result of teachers' Inservice training: reading, vocabulary, verbal skills, respect for school and learning, and self-esteem. Teachers also report a greater sense of professional gratification and self-satisfaction after applying Inservice methods.

Two to four days of training are provided for persons selected as Inservice Peer Leaders. (These are primarily classroom teachers who have had particular success in implementing Inservice methods in their classrooms and have been certified to lead awareness and staff development sessions for colleagues across the nation.)

Awareness materials are available at no cost. Implementation costs include Inservice Kits and Peer Leaders' daily fees and travel costs.

Project staff and Peer Leaders are available for awareness sessions at professional meetings and conferences. Peer Leaders are also available to conduct training workshops.

Contact   Dr. Ralph T. Nelson, Columbia Education Center, 11325 Southeast Lexington, Portland, OR 97266. (503) 760-2346, FAX (503) 760-5592.

Developmental Funding: USOE ESEA Title III.

JDRP No. 75-26 **(5/16/75)**
Recertified **(1/85)**

Learncycle: Responsive Teaching. An intensive teacher-training program developing flexible, effective skills for managing and teaching mainstreamed or high-risk students. Approved by JDRP for teachers of special education or main- streamed students grades K-9, and teacher trainers and consultants.

Description The program includes two levels of training. Learncycle presents a simple problem-solving method to define, analyze, and solve common student problems such as incomplete assignments, distractibility, disruption, isolation, and poor self-image. Participants learn how to assess the key "change factors" for each problem. Through lecture, demonstration, practice, and team task groups, they acquire a wide array of simple, teacher-tested ways to adapt curriculum, consequences, or their own behavior. Each teacher then puts together a short five-step plan to use back in the classroom. What implementation is chosen depends on students' needs and teacher preference. A unique feature is training of teachers in proven ways to enlist the support of a whole class for program success with one or two high-risk students. The overall problem-solving method allows teachers to adapt the program instantly to new situations. Awareness materials are available at no cost. Training is available at the adopter site or for a group of adopters at a common site (costs to be negotiated).

Contact   Effective Teaching Consortium (Etc . . .), P.O. Box 1896, Longmont, CO 80502. (303) 651-1751.

Developmental Funding: USOE ESEA Title III.

JDRP No. 74-53 **(5/24/74)**

Successful Inservice through Turnkey Education (SITE). A mathematics program for the development of higher-level thinking skills through the use of manipulative materials. Approved for elementary school teachers and supervisors (grades 2-6) and students of these participants.

Description The Successful Inservice through Turnkey Education (SITE) program is based on a problem-solving approach to learning new mathematical concepts and skills. SITE integrates content and methodology, using hands-on activities with a variety of manipulatives. Since teachers "teach as they were taught," the program uses processes and activities which are immediately applicable in the classroom, mesh with every textbook, and model the K-4 and the 5-8 NCTM Standards for Curriculum and Evaluation. Mathematics content (fractions, decimals, area, perimeter, volume, metric measure, graphing, geometry) is developed through a process approach (cooperative grouping, questioning strategies, guided discovery). SITE provides the printed instructional materials as well as the manipulatives needed in the classroom.

Effectiveness has been demonstrated in urban, suburban, and rural schools. Teachers' mathematical knowledge increases while enthusiasm and skill in teaching math is noticeably enhanced. Student growth in knowledge from pre- to posttest has been significant (at 0.05 level).

Initial training requires 3-5 full days. Periodic follow-up is recommended. Costs include: honorarium, travel, and per diem costs for SITE trainer(s); $95 per participant for workshop materials; one SITE Starter Kit for each adopting building ($415). First-level awareness materials are available at no cost.

Contact Dr. Barbara Berman or Dr. Fredda J. Friederwitzer, Co-Directors, SITE, Educational Support Systems, Inc., 446 Travis Avenue, Staten Island, NY 10314. (718) 698-3636, FAX (718) 370-3102.

Developmental Funding: USOE Metric Education Program.

JDRP No. 82-27 **(5/27/82)**
Recertified **(6/5/86)**

Section 2

Organizational Reform

* These programs are currently funded by the NDN.

Summary of Program Services for Section 2

Program	Page	Goal*	AWARENESS — Dissem. Funds Available		AWARENESS — Costs to Potential Adopter			AWARENESS — On Site Visitation Available		AWARENESS — Materials Available				TRAINING — Staff Available		TRAINING — Costs to Adopter			TRAINING — Certified Trainers Available	TRAINING — Training Time Required
			NDN	Other	Hon	Trav	Per Diem	Home Site	Adopt Site	Free Paper	Video	Film Strip	Other	Home Site	Adopt Site	Hon	Trav	Per Diem	State(s)	Day(s)
Administrative Cooperative in Education	2-6	3				✓	✓	✓		✓				✓					(none)	1
Classroom Organization... (COMP)	2-1	3	✓		✓	✓	✓		✓	✓	✓			✓	✓	✓	✓	✓	AR, CA, FL, HI, IN, KY, MD, MI, MS, NE, OH, PA, SC, TN, TX, VT, WI, WV, Guam, Saipan	3
More Effective Schools/Teaching Project	2-2	2, 3, 4	✓		✓	✓	✓	✓		✓					✓	✓	✓	✓	KY, NY, VT	14+
Outcomes-Driven... (ODDM)	2-3	3	✓		✓	✓	✓	✓	✓	✓	✓				✓	✓	✓	✓	AZ, MI, MN, NY, TX, UT, VA, WA	3+
Program for School Improvement, The (PSI)	2-4	2, 3	✓		✓	✓	✓	✓	✓	✓	✓			✓	✓	✓	✓	✓	GA	3+
Resident Supervisory Support for Teachers (RSST)	2-6	3		✓	✓	✓	✓	✓	✓	✓				✓	✓	✓	✓	✓	D.C., OH, ME, NY, PA, RI	2+
Sharing Successful Programs	2-7	3			✓	✓	✓	✓	✓	✓				✓	✓	✓	✓	✓	(none)	3+
Systemic Technology Planning to Support Education Reform (STPSER)	2-5	3	(info. not available)																	

* National Goals for Education—definitions for each goal can be found on pages 5-7.

Classroom Organization and Management Program (COMP). A supplemental program of six training modules to help teachers in grades 1-9 and other school staff improve their instructional and behavioral classroom management skills and/or help trainers train others in this skill area.

Audience Approved by PEP for regular classroom teachers in grades 1-9. Also intended for administrators, regional educational labs, state departments of education, and school staff developers who wish to design and deliver professional development workshops.

Description The Classroom Organization and Management Program (COMP) is intended to supplement other professional development activities and provides the necessary foundational management skills on which other academic and instructional programs must build. COMP provides teachers with management ideas and materials and involves them in activities directly relating these to classroom management. Program validated goals include improved student behavior and academic achievement.

The program has three focuses: planning, implementing, and maintaining classroom management skills. Training workshops (which either train teachers directly or train trainers to bring skills back to school systems) demonstrate models of a process that can be implemented in a school's own professional development program.

Workshops cover such elements as assessment and problem identification, research-based content presentations (using vignettes, case studies, films, and simulations), and formulation of implementation plans (with emphasis on teacher roles, responsibilities, and tasks).

Learning materials include two commercially published books (optional) and teacher manuals (required) which cover six modules: organizing the classroom, planning and teaching rules and procedures, managing student work, maintaining good student behavior, planning and organizing instruction, and conducting instruction and maintaining momentum.

Evidence of Effectiveness In evaluation studies, students who were in classes of teachers trained in the classroom management workshops made significantly higher gains on achievement tests than students in control group classes. Teachers who participated in training workshops used the effective practices to a greater extent, and students had significantly less off-task, less inappropriate and disruptive behavior, and had greater success in lessons.

Requirements All training must be conducted by certified trainers. Model 1 (Training of Teachers—9 to 25 participants) requires release time for a 3-day workshop (2 initial, 1 follow-up) and the assignment of a local coordinator to schedule visits to teachers' classrooms where follow-up and peer support is requested. Materials must also be purchased.

Model 2 (Training for Trainers—6 to 12 participants) requires prior training in Model 1, three consecutive days of release time for training, and practice with workshop materials. Materials must also be purchased.

Attendance of principals and other administrators at training sessions is highly desirable for both models.

Costs Training costs for Model 1 include materials ($35 per person for 12 to 30 participants), and trainer's fee (varies from $200 to $500 per day), travel, and lodging. Training costs for Model 2 include materials ($150 per person for 6 to 12 participants), and trainer's fee ($500 per day), travel, and lodging.

Services In addition to print materials, the program provides training for either teachers or trainers of teachers, plus follow-up training in subsequent years. Training can be scheduled in various locations to reduce costs. Awareness materials are available at no cost.

Contact Carolyn M. Evertson or Alene H. Harris, Classroom Organization and Management Program, Box 541 Peabody College, Vanderbilt University, Nashville, TN 37203. (615) 322-8100. E-Mail: harris@ctrvax.vanderbilt.edu

Developmental Funding: National Institute of Education, Arkansas State Department of Education, contributions from local school districts, Greeley (Weld Co.), CO, Kentville (Kings Co.), Nova Scotia.

PEP No. 89-9 **(5/11/89)**

More Effective Schools/Teaching Project. A program designed to increase academic achievement for all students and to improve the organization and delivery of instruction in schools throughout a district. The program uses a change process of systematic assessment, problem solving, and development of annual school improvement plans based upon research on effective schools and school improvement.

Audience Approved by PEP for all types of school districts.

Description The More Effective Schools/Teaching Project addresses the needs of improving achievement in the basic skill areas for all students and reducing the achievement gap between minority and nonminority students through training district-level, multirole planning teams and building-level, multirole school improvement committees. Teams and committees are trained to implement and maintain a data-based, data-driven school improvement process based upon the effective schools research. Annual plans are based on disaggregated student performance data and the results of a survey of faculty perceptions regarding the presence of correlates of effective schools. The project addresses a number of the National Goals for Education, in particular Goals 2, 3, and 4.

Evidence of Effectiveness Over a seven-year period: (1) there was a continued and significant increase in the proportion of students in the participating district scoring at or above the fortieth percentile and in stanines 7-8-9 on the Stanford Achievement Test in Reading Comprehension and Total Mathematics; and (2) the participating school district demonstrated significant improvement on the New York State Education Department Regents Exams in Math 9, Math 10, Math 11, Earth Science, Physics, and French. Improvements in institutional practices sustained over seven years included district adoption of new student outcome goals measured by standardized tests; creation of an on-going process for problem solving; formation of school improvement committees giving leadership roles to teachers; and attainment of the correlates of effective schools in participating schools.

Requirements The project requires active, visible endorsement and support by the district superintendent; designation of a district project coordinator; participation of teachers, administrators, parents, and, if desired, students on the district leadership team and school improvement committees and their participation in the training workshops; annual disaggregation of student achievement data and administration of a correlate needs assessment instrument; annual development of building school improvement plans and approval of them by the faculty; preparation and publication of an annual evaluation report; and follow-up consultation/technical assistance for the first two years of implementation.

Costs Costs vary according to district size, pay rates, and the amount of travel incurred by consultants. The approximate cost for starting the process is $25,000 to $30,000 per school district, usually spread over two fiscal years. Annual operation costs are directly related to local district decisions.

Services In addition to training and curriculum materials, follow-up consultation is available.

Contact Robert E. Sudlow, Spencerport Central Schools, 71 Lyell Avenue, Spencerport, NY 14559. (716) 352-0603. E-Mail: sudlow@aol.com

Developmental Funding: State and local.

PEP No. 91-24 **(4/92)**

Outcomes-Driven Developmental Model (ODDM). A comprehensive school improvement model using a systems approach to achieving excellence for all students, grades K-8.

Audience Approved by the JDRP (1985) & PEP (1994) for all schools and students K-8.

Description The Outcomes-Driven Developmental Model (ODDM) employs a systematic change process that is applied to all facets of school operation. Change in each area of school operation is always based on the best research literature. ODDM is a master plan for improving all facets of school operation to produce excellent student achievement for all students. The plan is a systems approach that avoids fragmented efforts. ODDM integrates the elements of good teaching, learning, and administration into an eminently usable model.

Evidence of Effectiveness ODDM succeeded in improving the achievement of JC students. Achievement in reading and math, K-8, served as the two key indicators of success in all areas of learning. In 1976, only 44% of all eighth grade students scored six months or more above grade level in reading; in math, 53% scored at this level. By May, 1984, 75% of all eighth grade students scored six months or more above grade level in reading (p>.001). In math, 79% scored at this level (p>.001). These gains in student achievement have persisted. Morale, climate, and staff effectiveness have also improved.

Requirements ODDM may be adopted by a single school district or by a cluster of school districts. Adopters must commit to receiving twenty-five days of training for two years.

Costs ODDM costs range from $20,000 - $25,000 for the first year of training and $10,000 - $15,000 for the second year (according to the number of participants).

Services Awareness materials are available at no cost. Visitors are welcome at JC or certified sites. Training is conducted at the adopter's site. Adopters receive training, implementation, telephone and mail correspondence, evaluation services, and a wide range of high quality training materials.

Contact Dr. Frank V. Alessi, Johnson City Central School District, 666 Reynolds Road, Johnson City, NY 13790. (607) 763-1200, Ext. 1252.

JDRP No. 85-7 (6/14/85)
Recertified (4/1/94)

Developmental Funding: Local, USOE. J

Program for School Improvement, The (PSI). A program designed to assist schools in developing a shared governance process for making decisions about school-wide improvements in curriculum, instruction, staff development, reorganization, and action research.

Audience   Approved by PEP for teachers and administrators at all levels.

Description   The Program for School Improvement (PSI) provides a framework of principles and premises for school improvement that has at its heart the condition that through collective choice and responsibility teachers share equally in decisions about school-wide teaching and utilize action research to evaluate the effects of these decisions upon students. The program aims to improve attitudes, achievements, and the quality of classroom and school life for all students; enhance the role of teachers as professionals in making instructional decisions; establish critical thinking and cooperation among school staff as they design, implement, and evaluate programs for school improvement; and establish better links between universities and public schools in evaluation, planning, and research.

PSI schools have been successful in reaching their individual goals, many of which have addressed the national goals. By implementing democratic procedures, League schools model the power of responsible citizenship (Goal 3).

Evidence of Effectiveness   Participating schools demonstrate improved performance, as determined by each school's individual goals for: (1) students (e.g., reduced dropout and retention rates, increased number of dropouts returning to school or gaining employment, and improved student achievement, higher completion rates on required basic skill tests for graduation, improved student attitudes towards learning); (2) teachers (e.g., increased conceptual thought and internal locus of control); and (3) schools (e.g., improved organizational climate, more positive parent attitudes, and winning competitive state, regional, and national awards).

Requirements   The organization of the work of PSI is through groups or clusters of schools. The make-up and size of these clusters and their school members may vary. Schools within these clusters provide assistance and support to each other. Adopting schools commit to the premises of PSI including voluntary participation, establishment of a democratic decision-making process over instructional and curricular initiatives, collection of data to assess the progress and effects of these initiatives, and participation with other League schools to share experiences with colleagues by receiving guests, participating in meetings, and making presentations.

Each adoption will be negotiated separately. Agencies that already have working relationships with clusters of schools best fit PSI's model.

Costs   (PSI is a nonprofit organization.) Cost will be negotiated through a single fee that covers all costs. Fees will vary depending on the size (may range from three schools to 20 or more) and level of assistance (number of days and trainers involved, as well as amount of support services needed). Existing agreements range from an annual single fee of $3,000 to in excess of $20,000 (these fees cover all expenses including travel).

Services   Awareness materials are available at no cost. Visitors are welcome at adopting school sites by appointment. Out-of-state awareness sessions may be arranged. Training is scheduled at a site convenient to the schools within a cluster. Training, implementation, follow-up, telephone and mail consultation, access to a national resource data base, and materials are provided to adopters.

Contact   **Lew Allen or Carl D. Glickman, University of Georgia, 124 Aderhold Hall, Athens, GA 30602. (706) 542-2516. E-Mail: lps@uga.cc.uga.edu**

Developmental Funding: University of Georgia, BellSouth Foundation, Georgia Leadership Academy, local.

PEP No. 90-2 **(3/19/91)**

Systemic Technology Planning to Support Education Reform (STPSER). A program to assist school districts in planning for the comprehensive technology infrastructure needed to implement educational reform programs.

Audience Schools, school districts and state departments of education that seek improved integration of educational reforms with the effective use of technology.

Description STPSER is a planning process that uses a collection of electronic information gathering templates/tools to assist the education community in developing technology-based education initiatives that can be integrated into a school curriculum. Using a consensus-building process, district staff are assisted in producing a five-year educational technology plan within a six-month period. The planning process consists of four phases. The first phase is the initial preparation and information gathering session. This phase is followed by a two-day orientation and needs analysis training which introduces the planning procedures and how to accomplish a needs analysis. The next phase gives consideration to the technology design and implementation process. The final phase provides trainer support and technical assistance, including electronic communications to assist with the production/adoption of the final document; phone consultation; and document editing, review and revision services. STPSER addresses National Educational Goal 3.

Evidence of Effectiveness Eleven claims of effectiveness were evaluated. Results show that a comprehensive technology planning process leads to significant improvements in six areas: development of curriculum and management of instruction; implementation of reform initiatives; district school management; internal communication practices; professional development opportunities; and funding for education technology. In addition, respondents from experimental group sites were able to identify additional benefits. STPSER has been adopted in 108 public schools, which includes a total student population of nearly 63,000 in rural, urban and suburban communities.

Requirements A willingness by the school district to allot three days of training for a designated team of central office and school-based staff. Willingness and participation by the district administrative leadership during the six-month development period. It is recommended that adopter sites use the Electronic Planning Workbook. Print versions of the Workbook are available, although it will increase paperwork and production time. To use the Electronic Workbook will require the availability of specific computer software (Microsoft Works).

Costs Start-up costs include district level training for a minimum of four and a maximum of ten professional staff participants. Two days of training are offered with one day of follow-up. Developer support for plan production is available at a negotiated cost, if requested. Operational costs represent normal print copying and disk reproduction for staff use. The five-year cost per student, depending on the number of students, will range from $.05 to $.26/student.

Services Trainer maintains a toll-free telecommunications support service for adopters that includes an electronic bulletin board, e-mail, and on-line conference capabilities. Toll-free telephone support is also available.

Contact John R. Phillipo, Executive Director; Mark Sherry, Technology Planning Program Director; Larry Vaughan, Senior Research and Evaluation Consultant, Center for Educational Leadership and Technology, 165 Forest Street, Marlborough, MA 01752. (508) 624-4877, FAX (508) 624-6565.

Developmental Funding: State, local, and in-kind.

PEP No. 94-13 **(5/1/94)**

Administrative Cooperative in Education. A multi-district cooperative program providing services to Chapter I teachers, students, and parents. Approved by JDRP for administrators, teachers, intermediate service agencies, and students in Chapter I programs.

Description The primary goal of Administrative Cooperative in Education (ACE) is to provide quality Chapter I services to rather sparsely populated rural districts, which are often too small to furnish all the necessary features of a successful mastery learning program.

ACE has four key elements: an administrative model, teacher in-service and evaluation, a materials resource center, and parent involvement.

The cooperative makes a cost-effective instructional materials support center a reality. Selected commercial materials for checkout and mass-produced teacher-made materials, accompanied by inservice on the efficient use of both, are a critical dimension. A well-defined staff development plan, evolving from identified needs based on developmental teacher evaluation, instructional strategy fidelity, and program objectives, guidelines, and regulations, is a second critical component.

Parents' participation in their child's instructional program is a priority. A variety of both school year and summer programs have been developed and instituted successfully through the combined efforts of the teachers across the districts.

Contact Norman Ronell, Program Director, ESU #7 Chapter I Cooperative, 2657 44th Avenue, Columbus, NE 68601. (402) 564-4414.

Developmental Funding: USOE ESEA Title I.

JDRP No. 78-197 **(11/17/78)**
Recertified **(11/84)**

Resident Supervisory Support for Teachers (RSST). An instructional support alternative designed to improve classroom instruction by training school personnel to utilize a nonjudgmental, nonevaluative process. For teachers, school administrators, and supervisory personnel.

Description Resident Supervisory Support for Teachers (RSST) is an instructional support process designed to improve classroom instruction by training existing school personnel to use an adaption of Robert Goldhammer's model with an emphasis on interpersonal communication skills, conferencing and data gathering techniques. The program helps teachers to capitalize on their strengths and compensate for weaknesses. It is designed to provide instructional support for effective, less effective, experienced and inexperienced teachers. This process may be utilized with instructors on all levels and disciplines (elementary, secondary, higher education). The ultimate goal of the training program is to provide each participating school with a cadre of peer coaches.

No special staff or facility is required to implement RSST. Persons interested in implementing the program must complete an initial two-day training session and a one-day follow-up session after implementation. The program is available for adoption by individual schools and/or school districts. Training manuals are $20 per copy.

Awareness materials are available at no cost. The program staff is available for awareness, training, and/or follow-up at the adopter site. Individual technical assistance is available as needed. Costs for all services are negotiable.

Contact Delores W. Hamilton, Director, Resident Supervisory Support for Teachers (RSST), Presidential Building, 415 12th Street, NW Room 1001, Washington, D.C. 20004. (202) 724-8550.

Developmental Funding: USOE Title IV-C.

JDRP No. 82-11R **(10/28/82)**

Sharing Successful Programs. Statewide procedures for validating, disseminating, and adopting educational programs.

Description Sharing Successful Programs (SSP) is an adaptation of PEP/JDRP and NDN procedures for validating, disseminating, and adopting educational programs. Promising educational programs are identified and provided with evaluation assistance, and reviewed by an external panel of trained reviewers who judge if the program has convincing evidence of success. Validated programs are reimbursed costs for providing awareness and training, and are given technical assistance in staff development techniques. School districts may adopt validated programs with local funds, or with funds secured by a grant process. A network of field agents helps school districts match needs with programs, and assists them in planning adoption strategies. SSP is composed of activities related to identifying exemplary programs, assessing the merit of those programs, preparing the staff of those programs to be effective in disseminating their programs, making programs available to school districts, and evaluating activities of the dissemination process. Implementing SSP can provide programs in four school districts for the same cost as implementing a development program in a single district. State Education Agencies are appropriate adoptors for SSP. An adoption of the complete model will require two years. Training required is five days for the complete model with two days for the initial stage.

Contact Laurie Rowe, State Facilitator, Room 974EBA, New York State Education Department, Albany, NY 12234 or Richard L. Egelston, Coordinator of Validation, Room 975EBA, New York State Education Department, Albany, NY 12234. (518) 473-1388.

Developmental Funding: ESEA Title IV, ECIA Chapter 2, EESA Title II, New York State legislative funds.

PEP No. 88-19 (11/1/88)

Section 3

Dropout Prevention/Alternative Programs

* These programs are currently funded by the NDN.

Summary of Program Services for Section 3

Program	Goal*	Page	AWARENESS										TRAINING						
			Dissem. Funds Available		Costs to Potential Adopter			On Site Visitation Available		Materials Available				Staff Available		Costs to Adopter			Certified Trainers Available	Training Time Required
			NDN	Other	Hon	Trav	Per Diem	Home Site	Adopt Site	Free Paper	Video	Film Strip	Other	Home Site	Adopt Site	Hon	Trav	Per Diem	State(s)	Day(s)
City-As-School (CAS)	2	3-1	✓	✓	✓	✓	✓	✓	✓	✓	✓			✓	✓	✓	✓		CA, NY	3
Coca-Cola Valued Youth Program, The	2	3-2	✓	✓		✓	✓	✓	✓	✓	✓	✓		✓	✓	✓	✓	✓	TX	3+
COoperative Federation... (COFFEE)	2	3-6			✓	✓	✓	✓		✓	✓		✓	✓	✓	✓	✓	✓	(none)	1
DeLaSalle Model	2	3-3			(negotiable)	✓	✓	✓		✓	✓		✓	✓	✓	✓	✓	✓	MO, OH, OK, OR, PR	2
Diversified Educational... (DEEP)	3	3-6			✓	✓	✓	✓		✓				✓	✓	✓	✓	✓	KS	3+
Focus Dissemination Project	6	3-7				✓	✓	✓	✓	✓					✓	✓	✓	✓	(none)	1-2
Graduation, Reality, And Dual-Role Skills (GRADS)	2	3-4	✓		(negotiable)	✓	✓	✓	✓	✓	✓			✓	✓	(negotiable)	✓	✓	NM, OH, WA	2
Intercept, Project	2	3-7			✓	✓	✓	✓	✓	✓	✓			✓	✓		✓	✓	(none)	3+
Public and Private School Collaboration	5	3-8				✓	✓	✓		✓				✓					(none)	3+
SCORE for College (SCORE)	3, 8	3-5	(info. not available)																	

* National Goals for Education—definitions for each goal can be found on pages 5-7.

City-As-School (CAS). An alternative program that combines academic learning with the world of work for high school students, including at-risk students.

Audience Validated by N.Y.S. and approved by NDN (U.S.D.E) for at-risk and gifted/talented adolescents in grades 9 through 12.

Description Features of City-As-School (CAS):

- A high school program which links students with hundreds of learning experiences throughout the community.
- Students spend up to 30-40 hours per week in learning experiences utilizing community resources of business, civic, cultural, social or political nature.
- Academic credit is granted for each learning experience successfully completed.
- Structured, student-centered Learning Experience Activity Packet (LEAP helps to identify and evaluate discrete areas of instruction in each resource.
- Students attend resources for one cycle (9 weeks) or two cycles and receive credit or no credit rather than letter or numerical grades.
- Specialized, small classes support activities at community resources.
- Weekly seminar groups serve as forum for discussions of guidance, academic and social issues.
- May be a stand-alone school, or a program within a school.

Evidence of Effectiveness

- Improvement in attendance;
- Increase in course completion rate of students;
- Better attitude toward schooling, career, and adults; and
- Evidence derived from school records, pre- and posttest comparison of a control group and use of likert-scaled instruments.

Requirements Three days of inservice training sessions in curriculum development and initial and ongoing program implementation is provided by CAS trainers at participating site or CAS in New York.

Costs Follow-up consultations are provided free of charge as an integral part of program implementation. Program evaluation services are also available in the form of a multifaceted, guided self-evaluation which can be administered at the adopting or home site. The all inclusive fee is $3,000-$3,500 (travel, lodging, trainer, materials), depending on the number trained, up to ten people.

Services All forms used to develop resources, publicity reports, pamphlets, catalogs, recruitment posters, evaluation instruments, and administrative materials included.

Contact William Weinstein, City-As-School, 16 Clarkson Street, New York, NY 10014. (212) 645-6121, (212) 691-7801, or FAX (212) 675-2858. E-Mail: bill.weinstein@nycenet.nycps.edu

JDRP No. 82-13 **(6/10/82)**
Recertified **(3/11/93)**

Developmental Funding: USOE ESEA Title IV-C and NYC Board of Education.

Coca-Cola Valued Youth Program, The. A cross-age tutoring program designed to reduce dropout rates among middle school children who are limited-English-proficient and at risk of leaving school, for grades 7-8.

Audience Approved by PEP for students in grades 7-8.

Description The Coca-Cola Valued Youth Program is unique in that tutors are limited-English-proficient students at risk of dropping out of school. When placed in a responsible tutoring role and supported in their efforts, tutors gain significant social and economic benefits. The program has three levels that incorporate all the major features of the model—philosophy, instruction, and support. The philosophical base consists of tenets such as all students can learn; all students, parents and teachers have a right to participate fully in creating and maintaining excellent schools; excellence in schools contributes to individual and collective economic growth, stability and advancement; and commitment to educational excellence is created by including students, parents and teachers in setting goals, making decisions, monitoring progress, and evaluating outcomes. The instructional strategy incorporates five major components including classes for tutors; tutoring sessions; field trips; role-modeling; and student recognition. The support strategy involves curriculum, coordination, staff enrichment, family involvement, and evaluation activities.

In 1992, the Coca-Cola Valued Youth Program was recognized by the Secretary of Education as a model dropout prevention program, meeting the National Goal for Education 2 of increasing the high school graduation rate to at least 90%.

Evidence of Effectiveness Student tutors participating in the program demonstrate a significantly lower school dropout rate than the comparison group and national rates; achieve significantly higher reading grades than the comparison group; show significantly greater gains on the Piers-Harris Self-Concept Scale than comparison students; and make significantly greater gains on the Quality of School Life Scale than the comparison group.

Requirements The model can be implemented by existing school staff. Six implementation guides (for the program administrator, the secondary principal, the elementary principal, the teacher/coordinator, the evaluation liaison, and the elementary receiving teachers) are available. Materials also include a family liaison guide and workbooks for each tutor in the program. While the materials provide the basics for adopting the program, schools are encouraged to plan adjustments in implementation. Elements critical to the success of the program include weekly classes for tutors with a minimum of 30 sessions per school year, a minimum age and grade difference of four years between the tutor and tutee, provision of a stipend, a flexible curriculum based on students' tutoring and academic needs, and a program staff dedicated and committed to the program's success. A minimum of ten training and technical assistance days are required.

Costs Cost per student/user (based on 25 tutors and 75 tutees) ranges from $150-$250, including tutor stipends, recognition awards, staff training, technical assistance, and evaluation.

Services In addition to training, technical assistance, materials, and evaluation, follow-up consultation is available.

Contact Josie D. Supik, Intercultural Development Research Association, 5835 Callaghan Road, Suite 350, San Antonio, TX 78228. (210) 684-8180, FAX (210) 684-5389.

Developmental Funding: Coca-Cola and
USDE Office of Bilingual and Minority Languages Affairs.

PEP No. 91-23 (4/8/91)

DeLaSalle Model. An individualized program of special services coupled with a core academic curriculum for students who have dropped out of grades 9-12 to help them improve their academic skills and complete their high school education.

Audience Approved by PEP for populations fitting the high school level (grades 9-12), with most students between the ages of 14 and 18. Students for whom the DeLaSalle Model is appropriate are those who have typically had poor or sporadic school attendance and low academic performance in their previous schooling.

Description DeLaSalle Education Center is a private not-for-profit agency which has served the greater Kansas City area since 1971. The goals of the fully accredited program are to increase school attendance, improve academic skills, and enhance self-esteem and educational attitudes in students who have dropped out of high school and have no other chance for completing an education.

DeLaSalle employs a variety of programming features and services within a comprehensive model to allow every youngster to be successful in his or her education. These include a supportive non-traditional school structure, a small student-teacher ratio, individualized learning, student contracting, intensive counseling, vocational skill training, and a diagnostic prescriptive teaching process.

The DeLaSalle Model provides a design for replication of educational strategies which reinforce the efforts called for by the National Goals for Education. Using the Model, any alternative school can develop an appropriate program within the framework of local needs and resources.

Evidence of Effectiveness Follow-up studies have shown that the DeLaSalle Model has enabled students to earn the high school diploma or GED certificate, and improve work skills and social adjustment. Improvements have been shown to be maintained long after program completion.

Requirements While DeLaSalle Education Center has developed its own facility apart from any traditional school, the Model it has developed could be incorporated into an existing school program or within a common campus. Minimally, the Model would require a separate wing or floor to accommodate its special focus. Size of faculty and staff would depend on enrollment. Beside the need for high-interest, low-skill level materials for classroom use, appropriate materials and space for vocational classes, and faculty training and inservice, there are no substantial differences in outlay between conventional programs and the Model program.

Costs Overall costs for implementation of the DeLaSalle Model are similar to costs in a public school system. Estimates for personnel and materials needed to serve 160 students: nine teaching positions, five support staff, three days of training annually, office space, classroom and vocational equipment, record-keeping and work supplies, and testing materials.

Services Initial awareness materials are available at no cost. Awareness and training sessions are available with costs to be negotiated, either at the home site or adoption site. Interested administrators are invited to visit DeLaSalle Education Center at any time. Adoption of the Model includes consultation and evaluation support for the first year.

Contact   Regina Hansen, DeLaSalle Education Center, 3740 Forest, Kansas City, MO 64109-3200. (816) 561-3312, FAX (816) 561-6106.

Developmental Funding: Mix of private and public funding (local and federal).   PEP No. 88-20 (7/21/89)

Graduation, Reality, And Dual-Role Skills (GRADS). A program to keep pregnant and parenting teens in school, with additional goals of encouraging good health care practices and helping young parents set occupational goals, for grades 7-12.

Audience Approved by PEP for all pregnant and parenting teens, male and female, in grades 7-12 from city, exempted village, local, and joint vocational school districts in urban, suburban, and rural communities.

Description Graduation, Reality, And Dual-Role Skills (GRADS) is a family and consumer-sciences instructional and intervention program. Regular GRADS classes are supplemented with seminars and individual projects. Teachers trained in the program serve one school or travel among three or four. The **instructional component** focuses on use of the 1300$^+$ page teacher-written *Adolescent Parent Resource Guide*, which provides the practical problems, concepts, and strategies which guide the development of skills in teenage parents. The guide discusses communication and skills necessary for effective problem solving in the teen family. It recognizes the stresses affecting pregnant teens, focusing on management skills required for teen family wellness. Central themes of the guide and the curriculum (which emphasizes practical problem solving) are the perennial and practical problems of the adolescent parent at home, school, and work; and the development of knowledge and skills to solve problems in real life, including identifying alternatives, examining consequences, considering personal goals and values, scrutinizing decisions, and taking morally defensible actions. The four content areas include positive self, pregnancy, parenting, and economic independence. Audio visuals, supplemental texts, and other materials are also part of the program. The **advisory committee component** and **home and community outreach component** seek to build strong relationships with students through home visits and/or contacts with family. Collaboration and agency linkages are necessary for addressing the obstacles teen parents face to being able to remain in school until graduation. The **evaluation/research component** seeks to identify and report student and program outcomes. All programs report outcomes, and a state and national report is published annually.

Evidence of Effectiveness Pregnant and parenting teens enrolled in the program are more likely to remain in school until graduation, during pregnancy, and after childbirth; they have also significantly increased their knowledge of positive parenting practices as measured by pre- and posttest instruments. Pregnant mothers are also more likely to deliver healthy babies than teens not enrolled in the program.

Requirements A certified family and consumer science teacher must secure the resource guide and attend a two-day inservice training. Needed equipment includes student tables and chairs, a teacher desk, file cabinets, lockable storage, audiovisual equipment, and a telephone for private conversation available at all times.

Costs Awareness presentation (one to two hours) costs consist of travel expenses for the presenter. Training (two days) costs consist of travel expenses for the presenter, and the purchase price of the *Adolescent Parent Resource Guide*, which must be obtained for each teacher or school team, at a cost of $78. Cost sharing may be requested for the *GRADS Implementation Notebook* (the training materials).

Services In addition to training and materials, the program provides updates, technical assistance, and processes for monitoring and evaluation of the program's effectiveness. Awareness materials are available at no cost.

Contact Sharon G. Enright, Ohio Department of Education, Division of Vocational and Adult Education, Room 909, 65 South Front Street, Columbus, OH 43215-4183. (614) 466-3046, FAX (614) 644-5702. E-Mail: ve_enright@odevax.ode.ohio.gov

Developmental Funding: Comprehensive Employment Training and Administration.

PEP No. 90-08 **(2/9/90)**

Audience Underachieving youth, especially high-risk students from language minority and diverse ethnic backgrounds, grades 7-12.

Description SCORE provides a comprehensive, holistic approach, training schools to institute a program incorporating appropriate placement, study skills, academic support, multiple modality teaching techniques, counseling, and mentoring. SCORE trainers work with schools to design a customized program for accelerating the achievement of high-risk youth, train staff, and provide follow-through support with a set of materials, workbooks, videotapes, and consultation. Students are heterogeneously grouped in a college core curriculum leading to university eligibility upon graduation. The program has five major components: (1) Tutoring and Study Skills; (2) Guidance; (3) Parents; (4) Motivational Activities; and (5) Summer Acceleration. Local trainers can be developed to inservice new staff and serve as program consultants. SCORE addresses National Educational Goals 3 and 8.

Evidence of Effectiveness Five claims of effectiveness were evaluated using case studies, pre/post test gains, and reversal of downward trends in college eligibility and college attendance. Each program component was evaluated for both individual and combined effectiveness. Results showed that high-risk students who participate in SCORE are successfully enrolled into a common core college preparatory curriculum; SCORE high-risk students enroll in colleges and universities at higher rates than their peers; students involved in SCORE test out of LEP programs at rates higher than their peers; SCORE schools decrease remedial course offerings and increase college preparatory curriculum; and schools that implement an effective SCORE program increase graduation rates.

Requirements SCORE can operate within existing school facilities using current curriculum and equipment. A director, teacher, tutors, counselors, and parent workers are required for implementation.

Costs Start-up costs include Adoption Training: $2000 for one three-day training on site. $250 per site (up to ten sites may be trained together) for materials. Actual travel expenses for the trainer. Study Skills Training: $1500 per site for one two-day self-contained training. $15 per participant for materials. Study Skills workbooks (English and Spanish versions) for student participants are approximately $5 per student. Supplementary teaching materials are approximately $500. Technical Assistance: SCORE recommends one half-day per site per quarter the first year, one day the second year, and participation in the trainer-of-trainers program once the program is operational. Adoption training materials include: Directors Guide, Staff Development Guide, and Resource Guide for the three day adoption training participants. Awareness videos on program overview and effective tutorials are available on a free loan basis. Supplemental curriculum materials for administrators, counselors, and teachers include research findings, teaching techniques/strategies, and teaching tools with a focus on language minority students and those at risk of failure. Reproduction masters are included for handouts and visual aids.

Services SCORE provides adopters with extensive staff development, staff and student materials necessary to run a quality program. Technical assistance, localized to site needs, is provided during implementation.

Contact Sharon Johnson, Director, Orange County Department of Education, 200 Kalmus, P.O. Box 9050, Costa Mesa, CA 92628-9050 (714) 966-4394, FAX (714) 662-3148.

Developmental Funding: ESEA, Title IV-C.

PEP No. 94-1 (**4/1/94**)

COoperative Federation For Educational Experiences (COFFEE). A comprehensive dropout prevention/ reclamation program for adolescents with histories of academic failure, truancy, poor self-concept, family problems, and social misconduct.

Description   COoperative Federation For Educational Experiences (COFFEE) is a regional, instructional, occupational training and counseling program for at-risk youth from seventeen school districts. The characteristics of this student population are as follows: histories of academic failure, truancy, poor self-concept, family problems, and social misconduct. The program integrates five components: an academic component—which provides relevant basic skills instruction based on an individualized education plan; an occupational component—which provides hands-on educational experiences in an adult-like work environment preparing students for the high-demand jobs of the 90's; a counseling component—which provides character building, occupational and emotional support utilizing existing state, regional, and local service organizations; a preemployment education component—designed to enhance the employability of at-risk students through classroom instruction and student internships; and a physical education component—which offers a program of recreational activities adapted to enable students to develop a sense of self-accomplishment and group cooperation. The occupational component includes training programs in the following areas: Computer Maintenance and Repair, Word Processing, Building and Grounds Maintenance, and Horticulture/Agriculture.

Contact   Edward Sikonski, Executive Director, Oxford High School Annex, Main Street, Oxford, MA 01540. (508) 987-6090.

Developmental Funding: Vocational Education.

JDRP No. 82-25 **(5/19/82)**
Recertified **(5/21/86)**

Diversified Educational Experiences Program (DEEP). A new method of organizing and managing an academic classroom, for grades 9-12.

Description   The major goal of the Diversified Educational Experiences Program (DEEP) is to develop an instructional process for secondary school classrooms that allows instructors to create an academic environment emphasizing success for every learner while decreasing learner hostility to educational institutions.

DEEP offers students and instructors a method of organizing and managing an academic classroom that differs from the usual classroom model. Students in the DEEP classroom identify needs, formulate objectives, develop tasks based upon these objectives, present group and individual projects based upon fulfillment of objectives, receive teacher debriefing following presentation of the projects, and participate in their own evaluations. DEEP offers learners in academic subjects alternative ways to create, gather, develop and display information. Extensive use is made of electronic and nonelectronic media. The role of the teacher is that of advisor, consultant, and learning-systems manager. The classroom is a workshop where students work cooperatively to complete tasks. Community resources are utilized.

The DEEP classroom is highly structured, but the structure is not the same as in the typical academic classroom. Teachers who demonstrate the ability and desire to change their methods of instruction are trained in the use of these new management techniques. They must be willing to teach one or more DEEP classes along with their regular classes. The teachers are trained as learning facilitators, and the conflict-management process is based on human relations and peer group interaction as well as on teacher-student interaction. Once the training has been accomplished, students can be enrolled in the program as part of the normal scheduling procedure. The program provides management charts and materials along with evaluation procedures.

Contact   J. Connett, Director, DEEP, KEDDS/Link, 412-18 South Main, Wichita, KS 67202. (316) 833-5100, FAX (316) 833-5103.

Developmental Funding: USOE ESEA Title III.

JDRP No. 76-82 **(6/23/76)**

Focus Dissemination Project. A successful secondary program for training teachers to deal with disaffected youth. Approved by JDRP for disaffected secondary students and all secondary educators, school board members, and community members who have an interest in developing local programs to meet the needs of the disaffected students in their settings.

Description Focus provides an alternative education plan for students who have been identified as disaffected, showing a lack of motivation, lack of confidence, and low self-esteem. The program effects responsible institutional change and positive student attitude and performance by helping students learn responsibility to self, school, and society. Through a group counseling experience, the peer group is guided to deal with the problems causing disaffection. Focus is a "school within a school" for secondary students who are not achieving or functioning in a way beneficial to themselves and/or those around them. The Focus program seeks to reduce student disaffection with school and learning, to improve each student's ability to relate effectively with peers and adults, and to give each student a reason to be optimistic about the future. Focus is a highly structured program offering courses in English, social studies, and math. Instruction in Focus classes is based on ability and need. Focus students take such classes as science, physical education, health, and electives in the regular school program. All Focus students are involved in a group counseling experience called Family. Each Family consists of 8 to 10 students and one teacher who meet together one hour daily throughout the year. Family attempts to help the student develop feelings of caring, self-worth, and concern for others. It includes examination of one's own behavior in relation to the reactions of others within an atmosphere of positive support from the group. Program effectiveness is measured in grade equivalency gains on standard achievement tests, reductions in negative behaviors and improved attendance and grades.

Contact   Don May, Focus Dissemination Project, Human Resource Associates, Inc., Suite 200, 201 North Concord Exchange, South Saint Paul, MN 55075. (612) 451-6840 or (800) 345-5285.

Developmental Funding: HEW, Youth Development Act.   JDRP No. 74-74 **(5/29/74)**

Intercept, Project. A positive program for intervention and remedy of students at-risk of suspension, truancy, dropout, academic failure, and behavior problems. Approved by JDRP for students in grades 9-12 who are considered high risk due to chronic academic failure, disruptive behavior, truancy, suspension, and dropout. Also used successfully for students in grades 4 through 8.

Description The basic premise of Project Intercept training is to restructure a school's teaching philosophies and to provide more effective techniques to deal with the at-risk student. The Intercept program is highly individualized and goals for each individual school are developed in concert with the participants of the project. Teachers, counselors, and administrators are trained as a team to approach all problems that affect at-risk students.

Project Intercept is a two-part program: one-half theoretical, one-half process. The program consists of a one-week training by Intercept master trainers followed by week-long visits throughout the year for on-line critiquing and demonstration teaching. One of the goals is to develop turnkey trainers for maintenance of the program at the original training site with possible expansion of the program to other schools in the system.

Contact   James E. Loan, M.A., Project Intercept, 1101 South Race Street, Denver, CO 80210. (303) 777-5870.

Developmental Funding: USOE ESEA Title-IVC.   JDRP No. 81-50 **(1/20/82)**

Public and Private School Collaboration. A program for students in grades 10 and 11; the Connecticut Scholars Program. A collaboration for the purpose of providing an opportunity for advanced residential study for academically promising urban school students.

Description Public Private School Collaboration makes connections and makes connections work. Where public and private schools have not traditionally joined forces, they do so within a collaborative framework. This allows them to apply their finest resources to meet significant needs. It also allows them to gain the support of leading corporations and foundations as well as research institutions and museums as they seek to respond to those needs.

The developer demonstrator has engaged in this work for over ten years. In Connecticut, Choate Rosemary Hall (a private boarding school) and the Connecticut Association of Urban Superintendents sponsor a five-week program of advanced residential study for students from Connecticut's 13 urban school districts. They have been joined by distinguished corporations (from AT&T to Xerox) and noted research institutions (from Brown University to the federal Star Schools Program). Students study topics ranging from Advanced Astronomy to Vectors and Matrices. They return to their schools encouraged by their accomplishments. Many other collaborative activities have flowed from this initiative and include programs for students and teachers alike.

Importantly, a collaboration does not have to involve a boarding school, urban schools, or huge foundation grants. It does require the full participation of public and private school partners, definition of genuine need, and the commitment to work together to find and apply resources to meet that need. After three and a half years, adoptions are now under way from Maine to California. They can be found in boarding schools, urban public high schools, day schools, elementary schools, and more. Winston Churchill once said that opportunity seeks not a "seat but a springboard." That is just what this program supplies.

Contact   Howard Hand, Director, Summer Programs, Office of Public Private Collaboration, Choate Rosemary Hall, Box 788, 333 Christian Street, Wallingford, CT 06492. (203) 284-5365.

Developmental Funding: Private sources.   JDRP No. 86-25 (**9/10/86**)

Section 4

Reading/Writing

* These programs are currently funded by the NDN.

Summary of Program Services for Section 4

Program	Goal*	Page	Dissem. Funds Available — NDN	Other	AWARENESS — Costs to Potential Adopter — Hon	Trav	Per Diem	On Site Visitation Available — Home Site	Adopt Site	Materials Available — Free Paper	Video	Film Strip	Other	TRAINING — Staff Available — Home Site	Adopt Site	Costs to Adopter — Hon	Trav	Per Diem	Certified Trainers Available — State(s)	Training Time Required — Day(s)
Books And Beyond	3, 6	4-1	✓		(negotiable)			✓	✓	✓	✓			✓	✓	✓	✓	✓	AK, AS, CA, CO, CT, GA, IA, IL, KY, LA, MA, MI, MN, MS, NC, ND, NE, NJ, NV, NY, OH, OK, SC, TN, TX, UT, VA, WI	<1-1
Computer Education for Language Learning (CELL)	3	4-2		✓				✓	✓	✓	✓		✓	✓	✓	✓			(none)	1
Cooperative Integrated . . . (CIRC) - Reading	3, 4	4-3	✓		✓	✓	✓	✓	✓	✓	✓			✓	✓	✓	✓	✓	AZ, CA, IN, MD, NY, PA, TX	2+
Exemplary Center for Reading Instruction (ECRI)	3	4-4	✓					✓	✓	✓	✓			✓	✓		✓	✓	AK, AR, CA, GE, LA, ME, MI, NE, NJ, NY, OH, OR, SC, SD, TN, TX, UT, VA, WI	3+
Flint Follow Through: The School Effectiveness Model	3,4	4-15		✓	(negotiable)			✓		✓				✓		(negotiable)			AZ, CA, MA, MT, OR, WA, Guam	2+
HOSTS (Help One Student . . .)	3	4-15	✓		(negotiable)			✓	✓	✓	✓			✓		✓			(none)	3+
Image-Making Within the Writing Process	3	4-5	✓					✓	✓	✓	✓			✓	✓	✓	✓	✓	NH	1½-2
Individualized Prescriptive . . . (IPIMS)	3	4-16			✓	✓	✓	✓	✓	✓	✓			✓	✓	✓	✓	✓	NY	1
Junior Great Books . . . (JGBC)	3	4-6						✓	✓	✓	✓				✓	(flat fee of $78/teacher trained)			(all states)	2
Keyboarding, Reading, and Spelling (KRS)	3, 6	4-7	✓					✓	✓	✓	✓			✓	✓	✓	✓	✓	AK, AL, CA, MI, NC, NE, OH, OR, SC, SD, TN, UT, VA, WI	<1-1

* National Goals for Education—definitions for each goal can be found on pages 5-7.

Summary of Program Services for Section 4 (cont'd)

Program	Goal*	Page	AWARENESS										TRAINING						
			Dissem. Funds Available		Costs to Potential Adopter			On Site Visitation Available		Materials Available				Staff Available		Costs to Adopter			Certified Trainers Available	Training Time Required
			NDN	Other	Hon	Trav	Per Diem	Home Site	Adopt Site	Free Paper	Video	Film Strip	Other	Home Site	Adopt Site	Hon	Trav	Per Diem	State(s)	Day(s)
Learning To Read Through the Arts Program	3	4-8			(negotiable)			✓	✓		✓	✓	✓	✓	✓	(negotiable)			CA, CO, FL, NC, NM, OK, WA	2
Multicultural Literacy Program (MLP)	3	4-9	(info. not available)																	
Profile Approach to Writing (PAW)	3	4-10	✓			✓	✓	✓	✓	✓	✓			✓		✓	✓	✓	CA, IL, OK, TX, WI, WY, Pacific Islands	1-3
QUILL . . .	3	4-16			✓	✓	✓	✓	✓	✓					✓	✓	✓	✓	KS, LA, MA, RI, SC	2
Reading Power in the Content Areas (RP)	3, 4, 6	4-11	✓		(negotiable)			✓	✓	✓	✓			✓	✓	✓	✓	✓	CA, CT, IL, KS, MA, MI, MN, OH, OK, TX, CNMI, GUAM	1-2
Reading Recovery	3	4-12	✓		✓	✓	✓	✓	✓	✓	✓	✓		✓		✓	✓	✓	(none)	9 months
Rural Schools Reading Project (RSRP)		4-13	✓		✓	✓	✓	✓	✓	✓	✓				✓	✓	✓	✓	IA, IL, MI, MN, OH	1-3
TV Reading S.T.A.R.	3	4-17				✓	✓	✓	✓	✓				✓	✓	✓	✓	✓	AL, CT, D.C., DE, MA, MD, NH, NJ, NY, PA, RI, VA	1.5
Writers Project, The	3	4-14	✓			✓		✓	✓	✓	✓		✓	✓	✓	✓	✓	✓	MO, NM, OH, WY	3+
WRiting Is Thorough and Efficient (WR.I.T.&E.)	3	4-17			✓	✓	✓	✓	✓	✓				✓	✓	✓	✓	✓	D.C., GA, HI, MO, NJ, TX, VA	2+

* National Goals for Education—definitions for each goal can be found on pages 5-7.

Books And Beyond. A program designed to motivate students in grades K-8 and their parents to become more discriminating in their allocation of time between recreational reading and television viewing.

Audience Approved by JDRP and PEP for students in grades K-8. Implemented successfully in all school settings and can be effectively used with bilingual students, non-English speaking students, Chapter I and learning disabled as well as mainstream and gifted students. Materials translated in Spanish.

Description Books And Beyond is designed to help students develop the *habit* of recreational reading, to involve parents in their children's reading activities, and to decrease indiscriminate TV viewing. Success-oriented strategies produce positive, long-lasting behavioral changes in regard to recreational reading. Success for each child is assured through self-paced procedures that allow for individual differences. Basic components include:

- A six to eight month read-a-thon based on at-home and in-school recreational reading with progress recorded on a colorful school bulletin board;
- Role-modeling by parents, teachers, and staff;
- Promotion of family literacy activities; and
- A unique TV component which promotes critical thinking and decision making regarding TV viewing and use of recreational free time.

This program addresses National Goals for Education 3 and 6 by encouraging students to develop the *habit* of reading and in doing so, improve reading and comprehension skills. This, in turn, broadens opportunities for students to *use their minds well* and *be prepared for further learning.* The program works to ensure that every child will become *a literate adult American, able to develop skills necessary to compete in a future world economy and to exercise the rights and responsibilities of citizenship.*

Evidence of Effectiveness Participants demonstrated significant gains in reading achievement when compared with a control group study as measured by the CTBS Reading Test. They also displayed increases in recreational reading, scope of reading, increased family literacy activities, and a decrease in time spent watching television.

Requirements A one-day training session and a Books And Beyond theme manual are necessary for successful adoption. The manual includes instruction for implementation, ideas for adaptations, graphic designs for bulletin boards, forms for student/teacher materials, and parent newsletters. Training topics include exploration school needs, reading strategies, record keeping, cost, evaluation, and activities for parent participation, developing discriminate TV viewing habits, and stimulating recreational reading.

Costs Typical training costs consist of travel expenses plus $300 per day honorarium for program staff. A network of more than 125 certified trainers exists nationwide. Training costs are negotiable with individual certified trainers. Costs for school implementation, including duplication expenses and incentives, are approximately $2.50 per student.

Services Program staff are available for awareness meetings (cost to be negotiated). Awareness materials are available at no cost. There are 25 National Demonstration Sites throughout the country available for visitation upon request. An awareness/training video is available for $20. Visitors are welcome at the program site by appointment.

Contact Ellie Topolovac, Director or Ann Collins, Coordinator, Solana Beach School District, 309 North Rios Avenue, Solana Beach, CA 92075. (619) 755-8000, 755-3823, or 755-6319 (for orders), FAX (619) 755-0449.

Developmental Funding: ESEA Title IV-C.   JDRP No. 84-8 (3/20/84)
Recertified (8/11/94)

Computer Education for Language Learning (CELL). A program of computer-assisted English-as-a-Second-Language instruction designed to increase the English reading and language arts competencies of Limited English Proficient (LEP) elementary school students.

Audience   Approved by PEP for LEP students with intermediate oral English proficiency levels in grades 1-5.

Description   Computer Education for Language Learning (CELL) provides a highly organized reading and language arts program using the inherent benefits of Computer-Assisted-Education (CAE) such as maintaining student interest with interactive learning and capitalizing on the students' natural excitement about computers and technology. The components of the CELL Practice are: (1) the CELL computer lab; (2) the Skills Prescription Guide which correlates commercial software to the ESL continuum and indexes software programs by difficulty level; and (3) the organization and communication system between the computer lab and the classroom. After students' needs and levels are diagnosed by the classroom teacher using Irvine Management System benchmark tests and teacher observation of classroom performance, the lab technician prescribes CELL software and activities coordinated with classroom instruction. Students use commercial educational software in 30-minute lab sessions four times per week. At the end of each skill segment, the students' skill acquisition is assessed and progress records are maintained. The teacher performs periodic checks to assure the application of newly acquired skills; and standardized forms are used to convey progress information between the teacher and lab technician. Students exit CELL when they achieve Fluent English Proficient status.

Evidence of Effectiveness   After eight months of CELL instruction, students in grades 1-5 achieve statistically and educationally significant gains in English reading and language arts as measured by the CTBS form U total reading and language scales. Analyses of NCE scores and effect sizes show that CELL students significantly close the gap between their English reading and language levels and those of the norm group. Equal program effect sizes are found in dissemination sites and the original site regardless of a school's high or low LEP concentration.

Requirements   A one-day inservice is conducted for lab technicians and a site contact person who is either the principal or a credentialed teacher. In addition, the computer lab requires three to eight computers (any combination of Apple IIe, Apple IIGS, and Macintosh) and commercial software as recommended by CELL.

Costs   Costs vary depending upon a school's hardware, software, and personnel needs. The estimated installation cost is $1040-$2040 per site ($21-$41 per student for 50 students per site), $100 for CELL manual and forms, $500-$1500 for commercial software. The cost estimate for subsequent years' operation is $120 per site: $100 for commercial software.

Services   In addition to training and materials, technical assistance is available on-call, replicating sites are updated on new software and technology available to them via the CELL Newsletter, and site visits/support are available.

Contact   Celia Edmundson or Brenda Dolan, Irvine Unified School District, 5050 Barranca Parkway, Irvine, CA 92714. (714) 733-9391 or (800) 237-CELL.

Developmental Funding: USDE ESEA Title VII,
Academic Excellence grant from OBEMLA, state, and local.

PEP No. 93-17 (**4/2/93**)

Cooperative Integrated Reading and Composition (CIRC) - Reading. CIRC is a comprehensive approach to instruction in reading and composition/language arts for grades 2-6. In CIRC Reading, students are taught in reading groups and then return to mixed ability teams to work on a series of cognitively engaging activities, including partner reading, making predictions, identification of characters, settings, problem and problem solutions, summarization, vocabulary, reading comprehension exercises, and story-realted writing.

Audience   Approved by PEP for students in grades three and four. Has been used successfully in grades 2-6.

Description   Cooperative Integrated Reading and Composition (CIRC) is a comprehensive program for teaching reading and writing/language arts. It has three principle elements: story-related activities, direct instruction in reading comprehension, and integrated language arts/writing. In CIRC, teachers use anthologies basal readers and/or novels, much as they would in traditional reading programs. Students are assigned to teams composed of pairs of students from the same or different reading groups. Students work in pairs on a series of cognitively engaging activities, including reading to each other; predicting how stories will end; summarizing stories to each other; writing responses to stories; and practicing spelling, decoding, and vocabulary. Students work in teams to understand the main idea and master other comprehension skills. During language arts periods, students also write drafts, revise and edit one another's work, and prepare to "publish" their writing.

In most CIRC activities, students follow a sequence of teacher instruction, team practice, peer preassessments, assessment, and team recognition. Students are not assessed until their teammates have determined they are ready. **Team recognition** involves giving certificates to teams based upon the performance of all team members on all reading and writing activities. Because students work on materials appropriate to their reading levels, they have **equal opportunities for success**. Students' contributions to their teams are based on their quiz scores and their final, independently written compositions, which ensures individual accountability.

CIRC Reading and CIRC Language Arts/Writing provide a structure for teachers to teach and students to learn which helps all students become more effective readers and writers.

Evidence of Effectiveness   The results of three separate studies indicate that CIRC has a consistent and educationally significant effect on the reading achievement of students in the elementary grades. More specifically, significantly greater gains were made in CIRC-Reading classes than control classes on the California Achievement Test's reading scales for comprehension and vocabulary, and on individually administered Durrell Informal Reading Inventory scales.

Requirements   CIRC-Reading requires two days of training for teachers and administrators, plus materials. Additional training/follow-up days are recommended. No additional staff is needed. For the installation year, materials costs are approximately $240 per class; for subsequent years, $100 per class.

Services   Awareness materials are available at no cost. Program staff members are available for awareness sessions, training sessions, and technical assistance (costs to be negotiated). Materials for anthologies, basals, and more than a hundred novels are available at a nominal cost.

Contact   **Anna Marie Farnish, CIRC, Center for Social Organization of Schools, The Johns Hopkins University, 3505 North Charles Street, Baltimore, MD 21218. (410) 516-8857, FAX (410) 516-8890.**

Developmental Funding: U.S. Department of Education.   PEP No. 88-06 (**4/27/88**)

Exemplary Center for Reading Instruction (ECRI). A program designed to identify critical teacher behaviors essential in preventing reading failure of students in grades 1-10. Inservice education for teachers based on the research findings on reading and other language arts.

Audience Approved by PEP for students of all abilities, grades 1-10.

Description Exemplary Center for Reading Instruction (ECRI)'s purpose is to teach teachers so they can use effective teaching strategies that prevent failure. These strategies include: eliciting accurate and rapid responses during instruction, establishing high levels of mastery, maintaining on-task behavior, integrating the teaching of language skills, using effective management and monitoring systems, varying schedules and classes so students can invest the time and energy needed to learn, and supervising students' hands-on activities and practice. Techniques are incorporated into reading, spelling, grammar, dictation, creative writing, and penmanship instruction, and are extremely effective in content instruction such as science and social studies.

Students' attention is sustained with the momentum of the teacher directives during instruction and reinforcement offered during practice time. Overt responses appeal to all preferred modalities of learning. Instruction is provided by ECRI so teachers can: utilize critical teacher behaviors identified through research, develop a management system for mastery and individualization, and teach reading and language skills effectively.

Teachers learn to teach word recognition, literal, interpretative, critical and creative comprehension, study skills, literature, and composition as they use basal readers, literature series, novels, content books.

Students demonstrate mastery through their participation in small-group discussions, writing, locating, organizing, and evaluating information.

ECRI students demonstrate competency in their ability to reason, solve problems, apply knowledge, read, write, and communicate (Goal 3). ECRI students remain in school longer because of their success in school and their higher academic scores (Goal 2).

Evidence of Effectiveness Regular education ECRI students demonstrate significantly greater gains ($p<.01$) on the reading subscales of standardized achievement tests than (1) comparison group students receiving their regular reading instruction and (2) expectancies derived from national normative data.

Special needs ECRI students (Chapter I, bilingual, remedial) and special education students (learning disabled) demonstrate significantly ($p<.01$) greater than expected gains (derived from national normative data) on the Total Reading composite scales of standardized achievement tests.

Requirements A 3-5 day preparatory seminar with one ECRI staff person for 35-40 trainees is desirable. The program includes lecture and practice sessions, preparation of materials for classroom use, and teaching students in a simulated setting. Following this, periodic visits by ECRI staff to trainees' classrooms to demonstrate, model, and monitor are encouraged. Additional 1-10 day seminars assist trainees to implement an integrated language arts program. The length of time to replicate the ECRI model varies. Existing district reading materials may be used. Supplies for teachers and pupils are those usually found in schools. ECRI has 16 self-instructional teacher texts that are used by teachers during inservice. No special staffing or facilities are required to implement ECRI.

Costs Some costs (honorarium, travel, expenses) can be negotiated through the NDN grant. Honorarium is $475/day. Required teacher texts are $195/teacher.

Services Awareness materials are available at no cost. Visitors are welcome by appointment at the program site and additional sites in other states. Program staff are available to attend out-of-state awareness meetings at no cost. Teacher of Teachers Conferences are held in August and September. Training, implementation, and follow-up services are available at the adopter site (costs to be negotiated) and at the program site.

Contact Ethna R. Reid, Reid Foundation, 3310 South 2700 East, Salt Lake City, UT 84109. (801) 486-5083 or 278-2334, FAX (801) 485-0561.

JDRP No. 74-48 **(5/23/74)**
Recertified **(2/13/90)**

Developmental Funding: USOE ESEA Title III, Private Sources.

Image-Making Within the Writing Process. A program that promotes literacy skills in elementary school-aged children through the integration of visual imagery throughout their writing process. Addressing National Goal for Education 3, Image-Making Within the Writing Process has proven its ability to increase students' academic achievement in writing by accessing visual and kinesthetic modes of conceptualization and to increase their ability to express ideas through the dynamic interweaving of visual imagery and the written word.

Audience While approved by PEP for students in grades 1-2, this program has been successfully implemented in grades 1-6.

Description Image-Making Within the Writing Process operates in the classroom as a part of the language arts program. Recognizing individual learning styles, the program defines all children as author/illustrators and draws young writers into a rich creative process using word and picture images to create outstanding published books. Children employ reading, writing, and oral language skills necessary to the development of literacy, gain access to visual and kinesthetic modes of thinking which serve to heighten their conceptualization process, and engage in higher level problem-formulating and problem-solving activities.

Through a series of process-oriented art activities, each child begins by creating a portfolio of hand-painted textured papers. These textured papers are used by the class to brainstorm "describing words" as well as to spark story ideas through free association. As children's imaginations are awakened, discovered creatures and settings become rich resources for imaginative stories. Children find stories hidden in their textured papers. When it is time for the children to begin the process of putting ideas down on paper, they are purposely not directed toward either writing first or making pictures first. Because verbal as well as visual modes of thinking are equally valued, young author/illustrators are given the license to follow their own creative process in story-making. In this way, they approach writing from a position of personal strength and enthusiasm.

Textured papers then become the raw materials for building colorful collage images. As children weave together story images in pictures and words, stories unfold through a lively interactive creative process. As stories evolve, children are taught how to "read" their collage images in order to increase descriptive detail and literary language in their writing. Collage images also provide a concrete tool for revision. As a result, completed published books are highly evolved in story line, descriptive language, and visual expression.

Evidence of Effectiveness Findings based on analytic scoring of writing samples demonstrate that participating students increase their academic achievement in writing, particularly in the areas of plot development, descriptive language, and overall imagination, and enhance their ability to express their ideas through the interweaving of word and picture images as compared to nonparticipating students.

Requirements Two-day and day-and-a-half trainings are available. A one-week lab school is available through the University of New Hampshire's Laboratory for Interactive Learning during the summer for teachers who would like more extensive training.

Costs An on-site two-day training (which can also be reorganized to fit into a day-and-a-half format) is available for a $700 consultant fee and a $45 per participant materials fee. The materials fee covers all the art materials used at the training and instructional materials to be used in the classroom. Complete classroom implementation packages (art materials for 25 students) valued at $180 are available for $120. Mini-kits of hard-to-find items, valued at $105, are available for $65. Custom-designed multi-classroom kits are also available to reduce costs.

Services In addition to training and curriculum materials, awareness presentations, an instructional videotape, and follow-up consultations are available.

Contact   Beth Olshansky, The Laboratory for Interactive Learning, University of New Hampshire, Hood House, 89 Main Street, Durham, NH 03824-3577. (603) 659-6018 or 862-3691.

Developmental Funding: Local, state, and numerous grants from private foundations.

PEP No. 93-11 **(3/26/93)**

Junior Great Books Curriculum, The (JGBC). A literature-based program of interpretive reading, writing, and discussion which partially replaces or supplements conventional instruction in literature and comprehension and also provides benefits in critical thinking.

Audience Approved by PEP for students in grade 3. Materials are available for grades 2-6. Related materials are available for grades K-1 and 7-12.

Description The Junior Great Books Curriculum (JGBC) is intended for use in up to five class periods of instruction per week for 12 or 24 weeks. The JGBC involves students in intensive collaborative guided practice in interpreting outstanding stories drawn from many cultures. It provides teachers with a method of identifying interpretive issues and formulating interpretive questions, stories suitable for intensive interpretation, and support materials to foster active reading, exchange of ideas, and rigorous individual thinking. For each story they read, students discuss and write about interpretive issues through a sequence of activities. In most activities, students form divergent interpretations, back up their interpretations with evidence from the text, and comment on each others' interpretations.

The Junior Great Books Curriculum promotes students' "ability to reason, solve problems, apply knowledge, and write and communicate effectively" (National Goal for Education 3).

Evidence of Effectiveness Students in the JGBC support their interpretations of stories with evidence from the text more frequently than students not in the JGBC, both during oral discussion and in written answers. Students in the JGBC also score at a significantly higher percentile rank on the reading vocabulary subtest of standardized reading achievement tests than students not in the JGBC.

Requirements The Great Books Foundation provides a two-day (ten-hour) required Basic Leader Training Course and optional one- or two-day Curriculum Training Course. For each semester there is a student anthology of twelve selections, student activity pages, and a Teacher's Edition of annotated student text and instructions for conducting activities. Weekly release time is recommended for teachers to prepare units together.

Costs One-time start-up costs per class are tuition for the Basic Leader Training Course at $78 per teacher and Teacher's Edition at $19.95 per semester. A Curriculum Training Course and on-site consultation are free for schools or districts using the JGBC with a large number of students. Student books, $9.95 each per semester, are softbound and recommended for use as consumables. Student activity books, $4.95 each per semester, are consumables, and may be duplicated.

Services In addition to training and materials, awareness presentations and follow-up consultations are available. Services are discounted for large adoptions.

Contact The Great Books Foundation, 35 East Wacker, Suite 2300, Chicago, IL 60601-2298. (800) 222-5870 (ask for the Foundation's coordinator for your state).

Developmental Funding: Great Books Foundation.

PEP No. 93-1 (2/10/93)

Keyboarding, Reading, and Spelling (KRS). A program which teaches students in grades 1-6 to use a microcomputer keyboard to learn to type, read, and spell.

Audience Approved by PEP for students grades 1-6. Supporting data also were gathered from students in grades 7-8.

Description Keyboarding, Reading, Spelling (KRS) is an instructional program that enhances reading achievement and keyboard skills. The program uses a phonetic approach to reading, with the microcomputer being an essential component of the instructional process. The computer does not replace the teacher in instructing, but rather provides opportunities for students to master skills through reinforced practice. The software runs on the Apple, Macintosh, and IBM PC-compatible computers and requires a single disk drive and DOS 3.3 or higher (on IBM PCs); a color monitor is preferred, but not required. KRS can be networked.

The program works whether one or more computers are available to a class or whether there is a computer lab in the school. Although the teacher teaches some skills, students are independent as they work at the computer.

KRS will help ensure students' competency in reading, writing, and communicating and adaptation to new technologies (Goals 3 and 6).

Evidence of Effectiveness Students in grade 1, using the typewriter version of the program, demonstrate reading achievement scores, as measured by the CAT, that are higher than scores of students in a true control group, at a statistically significant level ($p<.01$).

Students in grade 3, using the microcomputer version of the program, demonstrate reading comprehension and speed-and-accuracy scores, as measured by the Gates-MacGinitie Reading Tests, that are higher than scores of students in a nonequivalent control group, at a statistically significant level ($p<.01$). Typewriting and computer usage skills are also statistically significant for the experimental group when compared to the control group. Visual and auditory memory skills improved significantly.

Students in grades 1-6 using KRS demonstrate reading vocabulary, comprehension, and language skills scores, as measured by the Metropolitan Achievement Test, significantly higher ($p<.01$) than scores of control students who also spent an equal amount of time in the computer lab in other computer programs. Computer usage and typing skills are also statistically significant for the experimental group when compared to the control group.

Requirements A one-day preparatory inservice education program conducted by a Reid Foundation staff person is desirable. The program includes lecture and practice sessions. It would be advantageous to the trainees to have Apple, Macintosh, or IBM PC-compatible computers available. It is desired that data from pre- and posttests be sent to the Developer/Demonstrator.

Costs The basic program which includes four disks costs $180. Five sets of the four disks cost $468. Notify the Reid Foundation of which size disks ($3\frac{1}{2}$" or $5\frac{1}{4}$") are needed.

Services Awareness materials are available at no cost. Visitors are welcome by appointment at the program site and additional sites in other states. Program staff are available to attend out-of-state awareness meetings at no cost. Training can be done at the program site or at adopter sites. An awareness videotape is available for rental. At initial awareness and training sessions, time is provided without cost and expenses are negotiated. Training and awareness can take place the same day.

Contact Ethna R. Reid, Reid Foundation, 3310 South 2700 East, Salt Lake City, UT 84109. (801) 486-5083 or 278-2334, FAX (801) 485-0561.

JDRP No. 84-14 (**3/26/84**)
Recertified (**4/1/94**)

Developmental Funding: Local.

Audience Approved by PEP for children grades 2-7, including special education, and bilingual students who are reading at least one year below grade level.

Description At the developer sites, children in grades 2-7 are served, as well as special education and bilingual students. The program is also suitable for grades K-12, and adopters have used the program with those audiences. An overall interdisciplinary holistic approach to improving reading and writing is implemented through the integration of a total arts with a total reading program. Curriculum is developed based on themes. Listening, speaking, writing, and reading techniques are stressed in the reading-oriented art workshops, and a diagnostic/prescriptive approach to reading is employed in the reading workshops. Participating children meet with the artist teacher and classroom/reading teachers in whole class and/or small groups for an average of four hours per week. Students receive additional reading instruction for at least one and a half hours a week in reading-oriented arts workshops in such areas as dance, music, theater, crafts, sculpture, painting, printmaking, and photography. The resources of museums, cultural institutions, universities, resource centers, and libraries are used, and special programs related to the content of project workshops are scheduled for students on field trip/special event days. There is an annual Learning to Read Through the Arts exhibition of work by participating students and/or a Performing Arts and Film Festival. A series of parent workshops is also held. Preservice and inservice trainings are available.

By using the Learning to Read Through the Arts Program's methodology in a school's total educational program, students learn through a holistic, integrated, thematic experiential approach. Students are given the opportunity to apply their individual learning styles in improving their ability to read and write.

Through arts instruction, students inherently use the processes of analyzing, synthesizing, and evaluating by becoming involved in concrete hands-on experiences which assist them in the transfer of knowledge to abstract learning.

Evidence of Effectiveness Chapter I students in the Developer/Demonstrator Learning to Read Through the Arts Program have shown an NCE growth in reading from 4.0-9.9.

Requirements Reading teachers/classroom teachers, professional artists, and/or artist teachers are trained in the Learning to Read Through the Arts methodology. Teacher-made pupil-oriented materials, commercial materials, instructional devices, filmstrips, records, tape recordings, media libraries, books on the arts, and art and audio-visual supplies are used. Program hours and times are adaptable to adopters' needs and scheduling requirements.

Services Awareness materials are available at no cost. Visitors are welcomed at a program site by appointment. Program staff are available to attend out-of-state awareness meetings (costs to be negotiated). Training is conducted at the program site (adopter pays only its own costs). Training is also conducted at the adopter site (costs to be negotiated). Implementation and follow-up services are available to adopters (costs to be negotiated). Training materials and curriculum guides cost approximately $85 per teacher. Cost of program implementation depends on available personnel. Cost of art supplies and equipment depends on the reading-oriented workshops that are implemented.

Contact Mary Jane Collett, Director, **Learning to Read Through the Arts Program, Edtech Systems, Inc. , 35 Archer Drive, Bronxville, NY 10708-4601. Between 8:30-4:30 call (718) 935-4213, or phone/FAX anytime at (914) 738-5927. E-Mail: mary.jane.collett.@nycps.nycenet.edu**

Developmental Funding: USOE ESEA Title I.

JDRP No. 74-18 (**3/25/74**)
Recertified (**4/1/94**)

Multicultural Literacy Program (MLP). A program designed to be integrated with the reading and writing curriculum for students in grades 3-6.

Audience Classroom teachers in grades 3-6, special area teachers, Chapter 1 and ESL teachers.

Description The purpose of the MLP program is to incorporate: (a) the culture and language of culturally diverse students, as well as community participation, into the school's reading/literature program; (b) the active use of language to generate and construct one's own knowledge; and (c) an understanding of the relevance, reason, and need for cultural understanding and appreciation. Using a multicultural literature-based program bridges the gap between cultural experiences, prior knowledge, and verbal language/written text for culturally diverse and at-risk students. Teachers and students read multicultural stories; teachers further use a variety of literacy activities to enhance reading and writing performance. Program teachers receive instruction in methods and techniques to integrate multicultural literature-based activities into their reading program. New participants receive five days of inservice instructions throughout the year; veteran teachers receive three days during Years Two and Three of the program and may help conduct inservice sessions. Project directors visit each teacher's classroom bi-monthly. They demonstrate multicultural activities, collaborate with teachers, assist with adapting the activities to student needs, and observe teacher instruction. The learning materials include multicultural books, a Teacher's Manual, an Instructor's Manual to be used for conducting inservices, and basal reading texts or literature-based texts. Cultures represented among the multicultural books include African American, African, Arab, Asian, Hispanic, Native American, and European American. Monitoring and evaluation procedures are ongoing processes, which allow the program to be flexible and to match the context of the classroom, the school, and the community. MLP addresses National Educational Goal 3.

Evidence of Effectiveness Six claims of effectiveness were evaluated. Results of the analyses and teacher and student interviews consistently showed that the MLP had a positive impact on the students' reading and writing performance. The findings were consistent across three school districts and three years of implementation. Significant changes in teacher behavior and attitudes were also evidenced.

Requirements A bibliography of multicultural books; a Teacher's Manual of instructional activities; an Instructor's Manual of inservice activities; a classroom set of multicultural literacy books (25 titles per set); and one set of multiple copy books (25 in a set—same title—that can be circulated from classroom to classroom).

Costs Implementation and operation costs include training for teachers and the administrator or reading consultant; trainee travel cost to the Ypsilanti training session; release time (1 day per semester); honorarium and expenses for MLP program staff. Operation costs are estimated at $786 plus expenses per year.

Services Awareness materials are available at no cost. Project staff is available to attend awareness sessions (costs to be negotiated). Visitors are welcome at project site. Instruction is also available at project site (adopter pays own costs). Implementation, follow-up, and evaluation services are available to adopters. Costs for all services are negotiable.

Contact **Margaret A. Moore, Ph.D. and Barbara Diamond, Ph.D., Research and Special Projects, YCCB, 218 W. Cross, Ypsilanti, MI 48197 (313) 487-3260, FAX (313) 484-6471.**

Developmental Funding: U.S. ED Fund for the Improvement and
Reform of Schools and Teaching, Eastern Michigan University,
Ann Arbor Community Foundation

PEP No. 93-19R **(4/1/94)**

Profile Approach to Writing (PAW). A K-12 program designed to provide teachers across the curriculum with a standardized means to evaluate written assignments, reduce evaluation time, and increase the quantity and quality of feedback.

Audience Approved by the JDRP for all students grades 3-9.

Description Profile Approach to Writing (PAW) provides a reliable system for accurate assessment of writ- ing and meaningful feedback to students about their writing. The goals and objectives of the program are to

- Improve and measure student writing performance,
- Provide meaningful feedback for revision,
- Increase objectivity and reliability of readers, thereby standardizing writing evaluation, and
- Reduce teacher grading time.

Central to the program are the Composition Profile, a holistic/analytic evaluation instrument, and the Extended Criteria. Both were developed for three populations—elementary, middle school/junior high, and high school.

The Profile contains five components, each focusing on an important aspect of writing and weighted according to its approximate importance for written communication. The Content component concerns the **invention** of writing—having something to say. The Organization component addresses **disposition**, or the rhetorical principles for arrangement. Vocabulary, Language Use, and Mechanics together deal with **elocutio**—the linguistic and mechanical principles for effective delivery of discourse.

Year-long studies conducted in the College Station Independent School District, the Bryan Independent School District, and the Spring Branch Independent School District of Houston, TX found that using the Profile Approach to Writing:

- Evaluation provides an effective means to promote and show student writing progress,
- The program is effective with students of varying abilities,
- Teachers grade more uniformly and objectively than with impressionistic methods,
- Grading time is reduced significantly, yet students receive increased and more meaningful feedback with directive comments.

PAW addresses the third National Goal for Education in that the program helps students develop competency in their abilities to reason, solve problems, and apply knowledge through effective written communication. The program supports the goal's objective for significant increase in the academic performance of elementary and secondary students, and it provides a means of accountability.

Evidence of Effectiveness In school districts where the Profile Approach has been implemented, students in grades 3-9 have shown increased writing achievement. This achievement was measured using either the Profile scale or by the writing component of the Texas TAAS test.

Requirements Essential to the implementation of the program is teacher training in the use of the Profile and Extended Criteria and in the applications of each. The program can be implemented across the curriculum to provide standard grading criteria. In language arts and English classes, the program aids instructors in teaching the writing process and in assigning grades for writing. In other subject areas, the program provides for the inclusion of meaningful writing assignments and a guide for assessing them. It also reinforces the rules, conventions, and guidelines being taught in language arts. The program and the materials required for it can be transferred easily to other locations.

Costs Staff Training (20 participants in a 6- to 30-hour workshop), $350 per day; Travel and per diem expenses for one trainer (if needed), $340 (est.); Consumables, $15; Profile Package (pad of 100 Profiles, 25 Criteria Cards, and Profile Guide), $45.

Services Awareness materials are available at no cost. Visitors are welcome at three different demonstration sites by appointment. Program staff are available for awareness sessions (costs to be negotiated). Follow-up services are available to adopters. Summer institute costs differ from on-site workshop costs. Call for further information.

Contact **Jane B. Hughey, Director or Susan Vammen, Coordinator, 1701 Southwest Parkway, Suite 102, College Station, TX 77840. (409) 764-9765.**

Developmental Funding:
College Station Independent School District, in kind.

JDRP No. 86-32 (**10/30/86**)

Reading Power in the Content Areas (RP).
A staff development program that helps grades 6-14 content area teachers to increase student acquisition of knowledge through the use of acquired reading skills and minimize the gap between student reading abilities and reading requirements of printed instructional materials.

Audience Approved for grades 6-14. This program has been implemented in upper elementary, middle school, and postsecondary classrooms in both vocational and academic programs.

Description Reading Power in the Content Areas (RP) is a staff development program designed to raise content teachers' consciousness regarding the reading demands of course material. The goals of the program are to: (1) assist content area teachers in analyzing print requirements and student abilities in relation to the teaching of reading within the teaching of content; (2) provide content area teachers with information and practice in the use of practical teaching techniques to meet the needs of the first objective; and (3) increase student reading comprehension and learning of content.

The program consists of interrelated components. The instructor assessment component provides tools by which participants can assess their own teaching styles, skill levels, and effectiveness. Student assessment trains teachers to use formal and informal tests and inventories to assess the reading abilities of their students. Materials assessment provides teachers with the knowledge and tools, both manually and by computer, to analyze the reading levels of printed instructional materials, to apply this knowledge when selecting texts, and to modify and improve use of the print materials to fit students' reading abilities. The instructional strategies component focuses on practical activities in vocabulary, comprehension/thinking skills, and study skills that teachers can incorporate into the total curriculum. The ongoing inservice component provides procedures to infuse the reading strategies acquired into the total instructional curriculum as well as follow-up and evaluation services.

The training provided by RP provides secondary instructors with skills to assist students meet three of our National Goals for Education. Goals 3, 4, and 6 receive impact when teachers are well-trained and can provide students with challenging content and appropriate instructional strategies. Goal 3 looks for students to leave grade 12 competent in all subject areas; Goal 6 seeks a literate populace able to participate fully in their community and compete in a global economy. Goal 4 provides for professional development to our nation's educators. Since reading is one of the main factors in determining literacy and the ability to perform at the highest levels in the classroom, this program is well-suited to assist teachers and students as they seek these goals.

Evidence of Effectiveness In the most recent Reading Power in the Content Areas evaluation study (1994), students from diverse sites whose teachers were trained in and used RP concepts demonstrated significant gains in reading comprehension on norm-referenced tests. Comparisons with national and state Chapter I results showed that RP students achieved reading comprehension gains from one to two times those in the Chapter I programs. Additionally, over 25% of students with reading scores below grade level on the pretest increased performance to grade level pre-to-post. Complete data available upon request.

Requirements No new staff or special equipment are required. One staff person with a background in curriculum development and/or reading acts as coordinator. Administrators, content-area instructors, reading consultants, and other support staff should be involved. The D/D provides a training workshop lasting one to two days depending upon needs of the implementing site. Staff development time should be provided. Computer resources should be available.

Costs Training costs consist of a trainer fee for the days of actual training, travel and per diem expenses, and the purchase of the Reading Power in the Content Areas training manual. Some optional materials are available. Costs for all other program services are negotiable. Contact RP for specific figures.

Services Awareness materials are available at no cost. Visitors are welcome by appointment at the program site and additional demonstration sites. Program staff are available to attend awareness meetings. Training is conducted at the adopter site or a regional location. Implementation, follow-up, and evaluation services are available.

Contact Carol Burgess, The EXCHANGE, 2037 University Avenue S.E., Room 116, University of Minnesota, Minneapolis, MN 55414. (612) 624-0067, FAX (612) 471-9225 or 625-4880. E-Mail: burge003@maroon.tc.umn.edu

JDRP No. 74-45 (**5/14-15/74**)
Recertified (**4/1/94**)

Developmental Funding: USOE ESEA Title III.

Reading Recovery. A supplementary, one-to-one intervention program for the least able readers in the first grade to help them acquire and use fundamental reading and comprehension skills.

Audience The least able readers in first grade as determined by a comprehensive battery of individually administered diagnostic instruments.

Description Reading Recovery reduces reading failure through early intervention and helps children become independent readers. The goal is to bring the children to the average of their class or school by providing individually tailored 30-minute lessons. Reading Recovery supplements the regular reading program in a classroom. The specially trained teacher and child work together daily for one half hour, in which the child is involved in reading and writing experiences. Techniques include the reading of many "little" books to build confidence, daily writing, the re-reading of favorite books, and learning to hear sounds in words by writing simple stories. Reading Recovery focuses on providing opportunities for children to make their own links between reading and writing—and discover meaning. The integrated reading and writing lessons are tailored to build on what the child already knows while strengthening a self-improving system which leads to continued growth. The elements of the lesson are the same for each child, although the content differs with each child.

Evidence of Effectiveness First grade children improved their reading and writing ability after an average of 16.4 weeks, with 86% of the children reaching average levels of achievement for their class in reading. Replications across several thousand sites verify the consistency of the results. Growth in reading and writing is evidenced by statistically significant scores relative to an equivalent control group using a variety of writing and reading test elements. In addition, follow-up studies indicate that the majority of children released from the program continue to make progress and read with the average of their class through the second, third, and fourth grades without additional help.

Requirements For effective implementation, school systems should release one or two experienced individuals to attend a one year teacher-leader training program at a designated university. They will learn procedures for implementation, evaluation, and administration of the Reading Recovery program.

The teacher-leaders, upon returning to their home site, train other teachers in the Reading Recovery model. Release time for trained teacher-leaders and teachers in training (including arrangements for a weekly 2 1/2-hour class after school hours) is required.

Services In addition to negotiable costs for release time for teachers, installation of the one-way glass at the training site costs about $3,000, and books and materials cost about $2,000.

Awareness materials are available at no cost. Program staff are available for awareness presentations and training with all costs negotiable.

Contact   Dr. Carol A. Lyons, Gay Su Pinnell, or Dr. Diane E. DeFord, Reading Recovery Program, The Ohio State University, 200 Ramseyer Hall, 29 West Woodruff Avenue, Columbus, OH 43210. (614) 292-7807.

Developmental Funding: State of Ohio, Columbus Public Schools, National Council of Teachers of English, and private foundations.

PEP No. 87-11 **(4/20/87)**

Rural Schools Reading Project (RSRP). An instructional intervention and staff development program designed to improve reading instruction in elementary schools, thereby improving students' strategic reading abilities.

Audience Approved by PEP for students in grades K-6.

Description Rural Schools Reading Project (RSRP) addresses the access time and cost challenges of sustained, effective staff development in rural schools through the formation of school-based professional development leadership teams and integrated use of telecommunications technologies, both of which facilitate an innovative instructional intervention: strategic reading. With this approach, reading is taught as a thinking process, thus students and teachers learn how to plan, monitor, and evaluate their reading and instruction. Strategic reading stresses the interaction of text, context, and learner through the use of prior knowledge, text structure, inference, word meaning, and metacognition. This instructional approach focuses on building knowledge base and expertise within a school and across schools via face-to-face interactions and telecommunications. RSRP materials are designed for use in professional development activities and include a guidebook, audio tapes, a videotape, and overhead transparencies. The materials demonstrate the use of strategic reading with students, explain how to create an effective leadership team, and describe an implementation process designed to help the leadership team introduce strategic reading to school staffs.

Evidence of Effectiveness Analysis of audio recordings demonstrates that RSRP teachers use strategic reading instructional strategies approximately twice as often as non-RSRP teachers, and three-year RSRP teachers show higher levels of using strategic reading techniques than teachers in the project for one or two years. RSRP students score significantly higher than non-RSRP students on a reading strategies test.

Requirements RSRP implementation requires the Strategic Reading Project "basic kit" which consists of a handbook guide to planning, implementation, and evaluation; overhead transparencies for use in professional development sessions; a videotape and six (6) audio tapes illustrating classroom-based reading instruction. Additional products and services, including on-site and telephone technical assistance as well as evaluation services, are also available. A two-day RSRP preparation workshop is recommended for staff developers before specific planning for the program's first year begins. For each school, RSRP requires a video cassette recorder and TV, and audio cassette recorder.

Costs To start the project, schools need at least one "basic kit" as described above at a cost of $525. Additional handbook guides are $32.50 each. An introductory, one-day orientation workshop is highly recommended, at a cost of $500 plus expenses (travel, lodging, and food). Optional products and services include audio seminars ($15 connect fee plus $10 per person per seminar); technical assistance by telephone ($40 per hour); and on-site technical assistance (one trainer, $500 per day plus travel, food, and lodging expenses).

Services In addition to the above materials and training, follow-up consultation is available.

Contact Ernestine G. Riggs, Ph.D., Project Director, North Central Regional Educational Laboratory, 1900 Spring Road, Suite 300, Oak Brook, IL 60521-1480. (800) 356-2735, ext. 1085.

Developmental Funding: OERI Regional Educational Laboratory Rural Education Initiative.

PEP No. 91-15R **(4/8/91)**

Writers Project, The. An inservice program to increase student writing achievement for grades 4-12.

Audience Approved by PEP for teachers of students, grades 3-12, all ability levels and all subject areas. This program has been implemented K-12 in many districts.

Description The Writers Project's purpose is to increase student achievement in writing by effecting fundamental change in composition practices in the classroom and to sustain this change through an ongoing, system-wide writing improvement program. This process begins with a five-day WRITERS PROJECT WORKSHOP for teachers which consists of: (1) analyzing the current knowledge about effective teaching methodologies, (2) developing new strategies for teaching writing process and assessing student progress, (3) experiencing the writing process as a writer, and (4) designing a plan for implementing a writing program for students. The WRITING TO LEARN and the WRITING THROUGH HANDS-ON ELEMENTARY SCIENCE programs have been developed to give districts further options for reaching teachers in all subject and grade levels as well as all levels of background knowledge in writing instruction. The Writers Project offers a LEADERSHIP SEMINAR designed to develop local leadership for follow-up support. We attribute our long-term track record in such difficult areas as effecting and assessing achievement gain in writing to our model use of organizational change constructs.

Evidence of Effectiveness Results based on holistically scored writing samples indicate that students with trained teachers show statistical differences in their writing achievement when compared to students with untrained teachers.

Requirements Five days of training in the The Writers Project is recommended; a minimum of three days is required for adoption. Up to 30 teachers/administrators may be trained at one time. A larger group requires an additional project consultant. Adoptors should target two or more key teacher leaders for the initial training. It is recommended that the teacher leaders attend a Leadership Seminar given in the Ferguson-Florissant School District (or if more cost effective at the local site) to prepare them for the role of trainer in their district. A training manual for each participant must be purchased. No purchase of new student materials is required. This program may be adopted by a single district or a group of districts wishing to share one training site.

Costs Training costs consist of $350 per day expenses for presenters' fees plus all travel expenses. Training manuals are $20 per participant.

Services Awareness materials are available free of charge; awareness presentations are available on an expense-shared basis. Visitations are welcomed. Leadership Training Seminars are scheduled in March in the Ferguson-Florissant School District (located 20 minutes away from the St. Louis-Lambert International Airport). Arrangements may be made to conduct a Leadership Seminar at a local site.

Contact **Diane Scollay, Project Director, The Writers Project, Ferguson-Florissant School District, 1005 Waterford Drive, Florissant, MO 63033. (314) 831-4411, Ext. 279.**

Developmental Funding: USOE ESEA Title II and VII.

JDRP No. 82-26 (5/26/82)
Recertified (4/1/94)

Flint Follow Through: The School Effectiveness Model. A program developed for educationally and economically disadvantaged students. Approved by JDRP for grades K-3.

Description In practice since 1969, educationally disadvantaged students have grown significantly in basic skills development as well as in their ability to more accurately perceive themselves as worthy, capable people. Teaching materials are the highly structured, carefully sequenced, scripted lessons of *Reading Mastery*, and *DISTAR Language* and *Reasoning and Writing*. Increased achievement is attained by interactive teaching requiring a high degree of students' time on task; multiple-response techniques to increase guided practice of new skills; and criterion-referenced tests to monitor student progress. Reading skills are applied to novel studies in second and third grade. Parents become partners in the learning process through the home reading program. Results of the ITBS Achievement Test show student performance exceeding that of students in comparable schools.

A parent coordinator promotes an active parent education program. Group-level teacher materials are a one-time purchase at approximately $300 per curricular area. Consumable student materials are approximately $15 per student, per curricular area per year.

Program components are correlated but may be adopted individually based on LEA needs. An adopter must agree to a two-year implementation, provide pre- and posttest data, and purchase teacher and student materials. A one-day teacher training workshop per curricular area is required prior to implementation.

Classroom visitations are available by appointment. Teacher training and in-classroom consultant visits are provided by the sponsor (Dr. Gary Johnson).

Contact   Dr. Gary Johnson, Washington Research Institute, 150 Nickerson Street, Suite 305, Seattle, WA 98109. (206) 285-9317.

Developmental Funding: USDE Follow Through.   JDRP No. 77-122 **(8/17/77)**

HOSTS (Help One Student To Succeed). A structured mentoring program in Language Arts. The program targets compensatory students (K-12) who need assistance in reading, writing, thinking, and study skills. Approved by JDRP for "at-risk" students in grades K-12.

Description HOSTS (Help One Student To Succeed) is a structured mentoring program in language arts designed to reinforce the classroom teacher and reduce the workload, while improving student outcomes and containing costs. HOSTS does not require additional personnel, but works with existing compensatory staff, improving their efficiency and productivity.

Instruction is one-to-one. Mentor-friendly student folders, containing student learning assignments and activities, are prepared by the compensatory teacher, in cooperation with the classroom instructor, for each student and mentor. These folders act as roadmaps, guiding the mentor and reinforcing the classroom teacher's instruction, without creating an extra burden on the classroom teacher.

HOSTS is a continuous progress model and operates successfully with any assessments, curriculum, objectives and philosophies. The HOSTS database and software programs align the school and district's curriculum with any state or locally developed objectives, thus saving up to 80% of the teacher's time in planning.

HOSTS has received numerous awards for instructional leadership, including being selected as a national mentoring model by the U.S. Secretary of Education; a mentoring model for dropout prevention by the National Center for Dropout Prevention, Clemson University; and the Secretary's Excellence in Compensatory Education award as their state's exemplary compensatory program for Washington, Arizona, Montana, Texas, California, Hawaii, and North Dakota.

Contact   William E. Gibbons, Chairman, 8000 N.E. Parkway Drive, Suite 201, Vancouver, WA 98662-6459. (206) 260-1995 or (800) 833-4678, FAX (206) 260-1783.

JDRP No. 75-6 **(1/15/75)**
Recertified **(11/84)**

Developmental Funding: USOE ESEA Titles I, II, III, private and foundation.

Individualized Prescriptive Management System for Underachievers in Reading (IPIMS) Reading Center.
IPIMS Reading Center is not a text or a kit, but a model of an organizational structure for implementing a remedial reading/learning center for grades 7-12. Approved by JDRP for secondary students deficient in reading and other academic skills.

Description The Individualized Prescriptive Management System for Underachievers in Reading (IPIMS) Reading Center model is a highly effective organizational structure and management system for setting up and running a supplemental center in secondary schools. Its focus is on the improvement of academic achievement and the prevention of dropout among high-risk students. The center in Union Springs is staffed by reading teachers and paraprofessionals as well as student volunteers. The center in Niagara-Wheatfield is staffed by one reading specialist and several content area teachers. A wide variety of instructional resources is available; these materials are color coded into four reading levels. It is up to each individual district or building to set up and equip their own center with whatever materials they feel are appropriate. Once the center is established, it operates as follows:

> Students are identified and scheduled into the program. They are given further diagnostic testing and an interest inventory. Individual strengths and weaknesses are noted as well as personal interests. Individual prescriptions are written and implemented. Student progress is monitored by a criterion-referenced system. Parents, teachers, and students receive periodic progress reports. Students are posttested to determine achievement and future placement.

One of the unique adaptations of IPIMS in Union Springs is the addition of writing and math remediation which provides a flexibility that many districts need. The Niagara-Wheatfield Center also includes remediation in other core areas. With all the emphasis on dropout prevention and high-risk students, IPIMS can be a significant factor in academic improvement.

Contact Sidney J. Beckwith, Director, Union Springs Central School District, 27 North Cayuga Street, Union Springs, NY 13160. (315) 889-4117. Richard Leo, Trainer, Niagara-Wheatfield SHS, 2292 Saunders Seattlement Road, Sanborn, NY 14132. (716) 731-7372 or 731-7371.

Developmental Funding: PSEN funds, New York State; ESEA Title IV-C. JDRP No. 84-9 (3/23/84)

QUILL: Writing with Computers.

Description QUILL is a computer writing program that encourages students in grades 3-8 to use software for planning, composing, revising, storing, retrieving and printing written text. QUILL provides teachers with training and assistance to integrate the software into classroom writing instruction and writing in content areas. QUILL provides students with motivating writing activities in a structured, computer-based format, which allows for flexibility in addressing student ability and interest. QUILL provides teachers with tools to supplement and expand language arts and writing instruction, especially in the areas of expository and persuasive writing.

Intermediate level elementary students (grades 3-5) have significantly improved (p<.05) the quality of their expository writing, as measured by pre- and postwriting samples in comparison with a matched control group.

Quill training is done on an Apple IIe or GS computer using Bank Street WriterIII and The Wonderful World of PAWS. During one to two days of training teachers will:

- Learn to use word processing and typing tutorial software;
- Develop computer-based writing activities for their classrooms;
- Gain confidence in word processing.
- Get new ideas for writing instruction;
- Use the computer to edit and revise their own work; and

Costs for all services will be negotiated.

Contact Denise Blumenthal or Cheryl Williams, The NETWORK Inc., 300 Brickstone Square, Suite 900, Andover, MA 01810. (508) 470-1080.

Developmental Funding: U.S. Department of Education. JDRP No. 84-10 (3/30/84)

TV Reading S.T.A.R. (Scripts, Taping, Acting, Reading). Auditory and visual focus and practice improves student reading. Approved by JDRP for grades 4-8.

Description TV Reading S.T.A.R. (Scripts, Taping, Acting, Reading) uses popular commercial TV to teach academic and underlying psycholinguistic skills. Network videotapes with diverse production elements are used in the classroom or communication studio to provide concrete visualization and pronunciation of sophisticated vocabulary.

Lesson plans are prepared from the actual scripts used by TV producers and include skills related to social studies, oral language, reading, writing, and skills that affect learning rate such as memory, grammar, and visual and auditory integration. Teachers use rapidly paced oral response drills designed to increase accuracy in articulating, listening, handling complicated syntax, and master vocabulary meaning. Program techniques enable teachers to continuously assess lesson mastery, to correct responses, and to monitor student ability to transfer skills taught in the auditory-vocal channel to the visual-motor channel. Students move through increasingly difficult levels of reading material as they practice the previously taught strategies on supplemental material.

Teachers and students operate video cameras, VCRs, and TVs for use in learning, processing, and expressive activities. Students become camera persons, directors, technicians, and actors as they confirm their ability to read at the end of each session by videotaping and playing back their dramatizations. Students produce their own documentary on a topic related to the script. Significant student reading gains were duplicated by replicators representing a gamut of populations from grades 4-10 using standardized reading achievement tests. Costs include equipment, materials ($82 for year's lesson plans with matching script and tape), and training.

Contact   Jacqueline Van Cott, TV Reading S.T.A.R., S.T.A.R. Studio, 196 Laurel Ridge, South Salem, NY 10590-2409. (914) 533-6852.

Developmental Funding: USOE ESEA Titles III and IV-C.   JDRP No. 82-16 **(4/29/82)**

WRiting Is Thorough and Efficient (WR.I.T.&E.). Approved for grades K-12.

Description WRiting Is Thorough and Efficient (WR.I.T.&E.) is a writing program designed to improve students' writing competency and fluency in composing by using a process approach to writing that is developmentally tailored to students' needs, one of the major objectives of Goal 3 of the National Goals for Education. WR.I.T.&E. is a practical, classroom-level application of the writing process. It addresses the varying needs of primary, elementary, intermediate, and secondary levels. WR.I.T.&E. has three key elements: Curriculum, Training, and Support System.

- The K-12 curriculum is published as a *Curriculum Guide*, and is based on seven goals: Climate, Fluency, Audience, Writing Process, Writing to Learn, Literacy Skills, and Evaluation.

- The 15-hour staff training includes a published *Teacher Handbook*, and the support system is included in a *Management Handbook* for administrators. A handbook of mini-lessons for skills, strategies, and classroom management is also included.

WR.I.T.&E. program costs include training workshop, instructional manuals, student composition books, student publications, and an annual young authors' conference. Initial installation cost per student (N=600) is $20.

Contact   Monika Steinberg, Director, WR.I.T.&E., Educational Information and Resource Center (EIRC), 606 Delsea Drive, Sewell, NJ 08080. (609) 582-7000, FAX (609) 582-4206.

Developmental Funding: ESEA Title IV-C.   JDRP No. 84-12 **(3/26/84)**

Section 5

Humanities

* These programs are currently funded by the NDN.

Summary of Program Services for Section 5

Program	Goal*	Page	AWARENESS										TRAINING						
			Dissem. Funds Available		Costs to Potential Adopter			On Site Visitation Available		Materials Available				Staff Available		Costs to Adopter			Certified Trainers Available	Training Time Required
			NDN	Other	Hon	Trav	Per Diem	Home Site	Adopt Site	Free Paper	Video	Film Strip	Other	Home Site	Adopt Site	Hon	Trav	Per Diem	State(s)	Day(s)
Child Development Project (CDP)	3	5-1		✓	✓	✓	✓		✓	✓	✓			✓	✓	✓	✓	✓	(none)	~30 days, over 3 yrs.
First Level Language (Kindersay)	1, 3	5-2	✓						✓	✓	✓			✓	✓	✓	✓	✓	AK, CA, IA, IL, MN, MO, MS, NM, NY, OK, OR, PA, SC, SD, VA, WA	<1
Folger Library Shakespeare Education and Festivals Project	3	5-3	✓		(negotiable)			✓	✓					✓	✓	✓	✓	✓	CA, CO, D.C., MA, MN, NJ, NY, PA, TX, VA, VT	1
Hinsdale Central Foreign Language Program, The	3	5-4			✓	✓	✓	✓						✓		✓	✓	✓	(none)	2
Individualized Language Arts . . .	3	5-7			✓	✓	✓		✓	✓					✓	✓	✓	✓	GA, IA, IN, MD, MO, MT, NH, NJ TX	2
Kenosha Model . . .	3	5-7			✓	✓	✓	✓		✓					✓	✓	✓	✓	(none)	1
Scholars in the Schools (SIS)	3	5-5	✓		(negotiable)			✓	✓	✓	✓		✓	✓	✓	(negotiable)			(none)	1-3
Teaching Activities for Language Knowledge (TALK)	3	5-6			(negotiable)			✓	✓		✓			✓		(negotiable)		✓	AS, CA, CO, CT, FL, GA, HI, IL, IN, ME, MI, NC, ND, NE, NY, OK, OR, RI, SC, VT, WA, WI, WV	<1

* National Goals for Education—definitions for each goal can be found on pages 5-7.

Audience Elementary schools/districts. Approved by PEP for students in grades K-6.

Description The major goal of the Child Development Project (CDP) is to enhance prosocial characteristics in children as reflected in attitudes, motives, and behaviors, including consideration of and concern for others' needs, feelings, and welfare, and a willingness to balance one's own legitimate needs and desires with those of others in situations where they conflict. Another goal is to foster children's higher order learning and intrinsic motivation to learn.

The CDP program attempts to create a caring community in the classroom and school based on a shared commitment to prosocial, democratic values. It combines elements of traditional approaches to values education with those of more recent approaches derived from cognitive developmental theory—it helps children both to learn values through adult guidance, and simultaneously to develop values, through participating as a member of a mutually concerned, caring community.

CDP develops prosocial inclinations and behaviors through a variety of experiences, including opportunities to collaborate with others in the pursuit of common goals; to provide meaningful help to others and receive help when it is needed; to discuss the experiences of others and come to understand their feelings, needs, and perspectives; to develop and practice important social skills and competencies; and to assume responsible roles in the school community. These activities are incorporated into three components: Cooperative Learning, Developmental Discipline, and a Literature-Based Approach to Reading and Language Arts.

In the classroom, teachers give children active roles in creating a caring community; involve them in cooperative learning activities that focus on both academic and social goals; and use a reading/language arts program organized around whole works of children's literature that portray prosocial values and the ways they play out in daily life. The school-wide program consists of activities such as cross-age "buddies" and tutoring programs, community service and charity drives, and family film nights. Parents are also involved in a "family homework" program. Teachers' guides and other support materials are provided to link these activities into an overall, comprehensive program.

Evidence of Effectiveness Results of evaluations of CDP indicate that the program enhances students' interpersonal classroom behavior, social problem-solving skills, and commitment to certain democratic values. Program students have consistently demonstrated a better understanding of common interpersonal problems and a more thoughtful and sophisticated approach to solving them. Findings indicate achievement of a "self-other" balance. Positive effects were found two years after students left their elementary schools on conflict resolution skills, self-esteem, and involvement in extracurricular activities.

Requirements To effectively implement CDP, a school must make it a priority. On-going professional development is needed for teachers and administrators, to effect sustained improvement. This includes workshops along with regular opportunities for teachers to reflect on issues of philosophy and practice.

Costs Costs are individually negotiated with schools and/or districts depending on the program elements being introduced and the type of support, services, and/or materials required.

Services Staff development consultancy and planning assistance is available to schools and/or districts that have a sustained interest in and commitment to the program.

Contact Eric Schaps, Developmental Studies Center, 2000 Embarcadero, Suite 305, Oakland, CA 94606. (510) 533-0213.

Developmental Funding: William and Flora Hewlett Foundation; the San Francisco Foundation; the Robert Wood Johnson Foundation; the Danforth Foundation; the Stuart Foundations; the Pew Charitable Trusts; the John D. and Catherine T. MacArthur Foundation; the Annenberg Foundation; Spunk Fund, Inc.; the DeWitt Wallace-Reader's Digest Fund; the Louise and Claude Rosenberg Foundation; the Center for Substance Abuse Prevention, U.S. Department of Health and Human Services.

PEP No. 89-6 **(4/20/89)**

First Level Language (Kindersay). A program designed to facilitate oral language acquisition and an understanding of the basic language concepts and relationships needed to succeed in the more complex tasks of math and reading, prekindergarten to 1st grade.

Audience Approved by PEP for pre-primary students in pre-kindergarten, kindergarten, and transitional first grade, including those with developmental lags and learning disabilities.

Description First Level Language (Kindersay) is viewed as a basic part of a total language program and would naturally be accompanied by other informal language experiences. It provides a sequential curriculum and management system that provides for individual developmental growth and learning of basic language skills in conceptual language, auditory discrimination, and auditory memory. A child may work through as many as 72 lessons to reach advanced objectives. The step-by-step, closely sequenced lessons afford the child frequent experiences of success because higher level objectives are pursued when mastery of preceding skills is established. The curriculum is based on knowledge of developmental theory and cognitive growth. Lessons represent a three-part continuum: receptive language, expressive language, and concept-related activities. The sequenced objectives are also presented in strands so that the child does not reach an impasse in instruction due to a particular area of difficulty. Instructional periods take place on a daily basis for a period of 20-30 minutes. Children are grouped for instruction depending on their determined starting levels; there are typically three or four groups in a classroom. The well-documented lessons describe procedures and are accompanied by appropriate materials.

The program addresses Goal 3 of the National Goals for Education by helping to increase substantially the percentage of students who demonstrate the ability to reason, solve problems, and communicate effectively. The program has been used effectively with bilingual and ESL students.

Evidence of Effectiveness After one year in the program, participants demonstrated statistically significant and educationally meaningful gains relative to national norm groups and local comparison groups on three different measures of language-concept development.

Requirements The program requires no special staff or facilities. A maximum of one day of staff training is required. Administrators and para-professionals are encouraged to attend training sessions. A training tape, complete with manual, is available. One Kindersay materials kit is required per classroom.

Costs Training costs consist of travel expenses plus $150 per classroom for the Kindersay materials kit, which is nonconsumable.

Services In addition to training and materials, follow-up technical assistance is available if necessary. Monitoring and evaluation procedures are also provided. Awareness materials are available at no cost.

Contact   Mary A. Felleisen, PRIMAK Educational Foundation, 38 North Waterloo Road, P.O. Box 701, Devon, PA 19333. (610) 687-6252 or (800) 444-5729.

Developmental Funding: PRIMAK Educational Foundation.   PEP No. 88-11R2 **(2/13/90)**

Folger Library Shakespeare Education and Festivals Project. Based on the reality that one of the best ways to teach and learn about Shakespeare is to perform the plays. This program provides training in teaching techniques and materials to improve and enliven the teaching of Shakespeare.

Audience Approved by the JDRP for students grades 4-12.

Description The Folger Library Shakespeare Education and Festivals Project, an exemplary education program for grades 4 through 12, is devoted to providing effective and innovative strategies in the instruction of Shakespeare. These workshops emphasize a hands-on approach to literature incorporating a collaborative and cooperative approach to learning. Teachers are provided with methods that lessen the intimidation of the material and make Shakespeare more accessible to students. The festival process is not an enrichment activity, but rather a participatory approach to literature that leads students to a thorough understanding of Shakespeare's works. For a festival, students study, prepare, and perform a scene or scenes for an audience of their peers. Through this interactive, performance-based approach, students meet Shakespeare in the most historically accurate way.

The festival process meets Goal 3 of the National Goals for Education.

Requirements The Folger Library Shakespeare Education and Festivals Project can be replicated anywhere. The festival may involve one class or many classes, an entire school or several schools. The locations for a festival can be, and have been, as varied as a single classroom, an auditorium, a theater, a cafeteria, or a playground. Participants are trained in the use of Folger Library instructional approaches and materials, which include a comprehensive manual on teaching Shakespeare by performance and on festival planning.

Evidence of Effectiveness Cognitively, students are empowered to analyze literature and make decisions about language. Through this process, students gain a greater facility for language and become aware of the control they can exert over it. The project is beneficial to students of all ability groups and was recognized and commended by the Johns Hopkins Center for Schooling of Disadvantaged Students. Students become involved cognitively, affectively, and kinesthetically in their learning experience.

Costs The Folger Library has made every effort to keep implementation costs to a minimum. The consultant fee for each one-day workshop is $300. Each training manual is $30, one per participant trained. Trainings involve a minimum of 15 participants and a maximum of 30. Adopting sites pay travel expenses and per diem for the trainer's food and lodging. Depending on funding and a site's financial needs, travel costs are sometimes negotiable.

Services Awareness materials are available at no cost. Project site visits are welcomed, by appointment. Project staff are available for awareness sessions (costs to be negotiated).

Contact **Molly Haws, The Folger Shakespeare Library, 201 East Capitol Street, S.E., Washington, D.C. 20003. (202) 675-0373.**

Developmental Funding: State grants and the Folger Library.   JDRP No. 86-13 **(7/2/86)**

Hinsdale Central Foreign Language Program, The. A four-year, sequential high school foreign language program designed to increase students' language proficiency and awareness of the value and benefits of foreign language study extending well beyond the high school and as an essential element of lifelong learning.

Audience Approved by PEP for students in grades 9-12.

Description The Hinsdale Central Foreign Language Program provides a learning environment conducive to language acquisition and the development of cultural awareness; creates interest in further language study; develops goals and objectives communally; articulates within the department and with feeder schools; implements a variety of teaching strategies; conducts ongoing staff development; sustains effective departmental supervision; implements an enthusiastic public relations component; and maintains continuous intradepartmental communication regarding the effectiveness of daily and long-range activities. The program is not textbook or materials driven; any standard text may be adapted to achieve program goals. Daily, fifty-minute class periods exemplify the program's objectives of providing students a learning environment conducive to increasing achievement and developing interest in continuing language study. Elements of effective teaching are evident in daily and unit lesson planning. Learner activities are designed to allow for frequent, measured, graduated practice in communicative skills.

Evidence of Effectiveness Students participating in the program demonstrate significantly higher enrollment percentages than the comparison group and national averages; complete longer sequences of study than the comparison group; show significantly greater gains on standardized foreign language achievement tests than comparison students; and score higher on Advanced Placement Tests than the comparison group and national figures.

Requirements Familiarization with features such as the departmental philosophy, supervision, accountability, program evaluation, peer-counseling and public relations components can be achieved with one or two days of consultation. A complete curriculum guide is available, and no special facilities are necessary. A two-day inservice is recommended for start-up.

Costs Costs are the same as those normally associated with an increase in enrollment in an existing Foreign Language Department; if no department exists, the highest costs incurred will be for staff salaries. First-year costs are $385 per student (25 per class), which includes personnel, inservice, equipment, and materials/supplies. Second-year costs are estimated al $315 per student (two classes of 25 students).

Services In addition to training and curriculum materials, follow-up consultation is available.

Contact   Pierre B. Simonian or Donna L. Watkins, Foreign Language Department, Hinsdale Central High School, 55th and Grant Streets, Hinsdale, IL 60521. (708) 887-1340, Ext. 285.

Developmental Funding: Local and state.   PEP No. 91-5 (**2/19/91**)

Scholars in the Schools (SIS). A program to improve education in the humanities by involving university scholars in classroom instruction, program enhancement, and curriculum development in public and private schools, grades 7-12.

Audience Approved by the JDRP/PEP for all secondary schools.

Description The purpose of the Scholars in the Schools (SIS) program is to improve humanities education by involving university and other scholars with a Ph.D. or ABD in a discipline of the humanities in classroom instruction, curriculum development, program enhancement, and staff development. The program places humanities scholars in secondary schools (grades 7-12) for long-term residencies, usually 60-100 days during the 180-day school calendar, for a one-to-three year period. The scholars work with a team of teachers in each school to bring about **systemic** change; the program is **not** one of enrichment.

SIS is both fixed and flexible: It has key elements which should be an integral part of every program, yet is flexible so that it responds to local needs and requirements. For example, at each site a team of teachers is identified; these teacher teams recruit and select the scholar, usually from within the same geographic area; the teacher team and scholar comprise **the** change agent. Together they determine the needs to be met and develop a detailed plan which is implemented during the pilot period. The program is locale-specific as well as transportable. SIS meets specific needs in particular settings. Other features include summer workshops, short programs for credit, local symposia, and statewide and regional institutes.

SIS should be perceived as a process and a partnership, one that brings about improvement in the quality of humanities education by enhancing the professionalization of teachers in the humanities and aiding them in continued development in their discipline. SIS also explores a variety of techniques to facilitate the acquisition of knowledge in the humanities by students with many levels of abilities. SIS also encourages the cooperation of a variety of constituents in a school district's community and the development of networks among its various components.

Requirements The program may be implemented by all secondary schools, public or private. Program materials include a 30-page handbook which describes a variety of activities that can occur in the program as well as a step-by-step guide to setting a SIS program in place. Additional materials from three model sites—urban, suburban, and rural—are also provided in the *Project Sites Guidebook*.

SIS is easily transported, replicated, and installed in various school sites. This is evidenced by its implementation in dozens of sites of many varieties such as rural (in an area with such a sparse population that two counties join together in a school district), large urban, inner-city, suburban areas, and sites in multiethnic and culturally and demographically diverse settings throughout the country since 1978.

SIS installation and maintenance averages $4,000-$10,000 per year, per school site, to pay scholar stipends, provide honoraria, tickets, transportation, curriculum materials, and such. The cost may be reduced by utilizing emeritus faculty and by universities donating scholar time. Funding for the program has been accomplished through a variety of partnerships among schools, foundations, corporations, and other sources.

Services Awareness materials are available at no cost. The *Handbook*, *Project Sites Guidebook*, and *Video* are available at nominal cost. Program staff are available (cost to be negotiated). Visitors are welcome to program sites, by appointment.

Contact Ann M. Pescatello, Center for South Asia Studies, University of California-Berkeley, 865 Euclid Avenue, Berkeley, CA 94708. (510) 525-9611, FAX (510) 525-0940. E-Mail: a_pescate@inet.ed.gov

JDRP No. 86-22 **(7/9/86)**
Recertified **(10/31/87)**

Developmental Funding: Federal CCH, local, and private.

Audience Teaching Activities for Language Knowledge (TALK) was validated by the Joint Dissemination Review Panel for all elementary students grades K-3. Due to the current emphasis on oral language, TALK is now used in grades K-6, bilingual education, migrant education, special education, gifted education, and in some areas for adult education programs.

Description TALK was designed to improve the oral language skills of children kindergarten through third grades in lower socioeconomic area schools where there is an established need. Although the original program began in a lower socioeconomic school in Rockford, Illinois, it has been beneficial to children from all strata.

The methodology includes training a language specialist and participating classroom teachers of an adopting school district in the use of the *TALK* manual and suggested materials. The language specialist conducts 30-minute oral language lessons twice each week in each participating classroom. In addition, participating classroom teachers utilize the *TALK* manual of activities to conduct 30-minute follow-up oral language lessons twice each week. The approach encourages teachers to use a variety of techniques, implementing all modalities and utilizing positive reinforcement, as a means of stimulating oral language. A *TALK* manual includes lessons in listening skills, grammatical skills, describing and defining, personal and social awareness, choral speaking, story telling, creative dramatics and puppets.

At the end of a six-month period, the teacher should be capable of interfacing TALK with the classroom instructional program.

Evidence of Effectiveness TALK students have shown gains of 30% to 80% on standardized tests for receptive and expressive language. These highly significant gains have been obtained at all grade levels.

This program directly addresses Goal 3 of the National Goals for Education.

Students learn and apply effective oral language and communication skills. This substantially increases their ability to reason, solve problems, apply knowledge, and write and communicate effectively.

Requirements The adopting district provides a speech and language clinician or teacher with a background in language development or reading, one hour per week for each classroom receiving TALK. The TALK program can be utilized by a classroom teacher if speech and language staff are not available. After language specialists and classroom teachers have been trained in the program, they can train other personnel in the local district. TALK staff assist adopting districts in evaluating the effectiveness of the program as it is implemented.

Costs Each language specialist and classroom teacher must have a copy of the *TALK* manual, $50. A *TALK Training Manual*, $25, is suggested for each school district. TALK staff and Certified Trainers are available for trainings. Costs for these sessions are negotiable. Contact the TALK Director for specific figures.

Services Awareness materials are available at no cost. Visitors are welcome at the program site by appointment. Demonstration sites are available for visitation in most states. Program staff are available to attend out-of-state awareness meetings (costs to be negotiated). One-day training sessions are conducted at the program site or adopter site (costs to be negotiated). Implementation and follow-up services are available to adopters (costs to be negotiated). Video tapes for awareness and/or training are available on a no-cost loan basis. Statistical analysis of evaluation data is provided to all school districts submitting pre/posttest scores to the program office.

Contact **Stephanie Hendee, Director, National Training Network, P.O. Box 8057, Longmont, CO 80501. (303) 651-0833, FAX (303) 651-1044.**

Developmental Funding: USOE ESEA Title III.

JDRP No. 78-189 (**7/11/79**)
Recertified (**4/1/94**)

Individualized Language Arts: Diagnosis, Prescription, and Evaluation. A program combining a language-experience approach with techniques derived from modern linguistic theory to enhance skills in written composition. Approved by JDRP for grades 3-6.

Description The Individualized Language Arts: Diagnosis, Prescription, and Evaluation program has been used with grades 1-2, 7-12, college basic skills programs, adult education programs, special education programs, and independent and supplementary programs in written composition. At least three times a year, the teacher evaluates writing samples composed by students on self-selected topics. Utilizing criteria common to nearly all language arts programs, the teacher is then able to assign priorities to the needs of the whole class, groups of students, and individual youngsters. For each objective stemming from this diagnosis, a teacher's resource manual prescribes a variety of writing or revision techniques for all content areas involving writing. Motivation for writing is strengthened by a "communication spiral" that links composition to the other language arts and to real-life experience. A record-keeping system permits students, teachers, administrators and parents to observe growth in writing proficiency from month to month and grade to grade. The program can be combined readily with existing language arts curricula and materials.

Contact Jeanette Alder, Director, 29646 Buckingham, Livonia, MI 48154. (313) 525-9221.

Developmental Funding: USOE ESEA Title III.   JDRP No. 74-55 **(5/23/74)**

Kenosha Model: Academic Improvement through Language Experience. An individualized program to improve communication skills utilizing the language experience approach. Approved by JDRP for students grades K-2.

Description Public and nonpublic school classroom teachers refer low-achieving students to the Chapter I resource room for individual assessment. Following the educational assessment, the resource teacher selects those students with the greatest need. A Personalized Performance Plan is developed that considers the area of deficiency, the student's learning style and the instructional techniques to be followed in correcting the deficiency. The plan is flexible and can be modified as the needs of the student change. The language experience approach to instruction is utilized. Instruction follows the assumption that students can speak about that which they have experienced, write about that which they have spoken and read about that which they have written. Student authorship at all grade levels is requisite. At the parent project, a teacher and an instructional assistant serve each resource room. Instruction is individualized and takes place in small groups. This program serves approximately 1,400 students during the school year. Intensive inservice and parent participation are essential components of this program. Target schools are established by low-income guidelines. Students served are selected from those scoring in the 40 percentile or below on standardized tests. Kindergarten students are selected from those referred by classroom teachers. The model has been proven to be effective for limited English proficient students as well as the Chapter I target population. The approach is also used successfully to supplement the standard text in many reading/language arts programs.

Contact Audrey Hains, Director or Gloria Peterson, Curriculum Consultant, Kenosha Unified School District, 3600 52nd Street, Kenosha, WI 53144. (414) 656-6378.

Developmental Funding: USOE ESEA Title I.   JDRP No. 78-184 **(5/23/78)**

Section 6

Mathematics

* These programs are currently funded by the NDN.

Summary of Program Services for Section 6

Program	Goal*	Page	Dissem. Funds: NDN	Dissem. Funds: Other	Costs to Potential Adopter: Hon	Trav	Per Diem	On Site Visitation: Home Site	Adopt Site	Materials: Free Paper	Video	Film Strip	Other	Staff Available: Home Site	Adopt Site	Costs to Adopter: Hon	Trav	Per Diem	Certified Trainers Available: State(s)	Training Time Required: Day(s)
			AWARENESS											TRAINING						
Attainment of Algebra I Skills...	3, 5	6-1	(info. not available)																	
Calculator Assisted... (CAMEL)	5	6-13			✓	✓	✓		✓	✓				✓		✓	✓	✓	AZ, IL, KY	<1
Comprehensive School Mathematics Program (CSMP)	3, 5	6-2	✓		✓	✓	✓		✓	✓	✓		✓	✓	✓	✓	✓	✓	AK, AZ, CO, FL, IL, KY, MD, ME, MI, MN, MO, NC, NE, NY, OH, OK, OR, SC, VA, WA	(K-1) 1+ (2-3) 3+ (4-6) 4+
Decision-Making Math (DMM)	5	6-3	✓		✓	✓	✓	✓	✓	✓				✓	✓	✓	✓	✓	CA, HI, MA, MT, OR, SC	1
Diagnostic Prescriptive Arithmetic (DPA)	5	6-13				✓	✓	✓	✓	✓			✓	✓	✓	✓	✓	✓	AK, ME, MO, MT	2
Effective Videodisc Instruction in Core Mathematics Concepts	5	6-4	✓						✓	✓	✓				✓				(none)	<1
First Level Mathematics (Kindermath)	5	6-5	✓						✓	✓	✓			✓	✓		✓	✓	AK, CA, FL, IA, IL, MN, MS, NH, NM, NY, OK, OR, PA, SC, SD, TX, VA, WA, WV	<1
HOSTS Supplemental Math	5	6-14							✓	✓				✓					(all states)	3+
Maneuvers With Mathematics...	3, 5	6-6	(info. not available)																	
Mathematics Achievement through Problem Solving (MAPS)	5	6-7	✓						✓	✓	✓			✓	✓	(negotiable)	✓	✓	IN, MI, OH	5
Sci-Math	3, 5	6-8	✓		✓	✓	✓		✓	✓				✓	✓	✓	✓	✓	CA, CT, KS, KY, MA, NM, MT	<1
SEED, Project	3, 5	6-9	(info. not available)																	

* National Goals for Education—definitions for each goal can be found on pages 5-7.

Summary of Program Services for Section 6 (cont'd)

Program	Goal*	Page	Dissem. Funds Available		Awareness — Costs to Potential Adopter			On Site Visitation Available		Materials Available				Training — Staff Available		Training — Costs to Adopter			Certified Trainers Available	Training Time Required
			NDN	Other	Hon	Trav	Per Diem	Home Site	Adopt Site	Free Paper	Video	Film Strip	Other	Home Site	Adopt Site	Hon	Trav	Per Diem	State(s)	Day(s)
Skills Reinforcement Project (SRP)	5	6-10				✓	✓	✓	✓	✓	✓			✓	✓	(nego-tiable)		✓	CA, MD	2
Sound Foundations	5	6-11								✓				✓	✓	✓	✓		CA, IL, MI, NY	<1
Success Under-standing Mathematics (SUM)	3, 5	6-12				✓	✓	✓	✓	✓	✓		✓	✓	✓	✓	✓	✓	AL, HI, IA, IL, KY, MN, NY, SC, SD, VA	1-2
Systematic Teaching ... (STAMM)	5	6-14		✓	(nego-tiable)	✓	(nego-tiable)	✓	✓	✓	✓		✓	✓	✓	(nego-tiable)	✓	(nego-tiable)	CO, GA, MS, OH, RI, SC	1-2
Team Accelerated In-struction (TAI) ...	5	6-15			✓	✓	✓	✓		✓	✓				✓	(negotiable)			(variable)	1-2
Title I Mathematics ... (CAI)	5	6-15			✓	✓		✓		✓	✓			✓	✓		✓		(none)	2
Utilizing Computers ... (UCTSM)	5	6-16			✓	✓	✓	✓	✓	✓				✓	✓	✓	✓	✓	IL, NJ, TN	<1

* National Goals for Education—definitions for each goal can be found on pages 5-7.

Attainment of Algebra I Skills: Cord Applied Mathematics 1 and 2. A two-year secondary student program providing an alternative classroom experience to traditional Algebra I by offering to the student who learns best in a contextual manner real-life and workplace applications through hands-on activities.

Audience Learners with an eighth grade, pre-algebra math competency level. Without lowering skill standards, CORD Applied Mathematics challenges students from the middle fifty percentiles and enables them to enter mainstream science and math courses.

Description CORD Applied Mathematics is oriented toward the application and practice of mathematics concepts and skills in hands-on laboratories, and uses practical, world-of-work problems. The curriculum includes not only algebra 1 topics, but topics in geometry, trigonometry, probability, statistics, quality assurance and quality control, and computer programming. Each of the 36 units in the CORD Applied Mathematics learning materials is an integrated learning package made up of supporting parts: Video Program, Student Text, Teacher's Guide, and text sections such as Laboratory Activities, Student Exercises, Student Handouts, Problem Bank for End of Unit Test, and Glossary. Available for the entire program is an Overview Video, Implementation Resource Book, Multiple Choice Question Bank, and Student Resource Book. Audiovisual support is provided by a unit video program which introduces the math unit and sets the stage for the relevance of mathematics in the world of work. Hands-on Laboratory Activities make mathematics concepts come to life. CORD Applied Mathematics addresses National Educational Goals 3 and 5.

Evidence of Effectiveness Before beginning CORD Applied Mathematics, students on the average, have exhibited lower mathematical abilities than students in the traditional algebra 1 class. Algebra exit exam scores were analyzed from students representing twenty sites in thirteen states: results indicate no significant difference between the mean algebra test scores of the CORD Applied Mathematics 2 and algebra 1 classes.

Requirements Two major requirements of the curriculum are as follows: (1) teachers must attend a three-day training for each year of CORD Applied Mathematics, and (2) the class manipulatives must be used. Because the approach to teaching CORD Applied Mathematics courses is very different from the manner in which a more traditional math class is taught, proper teacher training is vital. Classroom equipment must be purchased and used to ensure course content is being taught as intended. Schools implementing CORD Applied Mathematics courses do not need a separate classroom exclusive to CORD Applied Mathematics because materials are transportable for each lab.

Costs To implement CORD Applied Mathematics, teacher training, classroom equipment, and text materials are necessary. The total cost for each year can range from approximately $1,900 to $3,200. After the initial investment in training and materials, subsequent annual costs are reduced to the minimal expense of consumables (generally less than $100 per classroom) and replacement of lost or damaged texts ($1.45 per student unit).

Services Awareness materials are available. Training is conducted at the CORD Teaching Center in Waco, Texas, or training can be arranged at other locations.

Contact Nancy Moore or Ann Ferrell, Dissemination Coordinators, (800) 231-3015, FAX (817) 776-3906; Dr. John Souders or Dr. Candace Todd, Curriculum Development CORD: Center for Occupational Research and Development, P.O. Box 21689, Waco, TX 76702 (800) 972-2766, FAX (817) 772-8972.

Developmental Funding: Center for Occupational Research and Development

PEP No. 94-15 (5/1/94)

Comprehensive School Mathematics Program (CSMP). An exciting, complete elementary-level mathematics curriculum with a focus on problem solving and concept development, promoting critical thinking as well as teaching basic skills.

Audience Approved as a complete mathematics curriculum for students of all abilities, grades K-6. Comprehensive School Mathematics Program (CSMP) addresses the objectives of Goals 3 and 5 of the National Goals for Education by strengthening mathematics education throughout the system, by improving student performance in mathematics, and by providing substantive mathematics background for teachers.

Description An underlying assumption of the Comprehensive School Mathematics Program (CSMP) curriculum is that children can learn and can enjoy learning much more mathematics than they do now. Unlike most modern programs, the content is presented not as an artificial structure external to the experience of children, but rather as an extension of experiences children have encountered in their development, both at the real-life and fantasy levels. Using a "pedagogy of situations," children are led through sequences of problem-solving experiences presented in game-like and story settings. It is CSMP's strong conviction that mathematics is a unified whole and should be learned as such. Consequently, the content is completely sequenced in spiral form so that each student is brought into contact with each area of content continuously throughout the program while building interlocking experiences of increasing sophistication as the situations become more challenging.

A feature unique to CSMP is the use of nonverbal languages that give children immediate access to mathematical ideas and methods necessary not only for solving problems, but also for continually expanding their understanding of the mathematical concepts themselves. Through these languages the curriculum acts as a vehicle that engages children immediately and naturally with the content of mathematics and its applications without cumbersome linguistic prerequisites. Other tools, such as the Papy Minicomputer, the hand-held calculator, various geometry tools, and random devices are used extensively throughout the curriculum to pose problems, explore concepts, develop skills, and define new ideas.

CSMP is flexible enough to facilitate whole-group, small-group, and individualized instruction. It is appropriate for all children including specialized audiences such as gifted, compensatory, and bilingual. It recognizes the importance of affective as well as cognitive concerns and has been developed and extensively tested in classrooms nationwide.

Evidence of Effectiveness CSMP students do better in applying mathematics to new problem situations and in using various reasoning skills. They learn traditional mathematics skills and concepts as well as or better than comparable non-CSMP students, and they show a higher level of enthusiasm and interest in mathematics.

Requirements School systems and CSMP agree on an implementation plan that provides for the training of teachers, the evaluation of the program, and support services. The school system appoints a local coordinator who maintains contact with CSMP as a member of the CSMP Network.

Costs Training costs are negotiable but usually include a trainer's travel expenses and/or training fee of $150/day. Workshop materials average approximately $5/participant. Complete sets of classroom materials for full class implementations cost (start-up) from $160 (K-level) to $460 (grade 6).

Services Awareness materials are available at no cost. With advance notice, arrangements can be made for visitors to observe the program in use in a variety of sites. Program staff are available to attend out-of-state awareness meetings. Training is conducted at the program site or at the adopter site. Implementation and follow-up services are available to adopters.

Contact Clare Heidema, Director, CSMP, 2550 South Parker Road, Suite 500, Aurora, CO 80014. (303) 337-0990. Voice Mail: (303) 743-5520. E-Mail: cheidema@mcrel.org

Developmental Funding: USOE ESEA Titles III & IV, National Institute of Education.

JDRP No. 78-169R (**3/17/78**)
Recertified (**4/7/92**)

Decision-Making Math (DMM). A program for improving students' capabilities in identifying, analyzing, and solving problems for grades 7-9.

Audience Approved by PEP for students in 7th and 8th grade math classes and 9th grade general or basic math classes.

Description Decision-Making Math (DMM) is a supplementary problem-solving program for grades 7-9 that teaches problem-solving and decision-making skills to develop students' mathematical power. DMM was developed by the Education and Technology Foundation to meet not only the needs of students so that they will be powerful problem solvers and effective decision makers, but also the needs of teachers who wish to create a problem-solving climate in the classroom. DMM directly focuses on the Curriculum and Evaluation Standards of the National Council of Teachers of Mathematics and the National Goals for Education. DMM addresses the need to create interactive classroom environments that encourage and develop more sophisticated mathematics skills of reasoning and communication. DMM brings to schools a proven and exemplary instructional program for both teachers and students that will provide:

- **Teacher training** that improves and enhances problem-solving knowledge and provides instructional techniques that infuse problem solving within mathematics;
- **Curriculum** in which students confidently learn and apply problem-solving skills and strategies on their own, in groups, and at home with parents;
- **Program assessment** to evaluate impact on student achievement and classroom implementation; and
- **Integrated follow-up activities** and technical assistance that ensure local and national institutionalization and help create systemic change.

The primary goal of DMM is to provide an integrated mathematics problem-solving program which allows students to go well beyond gains produced by existing programs. The emphasis of the program and the training is on process rather than solution. Cooperative learning and alternative assessment techniques are stressed throughout. A variety of methods is used to ensure understanding, such as: questioning and planning, interpreting and verifying, organizing and manipulating data, and analyzing and applying solutions.

The second major goal is to improve teaching skills and techniques to create classroom climates where students and teachers alike are required to communicate and reason with one another in a sophisticated manner. These higher levels of reasoning and thinking are developed through materials, investigations, teaching methodologies, and alternative assessment techniques utilized within DMM.

Evidence of Effectiveness DMM is an evaluated program that has demonstrated consistent and significant gains in student achievement as measured by Mathematics Concepts and Applications in the Comprehensive Test of Basic Skills (CTBS).

Requirements Adopting teachers use DMM approximately one-fifth of their class time to complement their regular math program. They attend a full day of inservice, acquire one complete curriculum set per teacher, and duplicate student materials. An additional one-day follow-up workshop is highly recommended to ensure successful implementation. Classroom adoption can be assessed using the DMM Criterion Reference Test. DMM may be adopted by a district, school, or individual teacher.

Costs Awareness materials are available at no cost. Initial adoption costs include the one-time purchase of the DMM Curriculum materials which consist of the *DMM Binder*, 16 *Student Guide to Problem Solving Workbooks*, and 128 *Strategy Practice Cards* for $99. Training costs are negotiated to include consultant fee and travel expenses.

Services Program services include a one-day training workshop, an optional follow-up workshop, quarterly mailings, assistance with program implementation and evaluation, and ongoing technical assistance. A Spanish translation of the Student's Guide is available. Interested educators are welcome to visit demonstration sites across the country. Program staff are available for awareness meetings and trainings which can be conducted at the adopting site.

Contact Kristine A. Shaff, Director, Education and Technology Foundation, 4655 25th Street, San Francisco, CA 94114. (415) 824-5911, FAX (415) 282-4294.

Developmental Funding: (info. not available).

JDRP No. 87-10 **(6/1/87)**

Effective Videodisc Instruction in Core Mathematics Concepts. A videodisc instructional program approved for students of all ability levels in grades 5-7, including remedial, mainstreamed, and mildly disabled students.

Audience Approved by PEP for students of all ability levels in grades 5-7, including remedial, mainstreamed, and mildly handicapped students.

Description The Effective Videodisc Instruction in Core Mathematics Concepts program enhances the ability of teachers to provide instruction in mathematics through the classroom use of videodiscs. The technology is used to emphasize prerequisite skills, providing systematic review and guided practice in small steps.

The teacher, using a handheld remote control, conducts the videodisc lesson while monitoring and supporting students. Videodisc demonstrations are briskly paced, with intensive questioning. Each lesson has five to seven major checkpoints; if students are experiencing difficulty, the teacher can provide additional guided practice through the videodisc. To ensure an emphasis on concept development rather than rote learning, two or three sets of parallel examples are available for reteaching.

The combination of quickly paced video demonstrations, intensive questioning, and increased presence of the teacher on the classroom floor all enhance academic learning time.

Each videodisc program consists of videodiscs, student workbooks, and a teacher's manual. Workbooks are primarily used for independent practice. During the interactive videodisc activities, most of the written student responses are made in notebooks. Student interaction is intensive, and demonstrations are rarely more than 30 seconds before a written response is required.

Evidence of Effectiveness Implementation of the program has consistently and substantively improved student achievement when compared with preexisting instructional programs. The program has shown considerable strength in addressing the needs of low achievers and mildly handicapped students. The program has supported regular classroom teachers' efforts to teach special education in the regular classroom.

Requirements Color television and videodisc hardware are required to implement the program. No additional personnel are required. Training is provided in the cost of purchasing the materials.

Costs Most Grade 5 implementation would use the fractions and decimals program, with a total of four videodiscs containing intense instructional support for more than 50 hours of instruction. Higher grades would add the 40-hour, three-disc word problems program. The typical Grade 5 costs would be $2,600 per building (three to four fifth grade teachers) and include the videodiscs, teacher's manual, 35 fractions workbooks, 35 decimals workbooks, and permission to copy workbooks. Videodisc players are $400-$650, and a color television monitor is needed. As a volume discount, a free videodisc player will be provided with every seven discs ordered.

Services Staff development (included in the cost of materials) involves an initial two-hour training session and an individual follow-up visit with the teacher during the second week. Included in each videodisc program is a placement test to check on skills development, a tool which can be used for management and monitoring.

Contact Alan Hofmeister, Technology Division, Center for Persons with Disabilities, Utah State University, Logan, UT 84322-6800. (801) 797-3718.

Developmental Funding: Federal Office of Special Education Programs.

PEP No. 89-11 **(5/17/89)**

First Level Mathematics (Kindermath). A comprehensive program in math fundamentals using concrete objects and actual physical operations for initial math instruction.

Audience Approved by JDRP and PEP for children in their first year of mathematics instruction, kindergarten or first grade.

Description The First Level Mathematics (Kindermath) program is diagnostic/prescriptive in nature, providing a sequential curriculum for individual developmental growth. The ninety lesson curriculum consists of the following nine components: same and different; patterns; sets zero to five; shapes; sets six to ten; numerals six to ten; signs; and addition/subtraction. Key elements of the program are developmental hierarchies, mixed instructional modes, and extended curriculum range. The program addresses Goal 4 of the National Goals for Education by providing special math emphasis in the earliest grades and increasing the number of teachers with a substantive background in mathematics.

The program has been designed to be used by both regular and special education teachers. Because it is available in Spanish, it is also appropriate for use in bilingual and ESL programs.

Evidence of Effectiveness As a result of participation in the program, children in their first year of mathematics instruction demonstrated statistically significant growth in knowledge of mathematics relative to national norms on three standardized tests of mathematics achievement.

Requirements Program may be implemented in an individual classroom, a single school, or a district. Teachers wishing to implement the program and management system should attend a training workshop, which is most often held at district or regional sites. Administrators and paraprofessionals are also encouraged to attend training sessions. A training tape, complete with training manual, is available.

One Kindermath kit is required per classroom. Materials are nonconsumable.

Costs Training costs consist of travel expenses for the trainer plus $75 per classroom for the one-time-only purchase of the classroom kit.

Services Awareness materials are available at no cost. Visitors are welcome by appointment at the program site and additional demonstration sites. Program staff are available to attend out-of-state awareness meetings. Training is available at the program site or adopter site. Implementation and follow-up services are available to adopters.

Contact Mary Alice Felleisen, 38 North Waterloo Road, Devon, PA 19333. (610) 687-6252 or (800) 444-5729.

JDRP No. 84-1 **(1/24/84)**
Recertified **(2/13/90)**

Developmental Funding: PRIMAK Educational Foundation.

Maneuvers With Mathematics Project (MWM). An innovative, calculator-intensive mathematics program for the middle grades.

Audience Students in the fifth through eighth grades of all ability levels.

Description The Maneuvers with Mathematics (MWM) program is designed to address the deficiencies in mathematical learning in the middle grades. It offers hands-on, problem-solving activities and makes full use of the scientific calculator as a tool to enable students to investigate. Each MWM module is a set of investigations, problems, and other learning activities that involves a specific body of mathematics. Students solve problems, make conjectures, reason, investigate mathematical relationships, look for connections among mathematical quantities, and use manipulatives. As they proceed, they communicate with each other and with their teacher about their thinking and ideas. The activities in a module engage students, stimulate their thinking, and make math interesting. MWM materials also incorporate several innovative techniques to help students gauge their own progress. The materials offer clear teaching plans, yet also encourage teachers to follow leads from student suggestions or from their own ideas. When MWM materials are coupled with a staff development program, teachers develop rich math classrooms that encourage discourse about mathematics, multiple solution paths to problems, and open-ended investigation. They serve as a means to stimulate and challenge a broad spectrum of students— including those who previously experienced little success in mathematics. At this time, seven modules are available: *Maneuvers With Angles*, *Maneuvers With Rectangles*, *Maneuvers With Triangles*, *Maneuvers With Circles*, *Maneuvers With Nickels and Numbers*, *Maneuvers With Number Patterns*, and *Maneuvers With Fractions*. MWM addresses National Educational Goals 3 and 5.

Evidence of Effectiveness When compared to a control group of fifth through eighth grade students, MWM students demonstrated significantly higher growth on a post-test consisting primarily of items from the Second International Mathematics Study and the National Assessment of Education Progress.

Requirements Teachers and administrators are encouraged to design a staff development workshop that fits their needs working with MWM staff. No special facilities are required.

Costs Start-up staff development costs include: an instructor ($400/day), travel expenses for an instructor, and teacher materials ($25/teacher/module); there are no annual operating costs. The start-up and annual operating implementation costs include student lab books ($150/class of 30). The cost of calculators, rulers and similar materials are costs that will be incurred either by the school or student.

Services The provision of follow-up support nationwide is being reviewed; in the Chicago area such support is being provided through various organizations.

Contact David A. Page, Project Director and Kathryn B. Chval, Associate Project Director, The University of Illinois at Chicago, 851 S. Morgan Street, (m/c 249) SEO 1309, Chicago, IL 60607-7045. (312) 996-8708.

Developmental Funding: National Science Foundation

PEP No. 94-3 **(4/1/94)**

Mathematics Achievement through Problem Solving (MAPS). The primary goals of this complete, one-year curriculum using teachers as facilitators are to increase the problem-solving ability and the conceptual understanding of mathematics in general mathematic students (typically 9th graders).

Audience Approved by PEP for first-year secondary general mathematics students (typically 9th graders).

Description The Mathematics Achievement through Problem Solving (MAPS) program is designed to replace the existing first-year secondary general mathematics program. The curriculum is grounded in the constructivist perspective, therefore, students build conceptual frameworks while they are engaged in activities requiring problem solving and decision making. The teacher functions as a facilitator rather than a disseminator. Extensive use of investigations and small-group problem solving enable students to construct generalizations of mathematical concepts and relationships. Students also learn to use calculators and computers as problem-solving tools. Learning materials consist of ten strands, including estimation and mental arithmetic, heuristic problem solving, number concepts, spatial visualization, including estimation and mental arithmetic, heuristic problem solving, number concepts, spatial visualization, probability, statistics, measurement, applied problem solving, intuitive algebra, and computer problem solving. This program strengthens mathematics education, which is part of the first objective of the national goals for science and mathematics education.

Evidence of Effectiveness Students participating in the program score significantly higher on a project-developed and validated criterion-referenced test of problem-solving ability, achieve consistently higher ratings in a content analysis of their work on the posttest, and score higher overall on the Indiana Statewide Test of Educational Progress (ISTEP) Mathematical Concepts and Applications subscore than comparison students in traditional general mathematics classes.

Requirements A five-day intensive workshop for teachers focused on understanding collaborative learning, the problem-centered curriculum, the constructivist perspective, and the classroom atmosphere needed to implement the MAPS program is required. Regular meetings with other MAPS teachers and attendance at a one- or two-day follow-up conference a year later is highly recommended.

Costs Training costs consist of $1600 plus travel expenses for presenters' fees and $50 per participant (typically 20 people) for workshop materials. Duplication expenses are $8 per student the first year and $4.50 per student in subsequent years. Manipulative expenses vary.

Services In addition to training and materials, MAPS provides newsletters, exchange visits, follow-up meetings, consultations, and classroom visitations.

Contact Jean Boddy, Mathematics Education Specialist, Department of Curriculum and Instruction, Purdue University, West Lafayette, IN 47907-1442. (317) 494-0803. William C. Kyle, Jr. (317) 494-5889.

Developmental Funding: Indiana Commission of Higher Education, Indiana Department of Education, and School Mathematics and Science Center at Purdue University.

PEP No. 92-6 **(3/92)**

Sci-Math. A curriculum model that bridges the abstract operations taught in mathematics and their applications in the sciences for average to above-average students in grades 7-10, and low achievers in grades 9-12.

Audience Approved by JDRP/PEP for grades 7-12, Sci-Math embraces mathematical techniques that can be applied by students of varying age and ability, from low achievers and the educationally disadvantaged to college-bound high school students in math, chemistry, and physics classes.

Description Sci-Math links the problem-solving skills utilized in mathematics with those needed in the sciences and in everyday life. Using the mathematics of rates and ratios, Sci-Math gives students problem-solving strategies which they can apply beyond their math classes to the sciences, social studies, home, and business. Sci-Math is ideal for teachers whose students say they can't do word problems because they just don't know where to start. Sci-Math promotes the National Goals for Education to increase student achievement in math and science and to strengthen math and science education.

- **Central Theme** The technique of factor analysis (also called dimensional analysis, labeled rates, and label canceling) is presented in discrete steps that build students' confidence in their problem-solving abilities. Sci-Math emphasizes essential problem-solving habits: to stay on track and find what a problem really asks for, to remember the importance of labels for data and answers, and to think of problem solving primarily in terms of relationships, not arithmetic calculations.

- **Applications** Teachers can easily implement Sci-Math as a mini-course, a supplement, or a parallel course. The program works well in cooperative learning environments. Advanced students of algebra, chemistry, or physics can assimilate the core Sci-Math ideas in as little as two weeks; for less advanced or younger students, teachers may spend three to six weeks, depending on the skill level they want to achieve. Teachers should note that Sci-Math does not expand the curriculum; rather, Sci-Math extends it by showing students new and efficient ways to solve the problems they already face.

- **Activities** More than 20 hands-on activities and experiments deal with situations at home, school, and business that are already familiar to students. Activity materials, such as rulers, string, and pressure gauges, are readily available and inexpensive.

- **Materials** Two editions of Sci-Math: Applications in Proportional Problem-Solving are available from Addison-Wesley. Module One is best suited to pre-algebra students; Module Two assumes familiarity with algebraic variables and graphing and charting techniques. Teachers' guides are available for each module, with all problems worked out in detail. The guides also provide record sheets, data, and answers to questions. The student texts cost about $8 per copy and are reusable. In addition, workshop participants receive numerous free worksheets and exercises which they can duplicate for classroom use.

Evidence of Effectiveness Grades 7-12 students of varying ability demonstrated significantly positive growth in proportional problem-solving skills on a validated criterion reference test.

Requirements Teacher training consists of one six-hour workshop that focuses on Sci-Math Module One. Participants should bring a Module One teacher guide and student book to the workshop. Workshop sponsors cover the cost of Addison-Wesley texts and the trainer's fee and expenses.

Services Awareness materials are available at no cost. Program personnel are available for one-hour awareness presentations when expenses are covered. Training costs are trainer's fee plus travel expenses, and $18 per participant (typically 20 people) for workshop materials. Duplication expenses are $3 per student each year. Program adopters receive follow-up assistance by phone or mail, and our newsletter, The Sci-Math Way, free of charge.

Contact   **Laura Dunn, Carolyn Hubachek, Co-directors, Sci-Math, Education and Technology Foundation, 4655 25th Street, San Francisco, CA 94114. (415) 824-5911, FAX (415) 282-4294.**

Developmental Funding: National Science Foundation.

JDRP No. 82-20 **(5/12/82)**
Recertified **(4/1/94)**

SEED, Project. A program designed to increase the number of students in grades 4-6 from low-income backgrounds who will graduate from high school with skills required for jobs, careers, further education, and leadership in a technological society.

Audience Students in grades 4 through 6, generally in schools with a predominance of Chapter 1 eligible students.

Description Project SEED brings specially trained mathematicians and scientists into low income elementary school classrooms to teach topics from algebra and higher level mathematics using a Socratic, group-discovery method of instruction. This question-and-answer approach encourages vigorous student discussion and high levels of participation from students at all ability levels. The lessons, which are supplementary to the regular mathematics curriculum, are designed to create a foundation for mathematical thinking, an enthusiasm for mathematical inquiry, and the self-confidence to overcome low achievement and a sense of academic inferiority. Conceptual understanding is emphasized and basic skills are reinforced. Project SEED instructors receive rigorous preservice and ongoing inservice training. They provide direct classroom instruction and inservice training for classroom teachers. Each class meets four days a week with additional time reserved for conferences with the classroom teacher, observation, and staff development. The classroom teacher is a participant and observer in the class during SEED lessons. Few learning materials are required since the instructors use their mathematics backgrounds to ask questions which guide students to discover mathematical concepts. Project SEED's national director oversees development in new locations and overall program implementation. A local project director and experienced mathematics specialists have responsibility for the daily program implementation. Project SEED addresses National Educational Goals 3 and 5.

Evidence of Effectiveness Rigorous longitudinal evaluations over a number of years in different locations with different instructors clearly demonstrate that Project SEED instruction has a positive impact on immediate mathematics achievement scores; that Project SEED instruction has a long-term impact on mathematics achievement; and that Project SEED students take more higher-level mathematics courses in secondary schools.

Requirements School districts are required to commit to implementing the program for a minimum of 3 years, subject to available funding, and to provide office and meeting space for project staff. Administrators work with project staff to identify target schools and classes. Teachers are required to meet regularly with project staff.

Costs Costs for personnel, training, materials and supplies are covered by the school district contract with Project SEED and will vary depending on the overall size of the program and class size. The average annual costs for a complete program of direct instruction, inservice, staff development and curriculum development when translated to a per student basis is estimated between $300-500.

Contact Helen Smiler, National Projects Coordinator, 2530 San Pablo Avenue, Suite K, Berkeley, CA 94702. (510) 644-3422, FAX (510) 644-0566. Hamid Ebrahimi, National Director, P.O. Box 830414, Richardson, TX 75083. (214) 358-2345, FAX (214) 479-1105.

Developmental Funding: Federal, state, and local sources.

PEP No. 94-5 **(3/4/94)**

Skills Reinforcement Project (SRP). A program which improves the reasoning ability and math achievement of talented students from culturally different and/or low income backgrounds. The Project's goals are to increase student participation in higher level mathematics classes, and in turn encourage currently underrepresented students to select college majors and careers in math and science.

Audience Approved by PEP for students in grades 5-7.

Description Skills Reinforcement Project (SRP) uses a diagnostic/prescriptive approach to mastery learning in an accelerated mathematics curriculum. The approach to instruction allows students to proceed at a flexible pace as new concepts and skills are mastered. Students work individually and in groups. The curriculum itself includes elementary arithmetic concepts and skills, more advanced skills, pre-algebra, and algebra. Supplemental program components include parent education and counseling, affective development (attitude, motivation, and discipline), and a supplemental language arts instruction to help students better understand and solve mathematical problems. SRP is ideally a two-year, 220-hour intervention consisting of 20 three-hour Saturday sessions during the academic year and a two-week summer residential program at a college campus. During the summer program, students are supervised and mentored by minority college students hired as residential assistants.

SRP was developed to enhance, enrich, and promote mathematics ability and skills in talented students often underrepresented in gifted and talented programs.

Evidence of Effectiveness After completing the program, the majority of students moved up substantially in percentile rank on both achievement and aptitude tests, with more students scoring above the 90th percentile after completion of SRP than before. Greater gains were made by students participating in the program for a full two years rather than a single year. Effect sizes for pre-post contrasts ranged from one to two full standard deviations.

Requirements Staff requirements include: site director and one resident assistant per 10 students (summer component); one teacher per 20 students, one teaching assistant per teacher (Saturday and summer component). With careful preselection of staff, training requires no more than one week. During the academic year, the Project requires classroom space and during the summer, access to a local college or university campus. Instructional materials include textbooks and project publications.

Costs Start-up costs are largely determined by the costs of staffing the program. Training costs $5,000 for start-up and $2,000 to operate the program. Materials and supplies cost $4,000 initially and $2,500 to operate the program. Total costs are estimated to be between $46,500 and $65,000 for a group of 45 students, and between $1,033 and $1,444 per student.

Services All aspects of the Project are described in published papers. Curriculum guides, teacher training materials, teacher, parent, and student handbooks, as well as an administrator's handbook on how to develop an SRP are printed and available.

Contact **Elizabeth Jones Stork, Associate Director, CTY, and Director, Western Region, Center for Talented Youth, Johns Hopkins University, Western Regional Office, 206 North Jackson Street, Suite 304, Glendale, CA 91206. (818) 500-9034.**

Developmental Funding: Private foundations.

PEP No. 93-4 (**2/10/93**)

Sound Foundations. A program developed to improve the achievement and attitude of high school remedial mathematics students by presenting concepts in the context of topics of interest to the age level.

Audience Approved by PEP for students and teachers in high school remedial, general, and basic skills math programs. Junior high schools and middle schools may also use the simulation in their seventh and eighth grade programs.

Description Sound Foundations replaces the traditional math curriculum for the target students but retains the traditional textbook for student practice. The program covers topics in the remedial math program by using a simulation format. Major topics include integers, rational numbers, graphing, measurement, geometry, probability, statistics, and consumer mathematics.

Sound Foundations is divided into ten milestones in a job simulation about a rock band: formation, equipment purchase, rehearsal, dance clubs, audio sales, airplay, publicity, local concerts, away concerts, and the national tour. Students are given a budget of $85,000 and must use creativity, management skills, and math concepts to successfully guide the band financially. Managers receive quality points based on their decisions. Students learn new math topics as they are needed in the simulation and work independently of each other.

The program includes a student book, teacher's manual, five decks of activity cards, 180 daily quiz masters, transparency masters, and test masters. An annual exchange of ideas occurs every fall in a newsletter circulated to users of the program.

Evidence of Effectiveness Remedial math students using the program show a greater increase in mathematics achievement and a positive increase in attitude towards success in mathematics, learn not to stereotype math as a male domain, and elect more quantitative courses in high school. Female students demonstrate a more positive attitude toward the usefulness of mathematics. Use of the program has increased the percentage of students passing state competency tests required for graduation, and has increased the percentage of students taking math electives.

Requirements A training workshop is required. A careful mix of structure and informality is also encouraged in the classroom.

Costs Costs for the program are $49.95 for a teacher's binder (which lasts for years), $11.95 per student book (which is consumable). Training costs consist of $400 plus travel/lodging expenses for presenter, plus $5 per participant for photocopying costs. Each participant must also purchase the student book and a teacher kit.

Services Awareness materials are available at no cost. An annual newsletter, which serves as a network for users, is available at no cost. It is called *Feedback*.

Contact   **Dr. Robert Gerver, North Shore High School, 450 Glen Cove Avenue, Glen Head, NY 11545. (516) 671-5500.**

Developmental Funding: Local.   PEP No. 90-05 (**2/6/90**)

Success Understanding Mathematics (SUM). A program designed to increase mathematical achievement of elementary school children through improved teaching practices.

Audience All elementary school children, including those who are achieving below grade level.

Description The program is based on the belief that children learn best when instructional methods match the ways in which they learn and on Piaget's research which showed that elementary school children need to manipulate concrete materials to understand math concepts. Program characteristics include:

- A problem-solving approach
- Emphasis on reasoning, number sense, and operation sense
- Use of manipulatives by students to make connections between math concepts, language, and written symbols
- Role of students—investigate, guess, check, reason, discuss
- Role of teacher—pose real-world problems, guide student learning by questioning

Program components include teaching methods that can be used with any textbook, management materials, and support for teachers. Publications include strategy books with suggested lessons and questions for teachers to use with their students, assessment inventories, record keeping forms, parent involvement materials, inservice materials, blackline masters, and a certified trainers' kit. SUM addresses National Educational Goals 3 and 5.

Evidence of Effectiveness Pretest and posttest data on a variety of mathematics achievement tests between 1987 and 1990 upheld validation studies done in 1980 and 1985. After one year of SUM instruction, students scored at significantly higher levels than would be expected by the test norms. Supplementary evidence included teacher questionnaires which showed that the SUM Program training was effective in influencing teachers to make the instructional changes recommended by the National Council of Teachers of Mathematics (NCTM) Standards. Student attitude surveys showed that students demonstrated positive attitudes toward mathematics. The program has been adopted in 43 states.

Requirements Teachers trained in the use of SUM teaching methods, the SUM manuals, and manipulative materials. The program may be implemented by a teacher, a school, or a school district. Student gains are evaluated with the adopter's assessment instruments.

Costs Implementation costs include a two-day workshop ($300/day plus expenses), participant materials (negotiable—approximately $105/participant), and follow-up technical assistance.

Services Awareness materials are available. Visitors are welcome by appointment. Training is available at the adopter's site. Follow-up workshops are tailored to meet teacher's needs. Ongoing consultant service is provided on site or by telephone.

Contact **Kathleen Bullington, Des Moines Public Schools, 1800 Grand Avenue, Room 343, Des Moines, IA 50309. (515) 242-7860, FAX (515) 242-7860.**

Developmental Funding: USDOE.

PEP No. 80-55R3 **(4/1/94)**

Calculator Assisted Mathematics for Everyday Living (CAMEL). A curriculum to increase the computation and application skills of general mathematics students in the 9th and 10th grades.

Description Calculator Assisted Mathematics for Everyday Living (CAMEL) is an individualized two-year program for those students who have had little or no success in mathematics. These students usually have computational deficiencies that preclude their mastering many of the "living skills" concepts that are part of everyday life for most people. CAMEL is based on the premise that these students can and will learn these concepts if the amount of computations is reduced. Students in a CAMEL classroom use calculators to perform the computations necessary to learn and apply these concepts. Paper and pencil computations are not excluded by use of the calculator. The program includes eight computations modules that the students must work using paper and pencil if they cannot demonstrate mastery of the skill on a pretest. Paper and pencil computations should take less than 20% of the students' time. While CAMEL was developed for use in a regular classroom and is primarily used there, the individualized nature of CAMEL makes it appropriate for any group that is highly transient and not well motivated.

The CAMEL program can be implemented by any math teacher. Teacher-student ratio 1:30 or less. A one-day training session is desirable. Each student in the program should have access to a calculator. A set of CAMEL materials is required and consists of eight computational modules, 31 applications modules, and two applications review modules; teacher and manager manuals; complete set of pre- and posttests with answer key. A management system to help the teacher is also part of the program.

Contact Shirley M. Menendez, Ph.D., CAMEL, 1105 East Fifth Street, Metropolis, IL 62960. (618) 524-2664, FAX (618) 524-2004.

Developmental Funding: USOE ESEA Title IV-C.

JDRP No. 82-5 (2/17/82)

Diagnostic Prescriptive Arithmetic (DPA). A basic arithmetic program with emphasis on developing, modeling and mastering the basic concepts and skills. Approved by JDRP for students functioning at grade levels 3-5.

Description Diagnostic Prescriptive Arithmetic (DPA) is a process-oriented program emphasizing the development and refinement of teacher modeling and questioning skills. DPA is an arithmetic program and includes counting, place value, addition, subtraction, multiplication, and division of whole numbers. Problem-solving skills are developed and reinforced through ongoing experiences with estimation and approximation, data collection, organization and interpretation, and real-life applications of arithmetic skills. Diagnostic tests for the major arithmetic topics (three levels) are used throughout the year to determine students' strengths and weaknesses both in concepts and skills. Prescriptions are then planned using the DPA Teacher's Manual, manual supplement, and other DPA resource materials. Each of the concept-developing and reinforcement activities in the Teacher's Manual has specific objectives related to the arithmetic instructional sequence and the diagnostic test items. The manual also includes descriptions of ongoing mathematics experiences, record-keeping procedures, classroom management techniques, and instructions for developing a variety of teacher-made materials. DPA can be used in self-contained elementary grade classes as the arithmetic component of the mathematics program or as a co-curricula remediation program (PSEN; Chapter I). Both approaches are essentially the same. A topic section of the DPA diagnostic test is administered, and the results are analyzed for group and/or individual needs. These data are recorded on the analysis chart, which aids the teacher in forming instructional groups and planning a program. Each student begins at his/her level of understanding. He/she may work with or without the teacher in a large group, small group, or independently. The student may use concrete materials for modeling a basic concept and may work with a DPA activity for reinforcing a new skill. The student may complete a written activity for practice or may help in the school by applying arithmetic to a real-life situation.

Contact Bonnie Hawthorne, Kessler School District #2, 2420 Choteau, Helena, MT 59601. (406) 442-0150. Sally Logan, 417 North Main, Louisiana, MO 63353. (314) 754-5953.

JDRP No. 74-68 (9/18/74)
Recertified (11/84)

Developmental Funding: USOE ESEA Title I.

HOSTS Supplemental Math. A supplemental program that provides students the opportunity to: learn to value mathematics; become confident in their own abilities; become a mathematical problem solver; learn to communicate mathematically; and learn to respond mathematically. Approved by JDRP for math instruction for elementary and junior high students.

Description HOSTS Supplemental Math is based on the belief that students need to learn mathematics in a way that is meaningful to them. The use of manipulatives and participative learning is highly stressed. Teachers are provided with lesson plans and activities for each objective which are designed to build a conceptual understanding before proceeding to the level of practice and application. The sequential system of objectives is aligned with the National Math Standards of the National Council of Teacher of Mathematics and covers nine levels, Readiness through Grade 8.

HOSTS Supplemental Math is compatible with all major math basal series. Lesson plans, activities, manuals, tests, and answer sheets are provided. Teachers also have access to the HOSTS computerized database and software that matches thousand of math resources, including literature, to state frameworks and local objectives. The HOSTS software also features a student record system, math problem generator, as well as a prescription program.

HOSTS Supplemental Math has been designed to offer teachers options to accommodate various learning styles and provide a fun-to-learn atmosphere for instructors and students.

Contact   William E. Gibbons, Chairman, 8000 N.E. Parkway Drive, Suite 201, Vancouver, WA 98662-6459. (206) 260-1995 or (800) 833-4678, FAX (206) 260-1783.

Developmental Funding: USOE ESEA IV-C and private.   JDRP No 82-8 **(4/9/82)**

Systematic Teaching And Measuring Mathematics (STAMM). A comprehensive outcome-based mathematics program resulting in high student achievement. Approved by JDRP for students of all abilities, grades K-8.

Description Systematic Teaching And Measuring Mathematics (STAMM) presents an elementary mathematics program that covers the curricula and the means necessary to assist in delivering NCTM's "Standards." Teachers can select from a variety of learning activities to provide for the needs of their students through a variety of concrete manipulatives, practice, problem solving, and enrichment strategies. STAMM provides students with varied opportunities to develop underlying concepts, and can be used in a variety of teaching styles (large group, cooperative grouping, departmentalization, individualized or labs). STAMM's flexible design fits into schools of all sizes and classroom structures. STAMM includes a management system which is organized around carefully designed learner outcomes. Student growth is monitored through postassessment strategies. Specifically, the program is delivered through the following STAMM materials: **Teacher Manual** (TM) - a resource book of *activity*-oriented ideas to assist the teacher in delivering the learner outcomes. **Student Booklet** - a set of student materials from which a teacher selects activities as needed to enhance development and practice of the learner outcomes by the students *after* they have received initial instruction. **Student Assessment Booklet** - criterion-referenced assessments to provide information about the student's progress on the learner outcomes utilizing alternative testing strategies.

These STAMM resource materials have been created to complement the existing textbooks, manipulative materials, and teacher-made resources. The Program is a cost effective way to support teachers. The primary program costs about $6 per child the first year and $3.50 maintenance, in contrast to many commercial primary level programs that typically cost $13-$15 per year.

Contact   Larry Bradsby, Director, STAMM, Jefferson County Schools, 1829 Denver West Drive, Golden, CO 80401. (303) 763-5650.

JDRP No. 76-87 **(6/23/76)**
Recertified **(12/84)**

Developmental Funding: USOE ESEA Title III.

Team Accelerated Instruction (TAI): Mathematics. Developed by R.E. Slavin and colleagues and approved by the JDRP for grades 3-6.

Description Team Accelerated Instruction (TAI): Mathematics is a program that helps teachers to meet the diversity of student needs within the math class. It combines quality interactive instruction with the power of cooperative learning to accelerate the achievement of all students, maximize teaching and learning time, enhance motivation and attitudes toward math, and improve students' social interaction.

Students receive concept instructions from the teacher in small homogeneous teaching groups. They then practice the skills learned in 4-5 member heterogeneous learning teams at their own pace on materials appropriate to their specific needs.

TAI: Mathematics instruction is organized into 13 paperbound nonconsumable student books. Each classroom set of books contains a range from advanced addition to pre-algebra.

The program also includes comprehensive teacher materials which make it easy for teachers to plan, teach, and manage the math program effectively.

TAI has proven effective in five field experiments which involved random assignment of classes to TAI or control treatments. Differences between TAI and control classes in grade equivalent gains on the Comprehensive Test of Basic Skills Mathematics Computations had a median ratio of more than two to one.

Awareness materials are available at no cost. Training is one to two days; follow-up advisable (costs to be negotiated).

Contact Barbara M. Luebbe, Director, TAI: Mathematics, Center for Social Organization of Schools, The Johns Hopkins University, 3505 North Charles Street, Baltimore, MD 21218. (410) 516-0370.

Developmental Funding: NIE and OSE.   JDRP No. 84-5 (3/23/84)

Title I Mathematics Computer Assisted Instruction (CAI). A diagnostic/prescriptive pull-out mathematics program with students receiving 10 minutes of daily concentrated drill on CAI. Approved by JDRP as a mathematics program for Chapter I students in grades 3-6.

Description Lafayette Parish had an effective diagnostic-prescriptive mathematics ESEA Title I pull-out program. In order to increase growth in mathematics, computer-assisted instruction was added to an already effective math program. The program is operated with close coordination of math-lab instruction and daily CAI drill. One day a week a Chapter I coordinating teacher provides individual instruction, where needed. The CAI program adjusts instructions to the level of the students and provides immediate feedback to the student. The CAI program provides daily, weekly, and monthly descriptions of progress and areas of difficulty which the classroom teacher can use to correct specific conceptual misunderstandings. Classroom instruction is imperative in providing conceptual understanding and remediation. Daily CAI drill provides the practice which Chapter I students especially need. This particular program was operated with 40 minutes a day of mathematics laboratory time and 10 minutes of CAI. Presently, it operates with 10 minutes a day of CAI and the services of a coordinating teacher one day a week. The particular program was devised by Computer Curriculum Corporation (CCC) of Palo Alto, California. The addition of CAI instruction produces significantly superior achievement when compared to standard mathematics laboratory instruction.

Math Lab-CAI can be adopted to supplement any regular program if 200 students are enrolled. Two to three days of inservice training are necessary. The program used Computer Curriculum Corporation Programs from Palo Alto, California. Correlation between your program and CCC must be established.

Contact John E. Martin, Supervisor, Federally Supported Programs, Lafayette Parish School Board, P.O. Drawer 2158, Lafayette, LA 70502. (318) 236-6907.

Developmental Funding: USOE ESEA Title I.   JDRP No. 82-46 (9/29/82)

Utilizing Computers In Teaching Secondary Mathematics (UCTSM). A program of microcomputer-based instructional materials and techniques to improve mathematics skills. Approved for grades 9-12.

Description The goal of Utilizing Computers In Teaching Secondary Mathematics (UCTSM) is to improve mathematics skills through the use of microcomputer-based instructional materials and techniques. The program's package consists of two teachers' manuals and six disks (for TRS-80 or Apple II computers) containing approximately 70 computer programs which encompass six areas of secondary level mathematics—Algebra I & II, Geometry, Trigonometry, Calculus, and Applied Mathematics. While some programs are tutorial in nature, others are drill and practice or simulations using graphics. The programs can easily be integrated into any traditional math curriculum without the need to hire any additional staff.

UCTSM addresses Goals 3 and 4 of the National Goals for Education by providing instruction and practice for students of all ability levels to increase their performance in mathematics.

Awareness materials are available at no cost. Training is available at the adopter site (all expenses, plus trainer's fee must be paid). Implementation and follow-up services are also available to adopters (trainer's fee and expenses must be paid). A fee of $150 is charged for the teachers' manuals and computer programs which are available.

Contact Monika Steinberg, Director, UCTSM, Educational Information and Resource Center (EIRC), 606 Delsea Drive, Sewell, NJ 08080. (609) 582-7000, FAX (609) 582-4206.

Developmental Funding: USOE ESEA Title IV-C.

JDRP No. 82-17 (**4/29/82**)
Recertified (**6/18/86**)

Section 7

Science/Technology

* These programs are currently funded by the NDN.

Summary of Program Services for Section 7

Program	Goal*	Page	Dissem. Funds Available: NDN	Other	Costs to Potential Adopter: Hon	Trav	Per Diem	On Site Visitation Available: Home Site	Adopt Site	Materials Available: Free Paper	Video	Film Strip	Other	Staff Available: Home Site	Adopt Site	Costs to Adopter: Hon	Trav	Per Diem	Certified Trainers Available: State(s)	Training Time Required: Day(s)
Capacitor-Aided . . . (CASTLE)	3, 5	7-1	✓	(info. not available)																
Conservation for Children	3, 5	7-2			✓	✓	✓	✓		✓	✓				✓	✓	✓	✓	CA, CO, MO, NJ	<1
Developmental Approaches . . . (DASH)	3, 5	7-3	✓	✓	✓	✓	✓	✓	✓	✓	✓			✓	✓	✓	✓	✓	AL, CA, HI, IL, KS, LA, MA, MI, MO, NC, NM, OR, PA, VA, WA	10
FISH BANKS, LTD.	3, 5	7-4	✓		(negotiable)			✓	✓	✓	✓		✓	✓	✓	(negotiable)			AK, CA, CO, CT, D.C., DE, FL, HI, IL, IN, KS, LA, MA, NC, NE, NJ, NH, NY, OK, OR, TX, VT, WA, WI	6 hours
FOR SEA . . . (Grades 1-6)	5	7-21			(negotiable)			✓		✓				✓	✓	(negotiable)			AK, CA, CO, CT, FL, HI, LA, ME, MN, NV, OR, SC, WA, WV	1
Foundational Approaches . . . (FAST)	3, 5	7-21		✓	(negotiable)			✓	✓	✓	✓			✓	✓	✓	✓	✓	CA, CT, FL, HI, IL, KS, ME, MN, MO, NC, NE, NJ, NY, PA, SC, VT, WA	10
Geology Is	5	7-22				✓		✓		✓	✓			✓	✓		✓	✓	CO, IL, NC	1
Hands-On Elementary Science	5	7-5	✓			✓	✓	✓	✓	✓	✓				✓	✓	✓	✓	AK, AZ, CA, CO, CT, HI, ID, IL, KS, MA, MD, ME, MI, MO, MT, ND, NH, NM, NV, NY, OK, OR, PA, RI, SC, UT, WA, Puerto Rico, Virgin Islands	2
Informal Science Study (IkSS)	5	7-6			(negotiable)					✓	✓				✓	(negotiable)			AZ, CA, CO, IA, ID, IN, KS, MT, NM, NV, OK, OR, PA, TX, UT, WA, WY	<1
Investigating and Evaluating Environmental Issues and Actions	3, 5	7-7	✓		(negotiable)			✓		✓	✓			✓	✓	(negotiable)			CA, FL, HI, IL, IN, KY, MD, MI, MO, OH, TX, VA	3+

* National Goals for Education—definitions for each goal can be found on pages 5-7.

Summary of Program Services for Section 7 (cont'd)

Program	Goal*	Page	Dissem. Funds: NDN	Dissem. Funds: Other	Awareness Costs: Hon	Awareness Costs: Trav	Awareness Costs: Per Diem	On Site Visit: Home Site	On Site Visit: Adopt Site	Materials: Free Paper	Materials: Video	Materials: Film Strip	Materials: Other	Staff: Home Site	Staff: Adopt Site	Training Costs: Hon	Training Costs: Trav	Training Costs: Per Diem	Certified Trainers: State(s)	Training Time: Day(s)
Iowa Chautauqua Program (ICP)	3, 5	7-8	✓		(negotiable)			✓	✓	✓	✓		✓		✓	(negotiable)			IA	3+
JEFFCO Middle School Life Science Program	5	7-9	✓			✓	✓	✓	✓	✓	✓			✓	✓	✓	✓	✓	CO, KS, MA, ME, WA	40 hours
Life Lab Science . . .	5	7-10	✓			✓	✓	✓	✓	✓	✓			✓		✓	✓	✓	CA, MA, MT, NC, PA	2
Marine Science Project . . .	5	7-22			(negotiable)			✓	✓	✓				✓	✓	(negotiable)			AL, CA, CO, CT, FL, HI, LA, ME, MN, NV, OR, SC, WA, WV	1
MECHANICAL UNIVERSE, THE: High School Adaptation	5	7-11	✓		✓		✓	✓	✓	✓	✓		✓	✓		✓		✓	AZ, CA, CO, FL, ID, IL, KS, MA, MD, ME, MI, MT, NE, NJ, NV, NY, OH, OK, OR, PA, TN, TX, UT, WI	3+
Pablo Python Looks At Animals	5	7-12	✓		(negotiable)			✓	✓	✓	✓			✓		✓	✓		NY	1-3
Physics Resources . . . (PRISMS)	5	7-13	✓			✓	✓	✓	✓	✓				✓		✓	✓	✓	(all states)	3+
Physics—Teach To Learn	5	7-14	✓			✓	✓	✓	✓	✓				✓		✓	✓	✓	CA, NY, PA, TN	1-2
Polar Regions, Project		7-15			✓	✓	✓	✓	✓	✓						✓	✓	✓	(none)	
Program for Access . . . (PASS)	3, 5	7-16	(info. not available)													✓	✓	✓		
Relationships and Math-Friendly . . . (RAMPS)	5	7-17	✓			✓	✓	✓	✓	✓				✓		✓	✓	✓	CA, CT, FL, KS, MT, PA	2
Science-Technology-Society . . . (PFTW)	3, 5	7-23			✓	✓	✓	✓	✓	✓	✓			✓		✓	✓	✓	CA, CO, IL, MO, NJ, TX, WA, WV, WY	1-2

* National Goals for Education—definitions for each goal can be found on pages 5-7.

Summary of Program Services for Section 7 (cont'd)

Program	Goal*	Page	AWARENESS — Dissem. Funds Available		AWARENESS — Costs to Potential Adopter			On Site Visitation Available		Materials Available				TRAINING — Staff Available		TRAINING — Costs to Adopter			Certified Trainers Available	Training Time Required
			NDN	Other	Hon	Trav	Per Diem	Home Site	Adopt Site	Free Paper	Video	Film Strip	Other	Home Site	Adopt Site	Hon	Trav	Per Diem	State(s)	Day(s)
Starwalk	5	7-23			(negotiable)	✓	✓	✓	✓	✓				✓	✓	✓	✓	✓		1
Stones and Bones	5	7-24			✓	✓	✓	✓	✓	✓		✓	✓	✓	✓	✓	✓	✓	(none)	1
STS Issues… (STSIS)	3, 5	7-18	✓		(negotiable)				✓	✓					✓	(negotiable)			CA, FL, HI, IL, MD, MO, OH, TX, VA	5+
Videodisc Instruction in Core Science Concepts	5	7-19	✓			✓	✓			✓	✓			✓			✓	✓	(info. not available)	<1
Wildlife Inquiry… (W.I.Z.E./Survival Strategies)	3, 5	7-20	✓	✓	(negotiable)			✓	✓	✓	✓			✓	✓	✓	✓		AL, AR, AZ, CA, CO, FL, GA, IA, KS, KY, LA, MT, NE, NJ, NV, NY, OH, OK, OR, TN, UT, VA, WA, WI	2

* National Goals for Education—definitions for each goal can be found on pages 5-7.

Capacitor-Aided System for Teaching and Learning Electricity (CASTLE). An innovative instructional module for use in high schools that can replace the electricity portion of any course for beginning physics students. Its instructional approach is an investigative, model-building mode of learning.

Audience High school students who are taking a beginning physics course at any level.

Description The CASTLE curriculum emphasizes small-group, hands-on investigations and discussion of electric circuits which students construct themselves. It is unique among instructional materials in electricity because of its use of capacitors and transient bulb lighting. Circuits are constructed with components contained in student equipment kits; the investigations are guided by a student manual, which is duplicated and distributed in the classroom. The experiments developed in the curriculum provide varying levels of investigation: concrete experiences that challenge battery-centered misconceptions in electricity; sensory experiences that stimulate construction of a visualizable model of current propulsion; and experiments that reveal the anomalous presence of distant action in circuits in order to provoke model criticism and foster revision toward a complete expert model. A teacher resource manual provides homework and quizzes for each section, visual aids and supplementary activities as well as information about misconceptions, classroom management, equipment issues, cognitive research, history of concepts, and mathematical representation. Management activities are minimal: assigning activities in the student manual, tracking equipment kits, and supplying replacement batteries and light bulbs. CASTLE addresses National Educational Goals 3 and 5.

Evidence of Effectiveness Four claims of effectiveness were evaluated using multiple choice diagnostic pre- and post-tests that focused on conceptual questions. The diagnostic was administered to classes of three groups of teachers: those who developed the curriculum; those who were trained in the use of the curriculum; and "control" teachers who used the traditional electricity curriculum. Scores for the three groups were compared. Results showed that the curriculum improved understanding of and confidence with circuit concepts significantly more than traditional instruction; dramatically improved the confidence of females with circuit concepts; and could be implemented without significant loss of effectiveness to teachers who did not participate in its development.

Requirements A three-day teacher training workshop is required for successful adoption of the program. Training workshops are scheduled periodically around the nation.

Costs Costs for training workshops vary. Teachers must purchase the curriculum guide ($40), and the CASTLE equipment kits are necessary for student laboratory work. For optimum effectiveness, one equipment kit ($56) is required for every two students. Annual operating costs are $10 per student for batteries, light bulbs and duplication of the student manual. Equipment kits, curriculum guide, and auxiliary apparatus are purchased through PASCO Scientific, Roseville, CA.

Services Awareness materials are supplied without cost. Different levels of staff development training are available upon consultation.

Contact Melvin S. Steinberg, Physics Department, Smith College, Northampton, MA 01063. (413) 585-3884, FAX (413) 585-3786. Camille L. Wainwright, Director of Teacher Education, Pacific University, Forest Grove, OR 97116. (503) 359-2205, FAX (503) 359-2907.

Developmental Funding: National Science Foundation

PEP No. 94-07 (**4/1/94**)

Conservation for Children. A practical, economical program to increase conservation awareness, understanding, and action of elementary school children through a variety of basic skill activities designed for use in the classroom.

Audience Approved by PEP for children in grades 2-6.

Description Through a variety of basic skill activities intended for use in the classroom, Conservation for Children teaches students about the interdependence of plants and animals, requirements of life, energy sources and use, pollution and other environmental problems, recycling, and other conservation concepts based on scientific principles. The grade-leveled conservation guides provide instructional materials which combine basic skill practice in the areas of language arts, math, social studies, science, and art with a conservation concept. Teachers can use the materials as a primary resource for teaching basic skills, as supplementary materials to a core program, as enrichment activities, skill review, or as independent units of study. **The program integrates conservation concepts as part of any regular classroom schedule.** Updated and revised in 1993-94 under a grant from the Environmental Protection Agency (EPA).

The goals and objectives of the program are to:

- Increase students' awareness, knowledge, and understanding of science based conservation concepts;
- Provide teachers with a curriculum program which will enable them to include conservation education in their daily instruction; and
- Provide schools with proven successful materials to enable them to meet local educational mandates and the requirements of the National Environmental Act, Public Law 101-619, enacted by Congress on November 16, 1990.

Evidence of Effectiveness Students in grades 2-6 who receive a minimum exposure of 30 minutes per week for one semester to the Conservation for Children materials, demonstrate a significantly ($p < .01$) greater knowledge and understanding of fundamental environmental and resource conservation concepts than groups of equivalent comparison students when measured by criterion referenced tests.

Requirements No special facilities are required. Six grade level sequenced guides are available (grades 1-6). Each guide contains 100 pages of appealing student skill sheets (40 in language arts, 25 in mathematics, 25 in social studies/science, and 10 in related activities such as art and music) emphasizing conservation topics such as energy use, animal habitats, rainforests, recycling, and land, air, and water pollution. Each guide also provides a quick reference table to correlate basic skills with conservation topics, a criterion-referenced test, and a class record sheet for tabulation of student need areas. In addition, the All Levels Guide supplement to the Conservation for Children program is a collection of activity ideas with instructions for arts and crafts, growing plants, music, reference lists of filmstrips and videos with conservation themes; contact information for conservation organizations, agencies, and other programs; low-cost (many free) materials to send away for; and extensive student and teacher bibliographies. A Crafty Ideas: Classroom Projects Using Recycled Materials supplement is also available. Materials are designed for schools which may lack the time, equipment, or funds to implement other conservation programs. Conservation for Children lessons require no additional equipment or changes in teacher methodology and a minimum of preparation time.

Costs Grade Level guides and the All Levels guide are available at $13.95 each. The Crafty Ideas supplement is $6.50. A complete set of materials (one of each title) is $90. All materials are distributed by Sopris West, Inc. In-service costs include consultant fee, travel, meals, and lodging.

Services Awareness materials are available at no cost. In-service training is minimal. Information as to how to use the materials, development of the concepts, basic skills-conservation topic correlation sheets, and criterion-referenced tests can be accomplished at regularly scheduled staff meetings or in-service days. Depending on the level of implementation and individual interests, between 2 and 4 hours of training are recommended.

Contact Marilyn Bodourian, Program Director, 13580 Thoroughbred Loop, Grass Valley, CA 95945. (916) 273-4197.

Developmental Funding: ESEA Title IV-C.

JDRP No. 83-12 **(3/4/83)**
Recertified **(12/1/94)**

Developmental Approaches in Science and Health (DASH). A comprehensive program designed to develop scientific literacy for K-3 students by facilitating the learning and application of basic concepts and skills in science, health, and technology in authentic and practical ways.

Audience   Approved by PEP for students in grades K-3.

Description   Developmental Approaches in Science and Health (DASH) addresses all six dimensions of scientific literacy advocated by *Project 2061, Science for All Americans;* restructures the curriculum by integrating science, health, and technology; is designed to meet the emerging standards for science education being developed by the National Research Council; provides effective, field-tested activities in an easy-to-use program; and is designed for national dissemination and implementation in diverse school settings. Students with wide-ranging backgrounds, abilities, and learning styles learn concepts and skills in contexts of authentic technological and scientific exploration, invention, and explanation, which provide models for thinking and problem solving. Individual and group activities focus on making sense of new information, making connections with what is already known, and then using new knowledge to expand understanding of the world. Materials are designed for use by classroom teachers or departmentalized science teachers and consist of grade-level teaching guides containing activities and support materials for teachers and students organized into ten clusters: Learning; Time, Weather, and Sky; Plants; Animals; Food and Nutrition; Health and Safety; Energy and Communication; Wayfinding and Transportation; Matter, Space, and Construction; and Conservation, Recycling, and Decomposition. Activities are designed to articulate with other subjects, including language arts, mathematics, music, art, social studies, and physical education.

Evidence of Effectiveness   Multiple sources of evidence (e.g., observations, artifacts, documents, and interviews) from seven case-study databases demonstrate that DASH students in grades K-3: (1) understand fundamental concepts, the use of basic inquiry skills and data gathering techniques, and the integration and application of concepts in science, health, and technology; and (2) are self-directed learners taking responsibility for their own learning as reflected in engaged learning time, planning and completion of tasks, and use of multiple resources. DASH teachers change their attitudes and approaches toward elementary science in ways that result in increased instructional time spent on science and focus on students' learning.

Requirements   Teacher participation in ten days of initial training and monthly staff development meetings during the first two years of implementation and the purchase of DASH and local materials.

Costs   Start-up cost for training and materials is $700-$800/classroom; second year cost is $200/classroom for materials and monthly staff development meetings; and subsequent yearly cost is $100/classroom for materials.

Services   In addition to training and curriculum materials, follow-up consultation is available.

Contact   **Donald B. Young, Curriculum Research and Development Group, University of Hawaii, 1776 University Avenue, Honolulu, HI 96822. (808) 956-6918, FAX (808) 956-9486.**

Developmental Funding: University of Hawaii; Hawaii State Department of Business, Economic Development, and Tourism; National Science Foundation; and Buhl Science Foundation.

PEP No. 93-13 **(3/26/93)**

FISH BANKS, LTD. A group role-playing simulation, assisted by one microcomputer, designed to improve environmental understanding and apply communication, group problem solving, and higher order thinking skills.

Audience   Approved by PEP for grades 9-12 and college students.

Description   FISH BANKS, LTD. creates profound insights into how depletion of natural resources can result from the interaction of ecological, economic, corporate, and psychological forces. It conveys factual knowledge about a major environmental issue and motivates students to be informed and effective citizens.

The FISH BANKS, LTD. simulation is a group process involving analytic reasoning, negotiation, and collective decision making. As an interdisciplinary model it provides linkages to environmental science, biology, economics, social studies, and mathematics. One teacher can run the program with 5-50 students. There are many teacher-selected extensions of this engaging exercise. A microcomputer is used by the teacher to analyze the effects of student decisions and produce yearly reports on corporate profitability and productivity of the fishery. Typically, role playing extends over six to ten cycles (years) and debriefing begins when teams realize the long-term consequences of short-term strategies. Many high school and college educators use FISH BANKS, LTD. to introduce systems thinking and systems dynamics modeling. FISH BANKS, LTD. helps students achieve National Goals for Education 3 and 5.

Evidence of Effectiveness   High school and college students who participated in the FISH BANKS, LTD. simulation show significantly greater gains on a program-developed test of knowledge and academic skills than comparison groups. Teachers have positive attitudes toward the simulation and certify the high level of student involvement and excitement.

Requirements   Adopting teachers or schools must purchase a kit consisting of a game administrator's manual; a materials manual, including masters for more than 50 overhead transparencies used in introducing and debriefing the exercise, and masters for all student handouts; a game board; wooden ships; fish money; and an IBM compatible or MAC program disk. A six-hour teacher training session is available. Access to a microcomputer and overhead projector are also necessary.

Costs   Start-up costs include $100 for the simulation kit and $15 to produce the overhead transparencies and student handouts. Training costs of trainer stipend (usually $250 for a full-day training) and travel, lodging, and meal expenses are negotiated between the program staff, state facilitator, and the local adopter. There is no charge for workshop materials.

Services   An awareness brochure can be requested at no cost. An awareness video is available through many state facilitators or it can be borrowed or purchased ($5) from the program. A sample role description is also sent upon request. Kits are available for preview. A table-top exhibit can be mailed for use at meetings or conferences. Program staff or certified trainers offer awareness, training, and follow-up support (costs to be negotiated). There are many possible formats for training: at an adopting site, inservice day, conference, etc.

Contact   Karen Burnett-Kurie or Dennis Meadows, Institute for Policy and Social Science Research, Hood House, University of New Hampshire, Durham, NH 03824-3577. (603) 862-2186. E-Mail: klbk@christa.unh.edu

Developmental Funding: Local.

PEP No. 91-12 **(3/19/91)**

Hands-On Elementary Science. An instructional program intended to provide elementary students with hands-on experiences emphasizing the processes of science as an approach to problem solving for grades 1-5.

Audience   Approved by JDRP for elementary teachers and students, grades 1-5.

Description   Hands-On Elementary Science provides elementary students with instruction that emphasizes the development of science processes as an approach to problem solving. In fostering positive teacher attitudes toward teaching science, it increased both the amount of science taught and the proportion of instruction dedicated to the processes of science. The curriculum employs a set of higher order processes at each grade level consisting of four basic units. The units consist of lessons concerning a unifying topic. The topic is based upon the skills identified for that grade level. First grade students work primarily on observation in the four units of seeds, patterns, magnets, and liquids. Second grade emphasizes classification skills through the study of insects, sink or float, measurement, and weather. In the third grade, experimentation skills are developed by units on flight, measuring, plants and structures. Fourth grade focuses on analysis in units on bio-communities, electricity, chemistry, and energy transfer. The fifth grade curriculum emphasizes application and consists of units on earth science, soil analysis, animals, and ecosystems. Since this is not a text program, all lessons are based upon hands-on activities supported and defined by curriculum guides at each grade level. They provide a sequence of basic lessons and incorporate all necessary materials to support the program lessons. A unique feature of the program is an optional package of materials students may request to work on over the summer.

Evidence of Effectiveness   (1) Students who have received at least one year of HOES scored significantly higher than students receiving a standard textbook curriculum on a performance based assessment. (2) Students and teachers who have used the HOES program for one year made significant gains on surveys which measured attitude and motivation toward science.

Requirements   Hands-On Elementary Science program is transportable to other sites where a commitment exists for hands-on science instruction. Teacher preparation consists of two days training prior to initiating the program followed by follow-up workshops which enhance implementation. Materials required include both a curriculum guide and a kit of materials of the appropriate grade level for each teacher.

Costs   The cost of the program in the installation year is approximately $17.50 per student (assuming 25 students per class in a school of 800 students and training 20 teachers). Subsequent years' costs to maintain the program through the replacement of consumable supplies equals $1.50 per student. Teacher guides are available for $37.50 each plus postage and handling, and kits are available from a national vendor at costs ranging from $465 to $615 depending upon the grade level.

Services   Awareness materials are available at no cost. Visitors are welcome by appointment at the program site and additional sites in their home state. Program staff are available to attend out-of-state awareness meetings (costs to be negotiated). Training is available at the program site and also at the adopter site (costs to be negotiated). Implementation and follow-up services are available to adopters (costs to be negotiated). Supplementary materials include the following: Spanish curriculum guides, Special Education Adapted curriculum; set of Summer Supplements; and a Trade Books Bibliography.

Contact   **Helen G. Herlocker, Dissemination Center for Hands-On Elementary Science, Carroll County Public Schools, P.O. Box 661, Hampstead, MD 21074. (410) 374-1358, FAX (410) 239-4373.**

Developmental Funding: Federal, state, and local.   JDRP No. 86-19 **(9/23/86)**

Informal Science Study (IfSS). A series of physical science mini-units for all students in grades 5-9, which are based upon students' recall and utilization of popular amusement park rides, sports, and playground experiences.

Audience   Approved by JDRP for all students in grades 5-9.

Description   To promote concept acquisition, Informal Science Study (IfSS) presents a series of physical and biological science mini-units which are based upon students' recall and utilization of popular amusement park rides, sports, and playground experiences. Learning activities are selected for their appeal and ability to provide concrete examples of otherwise abstract concepts. Topics include, among others: motion, speed, velocity, acceleration, relativity, forces, gravity, time, conservation of energy, frames of reference, fears, and phobias. Science processes include inferring, graphing, predicting, and forming hypotheses.

Each of the mini-units is designed around student dialogue, providing an introduction and review/application of both science and mathematics in low-key and nontechnical language. Science terms are introduced only after students recall previous experiences. In addition, several of the mini-units provide laboratory activities that employ toys (race cars, model rockets, etc.) and playground equipment. Mini-units include:

- *Physics of Fun and Play* is designed for any of grades 5-12. The focus is on the physics of amusement parks and sports. Slides and videotapes present the motion physics of amusement parks and playgrounds. Students are encouraged to apply motion physics ideas to each of the settings.

- *Science Safari and Toy Workshop* is designed for grades 5-9 and presents physics mechanics content and terms as well as pre-algebra mathematics exercises that allow students to deal with the quantitative elements of motion laws. A special part of this mini-unit focuses on common toys and their action in the orbiting space shuttle, Toys in Space.

- *Spaceflight Forces and Fears* is a two-part module that deals with the application of mechanics concepts on amusement park rides as they relate to the experiences of orbiting astronauts. Students (preferably in grades 7-10) also explore physiologic reactions to amusement park rides by comparing their simulated reactions to those of students who have ridden the rides.

- *Mechanics of Motion* is designed for high school physics classes. Students are required to use algebra and pre-calculus mathematics to focus on the design and operation of amusement park rides. Additional computer simulations are available for classes that have access to Apple II computers.

- *The Discovery Field Experience* focuses student attention on amusement park rides and sport activities. Slides, videotapes, and actual field experiences are emphasized for learners in grades 5-12.

Evidence of Effectiveness   With instructional periods from 1-3 weeks, students significantly increase knowledge and comprehension of science concepts, increase their analytic recall of science experiences, and demonstrate significantly increased applications of science concepts.

Requirements   Mini-units may be adopted individually or as a group. Teachers can be trained in four hours.

Costs   Training costs consist of a trainer fee for the days of actual training, and travel and per diem expenses. Material costs range from $50-$175 per school. Contact IfSS for specific figures.

Services   Awareness materials are available at no cost. Visitors are welcome to visit the program site by appointment. Project staff is available for awareness and/or training.

Contact   **Howard Jones, Director or Stephanie Hendee, National Training Network, P.O. Box 8057, Longmont, CO 80501. (303) 651-0833, FAX (303) 651-1044.**

JDRP No. 84-11 **(3/30/84)**
Recertified **(5/1/94)**

Developmental Funding: National Science Foundation.

Investigating and Evaluating Environmental Issues and Actions.
An interdisciplinary environmental issues and action curriculum focused on enhancing students' responsible behavior through the examination and evaluation of real life community-based environmental problems and issues, for grades 7 and 8.

Audience Approved PEP for students in grades 7 and 8. It has also been used with students in grades 5-6.

Description Investigating and Evaluating Environmental Issues and Actions consists of a series of six "modules" designed to introduce students to environmental issues, the skills needed to critically analyze and investigate issues, the skills needed for information processing, and those skills needed to evaluate and act responsibly on local issues. The curriculum can be infused into existing science, social studies, or language arts classes. In addition, it can be adopted for use in team-teaching and interdisciplinary situations. It is normally completed during one semester. Instructional activities involve students in problem-solving through a variety of interdisciplinary methods, including analyzing issues, utilizing questionnaires to collect and record data, producing and interpreting graphs, drawing conclusions and inferences, formulating and evaluating action decisions, and developing issue resolution plans.

This program directly addresses Goals 3 and 5 of the National Goals for Education. Students learn and apply problem solving, decision making, and citizen participation skills which demonstrably contribute to good citizenship, community involvement, and personal responsibility. Similarly, science education is strengthened as students learn and apply science concepts and principles to real life problems and issues.

Evidence of Effectiveness Students of all ability levels participating in the program show significantly greater gains in knowledge of responsible citizen action skills. Students identify more categories of citizenship action and report undertaking more actions and more types of citizenship behaviors on program-developed and validated instruments. Parents of students in the program report observing more overt citizenship behaviors on the part of their sons and daughters.

Requirements Materials include student edition and teacher edition worktexts. The development of a small library of issue-related videotapes, news articles, magazine articles and books is recommended, if not already available.

Two options for staff development include: (1) two three-day academic year inservices scheduled from one to four weeks apart or (2) a five-day summer inservice workshop. Both training formats allow participants to complete a small group issue-related assignment. During the staff development, teachers acquire and apply skills, participate in an issue investigation, prepare and communicate an implementation plan, and learn to function as consultants and facilitators to students.

Costs Start-up costs are $13-$15 per student. A training manual ($16) must be purchased for each participating teacher. Continued operational costs are $9-$10 per year, per student, if the consumable worktext is purchased each year. All training costs are negotiable with the exception of materials.

Services In addition to training and materials, follow-up consultation is available. Graduate credit may be available.

Contact **Stephanie Hendee, Director, National Training Network, P.O. Box 8057, Longmont, CO 80501. (303) 651-0833. Trudi Volk, Southern Illinois University, Carbondale, IL 62901. (618) 453-4214. John M. Ramsey, University of Houston, Houston, TX 77204. (713) 743-4966.**

Developmental Funding: National Science Foundation, Illinois Title II Grant.

PEP No. 90-19R (3/29/91)

Iowa Chautauqua Program (ICP). An inservice model for improving science teachers and science education programs.

Audience Approved by PEP for teachers of grades K-12.

Description The Iowa Chautauqua Program (ICP) provides a unique approach to science inservice education. Created out of the realization that most inservice programs fall short in terms of meeting the developmental needs of teachers, the ICP strives to empower science teachers to make science more meaningful and useful for their students. The Iowa Chautauqua Program is unique in that it provides ongoing support across a summer and an entire academic year to teachers in grades K-12 as they develop and assess strategies that match those which characterize a reform effort termed Science-Technology-Society (STS). The STS approach involves constructivist strategies to science teaching and can best be described as the teaching and learning of science in the context of human experience. Student ideas, questions and thinking are used to drive the lessons.

The goals of the ICP include: (1) improving teachers' confidence in teaching science; (2) making teachers' instruction more congruent with the features of basic science by focusing instruction on questioning, developing explanations, and devising tests for evaluating those explanations; (3) preparing teachers to facilitate student learning in multiple domains, concepts, processes, applications, creativity, attitude and world view of science—not the simple memorization of facts; and (4) developing teachers as leaders in science education reform. A comprehensive assessment methodology has demonstrated the effectiveness of the workshops in terms of behavioral, attitudinal, and achievement changes in both teachers and students. The ICP stands out as a dynamic model for others interested in transforming their science programs.

Evidence of Effectiveness Participating teachers expressed substantially more confidence in the teaching of science and in their understanding and use of basic science concepts than did a group of similar science teachers not enrolled in the program. Furthermore, students taught by ICP-trained teachers developed greater science process and application skills, creativity in approaching science problem solving, improved attitude toward science learning, and an improved understanding of science in the context of human intellectual development. Students learned basic science concepts at least as well as students taught with traditional materials and methods.

Requirements A one week summer leadership conference at the University of Iowa, and a two to three week summer workshop for new teachers in local setting. Participants must develop, use, and assess the effectiveness of newly learned teaching skills and teaching materials. Central school staff such as state, regional, or district science supervisors and college/university faculty should also be involved in the training and follow-up activities. A fall short course and a spring short course to follow up and evaluate the success of implementation is required.

Costs The cost of a single ICP series enrolling 30 teachers in Iowa is typically $46,500. Cost per student (K-12) in a classroom of 36 is approximately $43. Start-up costs include personnel (three Lead Teachers, three central staff, three scientists and others); stipends for teachers in the summer workshop; staff travel and per diem; and materials and supplies. Operational costs average about $4,000 for staff travel and per diem and for materials and supplies. The expenses vary in different states and years. The approach can be adjusted to match the available funds.

Services Training and related consultation as well as printed guides for leadership training, module development, changes in teaching strategies, and program assessment are available.

Contact Robert E. Yager, Director, Science Education Center, The University of Iowa, 759 Van Allen Hall, Iowa City, IA 52242. (319) 335-1189. E-Mail: robert_yager@uiowa.edu *or* reyager@blue.weeg.uiowa.edu

Developmental Funding: National Science Foundation, ESEA Title 2, Eisenhower Math and Science Program, local school districts, Iowa Utility Association, Environmental Protection Agency.

PEP No. 92-5 **(3/26/93)**

JEFFCO Middle School Life Science Program. A program that enables students to understand the human body, basic ecological principles, and issues associated with environmental problems; and to make decisions to improve health-related behaviors. This program is a year-long life science program for students in grades 7 and 8.

Audience Approved by PEP for students in seventh and eighth grades of all abilities who are involved in a year-long science program.

Description JEFFCO Middle School Life Science Program is a full year life science course which replaces the curriculum currently being used in general science or life science. It can also be used in an integrated science-health course or divided into units and used as part of a two or three year integrated middle school curriculum.

The program characteristics parallel those recommended by most national science education reform groups and would assist a district in meeting National Goal for Education 5.

Learner materials consist of a text that integrates laboratory activities and readings. Topics were defined by life science teachers based upon their experiences with students as well as on the recommendations of nationally recognized experts in middle school science curriculum. Content is delivered in a learning cycle that consists of three phases: exploration, concept formation, and application. In the exploration stage, students carry out an experiment or investigation. This introduces them to the phenomena and experiences that lead to concept development. Finally, students apply the concept in an application activity or discussion. Development of thinking skills is emphasized throughout the program.

Teacher materials include instructional procedures for effectively presenting activities, detailed answer keys, supportive background information, worksheet masters, overhead transparencies, and optional student activities.

Evidence of Effectiveness In terms of student acquisition of conceptual and factual knowledge, students in this life science course scored significantly higher on reliable locally developed tests. Higher performance of the treatment group was generalizable across ability levels, gender, and teachers.

Requirements A typical middle school science classroom/laboratory is required, including flat top tables, storage space, and at least one sink. In addition to basic science equipment and supplies (including light microscopes) some unique materials are required. An inservice program of approximately 40 hours is strongly recommended.

Costs For appropriately equipped schools, it costs approximately $800 to set up a classroom with the necessary unique equipment and nonconsumable materials. The *Teacher Guide* is $47.90 and the *Teacher Resource Book* is $79.90. Student textbooks cost $34.90 each. Training costs are $200 for registration plus travel, room, and board for the national workshop in Colorado. Local workshops can be arranged for the cost of presenters' fees and travel costs—about $200 per participant for a minimum of 15 people.

Services Visitors are welcome by appointment at the program site. Training is available at the program site, and also at the adopter site (costs to be negotiated).

Contact Judy Capra or Harold Pratt, Middle School Life Science, 7101 West 38th Avenue, Wheat Ridge, CO 80033. (303) 467-1184.

Developmental Funding: Local funding and National Science Foundation.

PEP No. 90-04 **(2/6/90)**

Life Lab Science Program. An applied science program emphasizing a hands-on, garden-based "living laboratory" approach to elementary science education in grades 2-6.

Audience Approved by JDRP for elementary students, grades 2-6.

Description The Life Lab Science Program strives to ensure students' future interests and success in science by improving student attitudes toward the study of science, and increasing students' level of knowledge and skill acquisition in science. The instructional approach is a combination of indoor and outdoor hands-on science activities with the key component being the garden lab (e.g., indoor grow box, greenhouse, planter boxes, vegetable beds, etc.). Students and teachers collaborate to transform their school grounds and/or classrooms into thriving garden laboratories for the application of scientific processes. In this setting students conduct experiments using the scientific method. They observe, collect and analyze data, establish worm colonies, raise vegetables, herbs and flowers, and have responsibility for maintaining their living laboratory. A structured course of study is followed in science, nutrition and gardening. Instructional time varies from two to four hours per week. Teachers are responsible for all classroom instruction and use *The Growing Classroom* curriculum guide for the bulk of their science lessons.

Life Lab Program is also developing a telecommunications system—E-WORLD—available to Life Lab teachers to support the networking of information regarding experiments such as plant growth or composting as well as teacher and student exchange of ideas, collaborative reports, and problem solving.

Evidence of Effectiveness Elementary students demonstrated significant gains in science achievement as evidenced by the California Test of Basic Skills Science Subtest, and the SAT and MAT in Science achievement. The Life Lab Program also fostered positive attitudes towards the study of science at all elementary grade levels, based on student surveys.

Requirements The critical learner setting is the "living laboratory" whether an indoor grow box, containers adjacent to the classroom, a greenhouse or a three-acre school farm. As such, all elements of the program are transportable. The primary curriculum guide is *The Growing Classroom*, which contains Science, Nutrition, and Gardening units and is accompanied by a scope and sequence. Prior to implementation, the project has a two-day workshop at the school site or project site that prepares teachers for using the project, teaching techniques, and the "living laboratory" approach. Following the initial training, staff development and project implementation become the responsibility of Lead Teachers in each school. Advance training is available and technical assistance will continue to be provided throughout the installation year. Adopters of the Life Lab Science Program typically generate a great deal of community support and resources. Cultivating the community is an important requirement of a successful adoption.

Costs The adopter is responsible for travel and per diem costs. Trainer fees are to be negotiated. Implementation costs vary by site and the extent of "living laboratory" development. *The Growing Classroom* curriculum must be purchased for each implementing classroom teacher.

Services Awareness materials are available at no cost. Visitors are welcome by appointment to visit project sites in their home state or out-of-state. Project staff are available to attend out-of-state awareness meetings (costs to be negotiated). Training is conducted either at the project site or the adopter site (costs to be negotiated). Follow-up technical assistance is also available.

Contact Lisa Glick or Roberta Jaffe, Life Lab Science Program, 1156 High Street, Santa Cruz, CA 95064. (408) 459-2001, FAX (408) 459-3483. E-Mail: lifelab1@eworld.com

Developmental Funding: ESEA, Title IV-C, Packard Foundation,
California State Department of Education, and National Science Foundation.

JDRP No. 86-17 **(9/10/86)**

MECHANICAL UNIVERSE, THE: High School Adaptation.

A series of 28 videotape modules developed for teachers and high school students to reinforce the major topics and concepts covered in most physics textbooks. Through the use of these audio-visuals with computer animation, complex principles are clarified. Historical milestones are reenacted throughout the series to emphasize the evolution of ideas and the connectedness of scientific discovery.

Audience Approved by PEP for all high school physics teachers and students.

Description THE MECHANICAL UNIVERSE: High School Adaptation presents an innovative approach for motivating students toward mastering a conceptual understanding of physics. The specified pedagogical style for a lesson - based on the Karplus Learning Cycle of exploration, concept development and application - begins with an appropriate introduction by the teacher followed by a segment of one of the modules and concludes with student activity in discussion, further lab experiences or another prescribed task for utilization of the concept presented. The complete module can take the student from a view of Galileo framing a thought experiment to close-ups of complicated experiments or modern nuclear laboratories - from animated cartoons of gravitational effects to three-dimensional computer graphics that come alive. Hence, the abstract concepts of physics are made more understandable. These visual images prompt the student's memory, imagination, and understanding as the narrative develops the typical (and not so typical) concepts of high school physics. The audio-visual materials in conjunction with the written Teacher's Guide and Student's Guide, encourage repeated viewings for an ever- deepening conceptual comprehension of the topics presented.

The written comprehensive Teacher's Guide includes (1) a specific plan outlining the necessary instructional procedures for the effective implementation of each module, (2) supportive background information to assist teachers in their own understanding of the physical concepts, (3) questions to explore common applications of the concepts, and (4) test questions for the assessment of student understanding.

These materials can replace traditional material being used for most physics topics typically presented in high school. The 28 topics available cover all but very few topics contained in a traditional physics course, with some topics, such as *Black Holes and Curved Space*, that are new to the typical course.

Evidence of Effectiveness Comparative studies between traditional materials and **THE MECHANICAL UNIVERSE: High School Adaptation** have revealed that **MUHSA** students express a greater interest in taking physics, as well as an improved confidence that they can succeed in physics. Students using **MUHSA** produced results with a mean score 11 percentile points higher than the mean score of students using traditional materials. The desired effectiveness can be expected when the prescribed pedagogical style is implemented.

Requirements A four-day workshop is available for teachers with a college major or minor in physics and five or more years of experience in the field of physics. Those teachers with less experience and/or college physics should take part in longer workshops that are offered at the University of Dallas.

Costs Purchase cost for the 28 modules is $525, which includes all videotapes, teacher's and students' guides, and duplication rights for the school. If the adopting site does not have a video cassette player and monitor, those must be acquired separately.

Services A sample module including the video and written materials can be obtained at no cost. Program demonstration sites in 24 states are open to visitors by appointment. Awareness and training workshops are available with costs to be negotiated. A support staff is available through the toll-free number (800) 526-8472.

Contact Beverly T. Cannon, Project Disseminator, Richard P. Olenick, Project Director, Department of Physics, University of Dallas, 1845 East Northgate Drive, Irving, TX 75062-4799. (800) 526-8472 or (214) 721-5072. E-Mail: tcannon@phys.udallas.edu *or* olenick@phys.udallas.edu

Developmental Funding: National Science Foundation.

PEP No. 88-18 **(11/1/88)**

Pablo Python Looks At Animals. An introductory science curriculum for children of all ability levels in grades K-3 combining hands-on, interdisciplinary classroom instructions and the scientific resources of zoos to teach fundamental science concepts and observation skills.

Audience Approved by PEP for students in grades K-3.

Description Pablo Python Looks At Animals utilizes a multimedia approach that encourages young children to explore the world, using all their senses. It meets the National Goals for Education by addressing the need for more and better ways to teach science and observation skills. The program is modular and flexible: it can be used as the entire science curriculum or a supplement. It may also be used to enhance the early childhood curriculum in all other areas such as understanding and expressing spoken language and developing reading, writing, math skills, art, and music. Pablo Python capitalizes on children's natural curiosity and love of animals and provides a foundation for future learning as it helps children develop self-esteem and competency in science.

The program consists of a series of six books, an audio tape of animal sounds, a video cassette, 48 student activity sheets, six colorful posters, parent handbook, and a teacher's manual. Each of the six main topics can be divided into units, with each unit involving two lessons. A variety of learning activities involve the children in small-group instruction and cooperative learning situations. Two to six zoo visits are encouraged. These thematic field trips relate closely to the content of the program materials and serve as the earliest and most enjoyable laboratory experiences for this age group.

Evidence of Effectiveness Students in K-3 classrooms implementing the Pablo Python curriculum program demonstrate a significant increase in acquisition of basic science concepts on program-developed and validated mastery scales and criterion-referenced tests, and a significant increase in their understanding of zoos as places to study nature and science. Teachers gain confidence in using the zoo as a science resource, increase their instructional repertoire, teach more specific science concepts, and teach science a significantly higher number of minutes per week.

Requirements The classroom teacher implements the program with the students and determines how much time to devote to a topic and to what depth it will be explored. Teacher training consists of a 18 hour interactive workshop. During training, teachers receive student materials, are given lesson plan suggestions for implementing the program in the classroom and at the zoo, actually participate in the student activities, discuss classroom management of the program, and increase their knowledge of science.

Costs The Teacher's Kit and classroom curriculum materials cost approximately $150 and include the book series, videotape, audio cassette, activity sheet masters, teacher's manual, and supplemental materials. Teacher Training Workshops, at regional sites or locally upon request, for 15-20 teachers with one staff trainer cost $155 per day per trainer, plus travel expenses. The total start-up cost estimate is $150 per teacher. Additional costs might be associated with zoo visits.

Services In addition to training and materials, follow-up assistance is available as are supplementary materials.

Contact Annette Berkovits, Vide President-Education and Project Director or Julie Gantcher, Program Dissemination Coordinator, Bronx Zoo/Wildlife Conservation Park, 185th Street and Southern Boulevard, Bronx, NY 10460. (718) 220-6856, 220-5131, or (800) 937-5131, FAX (718) 733-4460.

Developmental Funding: New York State Council on the Arts, Samuel and May Rudin Foundation, Louis Calder Foundation, and Liz Claiborne Foundation.

PEP No. 91-7 **(3/14/91)**

Physics Resources and Instructional Strategies for Motivating Students (PRISMS). A comprehensive physics program that stimulates students to develop reasoning and problem-solving skills while providing learning activities about practical applications of physics for grades 10-12.

Audience Approved by PEP for students in grades 10-12 with backgrounds in beginning algebra, especially for those students who need additional motivation to learn the concepts and practical applications of physics.

Description Physics Resources and Instructional Strategies for Motivating Students (PRISMS) blends exploratory activities, concept development and application activities into a learning cycle. The concepts addressed in the *PRISMS Teacher Resource Guide* are those typically included in most high school physics courses including kinematics, dynamics, work and energy, internal energy and heat, wave phenomena, electricity and magnetism, and atomic and nuclear physics. High interest activities involving cars, bicycles, balloon rockets, dart guns, sailboats, etc., are utilized to teach the major concepts in physics. Exploration activities encourage students to observe relationships, identify variables, and develop tentative explanations of phenomena. Concepts are introduced through the experiences in this exploration phase. The student tests the generalization through observations in the application stage.

For each of 125 activities there are student sheets and teacher notes including teaching strategies, sample observations and calculations, a summary of the concept or outcome of the activity, and time required to conduct the activity. In most cases, there are multiple activities to support the learning cycle. The activities in the guide are an appropriate replacement of traditional laboratory experiments rather than supplementary materials. Student evaluation aids include a check list of indicators of student involvement in the laboratory activities and a computer test bank of over 2,000 questions keyed to course objectives and ranked by levels of reasoning according to Bloom's Taxonomy of educational objectives.

Evidence of Effectiveness During one academic year of physics instruction, 10th - 12th grade students showed a significantly greater gain in physics achievement relative to a comparable control group which used conventional materials and teaching strategies. Gain was measured using two forms of the New York Regents Physics Examination on a pre-posttest basis. In addition, PRISMS students had higher gains in reasoning/science problem-solving skills compared to a control group which used conventional materials and strategies. Change was measured by using two forms of the Test of Integrated Process Skills (TIPS II) on a pre-posttest basis.

Requirements To implement the program, the normal science laboratory facilities should be available. Several optional activities are provided that use computers for data acquisition. The physics teacher should understand the teaching strategies and be familiar with many of the activities before implementing the program. Inservice training for one week or a total of 32 hours is required.

Costs PRISMS materials include the Teacher Resource Guide, two video tapes, and a test bank of questions for evaluating student learning at a cost of $175. Assuming 15-20 teachers attending a one-week training period, the cost for the training is approximately $150 per teacher.

Services Awareness materials are available at no cost. Training is conducted during the summer at the development site at the University of Northern Iowa. In addition, staff are available to conduct workshops at other locations with costs to be negotiated. For demonstration sites available for visitation near you, contact the PRISMS Program Office.

Contact Roy D. Unruh, PRISMS, Physics Department, University of Northern Iowa, Cedar Falls, IA 50614. (319) 273-2380. Tim Cooney, Earth Science Department, University of Northern Iowa, Cedar Falls, IA 50614. (319) 273-2918, FAX (319) 273-5813.

Developmental Funding: Iowa Department of Education and
U.S. Department of Education—Secretary's Discretionary Fund.

JDRP No. 87-4 **(5/28/87)**

Physics—Teach To Learn. This program uses computer simulations of the most difficult to teach concepts in physics to supplement the entire program of instruction in high school physics.

Audience Approved by PEP/JDRP for 12th grade physics students.

Description The Physics—Teach To Learn program provides teachers and students with instructional materials and processes that facilitate the exploration and illustration of physical events which are frequently misunderstood by students and difficult for the teacher to illustrate in the classroom. The program then tests the students' understanding and ability to make application of the physics concepts underlying those events.

The program's 23 instructional modules, each with teacher-controlled computer simulations and supporting curriculum materials, were developed by a committee of Los Angeles Unified School District master physics teachers with university support. They were designed to provide students with fundamental and qualitative understanding of physical events in selected topic areas. The computer simulations require the learner to make a judgment about a physical event. This judgment, based upon learner experience and/or observation, often reveals misconceptions based upon defective logic. After the initial judgment (pretest), the teacher then utilizes the computer simulation(s) to lead the student through the steps of exploration, development, and application. By using this step-by-step method, the teacher is best able to guide the correction of student misconceptions about the physical events under consideration. After this process has been completed, the student takes a formal paper/pencil posttest. Each topic is accompanied by extensive written curriculum material designed to enhance the teacher's ability to present the key concepts. The program also enables the teacher to have the computer print any screen display, both text and graphics, to generate additional student activity materials.

The Physics—Teach To Learn program meets National Goal for Education 5 by strengthening science education and increasing the number of students who complete high school physics.

Evidence of Effectiveness A "one group/pre-post" design was used to measure changes stemming from the intervention of the Physics—Teach To Learn program. The results provided compelling evidence that the program consistently influenced students' interest in and understanding of physics concepts.

Requirements The instructional modules that were developed by the Physics—Teach To Learn program were designed to be adaptable to any course approach and compatible with any textbook. The materials for the 23 content modules in the program's curriculum package have been assembled to facilitate dissemination and implementation. The package includes 5.25 inch computer disks which are designed only for use with the Apple IIc, IIe, and IIGS, a graphics printer, and a monitor. This software can also be run on an Apple IIc+ computer equipped with an external 5.25 inch drive. For classroom use, a 19-inch (or la. ;er) television is recommended to display the simulations. **No prior computer experience is necessary** to effectively use the program's computer software or curriculum materials. Experienced physics teachers can be trained in the philosophy, content, and use of the modules in one day. It is recommended that new and/or "crossover" teachers have access to two days of training.

Costs The Physics—Teach To Learn curriculum package is available for a cost of $325 plus shipping and handling. **The program does not charge a training fee.** Once the training has occurred and the package has been purchased, there are no other program costs to the user.

Services Awareness materials are available at no cost. Visitors are welcome by appointment at the program's demonstration sites. Program staff are available to conduct inservice training workshops. Training can be conducted at the program site or at sites selected by potential adopters or by NDN State Facilitators.

Contacts Pamela Williams, Director or Charles Schleiden, Disseminator, L.A.U.S.D./Physics-Teach To Learn, Bell High School, Bell, CA 90201-2594. (213) 773-2408 or 560-1800, FAX (213) 560-7874.

Developmental Funding: ECIA Chapter 2.

JDRP No. 86-16 **(9/25/86)**

Polar Regions, Project. An innovative, interdisciplinary science program for middle grade students emphasizing an investigative and problem-solving approach to the study of meteorology, oceanology, geology, and the exploration of the earth's Arctic and Antarctic regions.

Audience Approved by PEP for students in grades 5-8.

Description Polar Regions supplements and reinforces the existing science and social science curriculums and replaces outdated content areas related to the polar regions without requiring additional instructional time. It provides instructional materials for students and resource information for teachers to pursue a problem-solving, investigative approach to topics in: geology, meteorology, oceanology, biology, and the social sciences. The development and application of critical thinking skills and the involvement of laboratory activities are emphasized for the purpose of developing scientific content and concepts. Concepts are developed and reinforced relating to global geography and the exploration of the polar regions. The project's curriculum is divided into four units of instruction: Climate, Oceans, Land, and Discovery and Exploration.

Evidence of Effectiveness Students participating in the program at grades 5 through 8 make significantly greater gains in science knowledge and concepts on project-developed and validated criterion-referenced lists than comparison groups covering the same knowledge and concept areas using traditionally available curriculum materials.

Requirements The program may be taught in self-contained or departmentalized classrooms by science, social science, or environmental education teachers. Each of the four project curriculum units require an average of two to three weeks of instruction or 10 to 15 one-hour periods, depending upon student needs and instruction methodologies used. One six-hour inservice workshop is sufficient to prepare teachers for effective program implementation.

Costs Project Polar Regions' complete Curriculum Package is comprised of four instructional units, each with its own Teacher's Guide and classroom set of 30 nonconsumable packets of Student Background Information and Investigations. Twelve 11" x 14" Antarctica Study Prints and one Antarctica Filmstrip, both with Background Information and Discussion Questions, accompany the project's printed materials. The complete Curriculum Package, whose four units of instruction can be "modularized" to serve four separate classes of 30 students each at one time, is available for $1,050. A Teacher's Edition of the Curriculum Package with only one copy of all program printed materials, without the study prints or the filmstrip, is available for $100.

Services In addition to training and materials, an awareness packet is available at no cost. Visitors are welcome to visit the project's demonstration school site by appointment. Training workshops can be conducted either at the project site or at sites selected by potential adopters or by NDN State Facilitators. Project staff is available to attend awareness meetings out of state with costs to be negotiated.

Contact Donnalyn Jaque-Anton, Los Angeles U.S.D., Director of Professional Development, 450 North Grand Avenue, Los Angeles, CA 90012. Milton Anisman, Disseminator, Environmental Science Center, 6625 Balboa Boulevard, Van Nuys, CA 91406. (818) 997-2389.

Developmental Funding: ESEA Title IV-C and district.   PEP No. 91-21 (**4/3/91**)

Program for Access to Science Study (PASS). A program designed to enable underprepared college students to pass introductory science courses.

Audience Underprepared college students interested in pursuing science-based careers who are programmed by their academic advisors to take a preparatory course in science.

Description PASS is composed of a preparatory science course and a special counseling seminar. It is designed to address both aspects of student failure: academic underpreparation and social integration into college life. Both components are taught in tandem. Academic preparation includes problem-solving using chemistry and physics content. The curriculum is divided into cycles, each built around a single topic. A general problem set related to the topic and an illustrative lab experiment are introduced. Students perform the experiment, analyze the data obtained, work on a problem set based on the experiment, and take a quiz. Integration into college life is accomplished through the counseling seminar, which is designed to promote the student's ability to monitor, evaluate and adjust their behavior in order to achieve both their academic and personal goals. Using their experience with the science course, students learn how to manage their academic lives, assess their progress, and take responsibility for their actions rather than blaming circumstances. Learner activities emphasize problem-solving approaches in an interactive participatory setting. Management and staff activities include training sessions in the start-up phase of the project and consultative and feedback processes among the various project team members to ensure the student's individual needs are met. Program supervision and management takes 3-4 hours per week for each active staff member. Student recruitment is routine after the first year of operation. PASS addresses National Educational Goals 3 and 5.

Evidence of Effectiveness Claims of effectiveness were tested on data obtained between 1989 through 1992. Results showed that students enrolled in PASS have a higher retention rate than the general college population, performance level in PASS is a strong predictor of future performance, and successful participants developed the positive behaviors and attitudes that lead to future success.

Requirements Faculty interested in collaborating to meet the needs of underprepared students. Routine lab facilities, equipment and supplies sufficient to meet the science syllabus.

Costs There is no cost for installation or supervision of the program. Recurring operating costs are for instruction, training and supplies based on one section per semester. When science faculty teach the section as part of their regular course load, the program operates at a considerably lower cost.

Services Materials, staff development, and technical assistance are available for a fee.

Contact Michael Weiner, Professor, Chemistry Department, (212) 650-8337 or Millicent Roth, Professor, Department of Special Programs, (212) 650-6768, City College of New York, New York, NY 10031. FAX (212) 650-6107.

Developmental Funding: USDOE, Howard Hughes Medical Institute, National Science Foundation

PEP No. 93-18R (4/1/94)

Relationships and Math-Friendly Physical Science (RAMPS). A physical science course to enable 8th or 9th grade students to apply mathematics to introductory science with understanding and with skill. The book may be used as a sourcebook or student textbook and comes with an extensive teacher's guide.

Audience Approved by PEP in grades 8 and 9.

Description Relationships and Math-Friendly Physical Science (RAMPS) has incorporated its innovative mathematics treatment into a unit interfaced into a one-year physical science textbook that covers the usual science topics so as to increase students' understanding of both science and mathematics. All of the materials, both science and applied math, include many hands-on activities which are simple but make their point, use materials which are already available in the school or can be purchased in the supermarket, and are nonpolluting. The special materials include sections about organization of knowledge, science relationships and how they are expressed both mathematically and nonmathematically, problem solving, proportionality, and how equations show relationships. The content is easily learned both by student and teacher, and enables the student to be comfortable and understanding in the applications of mathematics to introductory science. Optional materials and activities enable the teacher to tailor the materials to the students. An extensive teacher's guide provides answers to all items, tips, demonstrations, discussions of all activities, additional optional activities, updates, and references. By learning the special methods and approach of RAMPS, students are helped toward achievement of National Goal for Education 5. Because of its interdisciplinary component, RAMPS can be effectively used as part of the effort for systemic change.

The RAMPS materials may be adopted whole as a student textbook. Instead, the teacher may use RAMPS as a sourcebook and extract the parts most useful and appropriate to the particular classroom and textbook in use.

Evidence of Effectiveness Students in grades 8 and 9 participating in RAMPS demonstrated: (1) higher levels of understanding of the mathematics used for science and (2) higher achievement in applications of mathematics to science than did comparison students in a traditional physical science course.

Requirements RAMPS material can be taught by any teacher of physical science, even if not mathematically knowledgeable. Teachers can easily learn the special material by reading the textbook and utilizing the Teacher's Guide. Two days of training are recommended to learn the special aspects of the materials; additional training for up to four days makes it easier for the teacher.

Costs Training costs consist of travel expenses and the cost for a RAMPS textbook and Teacher's Guide ($65). Operational costs total $4 to cover supplies for a class. When student textbooks are ordered in lots of ten or more (without the Teacher's Guide), they cost $18 each.

Services In addition to training, awareness materials are available. A newsletter with updates, suggestions, and new materials is sent out twice per year to adopters. Telephone help from project trainers is available. The project has a toll-free number which is provided to adopters.

Contact Madeline P. Goodstein, PRIMAK Educational Foundation, P.O. Box 701, Devon, PA 19333. (215) 687-6252. E-Mail: mgoodste@inet.ed.gov

Developmental Funding: Addison-Wesley Publishing Company and local.

PEP No. 91-IR (**4/8/91**)

STS Issues and Solutions (STSIS). A one-semester curriculum that focuses on the interrelationships among science, technology, and society and on the skills needed for the investigation, evaluation, and citizenship responsibilities associated with science-related social issues.

Audience Approved by PEP for grades 6-8.

Description STS Issues and Solutions (STSIS) provides training in the investigation and participation skills needed by a scientifically literate citizen. Following an introduction to science-technology-society interactions, the program prepares students to conduct investigations into issues related to those interactions in their own community or region. Science-technology-society issues, for example, include controversies over transportation safety, medical procedures, use of animals in research, and zoning or development decisions. Environmental issues, such as solid waste management, use of wetlands, asbestos in the workplace, and endangered species are also examples of STS issues which students might choose to investigate.

STSIS addresses Goals 3 and 5 of the National Goals for Education. With its major emphasis on science, technology, society, and their interactions, this program is an excellent example of authentic learning as students investigate science-related issues in their own community. Through their application of scientific concepts and principles in a meaningful community-based context, students recommend issue solutions and produce (and evaluate) action plans which help bring about those recommended solutions.

Evidence of Effectiveness Eighth graders in the STSIS program tested significantly higher on a postinstruction test using the Iowa Test of Basic Skills in both science and social studies than did students in a comparison group receiving traditional instruction. Students involved in STSIS received higher scores than comparison students on measures of overt citizen behavior, individual locus of control, group locus of control, knowledge and perceived knowledge of citizen action skills, and perceived skill in the use of citizen action skills.

Requirements Teachers must be trained in the STSIS model. Inservice training consists of a minimum of five days. Each participating student must have a consumable work text. It is also highly recommended that participating schools develop a library of issue-related videotapes, articles, and books.

Costs Training costs for a group of 30 teachers include two trainers at $250 per day per trainer, for five days, plus expenses. Assuming a 100 student load for each teacher, start-up costs are $12-$16 per student. Continued operating costs are $9-$10 per student per year for the annual purchase of the consumable student work text.

Services Training and consultation are available. Student consumable work texts are available for purchase.

Contact **Harold Hungerford or Trudi Volk, Science and Environmental Education Center, Department of Curriculum and Instruction, Southern Illinois University, Carbondale, IL 62901. (618) 453-4211 or 453-4214 or Stephanie Hendee, National Training Network, P.O. Box 8057, Longmont, CO 80501. (303) 651-0833.**

Developmental Funding: Private.

PEP No. 93-12 **(3/26/93)**

Videodisc Instruction in Core Science Concepts. An instructional system utilizing videodisc technology to enhance science teachers' capacity to reach diverse learners.

Audience   Approved by PEP for students in grades 5-12, including special education and Chapter 1.

Description   With the aid of a videodisc player, a teacher engages students in stimulating discussion, demonstrations, and individual work to learn challenging earth science and chemistry content. Teachers closely monitor student learning and reteach concepts to students needing additional direct instruction. The program is built around three major strategies: (1) maximizing learning time for the most important subject matter; (2) intensive student involvement in learning coupled with close monitoring of student progress and adaptation of teaching to prevent student failure; and (3) pedagogy and content organization stressing important, generalizable concepts and problem-solving strategies applicable to all students.

Evidence of Effectiveness   Students of diverse ability levels enrolled in the Videodisc Instruction in Core Science Concepts program achieved comparable gains in knowledge of core chemistry concepts to gains made by students in an Advanced Placement chemistry course. Students of diverse ability levels enrolled in the Videodisc program achieved substantially greater earth science knowledge, generalization, and problem-solving skills than did students in a traditional earth science course.

Requirements   An initial two-hour training for teachers is required, along with a follow-up visit with the teacher using the curriculum within two weeks after initial training. Schools must purchase a videodisc player, videodiscs for the "Earth Science" and "Understanding Chemistry and Energy" programs, teachers' manuals, student workbooks, release of copyrights to allow reproduction of the student workbooks, and staff development videotapes.

Costs   Approximately $5,000 per building.

Services   Training, videodisc programs, student workbooks, and teacher training materials are available.

Contact   **Alan Hofmeister or Judy Fifield, Technology Division, Center for Persons with Disabilities, Utah State University, Logan, UT 84322-6800. (801) 797-3718.**

Developmental Funding: USDE, Office of Special Education and Rehabilitative Services, state, local, and other sources.

PEP No. 92-9 **(3/26/93)**

Wildlife Inquiry through Zoo Education (W.I.Z.E./Survival Strategies). A life sciences program which improves understanding of concepts related to ecology, wildlife conservation, and species survival for students in grades 7-10.

Audience   Approved by PEP for all students, grades 7-10.

Description   Combining classroom study with the unique scientific resources available at zoos, Wildlife Inquiry through Zoo Education (W.I.Z.E./Survival Strategies) explores issues related to wildlife survival in the 21st Century. Using a nontraditional, multidisciplinary approach, the program improves understanding of concepts related to ecology, wildlife conservation, population biology, and species survival. Utilizing cooperative learning techniques and highly motivating hands-on activities that encourage decision making, the program develops an understanding that animals are members of populations that interact with one another and that ecological processes affecting animals also affect humans. Involving an average of 15 weeks of instruction, the program includes three visits to a local zoo or a suitable alternate site. Using highly motivating activities, multimedia materials, small-group discussions, zoo visits, and *Posterity*—a role-playing simulation, students are exposed to the scientific method and develop problem-solving skills, working towards solutions which cause the least disruption to the environment. W.I.Z.E./Survival Strategies educates young people to approach difficult problems analytically and to make decisions rooted in a firm understanding of scientific concepts. W.I.Z.E./Survival Strategies can serve on its own merits as an independent curriculum, or as a supplement to an existing life science or environmental education program. W.I.Z.E./Survival Strategies addresses National Goals for Education 3 and 5. The program exercises students' analytical and writing skills, preparing them to take responsible, proactive roles within their communities. W.I.Z.E./Survival Strategies builds students' self-confidence and an ability to make competent decisions. They delve into environmental issues and learn how to take action to solve complex problems. Students learn to arrive at the best solutions by considering the various economic and cultural issues that affect the environment locally, nationally, and globally. Since nationwide dissemination began in 1988, W.I.Z.E./Survival Strategies has demonstrated its ability to improve science competency in over 70,000 students nationwide.

Evidence of Effectiveness   Grade 7-10 students participating in W.I.Z.E./Survival Strategies for a period of 12-15 weeks scored significantly higher on a reliable locally-developed test of life science concepts than did a control group. This claim is based on an experimental and comparison group study of 16,000 students in 20 states. Further, students participating in W.I.Z.E./Survival Strategies also scored significantly better than the control group on two scales measuring mastery of specific science skills and knowledge areas taught in the W.I.Z.E./Survival Strategies curriculum.

Requirements   No special facilities are required within an adopting school. Access to a zoo, natural history museum, nature center, or wildlife area is recommended by the program. Although the detailed Teacher's Manual enables instructors to conduct the program successfully, training is encouraged for optimal implementation. Curriculum/learning materials include the following:

- 34 Student Resource Books
- 22 Photo Cards
- 136-page Teacher's Manual
- 96-frame filmstrip

- 6 sets of 24 illustrated Discovery Cards
- 41 worksheet masters to accompany lessons
- 2 sound cassettes
- *Posterity* (a wildlife management game)

Costs   Teachers who adopt W.I.Z.E./Survival Strategies must purchase a *Survival Strategies* classroom kit from Beacham Publishing at a cost of $325. Usually, one kit per school is sufficient. A kit provides all the necessary materials for a class of 34 students. Beacham Publishing does offer bulk discount rates for schools or districts that order more than three kits. Training costs include $155/day plus travel expenses plus the cost of one *Survival Strategies* kit to be used during the training. Two- to five-day training options are available.

Services   Program staff are available to attend out-of-state awareness meetings. Two to five-day training options are available in requesting districts and states throughout the year. Follow-up assistance is also available to adopters. Participants receive ample supplemental materials on a regular basis.

Contact   Annette Berkovits, Vice President-Education and Project Director of W.I.Z.E. or Donald Lisowy, W.I.Z.E. Dissemination Coordinator, Bronx Zoo/Wildlife Conservation Park, 185th Street and Southern Boulevard, Bronx, NY 10460. (718) 220-5136 or (800) 937-5131.

JDRP No. 86-6 **(4/9/87)**
Recertified **(3/25/93)**

Developmental Funding: National Science Foundation.

FOR SEA: Investigating Marine Science (Grades 1-6). Interdisciplinary, activity-oriented, marine education. Approved by PEP for all students, grades 1-6.

Description The nationally validated curriculum materials of FOR SEA are designed to equip students with the experiences and information necessary to make responsible decisions about the marine environment. Focusing on the development of basic science skills and knowledge, FOR SEA provides interdisciplinary, activity-oriented, marine education curriculum and teacher training. The magic draw of water provides incentive to teach and learn science. FOR SEA has been used successfully as a core curriculum and has likewise proven effective in a thematic/unit teaching strategy. Close proximity to seawater is not necessary to implement this curriculum in the classroom. Curriculum guides are available for grades 1-2, 3-4, and 5-6. Each guide contains teacher background for each activity, student activity and text pages, answer keys for student materials, and a listing of vocabulary words. FOR SEA is designed to be implemented in classrooms at a room, grade, school or district-wide level. Inservice training provides implementing teachers with an overview of the program, implementation procedures and hands-on activity sessions to familiarize participants with activities appropriate for their specific grade levels. Training can be provided for groups of 10-32 educators. Training agendas can be tailored to serve specific grade levels or include all teachers, grades 1-12. (Please see listing for Marine Science Project: FOR SEA, Grades 7-12.) A copy of the appropriate grade level curriculum guide must be purchased for each implementing teacher at $35.00 per guide. Student text materials in the guide are designed to be reproduced by adopting sites. Hands-on materials required in most activities are generally found in the school setting or are readily available at local grocery, variety, or pet stores. Start-up costs vary by site. Awareness brochures and samplers of curriculum are available.

Contact Marlene C. Holayer, Assistant Superintendent, Curriculum and Instruction, Olympic Educational Service District 114, 105 National Avenue North, Bremerton, WA 98312. (206) 479-0993.

Developmental Funding: USOE ESEA Title IV-C.

JDRP No. 81-37 **(81)**
Recertified **(3/88)**

Foundational Approaches in Science Teaching (FAST). A course in the concepts and methods of the physical, biological and earth sciences and their relation to the environment. Approved by JDRP for students in grade 7.

Description Foundational Approaches in Science Teaching (FAST) is a full-year course giving students a sense of the operations of the modern scientific community by involving them in typical science activities. FAST is laboratory- and field-oriented and designed for use with students who represent the full range of abilities and interests found in the typical middle/junior high school classroom. Instructional strategies are structurally sequenced to address differences in learning styles and to develop thinking skills. Students study three strands concurrently: physical science, ecology and relational study. The physical science strand introduces such concepts as mass, volume, density, buoyancy, physical and chemical properties of matter, pressure, vacuum, heat, temperature and energy; the ecology strand such concepts as ecology, plant and animal growth and development, weather and climate, field mapping and population sampling; the relational study strand such concepts as resource management, technology, environmental use, energy use and conservation. Student and teacher materials guide student investigations. The Student Record Book enables students to record a concise log of individual and class activities. A classroom library of Reference Booklets, which describe use of instruments, suggest experimental designs, outline experimental techniques, and provide necessary supplemental readings, helps students to practice the skill of using outside references to supplement information available from the investigations and Student Book. The Teacher Guide presents the logic connecting topics and sequences. Keyed to the investigations in the Student Book, the Teacher's Guide includes teaching suggestions, advice on classroom procedures, and detailed discussion of the conceptual and practical development of the students' investigations. Other materials for teachers include the Instructional Guide and Evaluation Guide.

Contact Donald B. Young, Co-Director, Curriculum Research and Development Group, University of Hawaii, 1776 University Avenue, Room CM117, Honolulu, HI 96822. (808) 956-7863, FAX (808) 956-9486.

JDRP No. 80-2 **(12/9/80)**
Recertified **(1/85)**

Developmental Funding: University of Hawaii.

Geology Is. An introductory geoscience course. Approved by JDRP for all students, grades 9-12.

Description Designed to become part of the secondary school curriculum, Geology Is provides geoscience learning opportunities not presently available in the science curriculum. A broad range of materials and media-delivery instruments allow for varied teaching and learning techniques. The technical aspects of course content and the social implications in the wise use of earth resources combine in an effective interdisciplinary approach. Awareness and understanding of geoscience processes make students more responsible consumers of earth materials and protectors of the environment.

The five distinct but related units of Geology Is are Introduction, Earth Materials, Observing the Earth, Internal Processes, and External Processes. These are subdivided into a total of 20 chapters. Although it is a two-semester course, parts can be taught as a semester offering. Each unit contains text material, lab exercises and activities, and objective and subjective tests. Slide-tapes, films, videotapes, and guest speaker presentations are offered, and students are encouraged to evaluate these. Small groups and individuals investigate topical areas for student-led class discussions. Off- and on-campus field experiences and resource personnel add another dimension to the text. Teachers are provided with a guide and an activities handbook as a supplement to the student textbook. Through study in this elective option, students can become more responsible consumers of earth resources and make informed decisions for the future regarding energy, geologic hazards, and land use.

Contact Rion D. Turley, O'Fallon Township High School, 600 South Smiley, O'Fallon, IL 62269. (618) 632-3507.

Developmental Funding: USOE ESEA Title IV-C.

JDRP No. 81-42 **(12/18/81)**
Recertified **(2/86)**

Marine Science Project: FOR SEA (Grades 7-12). A comprehensive, activity-oriented, marine science curriculum that teaches basic science skills and knowledge on or away from the coast. Approved by JDRP for all students, grades 7-12.

Please see page 7-3 for a description of the grades 1-6 program.

Description By the year 2000, three out of four Americans will live within an hour's drive of the sea or Great Lakes coasts. The impact on these coastal waters will be severe. The nationally validated curriculum materials of FOR SEA are designed to equip students with information necessary to make responsible decisions about the marine environment. FOR SEA provides comprehensive, activity-oriented, marine education curriculum to be used in addition to or in lieu of an existing science program. The magic draw of water provides incentive to teach and learn science. Close proximity to seawater is not necessary to implement this curriculum in the classroom. Curriculum guides are available for the following grade levels: 7-8 and 9-12 (Part I - Physical Oceanography, Part II - Marine Biology and Issues). Each guide contains a teacher background for each activity, student activity and text pages, answer keys for student activities, and a listing of vocabulary words for each unit.

Contact Marlene C. Holayer, Assistant Superintendent, Curriculum and Instruction, Olympic Educational Service District 114, 105 National Avenue North, Bremerton, WA 98312. (206) 479-0993.

JDRP No. 83-26 **(3/28/83)**
Recertified **(4/9/87)**

Developmental Funding: USOE ESEA Title IV-C.

Science-Technology-Society: Preparing For Tomorrow's World (PFTW). A multidisciplinary approach to problem solving and critical thinking designed to promote decision-making and problem-solving skills needed to deal with issues at the interface of science, technology, and society. Approved by JDRP for all students, grades 7-12.

Description In our increasingly complex technological world, issues and problems also become increasingly complex. Students need more sophisticated problem-solving and decision-making skills to deal effectively with current and future societal issues. The goals of the Science-Technology-Society: Preparing For Tomorrow's World (PFTW) modules are the development of logical, higher level thinking and social reasoning skills in the context of science, technology, and society. Serving as the guiding framework for the materials, activities, and teaching strategies, a sound instructional model is utilized to develop the skills necessary for students to move to higher levels of cognitive reasoning and citizenship. Designed to directly relate to National Goals for Education 3 and 5 related to citizenship, problem solving, and higher order thinking.

PFTW is comprised of a set of four independent curriculum modules. Topics covered include:

- Coastal Decisions
- Beacon City: An Urban Land-Use Simulation
- Space Encounters
- Decisions (a 12-topic cross discipline "sampler" module)

PFTW engages students in activities such as scenario writing, graphing, problem solving, conducting surveys, and futures forecasting, to add another dimension to existing curricula. Discussion and debate among students encourage critical self-evaluation and promote more complex reasoning ability and increased perspective-taking abilities. Depending on the modules selected and the course structure in which they are used, activities may be used in continuous sequence, interspersed throughout existing courses, or, as in the senior high grades, taught as discrete units of study. One- or two-day training is available.

Contact   David Lidstrom or Marilyn Bodourian, P.O. Box 1324, Grass Valley, CA 95945. (916) 273-4197.

Developmental Funding: USOE ESEA Title IV-C.   JDRP No. 81-10 **(12/15/81)**

Starwalk. A comprehensive earth/space science program for elementary students. Approved by JDRP for grades 3 & 4.

Description Starwalk provides instruction in Earth/Space science concepts to grades 2 to 5. Students receive a series of classroom lessons and activities structured around visits to a planetarium facility. Classroom lessons are designed as both pre- and postplanetarium visit in order to prepare students for their activities at the planetarium, and to consolidate and further the learning after the visit. Planetarium and classroom teaching guides provide the instructional materials for the lessons.

The availability of a planetarium facility, either fixed-base or portable, is required. Classroom materials are minimal, but should include an earth globe, celestial sphere, and earth/sun model. Recommended classroom instructional time is about 12 hours per level, including the planetarium lesson. Inservice training requires two-five days depending upon the implementation situation.

Awareness materials are available at no cost. Developer or certified trainers are available for awareness presentations and/or implementation training. All costs are paid by adopter. Training can be conducted at the adopter or program site, and is available throughout the year. Implementation follow-up services are also available. Additional grade-level materials are also available for grades 2 and 4.

Contact   Bob Riddle, Starwalk, Southwest Science/Math Magnet High School, 6512 Wornall Road, Kansas City, MO 64113. (816) 871-0913. E-Mail: starwalk@delphi.com

Developmental Funding: Title IV-C, state, and local.   JDRP No. 83-9 **(3/4/83)**

Stones and Bones. An innovative laboratory approach to the study of Human Emergence. Designed to enrich present modern or life science, biology, and physical anthropology courses. Approved for science students of all ability levels, grades 7-12.

Description Stones and Bones meets the needs of all ability students. The format is interdisciplinary in design and emphasizes active student participation through laboratory explorations. Modern (general) or life science and biology instructional units supplement, enrich, and extend current science curricula. Three instructional pathways emphasize the study of humankind:

- *Modern (General) Science Pathway:* Designed to motivate noncollege-oriented students. Each of the 20 laboratory explorations offers the general science student hands-on opportunities to investigate topics such as geologic time, measuring radioactivity, mapping, behavior of primates, and replica casts of fossil hominids. During this unit, students will also have an opportunity to simulate archaeological excavation.
- *Biology Pathway:* An overview of physical anthropology. The unit provides students with hands-on, in-depth experiences as a supplement to physical anthropology in biology textbooks. A series of 11 investigative explorations focuses on topics including primate behavior and distribution, interpreting archeological records, primate locomotion and morphology, and replica casts of fossil hominids. This approach reinforces and extends many basic concepts taught in the study of biology.
- *Semester Course Pathway:* This pathway in physical anthropology provides students the opportunity to study early origins of humankind in depth. Laboratory investigations pursue such topics as: phylogeny through time, continental drift, locomotion and behavior of primates, classification and morphology, as well as 14 fossil replica casts of Australopithecus, Homo erectus, Neanderthal, and Cro-Magnon.

Instructional materials for all three pathways are highly self-directive, requiring minimal teacher training. In addition to printed materials, cast replicas of fossil hominid casts and instructional materials used in the explorations have been validated to be scientifically accurate by the L.S.B. Leaky Foundation, Los Angeles County Museum of Natural History, and by world-recognized anthropoligists from various major universities.

Cost for implementing program: Modern Science Unit ($570.50); Biology Unit $1,065.50; Semester Course ($1,530.50). Training costs consist of: travel expenses; $200 per day honorarium; no charge for training workshop materials.

Contact   Milton S. Anisman, Director, Los Angeles Unified School District, Physical Anthropology Center, 6625 Balboa Boulevard, Van Nuys, CA 91406. (818) 997-2389 or (310) 472-6175, FAX (818) 774-9462.

Developmental Funding: USOE ESEA Title IV-C.   JDRP No. 82-29 **(5/26/82)**

Section 8

Social Sciences

* These programs are currently funded by the NDN.

Summary of Program Services for Section 8

Program	Goal*	Page	Dissem. Funds Available NDN	Dissem. Funds Available Other	Costs to Potential Adopter (AWARENESS) Hon	Trav	Per Diem	On Site Visitation Available Home Site	Adopt Site	Materials Available Free Paper	Video	Film Strip	Other	Staff Available (TRAINING) Home Site	Adopt Site	Costs to Adopter (TRAINING) Hon	Trav	Per Diem	Certified Trainers Available State(s)	Training Time Required Day(s)
Choices for the 21st Century	3	8-1	✓		✓	✓	✓		✓	✓				✓	✓		✓	✓	CT, MA, MO, NJ, NY, RI, VT	<1-1
Facing History and Ourselves . . .	3, 6, 7	8-2	✓		✓	✓	✓	✓	✓	✓	✓		✓	✓	✓	✓	✓	✓	CA, FL, IL, MA, MD, ME, NM, NY, TN	1-6
GeoGram, Project	3	8-3	✓			✓	✓	✓	✓	✓				✓	✓		✓	✓	(none)	1
History Theatre of Ideas	3	8-11			(negotiable)			✓		✓	✓			✓		(negotiable)			MA, MO	variable
Institute for Political . . . (IPLE)	3	8-11				✓	✓			✓					✓		✓	✓	AL, MT, NV, OK, OR, TX, UT	1-2
Kids Voting USA	3	8-4	✓		(negotiable)			✓	✓	✓				✓	✓	(negotiable)			(none)	<1
Law in a Changing Society (LCS)	3	8-12			✓	✓	✓	✓	✓	✓				✓		✓	✓		OR, NV, TX	1-3+
Law Related Education . . . (LEGAL)	3	8-5	✓	✓	✓	✓	✓	✓	✓	✓				✓	✓	✓	✓	✓	AK, AZ, CA, CO, HI, ID, NV, NY, OR, UT, WY	1
Life Unworthy of Life	3	8-6	✓		✓	✓	✓	✓	✓	✓	✓			✓	✓	✓	✓	✓	(none)	1
Past Is Prologue	3	8-12			✓	✓	✓	✓	✓	✓	✓			✓	✓	✓	✓	✓	AK, AZ, CA, CO, FL, GA, HI, ID, KS, NM, NV, NY, OK, OR, TX, UT, WY	1-3+
Preparing Instructional Teams To Teach Effective Citizenship Education	3	8-7	✓	(info. not available)																
Religion In Human Culture (RIHC)	3	8-13		✓	✓	✓	✓	✓	✓	✓				✓	✓	✓	✓	✓	(none)	1

* National Goals for Education—definitions for each goal can be found on pages 5-7.

Summary of Program Services for Section 8 (cont'd)

Program	Goal*	Page	AWARENESS											TRAINING						
			Dissem. Funds Available		Costs to Potential Adopter			On Site Visitation Available		Materials Available				Staff Available		Costs to Adopter			Certified Trainers Available	Training Time Required
			NDN	Other	Hon	Trav	Per Diem	Home Site	Adopt Site	Free Paper	Video	Film Strip	Other	Home Site	Adopt Site	Hon	Trav	Per Diem	State(s)	Day(s)
Respecting Ethnic And Cultural Heritage (REACH)	3	8-8	✓		✓	✓	✓	✓	✓	✓	✓			✓	✓	✓	✓	✓	GA, IO, KS, MO, MN, NC, NE, NJ, NY, OK, OR, PA, TX, WA	2
Save For America	3	8-9	✓						✓						✓				AL, CT, NH, NY, TX	.5
Teaching Geography: A Model For Action In Grades 4-12	3	8-10	✓	✓				✓	✓	✓				✓	✓	(nego-tiable)			(most states)	1
Teaching Individuals Positive Solutions.... (TIPS)	3	8-13			✓	✓	✓	✓	✓	✓				✓		✓	✓	✓	NJ, OH	<1

* National Goals for Education—definitions for each goal can be found on pages 5-7.

Audience Approved by PEP for students in grades 9-12.

Description Choices for the 21st Century is an ongoing series of supplemental curriculum units on current and historical international issues. Materials are designed to place special emphasis on preparing students to be participatory citizens. Choices units provide classroom teachers with the tools to raise foreign policy issues in the social studies classroom using a pedagogy that encourages critical thinking and student-centered learning. In addition to background readings and lesson plans, each unit provides a well-crafted framework of policy options on an issue, illustrating fundamentally different and feasible paths which U.S. policymakers could pursue. Each path contains its own distinctive pros and cons, risks and tradeoffs. Students must consider each option in the context of the history leading up to the issue and define and articulate their own judgment about the direction they feel U.S. policy should take. Each unit is packaged separately and includes a reproducible student text, complete lesson plans, student worksheets, and other handouts.

The Choices approach has also been applied to the study of key decision points in history. The drama of an historical era is recreated for students through an exploration of the options available to decision makers at a critical moment in time. By examining the decisions that were made and the ramifications, students to draw lessons from historical events such as the origins of the Cold War, the Vietnam War, and the collapse of Germany's Weimar Republic. Students are then challenged to apply these lessons to current national and international affairs. Each Choices unit is packaged separately and includes a reproducible student text and a teacher's resource book complete with lesson plans, student handouts and other references.

Evidence of Effectiveness Students who experienced the Choices curriculum learned factual information about the history and issues presented as well or better than did students in a traditional read-and-discuss curriculum. Students who worked with the Choices curriculum developed the ability to understand multiple perspectives, apply their analytic skills to new situations, and articulate and analyze the strengths and weaknesses of a reasoned opinion to a significantly greater extent than did students in more traditional programs addressing the same content matter.

Requirements Training is desirable, particularly for those with limited comfort or experience with interactive, student-centered learning. Adoption trainings require a minimum of two hours, however, a full day of training is best. The Choices program is developing a core group of experienced Choices teachers (Senior Associates) nationwide who can provide ongoing professional leadership to others, including workshops and inservice programs.

Costs Each curriculum unit sells for $8 and is reproducible on a standard copier. Duplication permission is granted. At 5¢ per page, student materials can be duplicated for $1.25-$2 per student. There is no additional expense for teachers to purchase and use Choices units. The Choices program currently charges a fee for training: $350 for a half day and $500 for a full day in addition to travel expenses. There is a charge of $20 per participant for training materials which include two complete Choices units.

Services Curriculum materials, training and follow-up consultation are available.

Contact Susan Graseck, Director, or Patricia Keenan-Byrne, Choices Education Project, Thomas J. Watson Jr. Institute for International Studies, Brown University, Box 1948, Providence, RI 02912. (401) 863-3155.

Developmental Funding: A combination of federal, state, and private sources including the Pew Charitable Trusts, United States Institute of Peace, and institutional support from Brown University and the Center for Foreign Policy Development.

PEP No. 93-10 **(3/25/93)**

Facing History and Ourselves: Holocaust and Human Behavior. A course of study using the history of 20th-century genocide to teach about the meaning of human dignity, morality, law, citizenship, and behavior for students in grades 8-11.

Audience Approved by PEP for students in grades 8-11.

Description Facing History and Ourselves: Holocaust and Human Behavior programs engage adolescent students of diverse backgrounds in an examination of racism, prejudice, and antisemitism. Within an interdisciplinary framework drawing upon adolescent development theory, the program encourages students to make the essential connection between history and the moral choices they confront in their own lives as citizens in a democracy. Facing History and Ourselves works in partnership with educators to create programs that address complex issues of citizenship and social justice.

The resource book, *Facing History and Ourselves,* helps students confront the complexities of history in ways that promote critical and creative thinking about the challenges they face and the opportunities they have for positive change. The book begins with short stories and autobiographical accounts that help students look at *ourselves*—who *we* are and how *our* identity is formed. The book then considers how three sets of ideas have shaped not only individual identity but also national identity, including that of the United States. Those ideas are *democracy, race,* and *nationalism.* The chapters that follow focus primarily on how those ideas influenced the decisions that led to the destruction of democracy in Weimar Germany and ultimately to the Holocaust. The book also relates those decisions to issues that affect students' lives today—particularly to issues of racism, antisemitism, violence, conformity, and power. That last chapters in the book take students from reflection to judgment, and then to action as they consider questions of right and wrong, guilt and responsibility. Those chapters also return to the themes of early chapters as students discover how the legacies of the past shape identity. Because *Facing History* is ultimately a study in human behavior, the book ends with a chapter entitled "Choosing to Participate." It features examples of pro-active and pro-social behavior. The resource book is cross-referenced to other publications, including *Elements of Time and Choosing to Participate*; the latter is a history of American volunteerism and community service.

The program uses the tools of the humanities and is interdisciplinary. It is specifically designed for adolescents in middle schools and junior and senior high schools. Its approach and methodology are broadly applicable to violence prevention, multicultural education, and critical thinking. The professional development activities offered employ an adult learning model that encourages the teacher to become a lifelong learner. Facing History and Ourselves views research through the teacher's lens and creates resources that can be used in conjunction with ongoing support to design effective courses for students in a variety of settings.

Evidence of Effectiveness Students who participated in Facing History and Ourselves units demonstrated: (1) greater knowledge of historical concepts than those not enrolled in the unit; and (2) increased complexity of interpersonal understanding compared with students enrolled in traditional Modern World History courses.

Requirements An individual teacher, team, school, or entire school district may choose to adopt a Facing History and Ourselves program (3-12 weeks), or adapt it to enhance existing courses. Teachers should attend a one- or two-day workshop or a six-day summer institute before piloting the classroom materials.

Services A team of national and regional program staff, as well as teacher trainers from public, private, and parochial schools are available for initial training, follow-up consultation, and continuing professional development activities. Brochures are available at no cost. Visitors are welcome at offices in Boston, New York, Memphis, and Chicago. The National Resource Center collects and distributes printed and audio-visual materials. Classroom visits to demonstration sites can be arranged. In communities where certified trainers are available, adult education courses and inservice programs are offered.

Costs Training costs consist of $500 per day plus travel and lodging for presenters' fees and $10 per participant (typically 20-40 people) for workshop materials. Costs can be negotiated depending upon available funds.

Contact Marc Skvirsky, Alan Stoskopf, or Margot Stern Strom, Facing History and Ourselves National Foundation, 16 Hurd Road, Brookline, MA 02146. (617) 232-1595.

Developmental Funding: USOE-ESEA Title IV-C.

JDRP No. 80-33 **(12/5/80)**
Recertified **(3/11/93)**

GeoGram, Project. An interdisciplinary curriculum program bringing together the studies of physical, cultural, and economic geography with map, graph, table, and chart skills, critical thinking, and expository writing for middle school students studying world history and geography.

Audience   Approved by PEP for students in grades 6-8.

Description   Project GeoGram provides effective supplementary materials designed to enable teachers to enhance instruction in physical, cultural, and economic geography, map/graph/table/chart skills, critical thinking, and expository writing for their middle school students. The Project's curriculum materials and instructional strategies, built upon the five themes of geography, that have since been adopted by the 1994 Geographic Education Standards Project, on behalf of the American Geographical Society and the National Council for Geographic Education et al., address key parts of the National Goals for Education centering around the need to have students demonstrate competency in geography and English. The Project's critical thinking thrusts help students prepare for responsible citizenship, further learning, and productive employment in our modern economy. Through the use of the Project's innovative instructional materials and teaching strategies, students "travel" and learn about selected areas of the world using nonconsumable "newsletters" and supporting curriculum materials which focus on basic geographical concepts about the areas of the world addressed in the Project's units. Supplementing each of the Project's units—America's Gateway Cities, India, China, Japan, Central America, and South America—adopters also receive student Reference Guides, with glossaries and crossword puzzles using key unit vocabulary words, teacher's Lesson Amplification and Implementation Guides, and all other necessary supporting materials including pre- and posttests. In implementing the Project, students are asked to use reading, writing, map, graph, table, chart, and critical thinking skills as they complete class work and homework activities, engage in collaborative projects, work with simulations, and complete individual assignments.

Evidence of Effectiveness   Students in middle school World History and Geography classes implementing the GeoGram curriculum demonstrated significantly greater gains on project-produced and validated criterion- referenced tests of geographical knowledge, and map, critical thinking, and expository writing skills; and scored higher on a standardized test of basic skills covering social studies, language arts, and reference skills than did those in comparison groups. Project field test results showed that teachers devoted more classroom instructional time to geography, critical thinking, and expository writing skills while using Project GeoGram materials and devoted more time to student-teacher exchanges; and that students showed increased concentration on classroom activities and greater time on task.

Requirements   GeoGram requires no change in staffing patterns. The Project's materials may be implemented as self-contained geography units, tracked into specific social studies content areas; or used as supplementary materials taught in a core program of social studies/English. The Project's six-hour staff development training workshop may be conducted at sites within the Los Angeles Unified School District, or at sites selected by potential adopters or State Facilitators.

Costs   A complete **Project GeoGram Curriculum Package**, with sets of 35 copies of each of the project's six curriculum units, published on color-coded, nonconsumable, 110 lb. "index" stock, and all student pre- and posttests, necessary supplementary unit materials, and a teacher's Lesson Amplification and Implementation Guide for the units, on regular 20 lb. stock, plus a three-ring binder **Teacher's Edition** containing a single copy of all project curriculum materials is available for a cost of $250. Schools possessing the curriculum package may purchase additional Teacher's Editions for $35.

Services   Project staff are available to conduct training workshops. Prospective adopters are asked to cover the travel and per diem costs necessary to conduct these workshops. The Project Awareness materials are available, on request, at no cost. A project quarterly . . . *Bulletin*, program updates, and other follow-up consultations are also provided at no charge.

Contact   Roberta Konrad, Coordinator, Leni Posner, Project Consultant, or Howard Lappin, Principal, Foshay Learning Center, Los Angeles Unified School District, 3751 South Harvard Boulevard, Los Angeles, CA 90018. (213) 730-0943, FAX (213) 733-2120.

Developmental Funding: ECIA Chapter 2 and LAUSD.   PEP No. 91-20 **(4/3/91)**

> **Kids Voting USA.** Addresses the national crises of low voter turnout through an innovative, community-based K-12 education program in which children actually accompany their parents to polling sites. Children participating in Kids Voting gain a sense of empowerment through extensive discussion of elections and candidates, casting a ballot, and identifying with the results of their election.

Audience Approved by PEP for students in grades K-12.

Description Kids Voting USA provides a grade-specific curriculum for grades K-12, equating to 6-12 hours of instruction, designed to supplement and enhance the civic education students receive at school and encourage critical thinking, creativity, and parental involvement. Students learn about their civic duty of voting and accompanying responsibilities; develop skills for obtaining information and making critical decisions; discuss candidates and issues in the classroom and home; and participate in creative ventures such as holding a press conference. The program culminates with students accompanying their parents to polling sites and casting ballots. The ballots are tabulated and results of this election are transmitted to the press, and released with official results. All components of the program specifically address Goal 3 of Goals 2000 with many school districts correlating the curriculum to the adopted state standards.

Evidence of Effectiveness In districts implementing the Kids Voting program, including the Kids Voting curriculum, students gained knowledge of elections/the electoral process; students participated in citizenship behaviors, such as voting at polling sites and discussing political candidates and ballot propositions at home; and parents increased their school involvement. Statewide voter turnout increased by 2.6%; precincts with districts implementing the program for one election demonstrated a voter turnout 5% higher than comparison precincts; and precincts with districts implementing the program for two elections demonstrated a voter turnout 2% higher than precincts implementing for just one election.

Requirements Formation of a community-based board of directors is required and should be comprised of business and civic leaders to function as the decision-making body responsible for: (1) inviting school districts to participate, based on funding and community representation; (2) "customizing" the curriculum to reflect each area's electoral process, regulations, and local issues; and (3) fundraising. Personnel needs include an executive director and staff consisting of clerical/support staff, regional managers, volunteer coordinator, election professional, public staff consisting of clerical/support staff, regional managers, volunteer coordinator, election professional, public relations consultant, and a distribution clerk to disseminate materials. Many of these positions can serve as "in kind" contributions from corporations. No specific training is required for regional managers, who serve as liaisons between the program and the educational community. Training totals approximately four days and consists of seminars the summer prior to the election and a "post-mortem" for executive directors afterwards.

Costs Adopting sites enter into an agreement with Kids Voting USA and pay a fee based on the number of students participating. The proposed schedule is: programs with less than 25,000 students pay $5,000; programs with 25,000-200,000 pay $10,000; programs with 200,000-400,000 pay $15,000; and those with more than 400,000 will enter into discussion with Kids Voting USA regarding fees. This entitles the affiliate to the copyrighted curricula, promotional packets, *Implementation Manual*, on-site consultation, and telephone consultation as needed. Cost per student is approximately $2.00-$3.00 based on program size. Kids Voting USA does everything possible to accommodate the needs of the affiliate.

Services In addition to standard training and materials, follow-up telephone consultation and additional training is available.

Contact Marilyn Evans, President & Executive Director, 398 South Mill Avenue, Suite 304, Tempe, AZ 85281. (602) 921-3727. E-Mail: averkamp@inet.edu.gov

Developmental Funding: Private corporations and donors, Maricopa County Board of Supervisors, Bureau of Indian Affairs, and Navajo County Board of Supervisors.

JDRP No. 92-11 (**4/92**)

Law Related Education: Goals for American Leadership (LEGAL). A curriculum to enable students to develop knowledge, problem-solving skills, and attitudes related to the functioning of the U.S. legal/judicial system for grades 5, 8, and 11.

Audience Approved by the PEP/JDRP for all social studies students, grades 5, 8, and 11, or those grades at which American history is taught.

Description Research has found that traditional teaching approaches have failed to improve students' knowledge of the processes of the U. S. legal/judicial system. The goals, therefore, of Law Related Education: Goals for American Leadership (LEGAL) are for greater attention to teacher training and implementation of specific and sequential approaches to law and civic education.

The first component of LEGAL's curriculum is the introductory unit that is taught in American history courses early in the school year. The unit consists of 10 lessons with teaching strategies that systematically and sequentially lead to the development of high level problem-solving skills. Teacher's manuals provide detailed lesson plans for this unit. The first four lessons enable students to discover that law affects their entire lives and that our Constitution and laws are based on societal and individual values. The fifth lesson presents situations to introduce the concept of legal values conflicts. The remaining lessons concentrate on the case method—analysis, formulation of issue and decision, and development of reasoning. The activities and examples are varied to meet the abilities of each grade level.

The second component is the bi-weekly lessons that teachers prepare to fit into existing state-mandated history course content. Each of these lessons reinforces the knowledge and problem-solving skills presented in the introductory units. Traditional curriculum content is therefore presented, but through LEGAL's teaching strategies.

Requirements The adopting district, or group of districts, should attend LEGAL's methods and materials. Adopting districts agree to infuse LEGAL into their existing American history curricula at the elementary and/or secondary levels through teaching the Introductory Unit and ten additional teacher-prepared infusion lessons during the remainder of the year. An administrator must be selected who will supervise training and act as local director throughout the implementation year.

Costs Generally, travel expenses for training sessions may be shared among the adopting districts, LEGAL's funding, and the State Facilitator's budget. Teacher's manuals, $5 each; student booklets, $1 each. Costs for training are to be negotiated.

Services Free awareness brochures are available. Awareness sessions, needs assessment surveys, three-day teacher training at the program or adoption site, follow-up technical assistance visits, pre- and posttests, and teacher and student materials at grades 5, 8, and 11 are supplied at various costs.

Contact James J. Carroll, Ph.D., Director, Syracuse University, 316 Lyman Hall, Syracuse, NY 13244. (315) 443-4720.

JDRP No. 81-39 **(1/28/82)**
Recertified **(3/31/92)**

Developmental Funding: USOE ESEA Title IV-C.

Life Unworthy of Life.   A coherent unit of study about the Nazi Holocaust for infusion of high school world history and other social studies courses.

Audience   Approved by PEP for students in grades 9-12.

Description   The Life Unworthy of Life curriculum is chronologically organized to fit world history courses. Lessons move from the aftermath of World War I, through the rise of Hitler and the Nazi Party, to the "Final Solution." The unit culminates with lessons about the consequences and implications of the Holocaust. The instructional approach is designed to stimulate active student participation in analysis of historical events and discussion of ethical issues pertaining to those events. Learning activities include viewing of videotaped survivor testimony, participation in authentic simulations, analysis of primary documents, discussion of ethical issues, and traditional outlining of short historical lectures. The instructor's manual provides teachers with lesson objectives, defines new terms, lists readings from the student text, and recommends a sequence of teaching steps including thought-provoking questions and answers and homework assignments.

Evidence of Effectiveness   Students participating in the program are significantly better able to express, in writing, consequences of indifference toward the mistreatment of others; demonstrate reduced prejudice toward minority groups; and show greater gains in historical knowledge of the Holocaust than comparison groups. Teachers using the curriculum are significantly more inclined and able to teach the topic of the Holocaust in depth than teachers in comparison groups.

Requirements   The program is a self-contained instructional unit comprised of a student textbook, instructor's manual, and five-part video of testimony by victims who survived the Holocaust. As part of their world history courses, teachers may incorporate all 18 lessons of the program or choose a shortened 11- or 5-lesson option. One to four weeks of in-depth instruction devoted to the Holocaust as a supplemental unit of study linked to the normal unit on World War II may be chosen. A one-day inservice teacher training program is available.

Costs   An examination set, including an instructor's manual, a 60-minute videotape, and one student textbook costs $95 (plus shipping). Complete classroom materials, including an instructor's manual, a 60-minute videotape, and 30 student textbooks, cost $295 (plus shipping). Additional textbooks are $7.50 (plus shipping). One-day inservice costs are negotiable.

Services   In addition to training and curriculum materials, follow-up consultation is available.

Contact   Peter Nagourney, Center for the Study of the Child, 914 Lincoln Avenue, Ann Arbor, MI 48104-3525. (313) 761-6440, FAX (313) 761-5629.

Developmental Funding: Private foundations.

PEP No. 91-8 (**3/14/91**)

Preparing Instructional Teams To Teach Effective Citizenship Education. A program that equips teams of educators to deliver a law-related education course that improves students' citizenship in grades 8 and 9.

Audience Approved by PEP for teachers, building administrators, and resource persons who will present the course to 8th and/or 9th grade students.

Description Many law-related education (LRE) courses exist with curriculum materials only, without a mechanism to change student attitudes and behaviors related to citizenship. In this program, educators are prepared to increase students' knowledge of the law and legal processes and reduce student delinquency by increasing law-abiding behavior. The program's team approach involves simultaneous training of teachers, building administrators, and police officers—all of whom are considered critical to the success of changing student attitudes towards delinquency. Teachers build their proficiency in instructional and classroom management strategies, including handling student debate. Police officers become adept at interactive teaching strategies, ways to deliver information to young students that law enforcement officials take for granted, and methods to help students realize that the officer's presence in the classroom is not an intrusion, but a learning opportunity. Building administrators are encouraged to be supportive and informed about the connections between the LRE course and their own actions (such as school governance). Training includes instruction, demonstration, practice, and debriefing. The preferred length of training is six days, with participation by police officers for at least two days. Participants receive a textbook and 200 pages of reference material including sample lessons.

Evidence of Effectiveness Eighth and ninth-grade students taught a one-semester LRE course by teams who have completed our training not only gain knowledge of the law and legal processes, but exhibit more favorable attitudes toward school, teachers, police, and law-abiding behavior, and less frequent delinquent behavior in and out of school than students in the same grades at the same schools who are taught conventional social studies or civics courses as measured by pre- and postprogram student questionnaires.

Requirements Minimal requirements include agreement by a local law enforcement agency to allow one or more officers to participate for at least two days of training and serve as co-teachers for two hours of classroom time per week, and commitment by one or more social studies teachers and one building administrator (per school) to attend six days of training and provide a nine-week LRE course. Costs for a typical four-person team from one school are $1,650, including all materials needed by team members but not student texts (estimated at $15 per student) or food, lodging, travel, team members' pay, and personal expenses. Costs for paying participating law enforcement officials for classroom participation must also be considered. Training takes place at the University of Colorado.

Services Awareness materials are available at no cost. Program staff are available to attend out-of-state awareness meetings (costs to be negotiated).

Contact   **Robert M. Hunter, University of Colorado, Center for Action Research, Bureau of Sociological Research, Campus Box 580, Boulder, CO 80309. (303) 492-6114.**

Developmental Funding: National Institute for Juvenile Justice and Delinquency Prevention, and Colorado Division of Criminal Justice.   PEP No. 88-09 **(3/15/88)**

Respecting Ethnic And Cultural Heritage (REACH).
A multicultural education program designed for infusion into the regular U.S. history and/or social studies. The program's intent is to increase the knowledge and understanding of cultural diversity in America, for grades 6-9, while increasing acceptance between members of different racial/ethnic groups.

Audience Approved by JDRP/PEP for all students, grades 6-9.

Description Respecting Ethnic And Cultural Heritage (REACH) is a nationally recognized multicultural education program designed for infusion into U.S. history and/or social studies curriculum. The program's goals are to increase knowledge and understanding related to cultural diversity while increasing social acceptance between cultural groups. The multicultural curriculum is designed around four phases:

- *Human Relations Skills:* Students participate in activities on self-awareness, self-esteem, interpersonal communications, and understanding group dynamics.
- *Cultural Self-Awareness:* Students conduct research on their own personal culture, family history, or community. This phase culminates with the Cultural Fair experience where each student presents a visual display at a major community event.
- *Multicultural Awareness:* Students study five booklets, the *Ethnic Perspective Series*. The booklets focus on U.S. History from different ethnic points of view. Listening tapes are available as an alternative to the booklets.
- *Cross-Cultural Experience:* Historical and cultural information in the booklets is made personal through dialogue and exchange with students and adults from different ethnic groups.

REACH is part of a four-unit multicultural/global training and curriculum organization, The REACH Center. Program units include High School REACH (high school), Project REACH (middle/junior high school), REACH for Kids (elementary), and REACH for Excellence (higher education/business).

Evidence of Effectiveness Students in REACH demonstrate statistically significant and positive changes in their attitudes towards other racial/ethnic groups, specifically in their expressions of social distance towards those groups.

Requirements REACH is usually implemented in all social studies classes at one grade level within the middle school/junior high. No special staffing or facilities are required. Participating teachers are trained by REACH staff or certified REACH trainers before using the materials in their classrooms. Training is typically over two days and a follow-up session is encouraged. Also, at least one classroom set of the *Ethnic Perspective Series* should be purchased.

Services Awareness materials are available at no cost. Program staff and certified trainers are available for out-of-town awareness sessions at the cost of travel and expenses. Follow-up consultation and monitoring are available to adopters. A 20-minute preview video explaining the program is available for the cost of postage. A trainer for trainers is also available.

Costs Training costs are negotiable but typically include travel, a $90 materials fee, and a $60 registration fee. Costs decrease as the number of participants increases. The materials include a teacher guide, the *Ethnic Perspective Series*, and workshop handouts. Also, at least one classroom set of the *Ethnic Perspective Series* should be purchased for each adopting school. Thirty sets of five booklets at $25 per set = $750 and includes a free set of the listening tapes and a free set of the Cultural Fair slides.

Contact   David Koyama, Director of Programs, The REACH Center, 180 Nickerson Street, Suite 212, Seattle, WA 98109. (206) 284-8584, FAX (206) 285-2073.

Developmental Funding: ESEA Title IV-C.

JDRP No. 84-16 **(6/29/84)**
Recertified **(3/25/93)**

Save For America. A program designed to teach students in grades 4-6 basic principles of personal economics and help them practice the skills they have learned by participating in a school-based banking program.

Audience Approved by PEP for all students grades 4-6.

Description Save For America is a school-based savings program sponsored by a bank but run by adult volunteers. Its purpose is to reinstill the savings habit in America's youth.

- DEPOSIT PROCESS
  Students Bank at School: Bank day is before school once a week. To make a deposit, students bring their money and savings register on Bank Day. Using Save for America software, and with adult supervision, students key in their deposit on the school's Apple or IBM computer. With a computer-generated receipt, a sticker, and the deposit recorded in their savings register, it's off to class for the new generation of savers!

  Electronic Data Processing: The Save For America data disk goes to the bank for processing. At the bank, a special program checks the disks for accuracy and prepares the deposits to be sent to the bank's mainframe computer or service bureau.

- CLASSROOM STUDIES
  Program Materials: Making a deposit is not enough to firmly establish the savings habit in the minds of American children. A Save For America curriculum has been designed to teach children why saving is important, how to save, and the mechanics of saving. This U.S. Department of Education approved curriculum is designed for use by teachers or parents.

- INCENTIVES FOR SAVERS
  Each time students make a deposit of any amount they receive a Save for America sticker to remind them to save again!

Evidence of Effectiveness Request a copy of the PEP report.

Requirements A sponsoring bank is required in order to implement the program.

Costs The bank pays all costs.

Services Awareness materials are available at no cost. The program staff is available for awareness sessions (costs to be negotiated). Implementation and follow-up services are available to adopters (costs to be negotiated).

Contact   Sherry Avena, 4095 173rd Place, S.E., Bellevue, WA 98008. (206) 746-0331, FAX (206) 562-8780. E-Mail: savena@inet.ed.gov

JDRP No. 85-6R **(4/2/85)**
Recertified **(3/5/92)**

Developmental Funding: Private sector initiative.

Teaching Geography: A Model For Action In Grades 4-12. A program designed to help teachers in grades 4-12 increase their competency and confidence in teaching geography. Inquiry-based learning methods are emphasized. The program is comprehensive and practical; it is designed for ease of understanding and adoption. The four program components are: Curriculum Guides; a Teacher's Handbook; Professional Development Workshops; and Support Services.

Audience Teachers in any discipline in which geography plays an important role; approved by JDRP for those teaching in grades 4-12.

Description Teaching Geography: A Model For Action in Grades 4-12 is one of the National Geographic Society's (NGS) comprehensive efforts—embodied in its Geography Education Program—to enhance the status and effectiveness of geographic education nationwide. Teaching Geography's materials and services can be effectively utilized in any course in which geographic concepts and skills play a part–such as history, other social studies, science or literature. Geography is one of the five subject areas in the national goals. The Teaching Geography program's goal is to help teachers increase their competence and confidence in teaching geography. Through a combination of materials, inservice workshops, and other support mechanisms, teachers learn to view geography in a conceptual framework based on five fundamental themes and to develop the ability to present geography in this context to their students. Using this approach to learning geography, students can both understand the importance of basic geographic observation–facts about location and place—as well as the more complex analytical concepts of geography relating to human interaction and development of the Earth. A major emphasis of the Teaching Geography program is the sharing of content, lesson plans, and teaching strategies that illustrate these five geographic themes: location, place, human-environment interactions, movement, and regions.

Teaching Geography workshop sessions use a basic framework of geography content and classroom-tested teaching strategies that can be tailored to the specific curricular needs of a state or school district. These are (typically) one-day workshops, combining short content presentations by professional geographers, with guided practice in hands-on teaching activity ideas by Teaching Geography teacher-consultants, who are exemplary graduates of NGS-sponsored geography institutes. A key support service of the Teaching Geography program is offered by access to NGS-sponsored state geographic alliances. These partnerships of classroom teachers, professional geographers, and other educators provide ongoing opportunities for instructors to contribute to the understanding of geography and how it is most effectively taught.

Evidence of Effectiveness Use of Teaching Geography program materials and services leads to positive changes in teachers' understanding of geographic content, of strategies to teach geography, and to increased confidence in teachers' abilities to teach the subject. Evaluative results indicate that teachers who have been trained to use the core content, methods, and materials show a change in performance and attitude that should have a positive influence on geographic learning among students in the classroom. In postactivity evaluations on both pilot programs and geography institutes, teachers were found to be better prepared in their mastery of geographic content and effective teaching strategies, more enthusiastic about teaching geography, and more confident of themselves as teachers.

Costs Costs vary for the different components of the Teaching Geography program. The handbook, *Directions in Geography: A Guide for Teachers,* costs $29.95, plus postage and handling. Most of the recommended teaching activities in the handbook can be carried out using standard, readily available classroom supplies. Other optional materials vary in cost. Teaching Geography workshop fees depend on the number of attendees and on cost-sharing arrangements with state facilitators.

Services Teaching Geography program awareness materials are available at no cost, as are Geography Education Program informational materials. Program staff or certified representatives are available to attend limited numbers of awareness conferences. Teaching Geography workshop training is conducted at adopter sites (costs to be negotiated). NGS-sponsored geographic alliances offer additional inservice training opportunities, alliance teacher-generated, state-specific curriculum materials, networking mechanisms, and multiweek Summer Geography Institute training, conducted at various university sites across the country.

Contact Charles E. Sterling, Teaching Geography Coordinator, Geography Education Program, National Geographic Society, 17th and M Streets N.W., Washington, D.C. 20036. (202) 775-6702.

Developmental Funding: National Geographic Society.

JDRP No. 87-14 (5/15/87)

History Theatre of Ideas. A program using dramatized events in state or local history to enrich grade 7-12 curricula and involve students in analyzing issues.

Description History Theatre of Ideas is a touring classroom drama/discussion program for students in grades 7-12. It provides an arena for the examination of relevant humanities issues. It serves as a model for using history in the introduction of political, social, and philosophical issues into the curricula.

The program's components include a brief historical drama depicting an event in state or local history. This is followed by a discussion between the students and the actors of the pertinent issues in the play. The actors retain their scripted identities throughout the classroom discussion. The teacher prepares students for the discussion by using study guide materials provided by the program.

The program's intent is to enliven humanities study for students. The program uses drama, discussion, and debate as teaching vehicles. Combining drama with discussion lends an immediacy and excitement to history teaching.

Awareness materials including a video (available on loan) are available at no cost. Visitors are welcome to the demonstration site by appointment. Program staff are available for awareness sessions. Training, technical assistance and manuals are available (costs to be negotiated).

Contact   Lorraine Keeney, History Theatre of Ideas, Rhode Island Committee for the Humanities, 60 Ship Street, Providence, RI 02903. (401) 273-2250.

Developmental Funding: NEH, state, and private.   JDRP No. 85-13 (**7/1/86**)

Institute for Political and Legal Education (IPLE). A secondary social studies program designed "to turn students on to active citizenship." Approved by JDRP for students of all abilities, grades 9-12. Materials have been used in grades 6-8.

Description Institute for Political and Legal Education (IPLE)/Model Congress introduces students in grades 6-12 to the American political, legislative, and legal processes. While usually incorporated in the social studies curriculum, the program can be used in a gifted program or as a club or other special interest option. IPLE/Model Congress is flexible enough to be implemented as a full year curriculum, a semester option, or as a single unit of study.

The curriculum, originally developed by IPLE staff and New Jersey teachers, stresses active participation by students through a variety of activities including role play, simulations, value clarifications, case studies and practical experiences. The core of IPLE/Model Congress is a simulation of the Federal Congressional process and this part of the program is particularly motivating for students. The research, writing, and debating skills and the self-awareness that the process generates, gives students tools they can use long after the simulation ends. In addition, by preparing students for responsible citizenship, IPLE addresses Goal 3 of the National Goals for Education.

Materials include *Voter Education, Model Congress Resource Manual, Techniques for Introducing the Law,* and *Individual Rights.* An additional volume, *Juvenile Justice,* is also available. While there is a logical sequence from one manual to another, each is independent and can be the basis of a separate elective course or be incorporated into an already existing course.

Materials may be used without training and are available outside New Jersey. Training for a group of six or more educators can be arranged upon request.

Contact   Rebecca McDonnel, Director, Institute for Political and Legal Education, Educational Informational and Resource Center, 606 Delsea Drive, Sewell, NJ 08080. (609) 582-7000.

Developmental Funding: USOE ESEA Title III.   JDRP No. 74-92 (**9/18/74**)

Law in a Changing Society (LCS). A social studies program designed to improve the citizenship skills and attitudes of students by providing them with an operational understanding of the law, the legal process, and its institutions. Approved by JDRP for teachers and their students in grades 5-12; also used with students in grades K-4.

Description Curriculum materials complement subjects traditionally taught in social studies classes. A broad range of topics and concepts is addressed in the units, in which constitutional issues and the functioning of our legal system predominate. Curriculum materials are activity-oriented, and legal content provides a natural vehicle for developing skills related to critical thinking and reasoning. The strategies encourage students to respond at higher thinking levels, consider alternatives and consequences, and evaluate both their own and society's solutions to the social, political, and economic issues that have been resolved through judicial questions. Students are exposed to the legal system's strengths and ways to participate in the system, and encounter positive experiences with functionaries in the legal system. The format of the classroom materials makes them easy to use. Each unit contains a detailed teacher's lesson plan, materials for students, and a handbook describing 31 strategies to be used. An important part of the curriculum is the use of community resources. The local bar association, police department, judiciary, and other legal agencies and groups provide resource speakers and field trip opportunities essential to the program.

Contact   Rhonda Haynes, Director, Law in a Changing Society, Law Focused Education, Inc., P.O. Box 12487, Austin, TX 78711. (800) 204-2222, ext. 2120.

Developmental Funding: Titles III, IV-C and LEAA.   JDRP No. 79-28 **(7/10/79)**

Past Is Prologue. A program teaching elementary students the procedures involved in operating a democratic government. Approved by the JDRP for students, grades K-6. Also used with students in middle and high schools (6-12).

Description Approved for K-6 in critical thinking and governance. Past Is Prologue uses three Native American Learning Stories from an Iroquois tradition, along with a Teacher's Guide. Students will learn how to effectively gather information, make clear decisions, and develop group consensus. The story Who Speaks for Wolf presents the multilevel concepts of the decision-making system of a democratic government. The Native American setting captures the interest of the young and involves them in the learning process. Teachers report enhanced listening and discussion skills and increased respect for each other and for other cultures. This program has been identified as meeting National Goal for Educational 3. Teachers report materials are equally effective with gifted, average, and disadvantaged students, and work well in the heterogenous and multicultural classroom. Well suited for use in an integrated curriculum as the thinking skills encouraged by Past Is Prologue relate to several elements. Each trainee must have both books, *Who Speaks for Wolf* and the *Teacher's Guide* ($24 per set)*. An audio cassette is also available ($15)*. Cost of personnel training is $450 - $900 per day plus transportation costs for a certified trainer. Awareness materials are available at no cost. Program site visits to model schools are welcomed, by appointment.

  * Educational discount available on materials.

Contact   Mobi Warren Phillips, Past Is Prologue, 10606 Benchmark Way, San Antonio, TX 78213. (210) 342-1223.

Developmental Funding: State and local.   JDRP No. 86-20 (7/9/86)

Religion In Human Culture (RIHC). A social studies program about religious traditions and topics. Approved by JDRP for students of all abilities, grades 9-12.

Description Religion in Human Culture (RIHC) is a semester-length, elective social studies course about religion for high school students. It consists of six instructional units which may be implemented wholly or in part. These include a unit on religious expression and five separate units on the Hindu, Buddhist, Judaic, Christian, and Islamic traditions. RIHC is a program for learning about religions and is intended to help students acquire greater awareness, understanding, and appreciation of religious diversity. The curriculum content is consistent with United States Supreme Court decisions that public schools shall neither teach nor practice religion but may teach about religion as it affects human history and culture. The overall objectives for the Religion in Human Culture series fall within four categories established by the National Council for the Social Studies Curriculum Guidelines. RIHC exposes students to religious diversity; develops attitudes of understanding and respect for the beliefs and practices of others; centers on the study of religions as part of the social studies curriculum; furnishes a total teaching package about the major religions of the world; follows an easy-to-use, lesson-by-lesson format; and emphasizes inquiry strategies, a developmental process, and substantive content.

Contact Wes Bodin and Lee Smith, Co-Directors, World Religions Curriculum Development Center, St. Louis Park Schools, ISD #283, 6425 West 33rd Street, Minneapolis, MN 55426. (612) 928-6733, (612) 928-6000.

Developmental Funding: USOE ESEA Titles III and IV-C.   JDRP No. 79-32 **(7/12/79)**

Teaching Individuals Positive Solutions/Teaching Individuals Protective Strategies (TIPS). A structured approach to teaching young people how to positively resolve conflict, to resist crime, and to protect themselves and their property. Approved by JDRP for fourth- and fifth-graders; curriculum has been developed for use in grades K-8.

Description Teaching Individuals Positive Solutions/Teaching Individuals Protective Strategies (TIPS) was initiated by a request from the Director of the Federal Bureau of Investigation (FBI) to translate the concept of crime prevention into an educational program. TIPS is an intervention program aimed at both the perpetrators and victims of crimes. The basic assumption of the program is that increased knowledge about crime prevention concepts will lead to more positive attitudes toward them and, subsequently, to improved behavior in dealing with them. The goals of the program are to promote and maintain positive student attitudes and behavior, while teaching students to responsibly insure the safety and welfare of themselves and others. These goals align directly with Goals 3 and 7 of the National Goals for Education in preparing students to become responsible citizens, more disciplined, and knowledgeable in positive conflict resolution.

Each grade-level curriculum is contained in a single manual ($7.50 each for grades K-5; $10.00 each for grades 6-8) that includes instructions for use, teacher information, reproducible student worksheets, and suggested supplementary information. Concepts presented are appropriate to the skill and reading level of each grade with more sophisticated materials added each year. Topical areas include positive conflict resolution; respect for rules, laws and authority; responsibility; and strategies in crime prevention. TIPS can be taught as a mini-course, a supplement to existing courses, an interdisciplinary unit, and as a focus for small-group discussion. Specific math, reading, and language arts skills are delineated for each lesson. Teacher-guided discussion is supplemented by student activities such as decision making, role playing, creative writing, vocabulary development, graphing, mapping and decoding.

Contact Monika Steinberg, Program Director, TIPS Program, Educational Information and Resource Center (EIRC), 606 Delsea Drive, Sewell, NJ 08080. (609) 582-7000, FAX (609) 582-4206.

Developmental Funding: USOE ESEA Title IV-C.   JDRP No. 82-21 **(5/12/82)**

Section 9

Health/Physical Education

* These programs are currently funded by the NDN.

Summary of Program Services for Section 9

Program	Goal*	Page	Dissem. Funds Available – NDN	Dissem. Funds Available – Other	Costs to Potential Adopter – Hon	Costs to Potential Adopter – Trav	Costs to Potential Adopter – Per Diem	On Site Visitation Available – Home Site	On Site Visitation Available – Adopt Site	Materials Available – Free Paper	Materials Available – Video	Materials Available – Film Strip	Materials Available – Other	Staff Available – Home Site	Staff Available – Adopt Site	Costs to Adopter – Hon	Costs to Adopter – Trav	Costs to Adopter – Per Diem	Certified Trainers Available – State(s)	Training Time Required – Day(s)
Athletic Health Care System	3	9-1	✓			✓	✓	✓		✓	✓			✓	✓	✓	✓	✓	CA, D.C., GA, MI, NE, NV, NY, OH, SC, TX, UT, VA, WA, WV	3+
CASPAR Alcohol and Drug Education Series	7	9-9			✓	✓	✓	✓		✓				✓	✓	✓	✓	✓	KY, MA	3+
CHOICE, Project	3	9-9			✓	✓		✓		✓		✓		✓		✓	✓		MI, TX	<1
Curriculum for Meeting Modern Problems...	7	9-10			✓	✓	✓			✓					✓	✓	✓	✓	(none)	2
Every Child A Winner ...(ECAW)	3	9-2	✓		(negotiable)				✓	✓	✓	✓			✓	(negotiable)			AL, FL, GA, KY, ME, VA	2
Growing Healthy®	7	9-10	✓		✓	✓	✓	✓	✓	✓	✓			✓		✓	✓	✓	AK, AR, CA, CO, FL, IA, IN, MA, MI, MN, NM, NY, OK, PA, SD, VA	3+
Healthy For Life (HFL)	7	9-3			✓	✓	✓	✓		✓				✓		✓	✓	✓	WI	3+
Know Your Body (KYB) School Health Promotion Program, The	7	9-4	✓		(negotiable)			✓	✓	✓				✓	✓	✓	✓	✓	(almost all states)	1-4
ME-ME Drug & Alcohol Prevention Education Program	3, 7	9-11		✓			✓	✓		✓	✓	✓				✓	✓	✓	AZ	1
Ombudsman	7	9-11			(negotiable)	✓	✓	✓		✓	✓			✓	✓	✓	✓	✓	AK, AS, AZ, CO, D.C., ID, KS, LA, NC, NE, NH, NV, NY, OK, OR, PR, SC, TN, UT, VA, WA, WY	2-3
Physical Management	7	9-12							✓	✓					✓	✓	✓	✓	IL, KY, ME	2

* National Goals for Education—definitions for each goal can be found on pages 5-7.

Summary of Program Services for Section 9 (cont'd)

Program	Goal*	Page	Dissem. Funds Available		Costs to Potential Adopter			On Site Visitation Available		Materials Available				Staff Available		Costs to Adopter			Certified Trainers Available	Training Time Required
			NDN	Other	Hon	Trav	Per Diem	Home Site	Adopt Site	Free Paper	Video	Film Strip	Other	Home Site	Adopt Site	Hon	Trav	Per Diem	State(s)	Day(s)
Social Decision Making and Problem Solving	2, 6, 7	9-5	✓		(negotiable)			✓	✓	✓	✓			✓	✓	✓	✓	✓	AZ, CO, NJ, NY, UT	3
SPARK: Sports, Play, and Recreation For Kids	7	9-6	(info. not available)																	
Stanford Adolescent Heart Health Curriculum		9-7	(info. not available)																	
Teenage Health Teaching Modules (THTM)	7	9-8	✓							✓				✓			✓		(all states)	2

* National Goals for Education—definitions for each goal can be found on pages 5-7.

Athletic Health Care System. A comprehensive system to prevent and manage athletic injuries in interscholastic athletic activity. Approved by JDRP for high school athletics— coaches, athletic directors, school nurses, certified athletic trainers, and student trainers.

Description Schools have the responsibility to operate safe athletic programs and to manage athletic health problems properly. This comprehensive risk management system serves to reduce liability. State-of-the-art sports medicine methods, adapted for the high school level, meet the educational, organizational and record-keeping requirements toward safer interscholastic athletic activities. The Continuing Education Committee of the American College of Sports Medicine has endorsed the efforts of the developer. The system includes:

- **Education** A 30-hour course for the entire "health care team" comprised of all coaches, the school nurse, certified athletic trainer (if on staff), and approximately 10 high school student trainers. The course provides common sense and knowledge in the areas of injury prevention, injury recognition, first aid, supportive taping, rehabilitation, and organization of the training room, as well as the importance and skills of record keeping. The laboratory portion of the course provides an ample 10 hours of demonstration by skilled health professionals who oversee the actual practice of the learned skills by participants. **The National Leadership Institute,** conducted for one week annually each summer in Seattle, focuses on the administrative skills of organizational management required for supervising and coordinating a system of athletic health care. The accompanying Administrative Manual explains the Athletic Health Care System philosophy and all procedures. Attendees become "Certified Administrators" for the Athletic Health Care System. Local leadership institutes can also be arranged.
- **Needs Assessment** considers the existing athletic program for safety and health care quality. School administrators and athletic staff receive a formal written report of the noted deficiencies and suggested corrective action plans.
- **Central Training Room** serviced by student trainers under adult supervision (preferably a Certified Athletic Trainer), with proper equipment, design and access for both boys and girls, provides services ranging from injury prevention, first aid, and rehabilitation for all student athletes. The Student Trainers Supervisor's Manual provides guidelines for selecting, utilizing, and evaluating student trainers.
- **Standardized Procedures** institute the daily use of written guidelines, checklists, protocols and record keeping. The Communications Manual explains the importance and use of special forms. Record keeping provides documentation and data for analysis.
- **Data Analysis and Observations** of each sport permit informative seasonal and year-end evaluative summaries on injury rates (injury surveillance system) and emergency preparedness/sideline safety for each sport. Through evaluation, quality assurance and accountability are maintained.

Evidence of Effectiveness Coaches and student trainers, after taking the course, show significant knowledge gains as well as greater concern and ability to recognize injuries. Participating schools demonstrate appropriate actions in emergency preparedness as well as effective organized management of injuries and health problems among student athletes.

Requirements Written support from school administration and local medical community; appointment of System coordinator for each school; assessment of the entire athletic program; required attendance by all coaches and student trainers at the educational session; formation of a central training room; appointment of student trainer supervisor; use of daily system procedures; accurate record keeping; full participation in the evaluative component of the system; a school-wide commitment to change; and attention to detail ensure successful implementation.

Costs Training costs for the five day course for coaches consist of $2500 for two instructors, plus travel costs for presenters and $50 per participant for course materials and supplies. Class size typically 20-30. Assessment Site Visit and 75 page written report $1000. National Leadership Institute (5 day course in Seattle—July 23-28, 1995) for one administrator, including room and board is $825. System supplies of forms and manuals is $435 initially, about $200 annually. Full evaluative services of sideline observation reports and injury surveillance data analysis are $60/sport/year—about $1000/year.

Services Awareness materials (literature and videotape) are available at no cost. Visitors are welcome by appointment at the program site and additional demonstration sites. Program staff welcome opportunities to attend out-of-state awareness meetings. Adoption services include: inservice training for System Administrator/ Coordinator (one person per school), preferably at summer National Leadership Institute in Seattle*; training for entire coaching staff and selected student trainers at the adoption site (approximately 20-30)*; system materials, manuals, record-keeping forms, guidelines and protocols; athletic program needs assessment report; evaluative services including injury data analysis, sideline safety observation reports; technical assistance and consultation as needed. Cost breakdown available upon request. *Three college credits (quarter system) are available for each course through the University of Washington.

Contact Stephen G. Rice, M.D., Athletic Health Care System, Division of Sports Medicine GB-15, University of Washington, Seattle, WA 98195. (206) 543-6734, FAX (206) 543-6573.

JDRP No. 82-37 (**7/21/82**)
Recertified (**5/1/87**)

Developmental Funding: USOE ESEA Title IV-C.

Every Child A Winner with Physical Education (ECAW). A developmentally appropriate physical education program which improves fitness, motor skills, and contributes to improved self-esteem and academic success for all children regardless of physical or mental ability, grades 1-3.

Audience   Originally approved by JDRP for students grades K-6, reapproved 1985 and 1991 by JDRP for grades 1-3. Components for grades 4-6 are still available and active.

Description   The Every Child A Winner with Physical Education (ECAW) program uses the concepts of space awareness, body awareness, qualities of movement and relationships as the basis for child-designed games, child-designed gymnastics sequences, and child-designed dance. The discovery learning or indirect teaching method is used to encourage critical thinking, one of the National Goals for Education. Children are given movement tasks which can be solved individually or within a group. Cooperation and competition are handled developmentally through educational games, educational dance, and educational gymnastics. Children are encouraged to reach their personal potential and winning occurs when each child does his or her best. A variety of solutions successfully answer each task posed by the teacher so children will not feel pressured or become embarrassed in the ECAW program. Inclusion has been a major focus of the program since its inception. Teacher implementers rate the program has a highly successful answer in physical education to meet special needs.

Training is designed to help classroom teachers, special educators, and physical educators implement the program. Phase I Training includes an accountability model for program implementation, teaching techniques for ECAW lessons, and training in program and fitness evaluation. Phase II Training (Continuation) provides more in-depth training and assistance in upper grade implementation. The program should be implemented first in K-3, with a plan for expanding to K-6.

Evidence of Effectiveness   Limited funds prevented a study of program effects on grades 4-6 in 1983. Therefore, JDRP reapproval covered only grades 1-3. However, the program has been successfully implemented in grades K-6 since 1974 in over 5,000 schools in 50 states, the Virgin Islands, and Canada. An evaluation (1983) involving a random sample of 3,800 students, pre- and posttesting using the Washington State Fitness Test, indicated significant gains (grades 1-3) in total fitness measures using a factor score composite. This same design was used to successfully recertify fitness in March, 1991.

Requirements   Program conducted by certified teachers. Pupil-teacher ratio 30:1. Training essential. Facilities needed are a multipurpose room or indoor area large enough for participation, as well as outdoor space to conduct lessons. A list of equipment, resource books, and training materials needed are available from the program.

Costs   Training costs consist of travel expenses plus trainer fees. Costs can be shared and negotiated.

Services   Awareness materials are available at no cost. Visitors are welcome at demonstration sites in their home state and out-of-state. Training may be conducted at the program site or adopter site. Program staff are available for awareness and technical training, implementation, and follow-up services.

Contact   Martha F. Owens or Susan B. Rockett, Every Child A Winner, Educational Excellence, Inc., P.O. Box 141, Ocilla, GA 31774. (912) 468-7098.

Developmental Funding: USOE ESEA Title III.

JDRP No. 74-60 **(6/6/74)**
Recertified **(3/29/91)**

Healthy For Life (HFL). A program designed to equip middle school students with the social competencies and life skills necessary to manage situations in which high risk behaviors are expected and rewarded by others. It seeks to improve health behaviors in nutrition, tobacco, alcohol, marijuana use, and sexuality.

Audience Approved by PEP for students in grades 6-8.

Description Healthy For Life (HFL) is a comprehensive program comprised of four components: (1) **Curriculum** that is cumulative, sequenced, and focused on health promotion lessons, activities, and teaching strategies; (2) **Peer Leadership** to employ students to teach through their words and actions; (3) **Family** to facilitate communication between the adolescent and one significant family member or other adult; and (4) **Community** to enlist community people actively working to reinforce the behavioral messages of the curriculum and launch an attack on the pervasive double-messages about the target behaviors that most communities transmit. Games, role plays, videos, cooperative learning activities, and hands-on demonstrations keep students engaged and participating. Homework, which involves students "interviewing" parents, encourages the sharing of family values and rules. Fifty-eight lessons are delivered sequentially in two distinct versions. The Age-Appropriate version provides lessons in sequence everyday for four weeks, first to one cohort of sixth graders and then to the same cohort as seventh and eighth graders. In this version, topics are addressed when they are most salient in the adolescent's life, and students build on their skills and experiences in previous grades. The Intensive version delivers the lessons in one sequential, twelve-week block to an entire cohort of seventh graders.

Evidence of Effectiveness Students participating in the Intensive version of HFL were significantly less likely to use cigarettes, more likely to eat more meals in a week, less likely to use smokeless tobacco, and scored significantly lower on an overall scale of substance abuse than students in control schools. Students in both treatment versions show movement in the positive direction on measures of alcohol and marijuana use and sexual intercourse rates.

Requirements At least two staff members need to participate in a 24-hour training. Time for Peer Leader training prior to and during the program must be in place. A partnership between the school and a parent or community group must exist. Two or three family or community leaders should attend the teacher training in order to become familiar with program goals/objectives and the Community Component protocol.

Costs Estimated total cost is $973.25 (per five classrooms of 25 students each and 18 peer leaders) to cover materials, Peer Leader certificates and prizes, films, nutrition unit, and student incentives. Cost for the 24-hour training session is $175 per person (assuming a statewide or regional training for up to 30 participants).

Services In addition to training and curriculum materials, follow-up consultation is available.

Contact Monica King, Pacific Institute for Research and Evaluation, 617 North Segoe Road, Suite 200, Madison, WI 53705. (608) 231-2334.

Developmental Funding: National Institute on Drug Abuse and local.

PEP No. 93-15 **(4/2/93)**

Know Your Body (KYB) School Health Promotion Program, The. A
multicomponent comprehensive school health promotion program for students in grades K-6 with the goal of empowering students with the skills they need to make their own positive health choices.

Audience   Approved by PEP for students in grades K-6.

Description   The Know Your Body (KYB) School Health Promotion Program consists of five basic components: (1) skills-based health education curriculum, (2) teacher/coordinator training, (3) biomedical screening, (4) extracurricular activities, and (5) program evaluation.

The curriculum and the teacher/coordinator training are considered the "core" components of the program, while the others are considered optional components or "enhancements." While implementation of the full KYB program is recommended, the program may be effectively implemented without the additional components. The American Health Foundation will assist schools to customize a program which best suits their needs, goals, philosophies, and capacities.

KYB curriculum materials include: Age-appropriate teacher's guides (grades K-6), student master sheets (grades K-3); student activity books (grades 4-6); a class Big Book (grade 1); and puppet sets (grades K-3). A comprehensive user's guide (Coordinator's Guide) is also available which provides detailed instructions for implementing all of KYB's program components.

The Program stresses individual responsibility for health and provides the basis for making health-promoting and disease-preventing decisions. Behavioral goals are geared toward outcomes that children of this age can realistically affect, such as breakfast and snack choices, and asking adults to not smoke in their presence.

It is recommended that the KYB program be taught a minimum of 40 minutes per week. Most teachers are able to use the program much more often because of its interdisciplinary approach.

The KYB program addresses the National Goals for Education in several ways. Through its substance use prevention, healthy relationship, and skill modules, the Program can help reduce drug use and violence (Goal 7). As part of the KYB training, program coordinators learn how to improve their school food service programs as well as how to achieve a smoke-free campus, thereby creating an "environment conducive to learning."

Evidence of Effectiveness   The results of several longitudinal evaluations have demonstrated that the KYB program has a significant positive effect on students' health-related knowledge, behavior, and biomedical risk factors such as serum cholesterol levels, blood pressure, cardiovascular endurance, smoking, and diet.

Requirements   Typically, the KYB program requires that a local program coordinator or trainer be trained by the American Health Foundation (AHF) staff. Once trained, this person can then conduct teacher trainings and support program implementation at their school site. The AHF hosts NDN-funded KYB Training Institutes biannually. The interaction of teachers, administrators, school food service personnel, and parents is key to the success of the Program. The involvement of local health agencies, hospitals, and health care professionals is also an important part of program effectiveness.

Costs   The first-year cost of the KYB core components is estimated to be $5 per student. In subsequent years this initial cost is reduced to $0 - 2 per student. Training costs consist of a $350 per diem plus travel expenses and workshop materials. (It is recommended that each participant have a teacher's guide [$40-$75] and a training packet [$15]).

Services   An awareness packet, which includes a sample module from the *Teachers' Guide*, is available for $5. The KYB staff will assist local coordinators with training, implementation, and evaluation of the program.

Contact   Jessica Cherry or Kerry Bozza, The American Health Foundation, 800 Second Avenue, New York, NY 10017. (212) 551-2507 or 551-2509.

Developmental Funding: National Heart, Lung, and Blood Institute, National Cancer Institute, and W.K. Kellogg Foundation.

PEP No. 89-1 **(3/24/89)**

Social Decision Making and Problem Solving. A program that teaches all children to "think clearly" when under stress. The program is curriculum-based and occurs in three developmental phases. The readiness phase targets self-control, group participation, and social awareness skills. The instructional phase teaches an eight-step social decision-making strategy to students. The application phase teaches children to use these skills in real life interpersonal and academic situations.

Audience Approved by PEP for teachers, administrators, guidance, child study team staff, and parents of children in grades K-6, both in regular and special education programs.

Description Social Decision Making and Problem Solving works by training educators and parents to equip children with skills in self-control and group participation, the use of an eight-step social decision-making strategy, and the practical know-how regarding the use of these skills in real life and academic areas.

The program is curriculum-based and occurs in three developmental phases. The readiness phase targets self-control, group participation and social awareness skills. The instructional phase teaches an eight-step social decision-making strategy to students. The application phase provides practice to help children apply these skills in real life interpersonal and academic situations.

The primary objective is to teach children a set of heuristic social decision-making thinking steps. Lessons are taught to the children on a regular basis by their classroom teacher. Extensive guided practice and role playing are used, as is skill modeling and the use of hypothetical social problem situations. Facilitative questioning and dialogue stimulates the integration of the techniques. And, cooperative group projects and writing assignments further advance that process.

The Social Decision Making program targets the National Goals for Education which address substance abuse and violence, the rights and responsibilities of citizenship, productive employment, and the critical thinking skills inherent in all aspects of academic and social learning.

Evidence of Effectiveness In pilot tests and published evaluations that have been emerging since 1979, teachers who were trained were found to improve in their ability to facilitate children's social decision-making and problem-solving. The children who received the program improved their social decision-making and problem-solving skills relative to control groups. Students also showed more prosocial behavior in school as well as greater ability to cope with stress upon their transition to middle school, when compared to control youngsters. Students who were followed up in high school showed high levels of positive, prosocial behavior and decreased anti-social, self-destructive and social disordered behavior when compared to controls.

Requirements At the building or district level, the school(s) is asked to form a Social Decision Making committee. This committee moves into a leadership role to provide guidance to the program's multiyear development as well as to provide consultation support to the teachers who are brought on board to teach the program. The committee should consist of some key teachers, representatives from the district/building administration, and such specialists as substance abuse counselors, guidance counselors and special education professionals.

Costs Training costs are negotiable and include a per diem plus travel expenses for the trainer and approximately $28 per participant (typically limited to 30 people) for workshop materials for a school building-based training. Costs for regional trainings may vary.

Services Awareness materials and presentations are available. Staff provide a two-day curriculum lab training workshop for those teachers and practitioners who will be teaching Social Decision Making directly to the students. Members of the Social Decision Making committee stay for a third day to prepare them for their role. Information is also available regarding how to bring parents on board with Social Decision Making. These trainings most often are offered on the school district site but are also available at our New Jersey location. All trainees become regular recipients of the program's newsletter, *The Problem Solving Connection*.

Contact John F. Clabby, Thomas Schuyler, or Linda Bruene, **University of Medicine and Dentistry of New Jersey-CMHC at Piscataway, 240 Stelton Road, Piscataway, NJ 08854-3248. (908) 235-4939** or Maurice Elias, **Department of Psychology, Rutgers University, New Brunswick, NJ 08903. (908) 932-2444.**

Developmental Funding: National Institute of Mental Health, William T. Grant Foundation, and Schumann Fund for New Jersey.

PEP No. 89-16 **(7/18/89)**

Audience Regular classroom teachers and physical education specialists in grades 3-6. The secondary audience is administrators, mentors, and supervisors who are responsible for physical education programs and instruction in elementary schools.

Description SPARK is a curriculum and staff development program designed to help elementary teachers provide quality physical education. Primary goals are to provide students with substantial amounts of physical activity through a program that can be implemented by trained specialists and classroom teachers. SPARK activities encourage maximum student participation during class time, as well as promote regular physical activity outside of school. The Physical Education Program promotes individual improvement, and students are encouraged to monitor their own progress. The curriculum calls for classes to be taught a minimum of 3 days/week throughout the school year. The yearly plan is divided into instructional units that are typically 4 weeks (12 lessons) in length. A standard 30-minute lesson has two parts: Type I Activities that focus on developing health-related fitness and locomotor skills and Type 2 Activities that focus on developing generalizable motor skills. The Self-Management Program is a classroom curriculum that teaches behavioral skills that are important for maintaining physical activity. Its emphasis is on behavior change skills rather than knowledge alone. The Teacher Training Program is designed to develop teachers' commitment to health-related physical education; help them understand SPARK curricular units and activities; and develop management and instructional skills for effective implementation. SPARK addresses National Educational Goal 3.

Evidence of Effectiveness SPARK is the product of a five-year National Institutes of Health grant and has been evaluated in a controlled trial. Current results show that students in the SPARK Program made significant improvements in cardiorespiratory fitness, muscular strength and endurance measures, and sport skills. In addition, teachers implementing SPARK provided significantly improved quantity and quality of physical education as evidenced by increased frequency and length of classes, fitness activities, skill drills, and the minutes children engaged in moderate to vigorous physical activity.

Requirements Commitment to quality physical education by the school district, site principals and teachers; commitment to training and follow-up consultations; and standard supplies and space to safely conduct active physical education.

Costs Costs depend upon location, number of teachers trained, amount of on-site follow-up desired, and available physical education supplies. Materials include SPARK Program video; physical education curriculum; self-management curriculum; black-line masters for student materials; and evaluation materials.

Services Awareness materials are available at no cost. Inservice training is provided at the adopting site. Costs include the Physical Education and the Self-Management curricula, trainer's honorarium, and travel expenses. Follow-up services for classroom teachers are strongly recommended.

Contact Dr. Thom McKenzie, Director, or Paul Rosengard, Coordinator, SPARK, San Diego State University, 6363 Alvarado Court, Suite 225, San Diego, CA 92120. (619) 594-4815, FAX (619) 594-4570.

Developmental Funding: National Institutes of Health.

PEP No. 94-6 (**3/1/94**)

Stanford Adolescent Heart Health Curriculum. A multiple-factor cardiovascular disease risk reduction/prevention curriculum for adolescents. Lifestyle factors such as cigarette smoking, diet, physical activity, and stress are targeted.

Audience Approved by PEP for students in grades 9 and 10.

Description The Stanford Adolescent Heart Health Curriculum is guided by social-cognitive theory and emphasizes self-regulatory skill development, building perceptions of self-efficacy, and social pressure resistance training. The curriculum consists of 16 classroom sessions, each lasting 50 minutes. It is divided into five component modules, Tobacco Use Prevention/Cessation, Physical Activity, Nutrition, Stress and Coping, and Personal Problem Solving, with the last module focused on intensive behavioral change. Each module provides students with: (1) information on the effects of different health practices; (2) normative information on the prevalence of unhealthy behaviors among peers; (3) cognitive and behavioral skills enabling them to change personal behavior; (4) specific skills for resisting social influences to adopt unhealthful habits; and (5) practice in using skills to improve performance. The curriculum features slide and music-slide presentations for most lessons, guided role-playing simulations, an introductory videodrama focused on personal choices and consequences, discussion sessions, and personal change student notebooks.

Evidence of Effectiveness Students participating in the program make significantly greater gains in knowledge of cardiovascular disease risk factors on program-developed and validated criterion-referenced tests; show beneficial physiologic/anthropometric effects in terms of resting heart rate, triceps skinfold thickness, and subscapular skinfold thickness; and are more likely to report that they would choose heart healthy snack items than a comparison group. A higher proportion of baseline "nonexercisers" participating in the program are classified as regular aerobic exercisers two months after completion of the curriculum; and more baseline "experimental smokers" participating in the program report quitting at follow-up and fewer report graduating to regular smoking than their comparison group counterparts.

Requirements Materials include a teacher guide, curriculum slides, introductory videodrama, and student handbook master. A computerized teacher training program with supplemental materials is available. Fifteen hours to complete the computerized training program and 45 minutes to prepare for each lesson are required.

Costs Start-up costs are $675 for equipment and $1000 for materials and supplies. An optional cost of $1400 for a Macintosh Classic with a computerized teacher training program and supplemental materials may be incurred.

Services In addition to training and curriculum materials, support materials for dissemination are available.

Contact Joel D. Killen, Ph.D., Stanford Center for Research in Disease Prevention, Stanford University School of Medicine, 1000 Welch Road, Palo Alto, CA 94304-1885. (415) 723-1000.

Developmental Funding: National Heart, Lung, and Blood Institute.   PEP No. 91-19 **(3/28/91)**

Teenage Health Teaching Modules (THTM). A comprehensive school health curriculum designed to provide adolescents with the knowledge, attitudes, and practices necessary to improve and/or maintain their health and well-being.

Audience Approved by PEP for grades 7-12.

Description Teenage Health Teaching Modules (THTM) is a series of 21 modules grouped by level for grades 7/8, 9/10, and 11/12. Modules range in length from six to fifteen class sessions, and address critical adolescent health issues such as violence prevention, tobacco, alcohol, and other drug use, and HIV/AIDS. THTM addresses National Goal for Education 6 by integrating injury/violence prevention and drug/alcohol prevention in a comprehensive school health curriculum.

Evidence of Effectiveness In a controlled evaluation study, THTM students had a strong, positive net gain in health knowledge. Compared to control groups, THTM students also had a net gain in health-related attitudes and total health practices.

Requirements No special facilities or equipment are necessary to implement THTM. THTM training for teachers implementing the program is strongly recommended. Contact Education Development Center, Inc. (EDC) for more information on teacher training. EDC sponsors a three-day training of trainers workshop.

Costs The cost of teacher training varies, depending upon who delivers the training. Individual modules may be purchased separately; the cost ranges from $15-$50. The total package for grades 7/8 is $300; the grade 9/10 package is $295; and the grade 11/12 package is $165. The complete package for grades 7-12 is $655. Orders above $3,000 receive a 25% discount. The cost of photocopying student handouts varies, depending upon how many modules are used at each grade level.

Services Training of THTM trainers is available from EDC, as are all curriculum materials. Teacher training is available from trainers located throughout the U.S.

Contact Lynn Watkins, Project Director, Education Development Center, Inc. (EDC), 55 Chapel Street, Newton, MA 02160. (800) 225-4276 or (617) 969-7100. E-Mail: lwatkins@edc.org

Developmental Funding: U.S. Department of Health and Human Services, Centers for Disease Control; U.S. Agency for International Development; U.S. Department of Justice; Metropolitan Life Foundation; Boston (MA) Department of Health and Hospitals; Michigan Department of Education and Michigan Department of Public Health; and Education Development Center, Inc.

PEP No. 93-14 (4/2/93)

CASPAR Alcohol and Drug Education Series. A curriculum to improve attitudes and cognitive knowledge related to alcohol and alcoholism. Approved for all students in grades 7-12.

Description The CASPAR Alcohol and Drug Education Series has modules for elementary grades K-3 and 3-6, intermediate grades 7-8, and high school grades 9-12. Each unit is designed for seven to ten 45-minute teaching periods, with flexibility for expansion or contraction. Factual information, personal and societal attitudes about alcohol, and decision-making and refusal skills are covered during the first six or seven periods, with alcoholism covered only during the last one to three periods when children who are experiencing family problems will be more ready to accept this information. The curricula emphasizes high student involvement through participatory activities such as debates, role plays, polls, drawings, and small-group discussions. Activities focus on real life issues and situations, and convey repeated and consistent messages about safe behavior and responsible decision making. Evaluation evidence from a number of sites indicates that proper implementation facilitates referrals increases knowledge and affects attitudes, and that these changes remain for at least a year. Published evidence also suggests that repeated exposure may decrease rates of problem drinking.

CASPAR has revised its curricula to include drug education units at all grade levels to be used in conjunction with its alcohol units. The drug lessons include participatory activities, age-appropriate information, and emphasize a nonuse message.

Contact   Priscilla J.G. Quirk, M.Ed., Associate Director, CASPAR Alcohol and Drug Education Program, 226 Highland Avenue, Somerville, MA 02143. (617) 623-2080.

Developmental Funding: (info. not available).

JDRP No. 82-42 **(10/28/82)**
Recertified **(6/23/87)**

CHOICE, Project. A cancer prevention program for students grades K-12. Approved by JDRP for students grades K-12.

Description Project CHOICE is a cancer prevention and risk-reduction curriculum for students in grades K-12. The program lessons are taught during a two-week time period at each grade level. The Project CHOICE curriculum consists of comprehensive, sequential units which promote three primary learning goals: (1) Students will learn cancer information and components of cancer risk; (2) Students will learn a rational process of information evaluation and decision making; and (3) Students will assume the locus of responsibility for behaviors leading to cancer risk-reduction and wellness.

The curriculum kits include original filmstrips, experiments, decision-making scenarios, group work, classroom reports, debates and discussions. The overall program emphasis is on positive health promotion, personal responsibility for health, the role of health professionals, and an understanding of risk and risk-reduction concept. The lesson themes attempt to replace a fear of cancer with a positive and active approach to maintaining health. At different grade levels the units deal with seven broad areas of cancer risk: Host Factors; Drugs—including alcohol and tobacco; Occupational Hazards; Stress; Environmental Factors—including radiation exposure; Nutrition; and Sun Exposure.

Not all cancers can or will be eliminated by cancer risk-reduction practices; therefore, students are taught to understand and recognize cancer warning signs, methods of early detection, appropriate treatment, and unproven methods of cancer treatment. By developing their own personal cancer risk-reduction plans, students enhance their awareness of their own responsibility for their health. Teachers are provided with complete lesson plans, student learning objectives, a *Cancer Resource Guide* with information that corresponds to lesson content, and all teaching materials.

Contact   Sarah Miller, Project Director, Project CHOICE-MP 951, Fred Hutchinson Cancer Research Center, 1124 Columbia Street, Seattle, WA 98104. (206) 467-4679.

JDRP No. 83-18 **(3/8/83)**
Recertified **(6/16/87)**

Developmental Funding: National Cancer Institute.

Curriculum for Meeting Modern Problems (The New Model Me—2nd Edition). Designed to help students understand the causes and consequences of behavior. Approved by JDRP for all students in grades 9-12. Used as a course in itself or to supplement existing courses.

Description The New Model Me—2nd Edition provides students with a basic understanding of why people behave as they do. It assists students in understanding the available alternatives for solving personal problems and the short- and long-term consequences of those alternatives. Dr. Ralph H. Ojemann's causal approach to behavior is the central theme of the 374-page student text. Young people increase their personal resources and improve their self-identity. They are given a framework for making constructive choices in critical decisions such as those regarding drug and alcohol use and conflict resolution. The student text, reproduced in its entirety in the teacher's manual, includes units on: *Human Behavior, Self-Identity,* and *Controls, Decision Making, and Change: The New Model Me.* The curriculum is student-centered, emphasizes esteem-building, has an attractive format, and a balance between structure and freedom for the teacher. It integrates the cognitive and affective domains, enhances reading skills, presents clear objectives, and highlights key words and phrases. It uses contemporary activities that are both personalized and integrated into the curriculum, provides ample opportunities for students to apply newly acquired knowledge, incorporates a balanced mix of text and visuals, and includes a practical teacher's manual containing a rich assortment of specially prepared materials to facilitate instruction. The New Model Me—2nd Edition fits well in social studies, language arts, health, home economics, psychology, orientation, vocational education, family living, special education, driver training, and a variety of programs for at-risk students.

Contact   John R. Rowe, Director, 15 Tuckaway Drive, Asheville, NC 28803. (704) 684-4543.

Developmental Funding: USOE ESEA Title III.   JDRP No. 74-73 **(5/29/74)**

Growing Healthy ®. A comprehensive health education program designed to foster student competencies to make decisions enhancing their health and lives. Approved by JDRP for grades K-6.

Description Growing Healthy includes a planned sequential curriculum, a variety of teaching methods, a teacher training program, and strategies for eliciting community support for school health education. Through group and individual activities, children learn about themselves by learning about their bodies. There is one 8-12 week unit for grades K through 6. Each grade studies a separate unit specifically designed for that age group. The units include an introduction of the five senses, feelings, caring for health, and general health habits; the senses of taste, touch, and smell and their roles in communicating health information; the emotions and communication methods with regard to sight and hearing; the skeletal and muscular systems; the digestive system; the respiratory system; the circulatory system; and the nervous system. Throughout all grades, health information about safety, nutrition, environment, drugs and alcohol, hygiene, fitness, mental health, disease prevention, consumer health wellness, and life style is explored and reinforced. Access to a variety of stimulating learning resources, including audio-visuals, models, community health workers, and reading materials, is abundantly provided. The curriculum is designed to integrate with the lives and personality development of children by providing situations in which they may assume responsibility, research ideas, share knowledge, discuss values, make decisions, and create activities to illustrate their comprehension and internalization of concepts, attitudes, and feelings. The curriculum has been developed to enhance other school subjects such as reading, writing, arithmetic, physical education, science, and the creative arts. Twenty-four separate studies have been completed including a ten-year longitudinal study. These studies indicate that Growing Healthy was effective in increasing health-related knowledge and providing positive health-related attitudes. Growing Healthy requires a school team comprised of two classroom teachers, the principal, and one or more curriculum support persons to receive training in the grade level being adopted.

Contact   Michele Reich, Director of Education, Evaluation and Training, National Center for Health Education, 72 Spring Street, Suite 208, New York, NY 10012. (212) 334-9470.

Developmental Funding: Grades K-3 JDRP No. 80-6 **(5/23/80)** Recertified **(12/12/84)**
HEW and U.S. Public Health Services.   Grades 5-7 JDRP No. 79-14 **(5/8/79)** Recertified **(3/1/85)**

ME-ME Drug & Alcohol Prevention Education Program. A school-based, multidisciplinary, year-long prevention program that helps improve children's self-esteem, their ability to solve problems and make responsible decisions, and increases their knowledge about the dangers of all drugs. Approved by JDRP for all students in grades 1-6.

Description The ME-ME Drug & Alcohol Prevention Education Program was developed to improve low self-esteem and other conditions found to be evident in most young people and adults who abuse drugs and alcohol. The program places great emphasis on enhancing the self-esteem of children during their formulative years when most of their learning and identifying who they are takes place. Children learn to make responsible decisions by learning how to predict the consequences of their choices and to recognize and resist negative peer influences. They receive the most up-to-date information about the dangers of all drugs including prescription, over-the-counter medicines, and alcohol. The ME-ME Program meets the **National Goals for Education** that pertain to: (1) **student achievement** and **citizenship**; and (2) **safe, disciplined, drug-free schools**. All classroom teachers (**K-6**) are responsible for implementing the program and coordinating their teaching styles with the program's goals. Activities are incorporated into **all areas of the curriculum** as well as **noncurriculum areas**. An entirely **new curriculum** has been written and **expanded** to include other areas of concern. A **parent component** has been added that includes areas not previously explored in other programs. All teachers must attend a **six-hour training** conducted at their site. **Program expenses include manuals for each teacher costing $48 per set ($18 for kindergarten teachers), travel, lodging,** and **meal expenses for the trainer.** Everything used in the program is found in the manuals. Technical assistance is available. General information about the program is available at no cost and program staff are **available to conduct awareness sessions**.

Contact   Artie Kearney, Ph.D., Executive Director, ME-ME, Inc., 426 West College Avenue, Appleton, WI 54911. (414) 735-0114 .

Developmental Funding: USOE ESEA Title III.   JDRP No. 75-47 **(5/15/75)**

Ombudsman. A school-based drug education/primary prevention program. Approved by JDRP for students of all abilities, grades 5-6.

Description Ombudsman is a structured course designed to reduce certain psychological and attitudinal states closely related to drug use. Through experiential activities, *Ombudsman* teaches healthy living skills and emphasizes information about drugs.

The course has three major phases. The first phase focuses on self-awareness and includes a series of exercises permitting students to gain a wider understanding and appreciation of their values as autonomous individuals.

The second phase teaches group skills and provides students with an opportunity to develop communication, decision-making, and problem-solving techniques that can be applied in the immediate class situation as well as in other important group contexts such as with family and peers.

The third phase is in many ways the most important: the class uses the insights and skills gained during the first two phases to plan and carry out the program within the community or school. During this phase, students have an opportunity to experience the excitement and satisfaction of reaching out to others in a creative and constructive way. The program is designed for thirty 50-minute implementation sessions.

Contact   Helen Harrill, Training Coordinator, The Drug Education Center, 1117 East Morehead, Charlotte, NC 28204. (704) 375-3784, FAX (704) 333-3784.

                                                                                    JDRP No. 78-194 **(6/12/79)**
                                                                                    Recertified **(1/85)**

Developmental Funding: HEW and National Institute on Drug Abuse.

Physical Management. Physical education designed to meet the needs of overweight students. Approved by JDRP for students in grades 10-12.

Description The Physical Management program was developed to give overweight students, grades 10-12, the knowledge and opportunity to interrupt the cycle of obesity and inactivity that prevents a fully healthy and effective lifestyle. The curriculum includes:

1. **Behavior change** - to replace inappropriate eating and exercise habits which have led to obesity and poor physical condition.

2. **Physical conditioning** - to enable students to evaluate their fitness and body composition, and design a conditioning program based on principles of exercise prescription.

3. **Nutrition education** - to provide practical nutrition education by teaching food group selection, portion control, and caloric density of foods.

4. **Positive image building** - to set the stage for positive change through goal setting, social skills, and assertiveness training.

Enrollees may earn either required or elective physical education credit. Physical Management can be implemented in schools of any size with minimal cost and adaption. No new staff or special facilities are required.

A complimentary awareness packet is available. Program staff are available to attend awareness and training sessions (costs to be paid by host).

Contact   Eileen Solberg, Director, Physical Management, P.O. Box 891, Billings, MT 59103. (406) 252-4822.

Developmental Funding: ESEA Title IV-C.   JDRP No. 84-3 **(3/13/84)**

Section 10

Multidisciplinary/ Cognitive Skills

Summary of Program Services for Section 10

Program	Goal*	Page	Dissem. Funds Available — NDN	Other	AWARENESS: Costs to Potential Adopter — Hon	Trav	Per Diem	On Site Visitation — Home Site	Adopt Site	Materials Available — Free Paper	Video	Film Strip	Other	TRAINING: Staff Available — Home Site	Adopt Site	Costs to Adopter — Hon	Trav	Per Diem	Certified Trainers Available — State(s)	Training Time Required — Day(s)
Adventure, Project	3	10-16				✓	✓	✓	✓	✓	✓	✓	✓	✓	✓		✓	✓	AL, CA, CO, CT, FL, GA, MA, ME, MI, NC, NH, NJ, NV, NY, PA, SC, SD, TN, VA, VT, ONTARIO, NEW ZEALAND, AUSTRALIA	3+
CHAPTER I H.O.T.S.: Higher Order Thinking Skills Project	3	10-1	✓	✓	(negotiable)				✓	✓	✓			(regional)		(negotiable)			AK, AZ, CA, CO, IL, IN, MA, ME, MI, MN, MO, NC, NM, NY, PA, TX	3+
CLIMB Plus	3	10-2	✓		(negotiable)			✓	✓	✓	✓			✓	✓	✓		✓	AZ, IL, KY, MO, NC, NJ, NY, VI	1
Computer Assisted Diagnostic Prescriptive ... (CADPP)	3, 5	10-3			(negotiable)				✓	✓	✓		✓	✓	✓	(negotiable)			FL, HI, IL, MS, NC, OK, PA, TN, WA, WV	1
Computers Helping Instruction ... (Project CHILD)	3	10-4	✓						✓	✓	✓				✓		✓	✓	FL	3
CReating Independence ... (Project CRISS)	3	10-5	✓	✓	(negotiable)			✓	✓	✓	✓			✓	✓		✓	✓	AR, AS, AZ, CO, CT, D.C., FL, GA, HI, IA, ID, IL, MA, ME, MI, MN, MO, MT, NC, NM, OR, RI, SC, TN, TX, UT, VA, VT, WI	2
Critical Analysis and Thinking Skills (CATS)	3	10-6			✓	✓	✓	✓	✓	✓	✓			✓	✓	✓	(negotiable)		HI, IA, MD, MN, NE, NJ, NM, NY, OH, UT	1
Davis County Indian Homework ... (IHC)	3	10-7	(info. not available)																	
Gulfport Follow Through ... (UGA)	3	10-16			✓	✓	✓	✓	✓	✓	✓			✓	✓	✓	✓	✓	GA, ID, MS, SC	3+
Increase Maximal ... (IMPACT)	3	10-8	✓		✓	✓	✓	✓	✓	✓	✓		✓	✓	✓				(none)	3+

* National Goals for Education—definitions for each goal can be found on pages 5-7.

Summary of Program Services for Section 10 (cont'd)

Program	Goal*	Page	Dissem. Funds Available (NDN)	Dissem. Funds Available (Other)	AWARENESS – Costs to Potential Adopter (Hon)	(Trav)	(Per Diem)	On Site Visitation (Home Site)	On Site Visitation (Adopt Site)	Materials (Free Paper)	Materials (Video)	Materials (Film Strip)	Materials (Other)	TRAINING – Staff Available (Home Site)	Staff Available (Adopt Site)	Costs to Adopter (Hon)	(Trav)	(Per Diem)	Certified Trainers Available – State(s)	Training Time Required (Day(s))
Institute for Creative Education (ICE)	3	10-17			✓	✓	✓	✓	✓	✓	✓			✓	✓	✓	✓	✓	AK, AZ, IL, KS, MI, NJ, NV, OK, OR, UT, WA, WY	2
Interdependent Learning Model (ILM)	1, 3	10-17		✓	✓	✓	✓	✓	✓	✓				✓	✓	✓	✓	✓	GA, NJ, NY	5
Kids Interest Discovery Studies KITS (KIDS KITS)	3	10-9			✓	✓	✓	✓	✓	✓	✓			✓	✓	✓	✓	✓	AK, AL, CO, GA, Guam, IN, KY, LA, MA, MN, MO, MT, NC, NE, NY, OK, OR, SC, TX, WA, WI	<1
Leflore County (Mississippi) Follow Through Project	3	10-18			✓	✓	✓	✓	✓	✓	✓			✓	✓	✓	✓	✓	MI, MS	3+
Literacy Links	3	10-10	✓		(negotiable)			✓	✓	✓				✓	✓	✓	✓	✓	AZ, ID, MI, MS, OK, SC, TX	1-3
Multicultural Reading and Thinking (McRAT)	3	10-11		✓	✓	✓		✓	✓	✓					✓	✓	✓		AR	9
Philosophy for Children	3	10-12	✓		(negotiable)			✓	✓	✓	✓			✓	✓	(negotiable)			CA, CO, HI, IA, IL, MA, MD, ME, MI, MN, ND, NJ, NY, OK, OR, PA, SC, TX, VA, WA, WI	2
Questioning and Understanding . . . (QUILT)	3	10-13	✓		(info. not available)								✓							
Student Team Learning (STL)	3, 5	10-18		✓	✓	✓	✓	✓	✓	✓				✓	✓	✓	✓	✓	CA, IN, LA, MD, NY, OH, PA, TN, TX	1-3
Study Skills Across the Curriculum	3	10-14	✓		✓	✓	✓	✓	✓	✓	✓			✓	✓	✓	✓	✓	AK, KS, MN, NE, NH, NY, OK, OR, WI	2
Systems Approach . . . (SAII)	3	10-19			✓	✓	✓	✓	✓	✓	✓			✓	✓	✓	✓	✓	(none)	2

* National Goals for Education—definitions for each goal can be found on pages 5-7.

Summary of Program Services for Section 10 (cont'd)

Program	Goal*	Page	AWARENESS														TRAINING			
			Dissem. Funds Available		Costs to Potential Adopter			On Site Visitation Available		Materials Available				Staff Available		Costs to Adopter			Certified Trainers Available	Training Time Required
			NDN	Other	Hon	Trav	Per Diem	Home Site	Adopt Site	Free Paper	Video	Film Strip	Other	Home Site	Adopt Site	Hon	Trav	Per Diem	State(s)	Day(s)
Talents Unlimited	2, 3, 5, 6	10-15	✓			✓	✓	✓	✓	✓	✓		✓	✓	✓	✓	✓	✓	AK, AL, AR, Canada, CO, CT, FL, GA, Germany, IA, ID, IL, IN, KS, KY, MA, MD, ME, Mexico, MI, MT, NC, ND, NH, NV, NY, OH, OK, OR, PA, SC, SD, TN, TX, UT, VA, WA, WI, WY	2

* National Goals for Education—definitions for each goal can be found on pages 5-7.

CHAPTER I H.O.T.S.: Higher Order Thinking Skills Project. An alternative approach to Chapter 1 for grades 4-6 in which compensatory services consist solely of higher order thinking activities.

Audience Approved by PEP for Chapter I students in grades 4-6 in both reading and math. This project has also been used successfully with Chapter I students in grade 7, learning disabled in grades 4-6, and gifted in grades K-2.

Description The CHAPTER I H.O.T.S.: Higher Order Thinking Skills Project (H.O.T.S.) replaces traditional drill and practice activities and content instruction in compensatory programs with thinking activities designed to generate the gains in basic skills expected from Chapter I programs. Students' thinking abilities and social confidence are improved in the process. The goal is to provide students with conceptual skills to learn the more sophisticated content of the upper elementary grade levels the first time it is taught in the classroom.

The program is conducted in a lab, equipped with Apple computers (Apple IIe, Apple IIgs, or Macintosh LC), with a detailed curriculum and a teacher trained in Socratic dialogue techniques. Computers are used to enhance motivation and improve students' ability to self-monitor their own comprehension. A detailed curriculum provides dialogues to improve the key thinking skills of metacognition, inference from context, decontextualization, and information synthesis. Students' increased abilities to articulate ideas and engage in sophisticated conversations enhance their language use and ability to learn content, with gains in both reading and math.

The program operates as a pull-out. Students are in the program for 35 minutes a day, four days a week, for two years. In the first part of the period, the teacher engages students in sophisticated conversations. Students are then given a challenge to solve using the computer. They later discuss their findings, approaches, and results. Teacher judgment determines the pace through the curriculum. Success is demonstrated by products generated by each student, how they articulate their findings, and the results they record.

H.O.T.S. directly addresses Goal 3 (Student Achievement and Citizenship. Activities in H.O.T.S. are specifically designed to increase cognitive development in ways that will transfer to gains in basic skill achievement, thus meeting the following Goal 3 objectives: (1) academic performance of elementary and secondary students will increase significantly and (2) students [will] demonstrate the ability to reason, solve problems, apply knowledge, and write and communicate effectively.

Evidence of Effectiveness As a result of participation in the program, Chapter 1 students in grades 4-6 improved their performance in reading and math to a greater extent than national averages and control groups, while also improving thinking ability as measured by the ROSS and "Inference from Context" measures. Improved self-concept and improved participation in content learning in the classroom were also evident. Studies were conducted in 11 schools encompassing a wide range of ethnic characteristics.

Requirements The program requires a computer lab, using Apple IIe, IIgs, or Macintosh LC computers, and an experienced teacher who is trained in Socratic coaching techniques. A week-long workshop is provided to train teachers in these techniques.

Costs Training, two year curricula, and support are a total of $1,600 for the first teacher trained at a school site. Each additional teacher trained for that school is $850. Support includes program research, telephone support, newsletters, and curriculum updates.

Services Awareness materials are available at no cost. Project staff is available to attend out-of-state awareness meetings and for training and technical assistance (costs to be negotiated).

Contact Christi Estrada or Dr. Stanley Pogrow, University of Arizona, College of Education, Tucson, AZ 85721. (602) 621-1305, FAX (602) 621-9373.

Developmental Funding: U.S. Department of Education and Ford Foundation. PEP No. 88-12 **(7/13/88)**

CLIMB Plus. Designed to improve a total school program in grades K-12 by integrating reading/writing, study skills, and mathematics across the curriculum through a comprehensive management system.

Audience PEP approved for all students K-12, including regular and ungraded classroom, Chapter 1, special education, at-risk, migrant, ESL, and after school programs for public and nonpublic school programs.

Description The goal of CLIMB Plus is to improve the performance of all students in reading, writing, study skills, and mathematics through the following components.

Curriculum framework, a coordinated program of instruction produced by teachers which includes:

- **Planning Arrays.** Identifies reading, study skills, and mathematic outcomes K-12.
- **Writing Bank.** Connects reading/writing/thinking and math skills to all content areas.
- **Assessments.** Provides ongoing information to assess student strengths and weaknesses through survey diagnostic and criterion referenced measures and a variety of performance based assessments incorporating portfolios.

- **Simplified Record Keeping System.** Monitors continuous student progress K-12. Available in a computerized format maining a complete history of students.
- **Strategies.** Combines skills and disciplines for an integrated, interdisciplinary approach.

Training, provides teachers with a systematic way to manage a student's instructional program in reading/writing and mathematics. Training includes:

- **Use of the Curriculum Framework.** A hands-on approach coordinating the CLIMB Plus framework into a school's materials, resources, objectives, and philosophy.
- **Procedures for Classroom Management and Implementation.** Teachers working collaboratively develop a classroom plan around the CLIMB Plus framework based on their materials, teaching style, and student needs and interests.
- **Active Learning Strategies and Models.** Mathematics-Congruent with NCTM Standards. Provides a hands-on approach moving from the concrete to linking to applied and mathematical problem solving. Reading/writing training integrated the CLIMB Plus framework into a whole language, literature-based, or basal approach. Training includes utilization of our Bank of Preparations for Instruction and writing strategies that go along with pieces of literature, themes, and content.
- **Content Reading and Study Skills Strategies for all Disciplines.**
- **Follow-Up Training.** Designed to meet the needs of adopting schools.

Management Design: Coordinates and Integrates Personnel, Materials, and Services.

- Provides a design for communication between classroom instruction and support services.
- Offers a system for coordination within and across grade levels and programs.
- Fosters a collaborative team approach to achieve instructional goals.
- Delineates roles for project coordination.

CLIMB Plus provides a means to tie together existing curriculum, textbooks, materials, goals and outcomes in a clear, concise program tailored to an individual school's needs. CLIMB Plus creates a cohesive curriculum framework for continuous student progress. The program addresses Goal 3 of the National Goals for Education.

Evidence of Effectiveness CLIMB Plus significantly increases and sustains the academic achievement of regular and compensatory education students in reading and mathematics, grades K-12, as measured by nationally recognized standardized achievement tests and as compared with national norms.

Requirements Teachers and administrators participate in training for effective utilization of CLIMB Plus curriculum and management design. Follow-up training sessions are recommended. Teachers must be supplied with the CLIMB Plus curriculum materials. The program can be adopted in reading/writing and/or mathematics at any or all grade levels and programs. CLIMB Plus can be implemented by a district, school, or a team of teachers.

Costs Start-up costs are approximately $85-$160 per classroom teacher for curriculum materials and supplies. Maintenance costs are minimal. Training costs are negotiable.

Services Awareness materials are available at no cost. Visitors are welcome at the Project site by appointment. Project staff are available to attend out-of-state awareness meetings. Implementation and follow-up services are available to adopters.

Contact Barbara Brenner, Director, CLIMB Plus, Middlesex Public Schools, 300 Kennedy Drive, Middlesex, NJ 08846. (908) 968-4494 or (908) 968-2666.

Developmental Funding: NJ TEEA R&D and USOE ESEA Title IV-C.

JDRP No. 81-44 (**1/28/82**)
Recertified (**3/25/93**)

Computer Assisted Diagnostic Prescriptive Program (CADPP) in Reading and Mathematics.
A computer managed program which generates educational plans as the basis for a diagnostic/prescriptive approach to instruction, used as a reading program for grades 3-9 and as a mathematics program for grades 3-7.

Audience Approved by JDRP as a reading program for grades 3-9 and as a mathematics program for grades 3-7.

Description Computer Assisted Diagnostic Prescriptive Program (CADPP) in Reading and Mathematics is a relational database software program that provides an alternative for teachers who manually prepare individual student prescriptions, by automating the task of preparing Individualized Educational Plans (IEPs). CADPP was developed for administrators, teachers, and parents of ECIA Chapter I students (formerly ESEA Title I) to meet Chapter I's federal requirement to develop and maintain an IEP for participating Chapter I students. Prior to the development of CADPP, IEPs were manually written, and required several hours of teacher planning and documentation. CADPP has now made available to educational programs an automated method for meeting the federal regulations of ECIA Chapter I and compensatory programs. CADPP's use of student prescriptions (IEPs), based on documented learner needs, has been automated to maximize instructional time and minimize the teacher's time-consuming, clerical activities. The relational database requires that the user customize CADPP to the local educational program by loading files with: (1) the adopter's learning objectives or curriculum; (2) learning characteristics of individual students served to include age, instructional level, and identified learning modality; and (3) concept-related characteristics of available instructional materials to include readability level, interest level, and learning modality. When the skills', students', and instructional materials' files are loaded in the database, customized prescriptions (IEPs) can be generated for each participating student. In addition to student IEPs, CADPP produces additional supplemental reports for school administrators and parents: (1) a skill mastery report, by student, for any time period indicated; (2) an instructional activities report by student, by skill, for any period indicated; and (3) an instructional materials report, by skill, by teacher. In addition to addressing Goals 3 and 5 of the National Goals for Education, CADPP program goals are to: (1) satisfy federal regulations governing the assessment, monitoring, and evaluation of compensatory education programs; (2) provide educators with an automated management system which minimizes record-keeping activities while maximizing the time available for instruction; (3) ensure that the pre- and posttest NCE gains in reading and mathematics for participating students will be greater than national average NCE gains; (4) maximize the use of existing available instructional materials and computer hardware, thus protecting the adopter's financial investments; and (5) enhance the educational service provider's current method for delivery of services.

Evidence of Effectiveness CADPP's claim is that participating students will exceed an annual NCE gain of zero. The trend for average gains in CADPP Reading programs has been greater than 5.0 NCEs, while the average gain in CADPP Mathematics programs has been greater than 7.0 NCEs. These results, when compared to the national NCE gains in compensatory education programs, are 90% greater in reading and 80% greater in mathematics.

Requirements CADPP operates on computers that read Apple BASIC and MS DOS (V 3.1 or greater). The Apple BASIC version requires two 5-1/4" disk drives; and the MS DOS requires a minimum 2 MB hard drive. Awareness materials (printed literature, a "boiler-plate" grant application document, and a 45-minute videotape) are available at no cost. A demonstration copy of the MS DOS version is available for $10. Program staff are available to attend out-of-state awareness meetings, conduct training at the adopter site, and to provide follow-up services to adopters. Training requires approximately three hours. No consulting fees are charged, and travel and per diem costs are negotiated with the user. A one-time fee of $99 is charged for the Apple BASIC version and $199 for the MS DOS version. In the commercial market, CADPP is comparable in design to Paradox, DataBase IV+, and R Base System V, systems that can cost the user up to $5,000 per school.

Costs Please see Requirements.

Contact   Debra J. Roberson, Technology in Education Corporation, Inc., 1844 West 85th Avenue, J-266, Merrillville, IN 46410. (219) 769-1712.

JDRP No. 79-15 (6/12/79)
Recertified (3/5/92)

Developmental Funding: USOE ESEA Title I.

Computers Helping Instruction and Learning Development (Project CHILD).
A computer-integrated instructional program for the elementary school. The goals are to: (1) modify the school structure and create classroom conditions conducive for learning with technology; (2) create cohesive units of work that foster strategies for thinking; and (3) realign curriculum for reading, language arts, and mathematics so as to cover legally mandated content while fully integrating computer technology into the curriculum.

Audience   Approved by PEP for students in grades K-5.

Description   Computers Helping Instruction and Learning Development (Project CHILD) seeks to modify the school structure and create classroom conditions conducive for learning with technology, create cohesive units of work that foster strategies for thinking, and realign curriculum for reading, language arts, and mathematics. It provides a system for fully integrating technology into reading, math, and language arts, and classroom management techniques for using computers and hands-on learning. It also offers strategies for teaming, cooperative learning, and parent involvement. Three classrooms form a Project CHILD cluster, grades K-2 or 3-5. Each of the three cluster teachers becomes a content specialist for one of the three Project CHILD subject areas in addition to being responsible for one grade-level classroom. Students from each grade in the cluster move among the classrooms to spend one hour per day working in each of the three subject areas. Thus teachers work in their specialty with the same students for three years. A Project CHILD classroom is organized with learning stations, and each has a computer station with 3-6 computers, a teacher station for small-group instruction, textbook and writing stations, and hands-on activity stations. Students follow a precise management plan for moving to the stations and set goals and record their activities in a book called a Passport. Required curriculum content is covered in six-week thematic units.

Project CHILD addresses the National Goals for Education by serving as an effective dropout prevention strategy; increasing the academic performance of elementary students; providing a systematic approach to develop reasoning ability, problem solving, decision making, and knowledge application; focusing on systematic approaches to writing and communicating effectively; and emphasizing mathematics concept development in the early grades.

Evidence of Effectiveness   School-by-school and pooled effect sizes by grade derived from standardized test score data reveal positive effect sizes in reading and math for CHILD students and significantly large effect sizes for students in lower-achieving schools and for those who participated for more than one year in the program. CHILD students have 2% fewer retentions overall, 6% fewer discipline referrals, and higher self-esteem and more positive attitudes toward school than non-CHILD students. Teachers express positive opinions toward the program.

Requirements   Two days of training are required for teachers and the principal before implementation of the program, with one day of follow-up training at midsemester. A computer aide is required in the primary cluster classrooms to assist children in doing tasks such as selecting designated software and reading lesson menus. Obtaining full support from the superintendent and district staff, school board members, and parents is advised.

Costs   Start-up cost for a six-classroom K-5 unit with 180 students for CHILD materials, training, and on-site support is $11,500. Cost for renewal materials is $1,000.

Services   In addition to training and materials, follow-up site visits and consultation are provided.

Contact   Sarah M. (Sally) Butzin, Daniel Memorial Institute, Inc., P.O. Box 13296, Tallahassee, FL 32317-3296. (904) 385-6985 or (800) 940-6985.

Developmental Funding: Florida State University College of Education and Florida Department of Education.

PEP No. 91-10 (**4/92**)

Audience Approved by PEP for all students in grades 4-12.

Description CReating Independence through Student-owned Strategies (Project CRISS) is designed to help students learn more effectively throughout the curriculum. Project CRISS focuses on teaching students how to learn through reading, writing, talking, and listening. Students learn to apply CRISS strategies in all subjects. The program focuses on the following areas:

- Principles and philosophy of learning.
- Identifying the author's craft and design.
- Understanding patterns and structure.
- Discussion—the conversation of learning.
- Active strategies for learning—generating background knowledge, concept mapping, free-form mapping, and summarizing.
- Organizing for learning—notes, charts, and story plans.
- Informal writing to learn—learning logs.
- Formal writing to learn—reports and essays.
- Authentic assessment strategies.

Project CRISS offers creative and motivating strategies for students in the regular classroom, and, in addition, is effective with special needs and "at-risk" students. The program assists teachers and students in integrating curriculum, and it is an invaluable tool for collaboration among teachers.

During the two-day training, participants have an opportunity to learn and practice the various reading and writing strategies using narrative and expository selections. Time is built into the training for teachers to develop learning activities with their own curriculum materials. No additional equipment or materials are required for the program to be successfully implemented.

Evidence of Effectiveness Students (grades 4, 6, 8, and 11) participating in Project CRISS demonstrate significantly greater gains ($p<.001$) in the retention of subject specific information than comparable nontreatment students when assessed by a free recall technique. Information measures also indicate that Project CRISS students apply more effective learning strategies on their own. In 1985, the JDRP validated Project CRISS as an effective, replicable program for grades 10-12; Project CRISS was revised and revalidated for grades 4-12 in 1993, based upon its continued excellence and effectiveness.

Requirements Project CRISS can be implemented by a district, school, or single classroom teacher; no special facilities or materials are necessary. Teachers and administrators participate in a two- or three-day inservice. An on-site program director is named to work with CRISS staff to develop an implementation plan for the adopting district. The district agrees to provide information on the extent and quality of implementation.

Costs Training costs consist of a per participant fee for training and materials plus the trainer's travel expenses, which are usually negotiated between the adopting district, Project CRISS, and the State Facilitator for NDN programs.

Services Awareness materials are available at no cost. Project staff and certified trainers are available to present awareness and training workshops. Visitors are welcome at the Project site or at any of the five national demonstration sites. Materials (including a 250-page training manual) are provided for each participant as part of the training. Implementation, follow-up, and evaluation services are available to adopters. Costs for all services are negotiable.

Contact Lynn Havens or Carol Santa, Project CRISS, School District #5, 233 First Avenue East, Kalispell, MT 59901. (406) 756-5011, FAX (406) 756-4510. E-Mail: csanta@inet.ed.gov.

JDRP No. 84-7R (2/26/85)
Recertified (3/1/93)

Developmental Funding: Title IV-C.

Critical Analysis and Thinking Skills (CATS). A program which teaches students how to apply critical thinking skills to problems and issues so that they will learn how to make more rational decisions and write persuasive essays.

Audience CATS has been approved by the JDRP as a program for high school students (grades 9-12) of all ability levels. CATS has been used with students in the lower grades.

Description The **goals** of the Critical Analysis and Thinking Skills (CATS) program are: (1) to help students learn and correctly use basic critical thinking skills so they can analyze issues and problems more effectively; (2) to help students learn and correctly use a decision-making process so they can make more rational decisions; (3) to help students become critical readers so they can decode and encode information more effectively; (4) to help students learn the composing process so they can write persuasive essays of high quality; and (5) to provide a way for gifted students to realize their intellectual and creative potential. CATS projects, which fall into two distinct phases, were developed to provide teachers with a practical and tested way for implementing CATS in the real world of the classroom. **Phase 1** (Defining and Evaluating). Students learn how to precisely define the issue at hand, evaluate the issue (i.e., how to obtain a wide range of relevant information), and then how to prioritize and assess the information for credibility. Students use the CATS six-step, decision-making process to define and evaluate the issue using specially formatted worksheets to complete the process. **Phase 2** (Writing and Revising). Students have on worksheets a highly organized version of the issue from which it is a relatively simple matter to write and revise a persuasive essay.

Students learn critical-thinking skills and how to apply these skills to issue analysis. These skills include: conceptual analysis, deductive and inductive reasoning, and priority analysis. Students are constantly called upon to analyze and synthesize their thinking. Students function at the evaluation level which most taxonomies identify as the highest of the higher order thinking skills. In addition, students are learning the important skills of critical reading and persuasive essay writing. In order to obtain benefits, students complete five CATS projects per semester. Since CATS is used as another teaching method in place of such things as lecturing and giving quizzes five times per semester, students do not suffer as far as acquisition of course content is concerned. However, with CATS, students gain an extra dimension for their education. CATS has been used in social studies, language arts, and related classes. Other adaptations are in progress at this time. CATS has developed special **Advanced CATS Projects** for the gifted student.

Evidence of Effectiveness CATS students make significant (p<.01) and large (greater than .8 standard deviations) gains as measured by the Critical Thinking Test (CTT) and the Essay. CATS students score significantly (p<.01) higher than comparison students as measured by the CTT and Essay. The magnitude of these differences was greater than .7 standard deviations.

Requirements Teachers receive CATS training in a one-day workshop. During the workshop, teachers complete a CATS Project (small-group work) and then learn how to use CATS in their classrooms. Follow-up can be accomplished in several ways; phone, mail, or on-site visit. CATS training requires no special equipment or facilities.

Services CATS staff and trainers certified by CATS can provide a variety of services to educators. Training, except in rare instances, is accomplished at the adopter site. Visitors are welcome at the program site by appointment. CATS staff will conduct awareness sessions anywhere in the U.S. or possessions (cost to be negotiated). Follow-up services as described above are provided (costs to be negotiated). Costs of a one-day workshop are: trainer=$250; travel, lodging, meals and other expenses=actual cost; materials=$45 per teacher. Included in the materials cost is the CATS Instructional Package, *Making Rational Decisions*, which is used both for the workshop and for classroom implementation.

Contact Terry P. Applegate or W. Keith Evans, CATS Program, 4988 Kalani Drive, Salt Lake City, UT 84117-6421. (801) 272-1877 or 277-7395, FAX (801) 272-1896.

Development Funding: USOE ESEA Title III.

JDRP No. 77-106 (**1/11/77**)
Recertified (**3/29/91**)

Davis County Indian Homework Centers Program (IHC). A tutoring program to increase the achievement scores of Indian students in the Davis County (Utah) School District.

Audience Indian students grades 1-12 who request or agree to be tutored.

Description The IHC provides tutoring to Indian students during after school hours at homework centers located in libraries of elementary and secondary schools. It is designed to provide one-on-one special help in reading, mathematics, and other subject areas according to the students' needs, and study skills. Students can enter the IHC program when the student requests tutoring; a teacher or administrator requests tutoring and the student agrees; or a parent requests tutoring. An individualized action plan is formulated for the student, and an appropriate tutor and tutor supervisor are responsible for implementing the plan. During the first two weeks of school, tutors and tutor supervisors are trained in academic learning styles and instructional methods, as well as Indian cultural heritages. Tutors are required to pass a test for cultural knowledge and instructional skills with at least an 85% level of proficiency and are provided additional training during the year. Four educational specialists offer supervision and training for tutors; two Native American Indians serve as consultants and trainers for the cultural heritage component. Tutor supervisors are responsible for monitoring and evaluating the ongoing operation with assistance from the parent committee of the Davis County Indian Parent Association. The IHC project has developed materials that include teacher aids, tracking systems for student progress and follow-up of tutors and tutor supervisors, mastery tests for knowledge of cultural heritage and instructional techniques, inservice procedures and materials, and evaluation and monitoring plans. IHC addresses National Educational Goal 3.

Evidence of Effectiveness The Stanford Achievement Tests (SAT) was the instrument used to measure student (grades 1-12) achievement gains. A pre- and post-test design was used. Supporting evidence was obtained through parent questionnaires. The treatment group sample included all of the Indian students who received at least 30 hours of tutoring over a 27 week period and who took both the pre- and post-tests. Results showed that students made significant gains in reading and mathematics. Gains were medium in magnitude at the elementary and junior high levels and large in magnitude at the high school level. The questionnaire showed that all parents had a positive attitude toward their children's involvement in the program and that they felt their children had gained in academic achievement.

Requirements For 60 students: ten qualified part-time tutors and one part-time tutor supervisor trained in Native American Culture for the Tribes represented in the geographic area to be served; access to elementary and secondary school libraries or media centers; Native American Indian Culture Kits; and criterion tests.

Costs Year one implementation and operation costs include program installation (3-day workshop and 5 follow-up days) estimated at $2,400 plus travel expenses of the trainer. For subsequent years, recurrent tutor training and follow-up costs are estimated at $1,000 plus trainer travel expenses. Staffing costs are estimated at $40,240 per year. Cost per student is $744 in the installation year and $721 in subsequent years. Materials and supplies are estimated at $1,000 per year.

Contact   **Bruce G. Parry, Project Manger, Davis County Indian Homework Centers Program, 2175 S. 1000 West, Syracuse, UT 84075. (801) 825-6512.**

Developmental Funding: U.S. ED ESEA Title IVC

PEP No. 94-18 (**5/1/94**)

Increase Maximal Performance by Activating Critical Thinking (IMPACT). A staff development program fusing critical thinking with content area instruction.

Audience Approved for students grades 6-9, and effectively used by teachers of students at all grade levels (K-college), subject areas, and ability levels.

Description Meeting national standards for basic skills achievement requires training in critical thinking. Increase Maximal Performance by Activating Critical Thinking (IMPACT) focuses on staff training to infuse the direct teaching of critical thinking into existing core subjects and across curricula areas. Program adopters are empowered to initiate classroom reforms in learning and instruction crucial to meeting the National Goals for Education, specifically Goals 3, 4, and 5 as identified in *America 2000*. IMPACT's instructional approach has three essential components: (1) a framework of 22 critical thinking skills, (2) a model lesson format, and (3) ten teaching behaviors that activate student use of critical thinking.

The IMPACT training and materials model proven methods for integrating subject-matter content with such thinking skills as Comparing and Contrasting, Classifying, Ordering, Patterning, Identifying Relevant and Irrelevant Information, Cause and Effect Relationships, and Predicting and Logical Reasoning.

Evidence of Effectiveness Program validation has shown that IMPACT students significantly ($p > .05$) outperform similar control students in mathematics applications, reading comprehension, and critical thinking skills after only one semester in the program.

Requirements The IMPACT Level I seminar is presented in six consecutive sessions, and includes: review of literature and research, lesson simulation, demonstration of technique, and group interaction. During Level I training, experts demonstrate teaching behaviors that engage and reinforce thinking skills (e.g., Cuing, Probing, and Reflection with wait-time). Trainees receive supervised practice for lesson reinforcement and integration. Following the seminar, participants further develop their skills by: (1) teaching the thinking skills listed in the IMPACT Universe of Critical Skills; (2) practicing the strategies using sample lessons published by Phi Delta Kappa; (3) observing each other teach IMPACT lessons in the classroom; (4) receiving/reviewing feedback on the peer-observation findings; and (5) creating original IMPACT-based lessons.

Teachers easily integrate the three key IMPACT components into their instructional program by first adapting sixty model practice lessons based on either Language Arts or Mathematics and then creating their own lessons. The curriculum materials, available only to IMPACT graduates, demonstrate both planning and instructional elements. The planning elements include: the identification of the thinking skills implicit in the standard curriculum, prerequisite thinking skills, behavioral objectives, materials, and equipment. The lesson design, based on the Hunter model, highlights the instructional elements of Orientation, Direct Instruction, Guided practice, and Closure.

IMPACT training occurs at two levels. First, for classroom implementation, the program recommends that a district enroll a team of at least two teachers and their site administrator in Level I training, an intensive 18-hour inservice (three days) that models the infusion of the IMPACT approach. Secondly, to become a Level II District/Site Trainer, a Level I graduate must have: (1) been appointed by the district; (2) taught 20 IMPACT lessons; (3) filed a plan to disseminate IMPACT within the district for two years; and (4) completed a Level II seminar.

Services Awareness materials are available at no cost. With advance notice, arrangements can be made for visitors to observe the program in use at demonstration sites located nationwide. Program personnel are available to make out-of-state awareness presentations. Training is conducted nationally at the program site, adopter sites, and prearranged advertised locations. IMPACT curriculum materials published by Phi Delta Kappa are available only to IMPACT Level I graduates. The registration and materials fee for Level I training is $350 per person, or $750 per team of three. The Level II training fee is $425 per person. When 25 or more attendees are enrolled, the registration fees defray all training costs. Awareness presentations, technical assistance, follow-up, and evaluation services are available to adopters on a cost-recovery basis. Three semester units of graduate credit are offered by the University of San Diego for completion of Level I and Level II training.

Contact S. Lee Winocur, Ph.D., National Director, IMPACT, Center for the Teaching of Thinking, 21412 Magnolia Street, Huntington Beach, CA 92646. (714) 964-3106. Phi Delta Kappa, Eighth Street and Union Avenue, Box 780, Bloomington, IN 47402-0789. (812) 339-1156.

Developmental Funding: USOE ESEA Title IV-C.

JDRP No. 83-17 **(3/8/83)**
Recertified **(6/12/87)**

Kids Interest Discovery Studies KiTS (KIDS KITS). A program to generate active, self-directed learning and higher levels of thinking, using organized sets of multimedia materials on topics of student interest, for grades 1-8.

Audience Approved by JDRP/PEP for students of all abilities, grades 1-8: has been used successfully with gifted and talented, Chapter I, educationally handicapped, and bilingual students, as well as regular classroom students.

Description Kids Interest Discovery Studies KITS (KIDS KITS) is a multimedia approach to gifted and talented education, special education, regular classroom instruction, and library media center activities. Based on a school-wide survey of student interest, kits such as Indians, Astronomy, and the Human Body are developed by the library media staff and teachers. Kits contain books, filmstrips, tapes, models, transparencies, etc., suitable for different grade levels, a variety of learning modalities, and a range of abilities. Integration of resources into KIDS KITS allows for immediate hands-on use of a variety of materials. There are four phases of student involvement: exploration, in-depth study, application, and sharing of information. Exploration allows students to become aware of topics of interest and resources available. During in-depth study, students ask and answer research questions by listening, viewing, reading, and writing. Students apply the information they have learned by creating a product or preparing a presentation. A wide variety of study products is encouraged, such as creative writing, transparencies, tapes, models, or filmstrips. Products may be added to the kits. Students are encouraged to share their learning. KIDS KITS relates to several of the National Goals for Education, but most directly to Goal 3. KIDS KITS is used by teachers to enrich instruction in all subject areas. The primary purpose of KIDS KITS is to enhance thinking skills. Higher levels of thinking are developed as students articulate questions, locate and use resources, organize information, and plan a presentation or product to demonstrate what they have learned. Engaging in this type of in-depth study develops the ability to reason and to write and communicate effectively. Problem solving and career education are integrated throughout the process. Attainment of Goal 2 is facilitated by assuring that all students experience challenge and success in their learning activities, thus developing or increasing positive attitudes towards school. Parent involvement is encouraged.

Evidence of Effectiveness Interview data for students in grades 1-8 have been collected at the original school and at 13 adoption sites located in eight different states. Sites vary from small rural to large urban. Analysis of the data indicated that with increased kit use students demonstrate: (1) greater specificity, complexity, and multiplicity in their descriptions of the purpose of their learning activities; (2) more awareness and use of learning resources; (3) a greater number of applications of information; and (4) a high level of interest and enthusiasm for research. The significance levels varied from .03 to .001.

Requirements Staff at the adopting school develop at least six kits, using a wide variety of print and nonprint materials. Much of this material already is found in most schools. Costs vary considerably, depending on the amount of new materials purchased. Each school identifies a coordinating team which receives four to six hours of training in kit materials selection, program management, implementation strategies, and evaluation. Teams should include the library media specialist/aide and one to three other staff members. Parents also may be included. Each team later conducts training at the building level. Students are trained in the use of KIDS KITS, operation of audio-visual equipment, and media production.

Costs Awareness materials are available at no cost. Appointments can be made for visitors to observe the program. Training can be conducted at the adopting school/district, other agencies, or at the original school. Purchase of one Program Manual ($25) per school is required. Optional purchases include Activity Cards, Discovery Cards (research questions), and Kit Development Guidelines. Follow-up services are available. Costs for all services (awareness, training, follow-up) include travel expenses and consultant fee for trainer.

Contact Jo Ann C. Petersen, KIDS KITS, 3607 Martin Luther King Blvd., Denver, CO 80205. (303) 322-9323, FAX (303) 322-9475.

JDRP No. 81-40 (**12/15/81**)
Recertified (**3/11/93**)

Developmental Funding: USOE ESEA Title IV-C.

Literacy Links. (Formerly *Reading Education Accountability Design: Secondary [READ:S].*) A performance-based reading education model which helps to overcome student reading deficiencies and improve achievement in reading and content subjects.

Audience Students of all ability levels, especially high-risk, grades five through twelve.

Description Literacy Links provides content area teachers with the necessary skills to develop instructional, interactive modules in vocabulary, comprehension, and study strategies using the content of their own courses. The modules are based on research-validated techniques, such as graphic organizers, feature analysis, and question clusters—techniques stressing ways of linking ideas and concepts. Module use is then coordinated through instructional approaches, cooperative learning, and problem-solving. Included are three major components: (1) teaching and modeling of reading, thinking, and writing strategies in all content areas; (2) inservice that focuses on both content and the processes of instructional delivery; and (3) an optional computer component for the development and delivery of customized learning activities. Program inservice benefits include: (1) development of instructional materials for immediate classroom use; (2) shared insights into reading problems and enhanced understanding of one another's subjects and how best to teach them; (3) familiarization with cooperative learning strategies; (4) teacher collaboration on mutually taught text units; and (5) awareness of a range of writing activities designed to enable students to organize and apply knowledge. Literacy Links supports National Educational Goal 3.

Evidence of Effectiveness Three claims of effectiveness were evaluated to examine the overall impact of the program on student achievement and teacher behavior. Eight studies at nine sites were conducted. Data from one study were pooled across multiple sites. Results showed statistically significant student achievement gains in content learning and reading ability, both for mainstream students and for those considered at-risk of academic failure. Moderate to strong effect sizes resulted in every study, across a diversity of districts, regions, and school populations.

Requirements Requirements necessary for implementing Literacy Links include: a three day training session; a maximum of twenty teachers and/or administrators per one trainer (preferably at least one English/reading teacher, at least one administrator, and a variety of content area teachers); one manual per participant; and one content area textbook per participant for the development of modules and related learning activities during and following the inservice.

Costs Start-up costs include: $1575 for training, and $400 for training materials for 20 participants. Total cost per student is estimated at $7.22.

Services Awareness activities, training sessions, and site visitations for a fee.

Contact Lynn Dennis, Director, Coeur d'Alene Public Schools, District 271, 311 North 10th Street, Coeur d'Alene, ID 83814. (208) 664-8241, FAX (208) 664-1748.

Developmental Funding: ESEA Title IV-C

Pep No. 94-17 **(5/1/94)**

Multicultural Reading and Thinking (McRAT). A staff development process designed to help teachers infuse higher order thinking skills and multicultural concepts into existing curriculum for all students and to measure progress through students' writing.

Audience   Approved by PEP for students in grades 3-8.

Description   Multicultural Reading and Thinking (McRAT) techniques are infused into the entire curriculum using available materials and resources. Instruction focuses on four kinds of reasoning—analysis, comparison, inference/interpretation, and evaluation—that students can use across the curriculum and that also transfer to practical situations. Teachers conduct a minimum of one McRAT lesson per week related to a multicultural concept, such as cultural diversity, cultural assimilation, or communication. During each lesson, students receive direct instruction on the use of thinking strategies through teacher modeling, explanation, guidance, and feedback. Each lesson guides students through an inquiry process involving nine components. All lessons feature sustained discussion and writing as vehicles for fostering critical thinking, and teachers use many tools to facilitate discussion and thinking including visual mapping and interactive strategies, e.g., cooperative learning and story retelling. McRAT lessons are often incorporated into thematic units of study involving parents and the community. Teachers use portfolios as systematic and organized collections of evidence to monitor and show student growth, to communicate student learning to parents, and to evaluate success in reaching instructional goals.

Evidence of Effectiveness   Based on analytic scoring of writing samples, McRAT students make significantly greater progress in their abilities to reason effectively and communicate their ideas in writing than students who receive typical classroom instruction. Follow-up studies indicate that McRAT students retain their learning and are able to perform at a higher level than students who do not receive McRAT instruction regardless of prior achievement level. Examination of teacher logs shows cross-curricular application of McRAT strategies.

Requirements   Teacher training requires release time for teachers to attend a minimum of nine days, of training scheduled at intervals during one year and the assignment of a local coordinator to provide monitoring, follow-up, and peer support. Principals' and other administrators' attendance at the initial three-day workshop is highly desirable. McRAT Resource manuals must be purchased for teachers. Participating districts must agree to collect and provide data on program effectiveness upon successful completion or training and classroom experience of 1 year, application may be made to participate in 6 additional days of training to qualify as a McRAT trainer.

Costs   For a maximum of 25 teachers, Year 1 implementation costs for 9 days of training are projected at $100/teacher for materials/supplies, $500/day for honoraria, and travel expenses for 3-4 trips.

Services   In addition to training and materials, follow-up consultation is available.

Contact   **Janita Hoskyn, Program Manager, Reading Program, Arkansas Department of Education, Room 401B, #4 Capitol Mall, Little Rock, AR 72201. (501) 682-4232 or (501) 225-5809.**

Developmental Funding: Chapter 2-ECIA, ADE (state), and Winthrop Rockefeller Foundation.

PEP No. 92-13 **(4/92)**

Philosophy for Children. A program that offers conceptual and cultural enrichment while providing skill improvement in comprehension, analysis, and problem solving. Specifically, the program develops reasoning competencies (e.g., inferring and finding underlying assumptions) and inquiry skills (e.g., forming hypotheses and explaining) for grades 3-7.

Audience Approved by the JDRP for elementary school children grades 3-7.

Description The classroom **community of inquiry** whereby children are encouraged to listen to and talk with their peers is the central feature of the Philosophy for Children program. This is not just another discussion format. Teachers are trained to become expert facilitators of substantive philosophical discussion about matters of concern to children. Why philosophy? Because the skills fostered by philosophical discussion are precisely those which cut across the various school subjects in which parents, teachers, and administrators want children to excel. This connection of the program with school subjects is borne out by the research indicated below. A short list of essential features of the program includes:

- The novel as text,
- The discussion method with philosophical ideas as content,
- Comprehensive instructional manuals with exercises to focus discussion,
- Training which allows teachers to become expert facilitators, and
- Attentive follow-ups to ensure teacher confidence and competence.

Since the **community of inquiry** is self-correcting, that is, individual opinions are continuously monitored by the community, children quite naturally come to recognize the procedures of critical thinking. This acquisition of procedures is reinforced, since sequentially arranged cognitive and reasoning skills are introduced in grades 3-6, and there is ample opportunity to **apply** the skills to concrete areas of concern to children throughout the 3-7 curricula. Additionally, children become creative as well as critical thinkers.

The pedagogical strategy of Philosophy for Children is to introduce children to standards of sound thinking through careful discussion of ideas. In this way, their reading, writing, speaking, and listening become infused with better reasoning, and this is then carried by them into other classrooms. Philosophy for Children is therefore critical thinking at its most thorough, aimed at producing reasonable students capable of good judgment when finding themselves in problematic situations. Philosophy for Children is especially germane to the first two objectives of National Goal for Education 3: (1) raising the overall academic performance of students; and (2) increasing the ability of students to reason, solve problems, apply knowledge, and write and communicate effectively.

Evidence of Effectiveness Students exposed to the program have consistently demonstrated significant gains in logic, reading comprehension, mathematics, and reasoning skills when evaluated with the California Test of Mental Maturity, the Metropolitan Achievement Test, and the New Jersey Test of Reasoning Skills, and when matched with equivalent comparison students. Populations have been heterogeneous, from all socioeconomic groups and of mixed ethnicity.

Requirements Training is required for all teachers who participate in the program. Guaranteed training must involve a certified trainer. Two follow-up visits by the trainer are strongly recommended; the first for the trainer to model the program in each class, while the second is for the trainer to observe the teachers.

Costs For a class of 25 students, the entire cost could be as little as $265 plus the cost of a substitute if needed. Follow-up activity is negotiable, but will not, in any case, require substitutes.

Services Awareness materials are available at no cost. Program or on-site training is available. Visitors are welcome by appointment to nationwide demonstration sites. In some cases, graduate credit can be arranged for inservice training.

Contact Matthew Lipman, Professor or Philosophy and Director, Institute for the Advancement of Philosophy for Children, Montclair State College, Upper Montclair, NJ 07043. (201) 655-4277, FAX (201) 655-5455. E-Mail: lipman@saturn.montclair.edu

Developmental Funding: NEH, USOE, ESEA Title IV-C, state, and private sources.

JDRP 86-12 **(7/2/86)**

Questioning and Understanding to Improve Learning and Thinking (QUILT).
A program designed to increase and sustain teacher use of classroom questioning techniques and procedures that produce higher levels of student learning and thinking.

Audience All teachers, K-12, in all content areas.

Description The QUILT program helps teachers improve the quality of questions they pose to students in order to create a more reflective classroom environment. QUILT incorporates research that links effective questioning to student learning and thinking. From deciding what's worth asking to providing appropriate feedback, QUILT represents a comprehensive approach to enhancing student engagement in learning through questioning. QUILT challenges teachers to rethink the standard approach to teaching and learning, in which students are passive learners. Through the QUILT program, teachers help students understand how questioning and answering can help them learn, teach students effective questioning strategies and techniques, and help students become active learners. The program, implemented over the course of an entire school year, is led by a school team (ideally composed of teachers and at least one administrator) trained to facilitate the QUILT program. The program promotes collaborative working patterns in the school and classroom as participating teachers learn through interactive instruction, discussion with colleagues, reflection on current practice, demonstrations, practice with feedback from a colleague, and classroom application. QUILT addresses National Educational Goal 3.

Evidence of Effectiveness Results showed that after one year of participation, teachers significantly increased their knowledge and understanding of effective questioning practices, and significantly increased their use of discrete questioning behaviors in a classroom setting. Students responded significantly more often at higher cognitive levels.

Requirements *Teachers:* Participate in the three-day Induction Training; implement QUILT behaviors in the classroom, which includes teaching effective questioning behaviors to students; attend seven collegiums, during which teachers review, plan for classroom application, share, and solve problems; and observe and receive feedback from a QUILT partner after each collegium.

Local school trainers: Attend a one-week training and a two-day "booster," plan and conduct the three-day Induction Training for school faculty, lead seven collegiums, and facilitate teacher efforts to partner and implement QUILT in the classroom.

Costs *Teacher materials:* ($25/teacher); *School materials:* ($250 includes eight videotapes, 149 overhead transparencies, and other materials); *Trainers:* ($625/person covers registration costs, including materials, for a weeklong training plus a two-day booster; additional costs are necessary to support the travel, room and board of local school trainers). *Optional costs* may include off-campus training facility, substitute teachers for partnering, stipends to school trainers, etc.

Services Awareness materials available at no cost. In addition to complete training and materials, program staff offers monitoring of program effectiveness and a newsletter for adopters. Technical assistance is available from staff (toll-free telephone). One national training for local teams is held in Lexington, KY the third week of June; additional trainings can be negotiated.

Contact **Sandra Orletsky, Project Director, Appalachia Educational Laboratory, P.O. Box 1348, Charleston, WV 25325. (304) 347-0400 or (800) 624-9120, FAX (304) 347-0487.**

Developmental Funding: U.S. ED Regional Educational Laboratory Program

PEP No. 94-14 **(5/1/94)**

Study Skills Across the Curriculum. An interdisciplinary program with the goal of improving students' study skills, thereby enabling them to be more successful in their middle and junior high content subjects, to be active and organized learners, and to be better prepared for the learning independence expected in high school.

Audience Approved by PEP for students in grades 5-8.

Description The Study Skills Across the Curriculum program is an interdisciplinary study skills program which provides a practical, effective vehicle for accomplishing school-wide improvement. The program model is firmly grounded in current educational research on effective middle school practices and is an excellent example of turning theory into practice. The program includes an alternative assessment package with guidelines for a study skills portfolio; a performance-based criterion-referenced test; and inventories for teachers, parents, and students to measure changes in study behaviors. The program also includes a parent component whereby parents are trained in the same strategies as their children so they can work with their children at home. The program's interdisciplinary model provides students with the consistency they need to reach their maximum potential as learners and to accomplish the national goal of student achievement and citizenship. Students cannot make a commitment to becoming a life-long learner, an important first step to productive employment in the Information Age, if they do not learn how to learn.

The curriculum is an interdisciplinary program consisting of a series of units, each with objectives and activities. Target skills include textbook format, time management and goal setting, learning from textbook materials, note taking from lectures and reading, test preparation, test taking, underlining/highlighting, listening, and library skills. A summary unit, "Becoming a Selective Viewer of TV," provides a model for the integration of the skills. Math activities have been added to each of the units in the notebook. These activities model for teachers lessons which require students to read, write, and speak mathematics. All the activities require students' active involvement, considerable modeling from teachers, homework, and writing assignments.

Materials are not workbook, fill-in-the-blank style; they are integrated into content area objectives and require the students to apply the target skills to their actual content course work. The materials can be used across disciplines in a particular grade or across several different grade levels within one building. The learning materials use sample lessons from social studies, science, and math textbooks to serve as models. The curricular materials include a pre- and postassessment for each skill, discussion questions, sample writing assignments, and transparency masters.

A team of teachers, an administrator, and, ideally, a parent attend the initial training. This team functions as a working committee to forge an implementation plan for a target grade level or building. The committee decides how best to integrate program goals into their local objectives and practices and how best to evaluate program implementation. After forging the building plan, the committee is expected to communicate regularly with staff colleagues and to maintain records of the implementation. A clearly delineated list of next steps, questions for consideration by the committee, and planning forms are included with the curricular materials. The program can be introduced intermittently throughout a quarter, semester, or school year in a variety of formats.

Evidence of Effectiveness Students who complete the program earn significantly greater gains on a program-produced and validated criterion-referenced study skills test, report greater gains in study skill behaviors, and demonstrate higher performance in their content courses.

Requirements Two days of training with an interdisciplinary team of teachers, an administrator, and, ideally, a parent from each building are required. Since ideally every teacher in a building plays one of two roles—the initial teacher of a strategy or the reinforcer—a day of follow-up is recommended consisting of a half-day inservice session on study skills for an entire faculty and a half-day follow-up meeting for committee members. Since the program requires an across-the-curriculum approach, more than one teacher from a building should attend training.

Costs The *Study Skills Across the Curriculum* manual costs $50 plus shipping. **Each** teacher who attends the initial training will need a copy of this manual. In addition a parent video and booklet, *Study Skills: The Parent Connection*, is available for $95 (booklet only for $7.50) and can be used in parent training sessions, on cable TV, or as a teacher training tool. The video and booklet are optional. Additional costs include travel expenses and consultant fee for the trainer. There are no recurring costs for the program.

Services In addition to training and materials, the program offers monitoring of the program's effectiveness and a newsletter for adopters. Awareness materials are available at no cost.

Contact Patricia S. Olson, Director, ISD 197-Study Skills Across the Curriculum, 1897 Delaware Avenue, West St. Paul, MN 55118. (612) 681-0844 or (612) 898-3002, FAX (612) 681-0879.

Developmental Funding: Local.

PEP No. 89-5R2 **(2/13/90)**

Talents Unlimited. A teacher training/learning model which integrates creative and critical thinking skills into the curriculum, for grades 1-6.

Audience Approved by PEP for grades 1-6. Data currently being gathered in kindergarten and 7th-12th grade implementations.

Description Talents Unlimited is a teaching/learning model which integrates creative and critical thinking skills into the set curriculum in any classroom arena. Based on the Multiple Talents Approach to Learning developed by Dr. Calvin Taylor at the University of Utah, this program increases student performance in specific TALENTS processes including Productive Thinking, Communication, Forecasting, Decision Making, and Planning with the Academic Talent as the frame of reference for all activities.

While Talents Unlimited indirectly addresses Goals 2 and 6 of the National Goals for Education, Talents Unlimited effects an immediate impact on Goals 3 and 5 which deal with specific content areas. Students improve in higher order thinking based on enhanced academic knowledge.

The model features three major components:

- Teacher Training - Professional development opportunity directed by certified trainers where teachers learn the TALENTS processes and strategies for classroom implementation.

- TALENTS Instruction - Lessons modeling TALENTS processes and technical assistance directed by a certified trainer which guide teachers as they generate meaningful, accurate activities to address curriculum and enhance thinking.

- Student Assessment - Instruments and activities, formal and/or informal which measure student performance in TALENTS thinking skills.

Evidence of Effectiveness When compared to a similar non-Talents Unlimited trained group, students trained in the Talents Unlimited model demonstrated significant gains in creative/critical thinking skills as measured by the program designed and validated criterion-referenced tests and the Torrance Tests of Creative Thinking: improved self-esteem as measured by the Coopersmith Self-esteem Inventory; and enhanced academic scores as measured on the Stanford Achievement Test.

Requirements A 12-16 hour inservice conducted by a certified trainer is necessary before teachers implement the Talents Unlimited program in their classrooms. After this initial training, teachers will need various forms of technical assistance to insure an accurate, effective program adoption.

Costs The costs for the initial teacher inservice (typically 30 people) to an adopter include travel, lodging and food for the consultant, and other travel expenses incurred, a consulting fee, and a materials fee per participant. A minimum of two days of training are required for classroom implementation. In addition, it is recommended that each adoption site purchase a Talents Activity Packet (TAP), a notebook of model Talents lessons available for $50, as a reference for all Talents-trained teachers.

Services Awareness materials are available at no cost. There are 12 National Demonstration Sites in the United States, which may be visited throughout the school year upon request to the building administration. Program staff is available to attend out-of-state awareness meetings (travel and per diem to be negotiated). Training is conducted either in Mobile or at the adopting school site. Implementation and follow-up services are available to adopters (all expenses to be negotiated).

Contact   **Brenda Haskew, Talents Unlimited, 109 South Cedar Street, Mobile, AL 36602. (205) 690-8060, FAX (205) 344-8364.**

JDRP No. 74-82 **(6/6/74)**
Recertified **(3/19/91)**

Developmental Funding: USOE ESEA Title III.

Adventure, Project. An interdisciplinary program involving experience-based learning in academics along with group problem solving and an alternative physical education program outdoors and indoors as well. Approved by JDRP for students of all abilities, grades 6-12.

Description Project Adventure is designed to infuse experiential learning into standard high school and middle school courses. For many students, learning is essentially a passive process offering little opportunity to take responsible action or to test abstract ideas in the real world. Project Adventure combines Outward Bound techniques and philosophy with a group problem-solving approach to learning and teaching. Small groups of students learn by working on specific reality-based tasks or problems in the community and the natural environment. The teacher's role is to state the problem and limits, giving students the responsibility for finding solutions. This approach has produced measurable improvements in self-concept, physical agility and competence. The project is made up of two separate components, which may be used singly or together: a physical education program involving initiative games, outdoor/indoor activities, and a Ropes Course apparatus; and an academic curriculum component designed to give hands-on experiences and a practical application of the basics. The program's aim is to educate the whole student through sound academics, physical activity, and learning activities that enhance self-concept. The project's strengths are its flexibility, the variety and quality of its curriculum models, and its ability to inspire and rekindle the enthusiasm of both teachers and students. The project offers five different initial training programs: academic, counseling techniques, physical education, professional development, and community partnerships.

Contact Dick Prouty, Project Adventure, Inc., P.O. Box 100, Hamilton, MA 01936. (508) 468-7981. Cindy Simpson, P.O. Box 2447, Covington, GA 30209. (404) 784-9310. Jim Grout, 116 Maple Street, Brattleboro, VT 05301. (802) 254-5054. Ann Smolowe, P.O. Box 14171, Portland, OR 97214. (503) 236-6765.

Developmental Funding: USOE ESEA Title III.

JDRP No. 73-4 **(4/9/73)**

Gulfport Follow Through: University of Georgia Model (UGA). Comprehensive education and intellectual model for developing cognitive and/or problem-solving skills for children of all ability levels in grades K-3.

Description The Gulfport Follow Through: University of Georgia Model (UGA) is based on the University of Georgia model. This program uses the assessment of cognitive level as a guide for establishing a learning environment that maximizes development of the thinking process. Learning activities are designed to encourage the child to experiment with problems and discover solutions; this type of experience enhances the shift from concrete to abstract levels of thinking. Based on the idea that learning occurs most easily when the child is an active agent in the process, all aspects of the classroom environment are designed in terms of three elements. The child is (1) presented materials just slightly more difficult than previously mastered (mis-match), (2) encouraged to choose his/her own method of problem solution (self-regulation), and (3) given time to manipulate learning materials (activity). Manipulative materials and activities that draw on the child's prior knowledge and experiences are essential to the program. Physical, concrete activities and materials involve children in constructing knowledge for themselves. Individual and small group instructional arrangements allow for active involvement, and permit the teacher to more effectively accommodate each child's cognitive and achievement levels and learning style. Teachers and instructional aides are trained to apply the model strategies to most of the currently used textbooks and materials in reading, language arts, science, mathematics, and social studies. Regular in-service training on teaching techniques and cognitive assessment is conducted with guidance from the university sponsor. Medical and dental health, nutrition, psychological and social services, and parent involvement are other essential elements of the University of Georgia model.

Contact Ronnie Barnes, Director, Gulfport School District, P.O. Box 220, Gulfport, MS 39502-0220. (601) 865-4672.

Developmental Funding: USOE Follow Through.

JDRP No. 80-51e **(2/2/81)**

Institute for Creative Education (ICE). A program that teaches a creative problem-solving process based in a sequentially ordered curriculum that integrates thinking skill development into a wide variety of subject areas.

Description The Institute for Creative Education (ICE) program is based on the belief that creative problem solving is essential to a quality learning experience. The program's process orientation, with a concentration on developing divergent thinking skills, gives students, in a nonthreatening atmosphere, the foundation for sound decision making and problem solving. The program's major goal is to develop students' abilities to respond to problems or tasks more fluently, flexibly, originally, and elaborately. This goal directly aligns with Goal 3 of the National Goals for Education for students to be able to more effectively reason, solve problems, apply knowledge, and write and communicate orally.

Unique to this program are the sequentially ordered activities or lessons that teach a process of creative problem solving that is clearly understandable to students and teachers. These curriculum materials ($65 per manual) are obtained at a two-day training workshop conducted by the Institute staff. During training, teachers experience the format of the curriculum and the basic elements contributing to the program components: productive thinking, reinforcement, and consciousness raising.

Contact Monika Steinberg, Director, Institute for Creative Education, Education Information and Resource Center (EIRC), 606 Delsea Drive, Sewell, NJ 08080. (609) 582-7000, FAX (609) 582-4206.

Developmental Funding: USOE ESEA Title IV-C.

JDRP No. 79-22 **(7/11/79)**

Interdependent Learning Model (ILM). This model uses instructional games and pupil self-management methods to teach children traditional academic skills and positive sociocultural attitudes and behaviors. Approved by JDRP for grades K-3. This model may also be implemented in grades 4-6.

Description The Interdependent Learning Model (ILM) is a comprehensive, structured approach to full-day instruction for children in preschool through the sixth grade. In model classrooms children are taught academic skills, positive values, and behaviors. The model's primary goals are to teach children to be independent; to behave interdependently, cooperatively, and responsibly; to have positive self-concepts and positive attitudes toward learning; to be effective communicators; to become skilled at reading, mathematics, writing, and learning how to learn; how to make rational decisions, keep records, schedule their time, and evaluate their work. Children in ILM classrooms learn by doing: through the use of games and play, through curriculum materials, peer teaching, and through the behaviors the teachers model for them. Teachers are trained to establish and maintain the model's classroom management system, which consists of: room arrangement; small-group instruction; pupil self-scheduling, record keeping, and self-evaluation; programmed instruction; curricula based on children's cultures, environments, and communities; and transactional instructional games. The curriculum materials designed for use in ILM classrooms include: Conservation Games, Street/Folk/Musical Games, Table Games, and the Integrated Skills Method Reading Program. Awareness materials are available at no cost. The model's results with children for nearly two decades demonstrates that it is an extremely cost-effective method for achieving the National Goals for Education. Visitors are welcome by appointment for guided classroom visits at the ILM elementary school or preschool demonstration programs in New York City, and at preschool programs in northern New Jersey. Training for administrators, supervisors, teacher trainers, and support staff is available at the University, at adopter sites, and at some current programs.

Contact Susan Courtney-Weissman, Interdependent Learning Model, Fordham University, 113 West 60th Street, Room 1003, New York, NY 10023. (212) 636-6494.

Developmental Funding: USOE Follow Through.

JDRP No. 77-121 **(8/17/77)**

Leflore County (Mississippi) Follow Through Project. A program based in part on the theories of Jean Piaget and the philosophy of John Dewey that blends open-ended, child-initiated activities with teacher-structured lessons. Approved by JDRP for K-3, school administrators, teacher trainers, paraprofessionals, and teachers.

Description The Leflore County (Mississippi) Follow Through Project employs the High/Scope cognitively oriented curriculum as a framework for education. This curriculum was developed by the High/Scope Educational Research Foundation of Ypsilanti, Michigan. Children assume responsibility for their own learning by planning self-initiated activities, carrying out their plans, presenting what they have learned, and sharing their experiences with others. Children become independent decision-makers and problem-solvers. Teachers structure specific learning experiences based on children's needs and their ability to learn a concept or skill. Adults help children apply acquired skills within student-initiated projects. Through this process, children become knowledgeable in the areas of writing and reading, mathematics, science, social studies, music, physical education, health, and safety. Recognizing that parental commitment to children's education is a major factor in a child's school success, the Leflore County (Mississippi) Follow Through Project has developed and implemented a parent program that takes the school to the home and brings parents to the school. Parents participate in classroom activities and workshops. Through these efforts, parents have contributed their knowledge, skills, and resources to the school's educational goals. Statistical analysis of test scores comparing Follow Through children's achievement over the last five years with those of non-Follow Through district students shows significant increases in the Follow Through children in reading, mathematics, and language.

Contact   Ann Adams, Educational Service Building, 1901 Highway 82 West, Greenwood, MS 38930. (601) 453-8566.

Developmental Funding: USOE Follow Through.   JDRP No. 77-123 **(8/18/77)**

Student Team Learning (STL). A set of instructional techniques in which students are placed in four- or five-member heterogeneous learning teams to master basic skills initially presented by the teacher. Approved by JDRP for students grades 3-12.

Description Student Team Learning (STL) is a set of instructional techniques based on years of research on cooperative learning at the Johns Hopkins University. STL consists of three major strategies: Student Teams Achievement Divisions (STAD), Teams-Games-Tournaments (TGT), and Jigsaw II. All three require students to work in learning teams that are heterogeneous in terms of academic achievement, race and gender. In STAD, students study with their team members following a teacher presentation. Students take quizzes individually to demonstrate how much they have learned. The individual quiz scores are summed to form a team score, and teams are rewarded for their performance. TGT is similar to STAD, except that students are actively engaged in an academic game instead of taking quizzes. In Jigsaw II, students become "experts" on topics relating to material they have read and teach these topics to their teammates. STAD is approved for language arts and TGT for language arts and math, and the STL program as a whole is approved for intergroup relations. STL can be used with the STL Teacher's Manual, 4th edition, and teacher-made curriculum materials. Inexpensive materials in many subject areas are available through the project. The techniques are very practical and easy to learn. They are in use in thousands of schools across the U.S. The effects of STL on intergroup relations are strong and consistent, because the team goal and team interactions allow students to view one another positively. Because the program is inexpensive, takes no more class or teacher time than traditional methods, and increases achievement as well as improving intergroup relations, it can be used as a regular part of class instruction in any subject.

Contact   Anna Marie Farnish, Director of Training Projects, Center for Social Organization of Schools, 3505 North Charles Street, Baltimore, MD 21218. (410) 516-8857, FAX (410) 516-8890.

Developmental Funding: NIE.   JDRP No. 75-81 **(75)**
Recertified **(4/17/79)**

Systems Approach to Individualized Instruction (SAII). A systematic instructional program in reading and mathematics. Approved by JDRP for students of all abilities, grades 1-6. It has also been used in other settings with grades 7 and 8.

Description Systems Approach to Individualized Instruction (SAII) has developed criterion-referenced tests and learning modules for 155 reading skills (e.g. readiness, phonics, syllabification, and structural analysis) plus 200 criterion-referenced tests and learning modules for the computational skills of mathematics.

The program has also developed sets of teacher questions and student worksheets to accompany over 400 paperback books (e.g., *Profiles in Courage, Henry Huggins, Little Red Hen*). Each set of questions has been divided into lessons with each lesson having questions on five levels of comprehension: recall, interpretation, extrapolation, analysis, and evaluation. A set of two handbooks is available to help the teacher manage the component parts. The program can be adapted to the areas of diagnosis (criterion-referenced—math and reading) or basic skill development (learning modules in reading and math comprehension components of reading).

A one- to three-day preadoption workshop is required. Consultant help is available. SAII is implemented by the regular classroom teacher. The reading component requires two teachers, the math component, one. Master tapes—available for reproduction—are required for the reading component.

Awareness materials are available. Visitors are welcome October through March. Training is conducted at the program site (adopting site must cover own costs). Training is conducted out of state. Program staff can attend out-of-state conferences. Print-ready sets of program materials are available at cost. Diagnostic tests: reading, $20; math, $24. Learning modules: reading, $70, math $120; comprehension questions, $165; games to accompany reading learning modules, $20.

Contact   Charles L. Barker, Josephine County School District, P.O. Box 160, Murphy, OR 97533. (503) 862-3111.

Developmental Funding: USOE ESEA Title III.   JDRP No. 73-15 **(4/5/73)**

Section 11

Early Childhood/Parent Involvement

* These programs are currently funded by the NDN.

Summary of Program Services for Section 11

Program	Goal*	Page	AWARENESS: Dissem. Funds Available NDN	Dissem. Funds Other	Costs to Potential Adopter Hon	Trav	Per Diem	On Site Visitation Home Site	Adopt Site	Materials Available Free Paper	Video	Film Strip	Other	TRAINING: Staff Available Home Site	Adopt Site	Costs to Adopter Hon	Trav	Per Diem	Certified Trainers Available State(s)	Training Time Required Day(s)
Cognitively Oriented . . . (COPE)	1	11-11						✓	✓	✓	✓			✓	✓	✓	✓	✓	AK, CA, IA, MN, MS, NM, OK, OR, PA, SC, WA	2
Early Intervention . . . (EISS)	1, 8	11-1	✓		(info. not available)														(info. not available)	
Early Prevention of School Failure (EPSF)	2	11-11				✓	✓		✓	✓	✓				✓	✓	✓	✓	49 states	2
Enriching a Child's Literacy . . . (ECLE)	1	11-2			✓	✓	✓	✓	✓	✓	✓			✓	✓	✓	✓	✓	(none)	2+
Family Intergenerational-Interaction . . . (FILM)	1, 6, 8	11-3	✓		(info. not available)															
Family Oriented . . . ("Seton Hall" . . .)	1	11-12			✓	✓	✓	✓	✓	✓				✓	✓	✓	✓	✓	(none)	2
High/Scope K-3 Curriculum	3	11-4	✓		✓	✓	✓	✓	✓	✓	✓		✓	✓	✓	✓	✓	✓	(none)	3+
High/Scope Preschool Curriculum	1	11-5	✓		✓	✓	✓	✓	✓	✓	✓		✓	✓	✓	✓	✓	✓	AL, AZ, AK, CA, CO, CT, D.C., FL, GA, ID, IL, IN, KY, MA, MD, ME, MI, MN, MO, MS, NE, NJ, NY, NC, OH, OK, OR, PA, SC, TX, VA, WA, WV, WI, WY, PRE	3+
Kindergarten Integrated Thematic Experiences (KITE)	1	11-6			✓	✓	✓		✓	✓	✓				✓	✓	✓	✓	AR, AS, CA, CO, D.C., DE, FL, GA, GM, IL, KY, ME, MI, NC, ND, NE, NJ, OR, WI	1
Mother-Child Home Program (MCHP) . . .	1	11-12		✓	✓	✓	✓		✓	✓	✓		✓	✓	✓	✓	✓	✓	IL, MA, NY, PA, SC, Bermuda, Canada, Netherlands	3+

* National Goals for Education—definitions for each goal can be found on pages 5-7.

Summary of Program Services for Section 11 (cont'd)

Program	Goal*	Page	Dissem. Funds: NDN	Dissem. Funds: Other	Costs to Potential Adopter: Hon	Trav	Per Diem	On Site Visitation: Home Site	Adopt Site	Materials: Free Paper	Video	Film Strip	Other	Staff Available: Home Site	Adopt Site	Costs to Adopter: Hon	Trav	Per Diem	Certified Trainers Available: State(s)	Training Time Required: Day(s)
On The Way to SUCCESS in Reading and Writing with Early Prevention of School Failure (Ages 4-7)	3	11-7	✓		✓		✓		✓	✓	✓				✓	✓	✓	✓	49 states, Pacific Rim, VI	1
Parents As Teachers	1	11-8	✓			✓	✓	✓	✓	✓	✓		✓	✓	✓	✓	✓	✓	CA, CT, DE, MO, NC, NY, OH, OK, PA, RI, TX	3+
Perception+	3	11-13				✓	✓	✓	✓	✓				✓	✓	✓	✓	✓	MD	1
P.I.A.G.E.T. (Promoting Intellectual Adaptation Given Experiential Transforming), Project	1, 3	11-9	(info. not available)																	
Portage Project	1	11-13		✓	✓	✓	✓	✓	✓	✓	✓			✓		✓	✓	✓	MS, NJ, NM, NY, OH, WA, WI	3+
Search and Teach	3	11-14				✓		✓	✓	✓	✓			✓	✓	✓	✓		GA, NJ, NY	2+
Webster Groves Even Start Program	1, 6	11-10	(info. not available)																	

* National Goals for Education—definitions for each goal can be found on pages 5-7.

Early Intervention for School Success (EISS). A program to provide teachers, support staff, and parents with basic knowledge of child growth and development and basic strategies for application in the kindergarten classroom.

Audience Kindergarten children, school teaching and support team, and parents.

Description EISS trains teachers, support staff and parents in: (1) basic knowledge of child growth and development; (2) successful strategies for large and small classroom settings; (3) support for teachers for transforming themselves from directors of instruction to facilitators of learning; and (4) practical tools for ongoing authentic assessment and effective instruction. EISS increases achievement, avoids grade-level retention, and reduces special education placements. A developmentally appropriate curriculum depends upon a well-trained school team which is provided through the EISS program. There are four distinct training components: organization and planning, assessment, strategies, and curriculum. EISS Certified Trainers work with schools to ensure the program is appropriate for its geographic, economic, ethnic, cultural and linguistic settings, as well as meeting State frameworks and mandates, district adoptions and requirements and school level content and objectives. EISS addresses National Educational Goals 1 and 8.

Evidence of Effectiveness Four claims of effectiveness were evaluated using a variety of methods. Results showed that kindergarten students after one year in EISS classes scored significantly better gains in receptive language, visual motor integration and achievement than comparison groups, and showed significantly fewer grade retentions than comparison samples. In a follow-up of a comparison study of at-risk (first quartile) students, an examination of reading scores found that the gains made by kindergartners in the program were maintained through grade three testing.

Requirements Commitment and openness to a developmentally appropriate philosophy and authentic assessment model is needed.

Costs The cost of training for the EISS program is approximately $3,010 for a school with four kindergarten classes. The cost, however, will be reduced after the first year through the EISS training-of-trainers model. Recurring costs will vary depending on staff turnover. EISS materials costs are minimal and usually limited to the first year. They include the *EISS Trainers Handbook, Legislative Annual Reports*; the *EISS Continuum* (includes explanatory parent brochures); *Parent Involvement Home Activities*; *Health Survey*; and an overview video tape. EISS also provides newsletters and a lending and video library.

Services Staff development training by EISS certified trainers; curricular and technical assistance from EISS project staff; access to eighty demonstration sites throughout California; access to a network of trainers and implementers; and training-of-trainers through the annual five day Trainers Institute.

Contact   **Dean Hiser, Orange County Department of Education, 200 Kalmus Drive, P.O. Box 9050, Costa Mesa, CA 92628-9050. (714) 966-4145, FAX (714) 966-4124.**

Developmental Funding: California Department of Education.   PEP No. 94-8 **(4/1/94)**

Enriching a Child's Literacy Environment (ECLE). A program of classroom and home instruction for teaching parents, teachers, and other care providers to develop oral language, thinking abilities, and motor skills in young children.

Audience Parents, teachers, and care providers and their young children (ages 6 months to 3 years) from varying economic levels and different cultural groups.

Description ECLE is an educational program that instructs parents, teachers and other care providers how to model various activities with young children six months to three years of age in order to promote psychomotor and cognitive development. Modeling techniques are practiced by parents and care providers under the guidance of ECLE teachers. One ECLE session averages 15 classes usually over a three-month time period. Classes are attended twice a week for 75 minutes. In at least four sessions, child care is offered so that parents and care providers can participate in special classes without the children. ECLE classes can be attended for as many as four sessions during a 12-month period and can be continued from one year to the next during the child's first three years. Parents and care providers are taught to develop children's large and small muscle coordination; oral language through sensory stimulation, print and number awareness; appreciation of literature; sensitivity to music and rhythm; and basic concepts. ECLE addresses National Educational Goal 1.

Evidence of Effectiveness Claims of effectiveness were evaluated by using pre and post treatment group measures contrasted with those from equivalent comparison groups and with normative data provided by the test developer. The sample used included five separate groups of students enrolled in the ECLE program from 1988 to 1993. The subscales of the Mental Development Index (MDI) and the Psychomotor Development Index (PDI) of the Bayley Scales of Infant Development were the tools used to measure projected growth. Results showed statistically significant gains made on both the MDI and PDI indices between the ECLE and comparison groups. On average, for every one month in the program, ECLE children showed more than two months of growth relative to the normative group.

Requirements Education providers who adopt ECLE are required to have their staff trained and to purchase implementation materials. Some equipment may need to be purchased or located, such as a balance beam, chinning bar, ramps, and common household items such as salt shakers, tongs, and cotton balls.

Costs All costs are in the start-up period: a two day-training session ($950); one follow-up visit ($475); $45 for the ECLE manual for each educator who teaches parents/care providers; five videotapes ($175), plus travel expenses for the ECLE consultant.

Services A two-day ECLE seminar covers the aspects of the program, materials to be used, observation of videotapes, evaluation, and ways to find parents and/or care providers for the classes. After program implementation, follow-up visits by an experienced ECLE consultant provide opportunities for new teachers to observe demonstrations with parents and children in their classrooms.

Contact Dr. Ethna Reid, Reid Foundation, 3310 South 2700 East, Salt Lake City, Utah 84109. (801) 486-5083, FAX (801) 485-0561.

Developmental Funding: U.S. ED FIRST Grant and Local Funds.

PEP No. 92-2R (3/1/94)

Family Intergenerational-Interaction Literacy Model (FILM). A family literacy program that works with all family members to increase the educational level of disadvantaged parents and children.

Audience All significant family members (i.e., mothers, fathers, and extended family) and their preschool children from culturally diverse environments, including high school drop outs and first generation immigrant families, who need education in basic school curriculum and parenting strategies.

Description FILM is a center and home-based program designed to work with family members to improve basic literacy, employment and parenting skills so they can better achieve educational, economic, social and family goals. During the school year, the project concurrently provides literacy services to parents and early childhood education to their children. Through the Adult Interaction classes, parents experience large and small learning groups, as well as interactive and self-directed learning through ABE, GED or ESL classes twelve hours per week while their children are in the Early Learning Center nearby. Parents also participate in Parenting Interaction Discussion Groups one hour per week. The Parent/Child Interaction Playgroup is a one hour session each week. Parents and children participate in a one hour Home Visit Interaction with a parent facilitator every week. MODELS (Model, Observe, Discuss, Explore, integrate Life skills, and celebrate Success), a teaching for success strategy, is integrated throughout the five elements of the program. FILM addresses National Educational Goals 1, 6 and 8.

Evidence of Effectiveness Three claims of effectiveness were evaluated in the areas of adult, preschool and parenting education. Results showed that FILM compares very favorably with other adult education programs in promoting academic achievement and GED acquisition. Preschoolers who participated in the Early Learning Center consistently scored higher on school readiness indicators than the comparison population; and teachers in advanced educational settings ranked FILM preschool graduates higher in academic performance and social skills than their peers. The positive results of parent education effectiveness were validated by student interviews, staff observation, written evaluation tools, and teacher reports of parent involvement in their child(ren)'s education.

Requirements It is recommended that all five FILM components be replicated: (1) Adult Interaction Education; (2) Parent Discussion Group; (3) Home Visit Interaction; (4) Parent/Child Interaction Playgroup; and (5) Early Learning Center. The comprehensive program requires a strong commitment to the philosophy of integrated planning by the staff.

Costs Awareness materials are available upon request at no cost. The training program recommended for adopters is a five day in-depth training with two or three trainers which will include a workshop for teachers as well as special assistance for administrators. Training fees will include $250 per day honorarium, travel, lodging and meals. Materials cost will be $60 per adopting site. Training materials will be provided at no cost to initial demonstration sites.

Services Awareness materials are available at no cost. Project personnel and certified trainers are available to conduct awareness meetings at project site, adopter sites or conferences. Visitors are welcome at project site by appointment. Training is available at project site or adopter sites. Implementation, follow-up and evaluation services are available to adopters.

Contact *Site Visit Information Contact:* **Mary Brown, FILM Supervisor, Capitol Hill Elementary School, 2717 S. Robinson, Oklahoma City, OK 73109. (405) 235-0801.** *Training Information Contact:* **Dr. Donna Richardson, Oklahoma City University, Division of Education, 2501 N. Blackwelder, Oklahoma City, OK 73106. (405) 521-5373.**

Developmental Funding: U.S. ED Even Start Funding.

PEP No. 94-2 **(4/1/94)**

High/Scope K-3 Curriculum. A comprehensive method for organizing and managing classroom environments and instructional activities to help at-risk students improve their school achievement and literacy skills by giving them opportunities to initiate and engage in learning activities that contribute to their cognitive, social, and physical development.

Audience Approved by PEP for students in grades K-3 and their families.

Description The High/Scope K-3 Curriculum views children as active learners who learn best when they themselves plan, carry out, and reflect upon activities. Teaching staff observe, support, and extend children's activities by maintaining a daily routine that permits children to learn actively and construct their own knowledge; arranging instructional activity centers in the classroom to provide learning experiences in math, language, science, art, social studies, movement, and music that match children's needs and address appropriate content, skills, and concepts in these areas; joining in the children's activities, asking questions that extend children's plans, and helping them think; organizing daily small-group instructional workshops involving concepts and skills in all of the content areas; and engaging children in key child development experiences that help them learn to make choices and solve problems. Other features of the program include a child observation assessment technique, an emphasis on parent involvement, and a nationwide training network.

Evidence of Effectiveness At-risk students in classrooms utilizing the High/Scope K-3 Curriculum score significantly higher on overall achievement and subtests in reading, language, math, science, and social studies on standardized achievement tests than comparison students in classrooms with a traditional K-3 curriculum.

Requirements No special equipment or materials are required beyond the computers and developmentally appropriate manipulative and print materials that should be present in all good K-3 classrooms. However, classrooms need to be rearranged into activity areas. Training is open to administrators and teaching and caregiving staff working with children five to nine years old in public and private elementary schools and day care centers and homes. Several training options are available for teacher training through High/Scope.

Costs The cost for two-day workshop activities is $125/person for groups of 40 or more. Handout materials are included in this fee. Services on a consulting or contractual basis are available according to local needs. Consulting fees and travel expenses are negotiated on an individual basis. Week-long institutes can also be scheduled for groups of 20 or more participants. Institute fees are $400/person plus travel costs for High/Scope staff. Customized implementation plans include training for up to three years with costs ranging from $28,500 to $65,000 depending upon location, group size, and duration of the training activities. Videotapes (five total) are recommended for each program at a cost of $450. Printed teacher curriculum guides and supporting materials are required for each classroom, at a cost of $230.

Services In addition to training and materials, follow-up consultation is available.

Contact   A. Clay Shouse, Director, Development and Services, High/Scope Educational Research Foundation, 600 North River Street, Ypsilanti, MI 48198. (313) 485-2000, FAX (313) 485-0704.

Developmental Funding: U.S. Department of Education, Follow Through Program, state, and other.

PEP No. 92-8 **(3/92)**

High/Scope Preschool Curriculum. Based on the child development ideas of Jean Piaget, the High/Scope Preschool Curriculum views children as active learners, who learn best from activities that they themselves plan, carry out, and reflect upon. The children are encouraged to engage in a variety of key experiences that help them to make choices, solve problems, and actively contribute to their own development.

Audience   Approved by JDRP/PEP for preschool children of all abilities.

Description   The High/Scope Preschool Curriculum is an open-framework model derived from Piagetian theory. The curriculum originated from one of the first early childhood intervention programs of the 1960s, the High/Scope Perry Preschool Project, and was further developed with funding as a demonstration project in the First Chance Network for handicapped preschoolers. Through designated key experiences for children, teaching and parenting strategies, and child-observation materials, the curriculum provides a decision-making framework. Within this framework, teachers design a classroom program that reflects the expressed needs and interests of the children being served. This approach emphasizes the identification of the child's status on a developmental continuum by examining his/her strengths and accomplishments. The project views discrepancies in behavior between disabled and nondisabled age peers as developmental delays, not as deficiencies. Basing their tasks on this orientation, teachers initiate developmentally appropriate experiences in the classroom that reflect the basic long-range goals of the project. These goals are to develop children's ability to use a variety of skills in the arts and physical movement; to develop their knowledge of objects as a base of educational concept; to develop their ability to speak, dramatize, and graphically represent their experiences and communicate these experiences to other children and adults; to develop their ability to work with others, make decisions about what to do and how to do it, and plan their use of time and energy; and to develop their ability to apply their newly acquired reasoning capacity in a wide range of naturally occurring situations and with a variety of materials. The plan-do-review sequence encourages children to achieve these goals by involving them in decision-making and problem-solving situations throughout the day. The teacher's role is to support the children's decisions and encourage them to extend learning beyond the original plan. Similarly, teachers rely on a basic room arrangement and daily routine designed to stimulate and support active learning.

Evidence of Effectiveness   Preschool programs using the High/Scope Preschool Curriculum have produced evidence that they improve children's school success, later socioeconomic success, and social responsibility. As compared to teacher-directed instruction, the High/Scope Preschool Curriculum has also been shown to lead to significantly lower rates of delinquency.

Requirements   The model can be used in individual classrooms as well as entire programs. Inservice training for teaching teams and program administrators is strongly recommended.

Costs   The costs for program implementation vary depending upon the number of teaching teams and children involved. However, the approximate cost per child for the initial year of implementation is $260 for personnel training and $195 for materials. Travel costs for the trainer are additional. Costs for the second and subsequent years also vary, but typically do not exceed $60/child. Cost calculations assume that the curriculum is being adopted by an existing program; personnel and facility costs for the classroom are not taken into account.

Services   Awareness materials are available at no cost. Visitors are welcome at the project site by appointment. Project staff are available to participate in out-of-state awareness meetings (fees and expenses to be negotiated). Curriculum workshops can be arranged as follow-up to awareness sessions at local sites (fees and expenses to be negotiated). Training is provided at the project site (fees and expenses must be paid). Additional inservice activities are also available.

Contact   A. Clay Shouse, Director, Development and Services, High/Scope Educational Research Foundation, 600 North River Street, Ypsilanti, MI 48198. (313) 485-2000, FAX (313) 485-0704. Philip Hawkins. (313) 485-2000, Ext. 252.

JDRP No. 79-9 (**3/28/79**)
Recertified (**3/9/92**)

Developmental Funding: USOE BEH.

Kindergarten Integrated Thematic Experiences (KITE). A program designed to increase reading and math achievement by promoting the acquisition of basic reading and math readiness and language skills while helping children develop a positive self-image.

Audience Approved by PEP for kindergarten—regular, and academically disadvantaged students (Chapter I and at-risk). The main components of this program have been used successfully for migrant, special education, bilingual education (Spanish) and ESL students in primary grades. The program is used in all 50 states, American Samoa, Guam, Saipan, and 14 foreign countries.

Description Kindergarten Integrated Thematic Experiences (KITE) effectively combines child-initiated and teacher-directed activities within a planned environment. This multisensory program utilizes oral language, manipulatives, music, and play.

KITE emphasizes all areas of development—cognitive, language, physical, and social-emotional. The varied KITE experiences integrate language arts, math, art, music, literature, social studies, science, drama, and physical education experiences. It assists teachers in moving from traditional toward **developmentally appropriate** practices.

Through developmentally appropriate activities, children use concrete objects, have meaningful interactions with materials, adults, and each other; and experience structured and informal oral language. These interactions enable children to assimilate abstract concepts.

Language and interest is stimulated by the use of imaginary outer space characters—*Astro* and *Astra*.

During teacher-directed instructional time, the program utilizes discovery with a game-like presentation of materials and positive teacher feedback. There is positive recognition of and a belief in the ability of each child to succeed. The contents of *Astro and Astra's KITE Motivational Bag* delight children and foster teacher creativity. Literature, poem charts, and math charts are used for whole language development. The program includes interactive large- and small-group activities.

The KITE program provides essential program motivation, contains lesson materials for the units, and stimulates curiosity in the children. *Astro* and *Astra* display various feelings, thus enabling the children to identify with them. The program promotes a thematic, developmentally appropriate, integrated curriculum.

Evidence of Effectiveness Regular and at-risk students demonstrate significantly greater positive academic growth on pre-posttest models. **Soft data**—teacher testimonials of child success and joy of learning with *Astro* and *Astra*, imaginary outer space characters. **Hard data**—NCE gains (info. available upon request).

Requirements The program can be implemented by a single teacher, whole school, or entire district. A one-day training session is required for adoption.

There is a one-time start-up cost for basic nonconsumable materials per classroom. Additional materials to enhance the program are available.

Costs **Materials**—Start-up (one-time expenditure) $134.50 per classroom; Awareness-negotiable. **Training**—One-day expenses and honorarium $300 (negotiable); two-hour training video-no charge (30-day loan).

Services Written awareness materials, a 50-minute video, and grant-writing packets are available. Program staff are available to attend out-of-state awareness meetings; numerous demonstration sites and certified trainers are also available. Training is conducted at the program or adopter site. Implementation and follow-up services are available to adopters (costs to be negotiated). A three- to four-day Certified Trainer workshop is held annually in the San Francisco area in the last week of June.

Contact Jeanne Stout Burke, Director, KITE, Sunshine Gardens School, 1200 Miller Avenue, South San Francisco, CA 94080. (415) 588-8082, FAX (415) 343-8720.

Developmental Funding: Local.

PEP No. 90-11 **(2/9/90)**

On The Way to SUCCESS in Reading and Writing with Early Prevention of School Failure (Ages 4-7). A holistic program approach to staff development in assessment and curriculum alignment from prekindergarten through second grade with a central goal to improve their schools and with a shared purpose to increase student learning and sustain program effects for at-risk children.

Audience Approved by PEP for children in kindergarten and after kindergarten for identified at-risk students (ages 4-7).

Description The program begins with educators serving kindergarten children participating in a two-day training program to learn a team approach: (1) to administering a normed assessment battery to all kindergarten children; (2) to use the data plus parent reports, transitional records, and other pertinent information to generate a computerized printout of each child's developmental learning profile (visual, auditory, language, and motor synthesis); (3) to correlate assessment outcomes and observations with developmentally sequenced learning concepts which can be used as a guide for charting progress; (4) to utilize program developed literature-based reading, writing, language, and thinking curriculum resources; (5) to monitor each child's progress using on-going portfolios and authentic performance assessments; and (6) to prepare written transitional reports for first grade teachers and parent conferences.

The child who is at-risk continued to participate in the program in first grade with age-and individual-appropriate initial and ongoing authentic assessments, literature-based curriculum resources, monitoring procedures, and parent involvement activities. A literacy-based reading and writing program reflects each child's interest and development. Reading and writing portfolios are continued in second grade.

The program celebrates the way children learn, recognizes each child's individuality, and has high expectations that a child will learn regardless of socio-economic status, language proficiency, parental involvement, experiential background, or ethnicity.

Evidence of Effectiveness Program evaluators demonstrated that, as a result of their participation in EPSF in kindergarten (1985-86) and On the Way to SUCCESS in first grade (1986-87), students at-risk of academic success in kindergarten and first grade could not be distinguished from their typical or average second grade peers on the basis of scores from tests administered in 1988. The robust effects of the program were demonstrated by the statistically significant and educationally meaningful gains of a demographically diverse group of students from 11 districts in nine states. The project has an unparalleled history of success: twenty years of documented student, teacher, and parent impact by constantly updating the program as a result of research and experience.

Requirements The EPSF kindergarten program requires two days of training. The On the Way to SUCCESS in first grade requires one day of training.

Costs The EPSF kindergarten program is a **one time cost** of $600 per **building** and the On the Way to SUCCESS first grade program is a **one time cost** of $145 per **classroom**.

Services The program provides awareness materials and presentations at no cost. Initial and sustained staff development are provided by sharing cost. State consortium meetings and leadership conferences are sponsored throughout the year at various locations.

Contact   Luceille Werner, National Director, Peotone School District 207U, 114 North Second Street, P.O. Box 956, Peotone, IL 60468. (708) 258-3478 or (800) 933-3478, FAX (708) 258-3484.

Developmental Funding: USDE ESEA Title III (EPSF);
USDE ESEA Title I (Migrant); USDE (SUCCESS).

PEP No. 90-17 **(6/11/90)**

Parents As Teachers. An early parenting program that provides comprehensive services to families from the third trimester of pregnancy until the children are three years of age. The program is designed to help parents give their children a solid foundation for school success and to form a closer working relationship between home and school.

Audience Approved by PEP for parents/guardians of children below the age of three.

Description Parents as Teachers is designed as a primary prevention program for all families aimed at helping parents give their children a solid foundation for school success and at forming a closer working relationship between home and school. It is based on the philosophy that parents are children's first and most influential teachers. As a parent involvement program from the earliest years, Parents As Teachers directly impacts the first National Goal for Education addressing school readiness. Parent educators trained in this model deliver family services using the Parents As Teachers curriculum, which includes information on child development and guidance in fostering a child's development. Services include regularly scheduled personal visits in the home, parent group meetings, periodic screening and monitoring of educational and sensory development, and access to a parent resource center.

Evidence of Effectiveness Children of parents participating in the program score significantly higher at age three on the Kaufman Assessment Battery for Children and the Zimmerman Preschool Language Scale, and score significantly higher at the end of grade one on standardized tests of reading and mathematics than the comparison and nationally normed groups. After three years in the program, parents demonstrate significantly more knowledge on program-developed and validated scales of child development knowledge and child-rearing practices; are more likely to regard their school district as responsive to a child's needs; and are more likely to have children's hearing professionally tested than the comparison parents. The greater the parent participation in the program the better children performed on measures of intellectual and language development. At the end of grade one, parents who participated in the program were found to be significantly more involved in their children's school experience than were comparison group parents.

Requirements Program services are offered through the school district for a minimum of eight months, preferably year round. The comprehensive program requires strong commitment to the philosophy of the program; availability of parent educator(s) with skills necessary to work with parents in a supportive learning environment; training for the parent educator(s); facilities for parent group meetings; and financial resources to support the parent educator(s) in the work of the program.

Costs Start-up cost is $2,725 for training and materials/supplies. Operation costs for 12 months are estimated at $562 per family (assuming a 60-family load per full-time parent educator), and include parent educator salary, travel, and additional materials/supplies. This assumes school district contribution of space, clerical assistance, and program administration.

Services In addition to training and curriculum materials, consultation and follow-up services are available through the Parents as Teachers National Center.

Contact Mildred Winter, Director, Parents as Teachers National Center, Inc., 9374 Olive Boulevard, St. Louis, MO 63132. (314) 432-4330 or Sharon Rhodes, Program Development Director.

Developmental funding: Title IV-C ESEA, Danforth Foundation, state, and local.

PEP No. 91-2 (**2/19/91**)

P.I.A.G.E.T. (Promoting Intellectual Adaptation Given Experiential Transforming), Project. A program to develop English language and cognitive competencies in bilingual preschool children whose native language is Spanish using a school-home setting.

Audience   Approved by PEP for preschool and kindergarten children and their parents.

Description   Project P.I.A.G.E.T. (Promoting Intellectual Adaptation Given Experiential Transforming) is based on three interrelated components. The teaching method includes one bilingual teacher and an aide per classroom trained in using 22 Piagetian-derived teaching strategies. Secondly, the bilingual aide helps Limited English Proficient (LEP) parents develop a meaningful educational home program that reinforces the learning concepts taught at school. The aide works half-time in the classroom and half-time visiting the homes to train parents. The third component is the academic assessment of the classroom children and parents' skills. The curriculum includes 90 concepts; use of Daily Activity Plans and Daily Observation Cards emphasizing diagnosis and prescription; and classroom activities grouped at learning centers including manipulation of objects, exploration and dramatic play, and other individualized activities.

Evidence of Effectiveness   Limited English speaking students who participate in Project P.I.A.G.E.T. for one year achieve significantly higher gains than a comparison group on tests of receptive language and reading readiness. Students also achieve greater than the norm in NCEs in English language reading, language, and mathematics by the time they are in fourth grade and these gains are sustained through grade 6.

Requirements   The minimum user requirements include two days of initial training with two days of follow-up training. Each classroom must have bilingual/bicultural professional and paraprofessional staffing. Implementation of the home component consisting of monthly home visits by the paraprofessional is also required.

Costs   Costs per classroom include two days of training for a teacher and an aide at a cost of approximately $300, materials cost of $800-$900 to include manual, workbooks, tests, and materials reproduction and, in most cases, the additional cost of an aide in the classroom at the prevailing wage rate. Travel costs of approximately $400-$500 per year should be anticipated for implementation of the home component.

Services   In addition to training and materials, follow-up consultation is available.

Contact   Iris Cintron, Bethlehem Area School District, 1516 Sycamore Street, Bethlehem, PA 18017. (215) 861-0500 or Dr. Thomas Yawkey, Department of Curriculum and Instruction, 159 Chambers Building, The Pennsylvania State University, University Park, PA 16802. (814) 863-2937.

Developmental Funding: USDE ESEA Title VII Bilingual Education.   PEP No. 92-19 **(2/10/93)**

Audience Families with young children (birth to 7 years of age). Families utilizing the services of the program have typically experienced difficulties in early adolescence such as teen pregnancy, single-parent homes, poverty, low literacy skills, high school dropouts, abusive relationships, and low self-esteem. Many of these adults are striving to "break the chain" for themselves and their children—to raise their educational level in order to receive better opportunities in the working world and to give their children an "even start" with their peers in school.

Description Even Start offers families integrated educational opportunities through a Family Learning Center, home-based activities, and collaborative services of community organizations and agencies. The model provides teaching and learning strategies that focus on family strengths and needs. The Family Learning Center (FLC) provides a setting that combines adult education, early childhood and parent education, and parent-child interaction. Adult activities include basic education, GED studies and computer skills, parenting or life skills and pre-employability instruction. Educational activities for children are designed to develop pre-literacy skills, such as social interaction and language development. Parent and child activities can be duplicated at home and include reading, drawing, story-telling, arts and crafts, and others. Home-based instruction supports the belief that families function as a unit and that attention must be focused on the child's home environment. Families receive 4 to 8 visits/year and parent-child activities, child activities, and parenting resource materials are taken into the home. Collaborative services are combined efforts with community agencies and organizations that ensure providing families with comprehensive services. Examples of the types of agencies and organizations that are brought into collaborative efforts are hospitals, legal services, churches, community colleges, and local universities. Support services include door-to-door transportation, meals, information and referrals, center and home-based counseling, and special family events/field trips. Webster Groves Even Start addresses National Educational Goals 1 and 6.

Evidence of Effectiveness Claims of effectiveness were evaluated by data collected on test scores, self-reports, and participant ratings by parent educators. Results showed that adults attending the FLC showed significant increases in passing the GED and parenting knowledge and skills. Those parents who were active in the program took more responsibility for their child's growth and development and achieved their personal goals. Outcomes for children showed that those attending the FLC significantly increased their receptive vocabulary and were equal to other children in preschool skills when they entered kindergarten.

Requirements School or related facility adequate to serve 15-30 families (including GED education room, computer lab with at least 7 computers and software, infant, toddler and Pre-K classrooms, and adequate office space); staff (program coordinator, secretary, parent educators, family educator, family advocate, early childhood classroom teachers, and aides to staff 4 classrooms, computer instructor, and ABE/GED instructor); a home component consisting of 4-8 home visits/year; seven days of training in family literacy, home visitations, and developing a Family Learning Center; follow-up training sessions in operating a FLC; and continuing inservice of staff.

Costs Costs include personnel (approximately 10 full and part-time); materials and supplies; training; and services (e.g., meals, rent and utilities, travel, etc.). Estimated costs for the start-up and follow-up years are approximately $200,000/year based on servicing approximately 50 families per year.

Services Initial training (7 days) is provided by the Webster Groves Family Learning Center Coordinator and a trained staff member; follow-up sessions (two 2-day sessions) are conducted by one staff person.

Contact   Diane Givens, Coordinator, 9153 (R) Manchester, Rock Hill, MO 63119. (314) 968-5354, FAX (314) 963-6411.

Developmental Funding: U.S. ED ESEA Even Start and local sources.   PEP No. 94-16 **(5/1/94)**

Cognitively Oriented Pre-Primary Experience (COPE). A comprehensive, sequentially programmed, pre-primary curriculum and management system that provides for individual developmental growth and learning of basic readiness skills.

Description Cognitively Oriented Pre-Primary Experience (COPE)'s wide range of activities and objectives (3-6 years developmentally) makes it effective for use with pre-primary children from varied socioeconomic backgrounds and with varied learning needs. It is appropriate for students in pre-kindergarten, kindergarten, and early first grade, including those with developmental lags and learning disabilities. The program is diagnostic/prescriptive. Based on the child's skills and development at entry, he/she works through a series of activities to reach advanced objectives. With its well-defined, step-by-step, closely sequenced levels, the curriculum is extremely helpful both in determining a child's needs and in stimulating outstanding intellectual and language growth. Each level is essentially a mini-lesson plan complete with objective, materials, method, and evaluation. Children pursue the objectives through individualized, small-group, and large-group instruction as well as in free-inquiry situations. The program contains lessons in perceptual-motor, conceptual language, math/science development, as well as social studies, health/safety, art, and music. Teachers, paraprofessionals, and parents who attend a COPE workshop not only learn to use the curriculum materials, but also come to understand how to put the program to use in their own particular situations. The program addresses Goal 1 of the National Goals for Education by providing a high quality, developmentally appropriate program that helps prepare children for school and also provides support and training for parents. Training, implementation, and follow-up services are available to adopters (costs to be negotiated). One set of curriculum materials is required per classroom.

Contact   Mary Alice Felleisen, Director, COPE, 38 North Waterloo Road, Devon, PA 19333. (610) 688-7993 or (800) 444-5729.

Developmental Funding: USOE ESEA Title III.   JDRP No. 75-49 **(5/16/75)**

Early Prevention of School Failure (EPSF). This program is designed to prevent school failure by identifying the developmental levels and learning styles of children ages four to six years. A follow-up program is also provided (see On The Way to SUCCESS).

Description Early Prevention of School Failure (EPSF) has demonstrated that the assessment tools, conferencing, and effective teaching strategies prevent children from failing academically. The EPSF program identifies every child's developmental level in language, auditory, visual, and motor areas as well as their learning style. The norm-referenced assessment instruments and observational procedures have been selected and/or developed to assess: (1) the developmental levels of children's language, auditory, visual, and motor synthesis; and (2) each child's experiential background. The computer printout reflects: (1) the developmental age of each child compared to a norm group of the same age; (2) what a child can do (criterion-referenced); and (3) observations by teachers and parents. Portfolios are maintained on at-risk students. The strategies include a literature-based reading and writing program, themes and units, higher process thinking activities, and researched steps for teacher-directed instruction of children with similar needs. The program is based on child growth and development and the principles of learning which focus on different rates of learning and different learning styles. EPSF was developed on a sound foundation of learning research and child growth and development. The research on over 100,000 children in ongoing yearly EPSF evaluations has demonstrated a seven-year developmental age span in a class of 25 entering-kindergarten children. A third longitudinal study, conducted in 1985 through 1988 in 11 districts in nine states, demonstrated statistically significant and educationally meaningful gains. A fourth longitudinal study began in 1992 in 16 diverse school districts.

Contact   Luceille Werner, National Director, Peotone School District 207U, 114 North Second Street, P.O. Box 956, Peotone, IL 60468. (708) 258-3478 or (800) 933-3478, FAX (708) 258-3484.

Developmental Funding: USDE ESEA Title I (Migrant); USDE (SUCCESS).   JDRP No. 74-46 **(5/15/74)**
Recertified **(4/19/77)**

Family Oriented Structured Preschool Activity (FOSPA). ("Seton Hall" Program). A program that prepares the parent to be the child's first and most significant teacher.

Description Family Oriented Structured Preschool Activity (FOSPA) is based on research findings that support the fact that the early years are critical to a child's development. Goal 1 of the eight National Goals for Education adopted by the National Governor's Association stresses that all children in America will start school ready to learn. The State of Minnesota also challenges educational institutions to empower parents to fully support all participants in their children's learning and development. Therefore, it is believed that parents as their children's first and most significant teachers, can benefit when the educational community is willing to help them in their parenting role. The FOSPA program, begun in 1972, focuses on: the quality of the parent-child relationship; the development of a competent and resourceful child; and supporting parents in their parenting role. FOSPA is designed to involve parents and their child the year before kindergarten entry in activities that will begin to prepare the child for kindergarten. Parents accompany their child to the neighborhood elementary school once a week from September to May for two-hour sessions. While at school, parents work and play with their child at learning stations set up in basic skill areas within an environment designed to meet the developing needs of the whole child. Parents observe formal model teaching and informal child-teacher interaction, and participate in a discussion group facilitated by a licensed parent educator. In this supportive, caring environment they learn about their child's development and share ideas and concerns about parenting. During this time children have a preschool experience with a qualified early childhood educator. Take-home activity kits are designed to promote parent-child interaction and growth in basic skills based on a validated assessment of the child's skills. Both parent and child grow in confidence as they participate in the program. This atmosphere of trust between home and school that parents develop continues when the child enters elementary school. This model has been adapted to use with Early Childhood Special Education, single parent groups, parents and young children infant through age three, parents with literacy needs, English as a Second Language groups, teen parents, and groups designed for dads. A two- to three-day training is available for adopters.

Contact Jeanne Hoodecheck, Program Director, District #742 Community School, 820 8th Avenue South, St. Cloud, MN 56301. (612) 253-5828.

Developmental Funding: USOE ESEA Title III.

JDRP NO. 75-48 **(5/15/75)**

Mother-Child Home Program (MCHP) of the Verbal Interaction Project, Inc.
A nondidactic, home-based program to prevent educational disadvantage in two- to four-year old children of parents with low income and limited education, and to foster parents' literacy and self-esteem, by enhancing parent-child verbal interaction. JDRP approved for two-year olds at risk for educational disadvantage.

Description The Mother-Child Home Program (MCHP) of the Verbal Interaction Project, Inc. theory is that cognitive and social-emotional growth results from the playful exchange between parent and child of conceptually rich language around permanently assigned curriculum materials (books and toys). In twice-weekly play with these materials in Home Sessions, "Toy Demonstrators" (home visitors) model for the parent a curriculum of verbal and other positive interaction with their children. Weekly Guide Sheets contain a fun-filled curriculum illustrated by the current book or toy. Among 29 adoptions, children at risk for educational disadvantage at age two were no longer so after two years of the MCHP. Program graduates met national achievement test norms in elementary school and graduated from high school at a normal rate. Effectiveness evidence and adoption training information are available at the National Center for Mother-Child Home Program.

Contact Dr. Phyllis Levenstein, Director, National Center for Mother-Child Home Program, 3268 Island Road, Wantagh, NY 11793. (516) 785-7077. (Affiliated with the State University of New York at Stony Brook.)

Developmental Funding: USOE, NIMH, Carnegie Corporation of NY, Rockefeller Brothers Fund, etc.

JDRP No. 78-165 **(11/27/78)**

Perception+. A prerequisite to any formal learning discipline. Approved for kindergarten (Level I) and first grade (Level II).

Description Perception+ addresses the student's ability to learn. It is based on the premise that learning can be learned as a skill. Perception is not a reading, writing, or arithmetic program; it prepares students to learn to read, write, and do arithmetic. It is not a remedial program, but it has been used for remediation. It is designed to be introduced at the kindergarten level, but is being used effectively from preschool to junior high, in regular and special education classrooms. Perception + addresses Goal 3 of the National Goals for Education as a prerequisite for young students to demonstrate more competency in learning to read, write, and compute.

Perception+ is perceiving: seeing what is looked at, hearing what is listened to, feeling what is touched. These are fundamental requisites for learning, the foundation for the "basics", and they are attainable through the 15-minute Perception+ lessons, given three times a week throughout the school year. An entire class, not just those identified as having perceptual deficiency, participates as a group. The teacher offers experiences, and the students describe them in their own words. Perception+ is also processing. Unprocessed information is meaningless and irrelevant. In each lesson of the Level I and II instructional units ($80 per level), Perception+ students continually process data. They analyze, relate, compare, judge, sequence, decode. They critique and self-correct. They internalize information through their individual and group interaction with experiences. The teacher functions as the provider of experience and director of the process of internalization, not as an expositor of information. The Perception+ program provides children with the means for making information meaningful. Finally, Perception+ is applying information that has been internalized and can be easily and readily applied.

Contact Monika Steinberg, Program Director, Perception+, Educational Information and Resource Center (EIRC), 606 Delsea Drive, Sewell, NJ 08080. (609) 582-7000, FAX (609) 582-4206.

Developmental Funding: USOE ESEA Title III.

JDRP No. 74-78 **(6/7/74)**

Portage Project. A family-guided, home-based program to serve children with disabilities, from birth to 6, and their families.

Description The Portage Project is a home-based intervention program for young children with disabilities and their families. The family-guided model, whether employed totally in the home or in a classroom-home combination program, centers on a home visitor assisting caregivers in identifying and addressing IEP/IFSP goals of the child and family based on the child's developmental needs and the desires, interests, and cultural mores of the family. The child's goals are implemented through naturally occurring activities that the child and caregiver participate in on a daily basis. Play activities are also used as a means of addressing child goals and enhancing caregiver-child interaction. The Portage Model addresses the first of the National Goals for Education by helping parents support their preschool child's development and, in this way, helping to prepare children for school. Results of the Portage Project model at the original demonstration site and at replication sites indicate that through this program young children can progress above their expected developmental level and families can gain skills to enhance their child's development. The model is appropriate for use in a variety of settings including preschools, prekindergartens, infant programs, and Head Start programs. Administrative commitment to a family-guided intervention model that addresses child and family goals is a prerequisite for successful implementation of the Portage Model.

Contact Julia Herwig, Director, Portage Project, P.O. Box 564, Portage, WI 53901. (608) 742-8811, FAX (608) 742-2384.

JDRP No. 75-75 **(11/10/75)**
Recertified **(1/85)**

Developmental Funding: USOE and SEP.

Search and Teach. An interdisciplinary model for the prevention of learning disorders.

Description The program provides a two-part approach to the prevention of learning disabilities: scanning and intervention. Scanning locates vulnerable children through SEARCH, an individual 20-minute test administered by teachers and educational assistants to all children in kindergarten or early in first grade. SEARCH taps the neuropsychological precursors of learning problems in young children, yielding data required for setting intervention priorities, and building teaching plans to guide intervention. Raw test scores may be evaluated either by age or local norms. Age norms permit comparison of a child's score with a broad reference group: the standardization sample of 2,319 children from intact kindergarten classes in inner-city, suburban, small-town, and rural areas. Local norms permit comparison with the immediate peer group with whom children will be learning in their own schools. Intervention is based upon TEACH, a prescriptive approach that helps to meet the educational needs defined by SEARCH. TEACH tasks are organized into five clusters relating to SEARCH components; tasks have been chosen for their experimentally demonstrated contribution to the job analysis of reading. The 55 tasks proceed through three stages of increasing complexity: recognition-discrimination, copying, and recall. Mastery criteria are provided to ensure automaticity in the application of these skills in reading and the language arts. TEACH provides a two-part sequence of activities with emphasis on accuracy of perception in the first part and on intermodal and prereading skills in the second.

Contact   Rosa A. Hagin, School Consultation Center, Fordham University at Lincoln Center, 113 West 60th Street, New York, NY 10023. (212) 636-6484 or Archie A. Silver, Department of Psychiatry, University of South Florida Medical School, 3515 Fletcher Avenue, Tampa, FL 33613. (813) 972-7062.

Developmental Funding: USOE BEH Title VI-G.   JDRP No. 79-33 (9/12/79)

Section 12

Special Education

* These programs are currently funded by the NDN.

Summary of Program Services for Section 12

Program	Goal*	Page	Dissem. Funds Available: NDN	Dissem. Funds Available: Other	Costs to Potential Adopter: Hon	Trav	Per Diem	On Site Visitation: Home Site	Adopt Site	Materials: Free Paper	Video	Film Strip	Other	Staff Available: Home Site	Adopt Site	Costs to Adopter: Hon	Trav	Per Diem	Certified Trainers Available: State(s)	Training Time Required: Day(s)
Achievement-Based Curriculum (ABC) - Project I Can	3	12-10				✓	✓	✓	✓	✓	✓		✓	✓		(negotiable)			CA, CO, FL, IL, IN, MD, NM, NY, NC, OH, OR, OK, TX, UT, WI, VA, WI	3+
ADAPT, Project	3	12-1	✓		(negotiable)			✓	✓	✓	✓			✓	✓	(negotiable)			AK, AR, CO, VT	2
All Children Totally Involved . . . (ACTIVE)	3	12-10			✓	✓	✓	✓	✓	✓	✓			✓	✓	✓	✓	✓	AL, AZ, OK, OR, WA	1
Developmental Therapy Model	1,3	12-11			✓	✓	✓	✓	✓	✓				✓	✓	✓	✓	✓	(none)	3+
Early Recognition . . . (ERIN)	1	12-11				✓	✓	✓	✓	✓				✓	✓	✓	✓	✓	MI, OH	3+
Elsmere Project	3	12-12			✓	✓	✓	✓	✓	✓				✓	✓	✓	✓	✓	D.C., FL, NC	2
INSITE Model	1	12-2	✓	✓	(negotiable)			✓	✓	✓	✓				✓	(negotiable)			AL, CA, FL, GA, IA, MA, MI, MN, MO, NM, OK, PA, SC, TN, TX, UT, WV	6
Lab School of Washington, The (LSW)	3	12-3	(info. not available)																	
Mainstream Amplification . . . (MARRS)	3	12-4				✓	✓	✓	✓	✓	✓	✓		✓			✓		CA, IL, IA, MN, MS, NE, OH, UT, WA	<½
Modification of Children's Oral Language	3	12-12				✓	✓	✓	✓	✓	✓			✓	✓		✓	✓	(all states)	1
Multi-Agency Project . . . (MAPPS)	1	12-5		✓		✓	✓	✓	✓	✓	✓			✓	✓		✓		AK, CA, ID, NV, WY	2
Precision Teaching Project	3	12-13			✓	✓	✓	✓	✓	✓			✓	✓	✓		✓	✓	CO, FL, MT, UT, WA	1
Programming for Early Education . . . (PEECH)	1, 7, 8	12-6	✓		✓	✓	✓	✓	✓	✓	✓		✓	✓	✓		✓	✓	AR, IL, MS, OK, SD	2+

* National Goals for Education—definitions for each goal can be found on pages 5-7.

Summary of Program Services for Section 12 (cont'd)

Program	Goal*	Page	AWARENESS — Dissem. Funds Available		AWARENESS — Costs to Potential Adopter			On Site Visitation Available		Materials Available				Staff Available		TRAINING — Costs to Adopter			Certified Trainers Available	Training Time Required
			NDN	Other	Hon	Trav	Per Diem	Home Site	Adopt Site	Free Paper	Video	Film Strip	Other	Home Site	Adopt Site	Hon	Trav	Per Diem	State(s)	Day(s)
Regional Program for Preschool Children with Disabilities	1	12-13				✓	✓	✓	✓	✓	✓	✓		✓	✓		✓	✓	CT, NY, TX	1-3
SKI-HI Outreach	1	12-7	✓	✓	(negotiable)			✓	✓	✓	✓		✓		✓	(negotiable)			AR, CT, FL, GA, HI, IN, KY, LA, ME, MI, MN, MO, MS, NE, NM, NV, NY, OH, OK, SD, TN, TX, UT, WI, WV, CD (Ontario)	3+
Systematic Screening ... (SSBD)	3	12-8	✓		(negotiable)					✓	✓		✓		✓	(negotiable)			CA, CO, KY, LA, MT, OK, OR, PA, UT, WV	1
Teaching Research ... (TRIP)	1	12-14		✓	(negotiable)			✓		✓	✓		✓	✓			✓	✓	KS, SC	3+
Youth Transition Program (YTP)		12-9	(info. not available)																	

* National Goals for Education—definitions for each goal can be found on pages 5-7.

ADAPT, Project. A comprehensive, replicable service delivery model for secondary and postsecondary learning disabled students ages 12 through 21. The project increases the number of students receiving full-time service in the educational mainstream, reduces the dropout rate of learning disabled students, and improves their basic academic skills.

Audience Approved by PEP for secondary learning disabled (LD) students (grades 6-12) and learning disabled adults in postsecondary vocational education programs.

Description Project ADAPT augments a school's existing LD service delivery system, improving the structure by increasing knowledge, skills, awareness, communication, and coordination. Central to the program is the concept of producing student outcomes through two key elements: changing the way teachers teach (Teacher ADAPTation) and changing the way students learn (Student ADAPTation). A two-day training for resource room personnel, a team of content area teachers, and support staff is the initial activity. The returning team works to modify existing structural and attitudinal barriers.

Three key areas for teacher adaptation are utilized: teaching skills, curricula and materials, and collaboration. The project training process instructs teachers in using alternative organization, management, presentation, practice, and assessment techniques to adapt the regular classroom environment for the LD student. All teachers learn to assess both their curricula and their teaching materials for appropriateness.

Student adaptation is in the domain of the resource teacher. The two program components focus directly upon the needs of secondary and postsecondary LD students: re-teaching and adaptive skill instruction. The goals are to remediate basic skill deficiencies and to equip learners with skills that will transfer to the regular classroom and the world of work.

Evidence of Effectiveness Twenty-two percent of learning disabled students were mainstreamed on a full-time basis after one year in the project; 43 percent after two years (national mainstreaming rate is 15 percent). Fewer than five percent of LD students dropped out of school (national rate for LD student is 38 percent). LD students in the program achieved greater than expected gains in basic academic skills.

Requirements For schools that have an LD program, no special staff are required. Two days of training for the core group are required. The major prerequisite is a moderate level of staff commitment. Minimal equipment and supplemental materials for students are suggested.

Costs The costs for adopting the project are travel, lodging, and per diem for one trainer during the two-day training, training manual ($25.00) for each participant, and a training fee (to be negotiated).

Services Awareness materials are available at no cost. The project staff is available for awareness sessions (costs to be negotiated). Implementation and follow-up services are available to adopters (costs to be negotiated). Statistical analysis of evaluation data is provided to all school districts submitting pre-posttests scores.

Contact Celia Meyers, 123 East Broadway, Cushing, OK 74023. (918) 225-1882, FAX (918) 225-4711. E-Mail: cmeyers@inet.ed.gov

Developmental Funding: Title VI-G Child Service Demonstration Center, state, and Office of Special Education and Postsecondary Demonstration Projects.

PEP No. 90-06 (2/9/90)

INSITE Model. A home-based program to help parents and others identify children from birth to age 5 who are multidisabled with sensory impairment to receive home programming to facilitate their optimal development.

Audience Approved by PEP for families who have infants or young children (0-5 years) with multihandicap sensory impairments and other disabilities.

Description The major goal of the INSITE Model program is to identify families with young children who are multidisabled with sensory impairment as close to their birth as possible and provide their families with complete home programming that will facilitate the children's optimal development.

Specific goals for the program are: the child will be able to interact meaningfully with other persons in the home and with objects in play; use residual sight and/or hearing as well as possible; build a communication system to convey his/her basic wants, needs, feelings, and observations; and reach the highest level of independence possible. The family is encouraged to have a warm, positive relationship with the child; understand the child's disabilities; provide a stimulating interactive home environment; and develop the skills and knowledge necessary to assist in setting goals for their child.

Elements of the program include identification and screening, direct services, support services such as physical and occupational therapy and medical services, and a program management system. All aspects of service are provided either directly or indirectly by INSITE support staff.

Evidence of Effectiveness A national data system collects yearly information on demographic status and child/parent progress for all participating adoption programs. Documented outcomes and benefits: (1) gains in five developmental areas (motor, perception, daily living, cognition/communication/language, and socialization) by children in INSITE programming are higher than would be expected due to maturation alone; (2) rate of growth in these areas accelerates during INSITE intervention; (3) families receiving INSITE services keep their children at home rather than placing them in institutions; (4) parents acquire skills they can use to facilitate their children's development; and (5) parents themselves perceive a significant improvement in their abilities to manage and promote their children's development.

Requirements Minimal requirements for program implementation include one full-time or part-time parent advisor to make weekly home visits, basic training for six days, a two-volume *INSITE* manual and other teaching/testing materials, support staff and materials, and a supervisor (for larger programs).

Costs Cost per child for 11 months of service is approximately $1,925 including direct and indirect costs.

Services Awareness materials are available at no cost. Visitors are welcome by appointment at demonstration sites in their home state and out of state. Program staff are available to attend out-of-state awareness meetings (costs to be negotiated). Training is available at adopter sites (costs to be negotiated). Implementation and follow-up services are available to adopters (costs to be negotiated).

Contact Don Barringer, Director, SKI-HI Institute, Utah State University, Logan, UT 84322-1900. (801) 752-4601, FAX (801) 755-0317.

Developmental Funding: U.S. Office of Special Education, Handicapped Children's Early Education Program, and the Utah State Legislature.

PEP No. 89-3 **(3/24/89)**

Lab School of Washington, The (LSW). A program designed to offer comprehensive educational services that meet the needs of learning disabled individuals preschool through young adult.

Audience Children and young adults (10-18) with average to superior intelligence with severe learning disabilities.

Description LSW is the only program in the U.S. that uses integrated arts and academic clubs to teach learning disabled students content area curricula and basic skills in a regular classroom setting. A multisensory and experiential approach form the program's foundation. Through diagnostic-prescriptive methods, the teaching staff seeks ways by which each student learns, discovers each student's strengths and interests, and experiments until effective techniques are found to help the student learn. The LSW program operates on a 182-day school year, 8:30 a.m. to 3:30 p.m. The program is complemented by an after school program from 3:30 to 6:30 p.m., a career and college counseling program, a tutoring program, and a range of diagnostic and related services program. The LSW class range is from 11:1 student-teacher ratio in the elementary and intermediate programs to a 5:1 ratio in the secondary programs. Students are immersed in the arts and academic clubs. The arts areas deal with symbols, patterns, and problem solving. In an academic club, higher order skills and sophisticated, content-based subject matter are taught through a dramatic framework, visual, and concrete materials. Each club for the elementary and intermediate age levels provides total immersion in a topic and follows a developmental sequence based on child development and the development of human history. Students progress from the Cave Club (first grade) to the Industrialists Club (sixth grade). The club approach is utilized in different ways in the secondary program (i.e., Humanities, Restaurant Programs and the School Store). LSW addresses National Educational Goal 3.

Evidence of Effectiveness Two claims of effectiveness were evaluated and were complemented by LSW staff profiles of students and alumni to illustrate the individual impact of the program's approach. Results showed that LSW students demonstrated significant gains in key academic skills, specifically reading comprehension and mathematics reasoning, as measured by standardized norm-referenced achievement tests, and they showed greater academic and personal success than similar learning disabled students nationally.

Requirements A team configuration composed of an administrator, content area teacher, special education teacher, art teacher, and related services personnel. One calendar year for a leader of a team of professionals from a potential adopting school or district who will be enrolled and complete the Master's program in Special Education: Learning Disabilities at The American University. Other team members will need to spend one summer at the LSW campus in intensive training.

Costs Release time for professionals to attend the training program. Tuition, travel, living expenses. In-service time for participants and other staff on location. Program materials will vary depending on the location of the adopting site. The program materials include audio, video, and a computer software program developed by students.

Services Ongoing staff in-service training; graduate training in conjunction with The American University; and LSW workshops.

Contact Sally L. Smith, Founder and Director, LSW; Professor, The American University, 4759 Reservoir Rd., NW, Washington, D.C. 20007. (202) 965-6600, FAX (202) 965-5105.

Developmental Funding: National Endowment for the Arts and private funding.   PEP No. 93-9R2 **(5/1/94)**

Mainstream Amplification Resource Room Study (MARRS). Sound field amplification technology used to enhance instruction, lessen teacher voice fatigue, and improve academic achievement in reading and language arts for students in grades K-6.

Audience Approved by JDRP for improvement of teaching and quality of instruction in reading and language arts for all students but especially students with mild hearing losses (MHL) grades K-6. The program has been used in regular and special education classrooms early childhood through grade 12 for instruction in all subject areas.

Description The Mainstream Amplification Resource Room Study (MARRS) program uses sound field amplification of the regular or special education teacher's voice in the presentation of the school's regular curriculum. Amplification equipment is installed in the classroom and the teacher wears a wireless FM microphone which permits freedom of movement in the classroom. The amplification allows the instructor to maintain a consistent signal approximately 10 decibels above the noise level in the classroom. Thus an improved listening environment is created for all students. Amplification enhances the clarity of oral instructions, promotes student attention, lessens teacher voice fatigue and increases academic achievement scores, particularly for students with mild (MHL) hearing losses who are to be found in all classrooms.

Data from the original study suggest 30% of all students in regular classrooms and as many as 75% of special education students have educationally significant hearing losses, many of which are undetected by routine school hearing screenings. MARRS provides a cost-efficient alternative/supplement to resource room instruction for mainstreamed mildly disabled students as well as an effective environmental modification to benefit all students and teachers. Statistically significant gains in academic achievement are demonstrated by target students in the least restrictive environment at a fraction of the cost of resource room intervention.

In the 1-86 validated study using data from four adopting districts, a pre-post experimental-control group design was utilized to demonstrate that K-6 target students (MHL) receiving instruction in standard classrooms equipped with sound field amplification make statistically significant greater gains in standardized achievement scores than do target students in control (nonamplified) classrooms ($p<.05$).

Requirements No special staff, facilities, or curriculum materials are required. The program is designed to enhance the ongoing curriculum, improve teaching, and create an improved listening/learning environment for all students. The adopting district purchases sound amplification equipment which is installed in classroom(s). Following a brief inservice, teachers use amplification for oral instruction.

(1) One-time purchase of sound field equipment, which can be used for years with minimal ongoing costs. Cost per student varies with the number of children in amplified classrooms and decreases with subsequent years as equipment continues to be used. (2) Portion of costs (to be negotiated) for installation and inservice of local staff by program personnel. Release time for teacher inservice is not ordinarily required.

Services An NDN funded Developer/Demonstrator program. Awareness materials are available at no cost. Visitors are welcome at program sites any time. Program staff are available to attend out-of-state awareness meetings (costs to be negotiated). Training is conducted at the program site (costs to be negotiated). Implementation and follow-up services are available to adopters.

Contact   Helen Ray, Director or Carole Rash, Associate Director, MARRS, Wabash and Ohio Valley Special Education District, Box E, Norris City, IL 62869-0905. (618) 378-2131.

Developmental Funding: USOE ESEA Title IV-C.

JDRP No. 81-27 **(7/28/81)**
Recertified **(3/5/92)**

Multi-Agency Project for Pre-Schoolers (MAPPS). A program that provides instructional materials, training, and follow-up technical assistance to schools and agencies that serve infants and preschool children with disabilities.

Audience Approved by JDRP for children with disabilities, birth to age 5.

Description The Multi-Agency Project for Pre-Schoolers (MAPPS) is a home- and center-based intervention program for infants and preschool children with disabilities and their families. The MAPPS model enables parents, paraprofessionals, and teachers to intervene successfully with a minimum of training. To accomplish this, parents and other personnel are trained to use specific, detailed curricula as a guide for teaching young children. In addition to home-based training, the MAPPS model enables delayed children to be mainstreamed into existing preschool and day care services by training staff in specific intervention strategies. Originally, the MAPPS model was designed for use in rural/remote areas; more recently, urban and minority populations, including Native Americans, are using the MAPPS model successfully.

A key component of the MAPPS model is the Curriculum and Monitoring System (CAMS), which covers five curriculum areas: cognitive, language, motor, self-help, and social skills. CAMS covers skills normally learned from birth to five years of age and each skill has been task-analyzed. The curriculum areas are designed to be free of jargon and to allow individual objectives to be photocopied for use by the parents, caregivers, or teachers working directly with the children. CAMS is designed to be a tool for teachers and parents, guiding them in individualizing a child's curriculum and monitoring the child's progress. Because CAMS is a tool, it is meant to be flexible so that individualized adaptations can be made to accommodate:

- The educational philosophy of teachers and families,
- The child's cultural background, and
- The child's type and level of disability.

The revised CAMS also includes easy-to-use scoring sheets that allow for reassessment of the child's progress in each developmental area. New developmental charts have been developed for use with parents to provide a broad overview of a child's development.

Evidence of Effectiveness Preschoolers who were taught using the CAMS curricula performed significantly better on the Battelle Developmental Inventory than a comparison group who were taught with an alternative curriculum.

Requirements The model can be used by parents, preschools, and any agencies serving infants and preschoolers with disabilities. If the model is adopted by a preschool or an agency, one teacher/monitor is required on a half-time basis to serve approximately 20 children. Speech, O.T., P.T., and psychology personnel should be available for consultation. Training for preschools and agencies consists of one to two days at the replication site depending upon the experience and background of the persons being trained.

Services Awareness materials are available at no cost. Visitors are welcome by appointment. Training workshops are conducted at the adoption site with costs negotiated between the cooperating agencies. The cost of a complete set of the CAMS curriculum which covers the five developmental areas mentioned above is $70. One set is necessary per teacher/classroom. Follow-up visits and telephone consultation are available. A videotape is available which provides a project overview and suggestions for using the CAMS curricula.

Contact **Glendon Casto, Director, Utah State University, Center for Persons with Disabilities, Logan, UT 84322-6580. (801) 750-2000.**

JDRP No. 80-7 **(6/17/80)**
Recertified **(4/1/94)**

Developmental Funding: USOE BEH.

Programming for Early Education of CHildren with Disabilities (PEECH). An individualized educational program designed to enhance the development of preschool children with mild to moderate disabilities, ages 3 to 5.

Audience Approved by PEP for children with mild to moderate disabilities, ages 3 to 5.

Description The Programming for Early Education of CHildren with Disabilities (PEECH) program provides training and technical assistance to early childhood programs which serve children with mild to moderate disabilities ages 3 to 5. By adopting PEECH, an exemplary program for young children and their families can be developed. The educational needs of the children are determined by utilizing an ongoing assessment instrument which evaluates fine motor, gross motor, language, general knowledge and school readiness, social, and self-help skills. The philosophy of the PEECH model includes a low student/teacher ratio, a positive approach to behavior management, extensive training and involvement of paraprofessionals as teachers, a carefully structured learning environment, and careful planning and evaluation of daily individualized teaching sessions. Individualized family involvement is included as an integral part of the model.

The PEECH NDN program serves three of the National Goals for Education: #1, children starting school ready to learn; #7, educators receiving professional development opportunities; and #8, parents participating as partners in their child's education. PEECH provides a developmentally appropriate program for preschool children, workshops specifically designed for staff development in all areas of preschool education and a systems approach to parent involvement in the program.

Evidence of Effectiveness Children aged three to five with mild to moderate disabilities who have preschool programming using the PEECH model show improvement in receptive and expressive vocabulary. This improvement is shown by: (1) greater gains in receptive and expressive vocabulary than would be expected on the basis of maturation at their preintervention rate of development; (2) accelerated rates of development during intervention; and (3) moderate to large effect sizes.

Children aged three to five with mild to moderate disabilities who have preschool programming using the PEECH model also improve in social competence. This improvement is shown by: (1) statistically significant differences between pre- and posttest scores on an instrument measuring teachers' ratings of children's social competence; and (2) moderate to large effect sizes.

Requirements Administrative commitment to program review and assessment, staff development based on a needs assessment, integrated preschool classes, and parents as partners in education are prerequisites for successful implementation of the PEECH Model.

Costs Adoption sites pay $100 to help defray the printing costs of the training manuals which the Certified Trainers use for workshops. Travel costs for the coordinator will be negotiated with the SF. Adoption sites must have an ongoing assessment tool in place. (If one is not being used, the cost of a new assessment tool would be approximately $300.)

Services Two or three day adoption training sessions in the PEECH Model components are usually conducted in individual states. Periodically training sessions are scheduled at the University of Illinois. The State Facilitator assists with the identification of personnel who become Certified Trainers and assume responsibility for coordinating services, conducting training sessions with the site staff, and acting as liaison with the PEECH Coordinator.

Contact Tess Bennett, Director, or Marge Stillwell, Coordinator, PEECH, Department of Special Education, University of Illinois, Colonel Wolfe School, 403 East Healey, Champaign, IL 61820-5598. (217) 333-4890, FAX (217) 333-4293.

JDRP No. 75-74 **(11/10/75)**
Recertified **(3/9/92)**

Developmental Funding: USOE, SEP, and NDN.

> **SKI-HI Outreach.** A comprehensive program that provides screening, audiological, diagnostic, assessment services, and complete home intervention resources for children who are deaf or hard of hearing, birth to age 5, and their families.

Audience Approved by JDRP/PEP for families with infants and young children, birth to age 5, who are deaf or hard of hearing.

Description SKI-HI Outreach is a comprehensive program that provides screening, audiological, diagnostic and assessment services and complete home intervention programming for children who are hearing impaired (birth to age 5) and their families. It provides a family-centered, team management approach.

The program is designed to provide services to a state-wide or large population area; however, SKI-HI effectively meets the needs of regional, district, rural, small and private agencies.

A complete home intervention resource manual is provided. It includes the main program areas of hearing aids, communication, auditory development, and both total communication and aural/oral language, as well as resources on Cued Speech and American Sign Language. Training in the SKI-HI model covers delivery for these programs, as well as the roles and functions of a Parent Advisor. Psychological, emotional, and child-development support are provided for parents in the home. Weekly and comprehensive quarterly assessment of child and family is performed. Parent advisors living in the area visit homes weekly to deliver the curriculum, which is targeted for families. A format for home visits is provided.

Elements of the program include identification, screening, program management, and a support system of ongoing audiological services, a hearing aid evaluation and loaner system, video units and tapes for total communication, hearing-aid molds, psychological services, and parent group services. Careful planning for transition to the next educational environment is included.

Evidence of Effectiveness A national data system collects yearly information on demographic status and child/parent progress for all participating adoption programs. Documented outcomes and benefits: (1) the rate of children's gain in language development is greater during SKI-HI intervention than would be due to maturation alone (12 to 16 months language growth in 9 months of intervention); (2) children demonstrated increases in auditory, communication-language, and vocabulary levels; (3) parents acquire skills needed to facilitate the development of their children; and (4) children receiving SKI-HI programming are identified as having a hearing loss at an early age (a median age of 17 months).

Requirements One full-time or part-time professional to make weekly home visits is the minimum requirement. This person must have basic SKI-HI training. Travel is necessary. For maximum effect, a hearing-aid bank, hearing screening, and audiological, psychological, and child development services should be provided. Earmolds, library books, video-playback units, and total communication tapes should be provided. In larger programs, supervision and administration are necessary. The program should participate in the SKI-HI data collection and evaluation system.

Costs Complete services for 11 months (including all direct and supportive services) cost approximately $1,549 per child. Start-up costs are minimal.

Services Awareness materials are available at no cost. Visitors are welcome by appointment at the program site and additional demonstration sites in their home state and out of state. Program staff are available to attend out-of-state awareness meetings (costs to be negotiated). Training is available at adopter sites (costs to be negotiated). Implementation and follow-up services are available to adopters (costs to be negotiated).

Contact Don Barringer, Director, SKI-HI Institute, Utah State University, Logan, UT 84322-1900. (801) 752-4601, FAX (801) 755-0317.

Developmental Funding: U.S. Department of Education, Bureau of Education for the Handicapped.

JDRP No. 78-192 (7/13/78)
Recertified (2/19/91)

Systematic Screening for Behavior Disorders (SSBD). Provides a solution to the problem of under-referral of students who may develop behavior disorders by giving regular classroom teachers uniform behavioral standards for use in reducing the idiosyncratic nature of teacher referrals.

Audience Approved by PEP for students in regular elementary grades (K-6) who may be at risk for developing either externalizing or internalizing behavior disorders.

Description Systematic Screening for Behavior Disorders (SSBD) provides a solution to the problems of under-referral of students who may develop behavior disorders by giving regular classroom teachers uniform behavioral standards for use in reducing the idiosyncratic nature of teacher referrals. This mass screening process, which occurs early in a child's school career, is a multiagent, multimethod approach.

The screening occurs in three stages: teacher nominations of groups of children whose characteristic behavior patterns most closely resemble profiles of behavior disorders occurring in the school setting and ranking of those students; screening of students in terms of behavioral severity and defining the content of their behavior problems using a series of ratings items and systematic observation of students using a classroom code and a playground code.

SSBD has been constructed under the following beliefs: teachers in least restrictive environments are more likely to refer pupils who exhibit externalizing behaviors that they perceive as aversive, while under-referring pupils with internalizing disorders; teacher rankings and ratings combined with direct observation is necessary to assess pupil behavior; and academic engaged time and peer-related social behavior are important indicators.

Evidence of Effectiveness In six separate studies, SSBD provided a reliable procedure for systematically screening and identifying elementary school students who demonstrate potential behavior disorders. In six additional studies, SSBD proved to be an accurate procedure that discriminates potential behavior disorder students from nondisordered or nonat-risk students within regular classrooms.

Requirements The only major requirement is mastery of the classroom and playground observation codes in stage three of the screening and identification process.

Costs Costs to an adopting district involve purchase of materials ($195 per building) and training ($400 per day). Consumable products are minimal and no special staff, equipment, or facilities are required.

Services Awareness materials are available at no cost.

Contact Rebecca Williamson, P.O. Box 18466, Boulder, CO 80308. (303) 651-1751. Dr. Herbert Severson, Oregon Research Institute, 1899 Willamette, Eugene, OR 97401. (503) 484-2123.

Developmental Funding: Federal, state, and local.

PEP No. 90-01 **(2/8/90)**

Educational Programs That Work (1995)

> **Youth Transition Program (YTP).** An interagency, collaborative service delivery model designed to improve school to work transition outcomes for students with disabilities.

Audience Approved by PEP for students with disabilities, ages 16 through 21, who are eligible for Vocational Rehabilitation services, in transition from school to community, and able to become competitively employed without long-term support.

Description Developed collaboratively by the University of Oregon, the Oregon Vocational Rehabilitation Division (OVRD), and the Oregon Department of Education, YTP enhances disabled students' ability to enter and retain meaningful, competitive employment after leaving school. Students typically enter YTP during their junior or senior year of high school, and continue for the first one to three years out of school, depending on individual needs. The model includes two major program components: (1) an in-school component; and (2) a post-school component. The YTP team works with each student to: develop an individualized transition plan leading to an employment outcome; place students in paid community employment with job-related instruction; and provide follow-up services for two years following student exit from the program. The services are provided jointly by school and vocational rehabilitation staff.

Evidence of Effectiveness Evaluation data support project claims that students who participated in YTP achieved substantially greater employment outcomes compared to employment status prior to the program. Gains were maintained after leaving the program, as measured by periodic follow-up interviews. The employment outcomes achieved by YTP students were superior to the outcomes achieved by three external comparison groups. These included: (1) a statewide sample of school leavers with disabilities in Oregon who did not participate in YTP; (2) a statewide sample of non-YTP Vocational Rehabilitation clients in Oregon; and (3) a nationwide sample of school leavers with disabilities. Outcomes were also examined for two sub-groups of YTP, those who were at-risk and those living in rural areas. Outcomes for each sub-group of students compared favorably with their non-at-risk and non-rural counterparts.

Requirements State and local commitment to a new collaborative service delivery model. In Oregon, the YTP involved collaborative administration and financing. Participating school districts supported the salary and fringe benefits of the teacher reassigned to coordinate YTP. The provision of services was supported by OVRD through the award of contracts to local school districts. The University of Oregon was responsible for the materials, training and technical assistance, and evaluation activities. However, the program may be implemented either as a statewide program or by local school districts without a state support structure. Available materials include the YTP Procedures Manual, describing in detail each phase of the YTP process, and "how to" steps for making YTP work in local communities; and the YTP Management Information System, a computerized software program, developed to evaluate the on-going program impact and outcomes.

Costs Costs vary by site and include: (1) salaries/fringe benefits for YTP Coordinator; (2) wage/fringe benefit costs for Transition Specialists; and (3) materials, supplies, and local travel costs. Across time and sites, the average cost per student has been approximately $3,000.

Contact Dr. Michael Benz, Associate Professor, 175 College of Education, 5260 University of Oregon, Eugene, OR 97403-5260. (503) 346-1408, FAX (503) 346-5818.

Funding: Federal, state, and local sources.

PEP No. 94-19 (**12/94**)

Achievement-Based Curriculum (ABC) - Project I Can. Improving the quality of physical education instruction for ALL students preschool through secondary. Approved by JDRP/PEP for teachers (special education, physical education, adapted physical education, and/or combinations) of disabled children in special and/or regular educational programs.

Description The Achievement-Based Curriculum (ABC) - Project I Can model has five major components to help teachers implement quality school programs: assess, prescribe, teach, evaluate, and plan for essential objectives in physical education for children and youth from near zero to functional level of competency. The curriculum materials (I CAN) represent a bank of 200 student performance objectives for qualitative assessment, prescriptive instruction, evaluation, student reports, and a computer management system for the school program.

The ABC model can be: (1) implemented without exotic equipment or facilities; (2) implemented by classroom teachers, physical education specialists, or combinations; (3) adapted to local needs and resources to either develop a comprehensive mastery in learning program, preschool through high school, or supplement an existing program; and (4) implemented by the user in compliance not only with P.L. 101.476 but also in response to school reform movements—pursuit of equity and excellence in American schools for all students.

An ABC videotape is available. Training costs are shared among the school/district, State Facilitator Project, and the ABC Project.

Contact   Luke Kelly, Ph.D., Project Center, University of Virginia, Curry School of Education, Ruffner Hall, 405 Emmet Street, Charlottesville, VA 22903. (804) 924-6192.

Developmental Funding: USOE OSE and state.

JDRP No. 81-13 **(6/11/81)**
Recertified **(6/85)**

All Children Totally InVolved in Exercising (ACTIVE). A diagnostic/prescriptive physical education program for disabled and normal individuals. Approved for disabled, ages 6-60, nondisabled, grades K-9.

Description All Children Totally InVolved in Exercising (ACTIVE) has been developed to serve disabled individuals, but is equally applicable to slow learners and normal and gifted children. ACTIVE offers a training program to provide teachers with those skills/strategies necessary to implement an adapted physical education program, diagnostic/prescriptive curriculum manuals and materials addressed to the entire gamut of disabled conditions, and consultant services to assist implementers during the installation phase. Program strengths include extreme flexibility for adoption/adaptation, a total curriculum package that can be implemented immediately at minimal cost, compliance with the federal mandate requiring "written education programs for the disabled population," unlimited support services to enhance successful implementation, and accountability features to enhance administrator/community support. Student instruction is based on instruction format (i.e., the program is structured to ensure that trainees acquire the skills, knowledge, and attitudes stressed), with emphasis on trainee exposure to disabled individuals in a field setting. Participants are trained to diagnose and assess pupil strengths and deficiencies and to prescribe motor, perceptual-motor, physical fitness, posture, nutrition, and diaphragmatic breathing tasks accordingly. ACTIVE has developed low motor ability, low physical vitality components for mentally retarded, learning disabled, and emotionally disturbed student populations. No special facilities are required. Comprehensive programs can be initiated in limited space.

Contact   Joe Karp, Director, ACTIVE, 13209 NE 175th, c/o Sorenson Building, Woodinville, WA 98072. (206) 485-0427.

Developmental Funding: USOE ESEA Title III.

JDRP No. 74-97 **(9/18/74)**
Recertified **(1/85)**

Developmental Therapy Model. A therapeutic program that offers a developmental curriculum to severely emotionally disturbed or autistic children, their parents, and teachers.

Description The Developmental Therapy Model is a therapeutic curriculum for social and emotional growth which can be used in a variety of settings or as originally designed, in a special classroom setting with groups of four to eight individuals. On the assumption that children with disabilities go through the same stages of development that normal youngsters do, but at a different pace, the curriculum guides treatment and measures progress by focusing on the normal developmental milestones that all children must master. It is composed of four curriculum areas (behavior, communication, socialization, and preacademics/cognition) arranged in five developmental stages, each requiring different emphasis and techniques. Special services to parents are an integral part of the approach. Developmental Therapy also emphasizes concurrent placement with children without disabilities. This mainstreaming aspect of the Model requires that regular school experiences mesh smoothly with intensive Developmental Therapy experiences. Resources are available that emphasize how to plan, implement, and evaluate an Individualized Education Program (IEP) using the developmental approach. The Developmental Therapy Model offers four types of technical assistance (information dissemination, program planning and design, training, and program evaluation). Program staff provide assessment of training needs, design an inservice instructional sequence, and implement the training program at the agency site with periodic visits. The Developmental Therapy Model, through enhancing social-emotional growth and self-esteem, addresses directly the National Goals for Education 1, 2, 3, and 6.

Contact Karen R. Davis, Director, Developmental Therapy Program, 191 East Broad Street, Suite 309, Athens, GA 30601-2801. (706) 369-5689, FAX (706) 369-5690.

Developmental Funding: USOE BEH.   JDRP No. 75-63 **(9/3/75)**

Early Recognition Intervention Network (ERIN). A curriculum/ assessment program for teachers, coordinators, and parents to assist young children with special needs in regular and special education settings. Approved by JDRP for children ages 3-7 with mild to severe disabilities in mainstream or special settings, programs for regular and special teachers, program coordinators, and parents.

Description The Early Recognition Intervention Network (ERIN) system is used in both special preschool classroom/home programs serving children with moderate to severe special needs and in regular early childhood (nursery, Head Start, day care) and primary (K-1) programs serving mainstreamed mild to moderate special needs children integrated with their peers. When adopting, each teacher implements a program of observation and curriculum modification for children with special needs. A local coordinator is trained to take over local training and monitoring of the program. The ERIN training program for adults (special or regular teachers and coordinators) provides the equivalent of three to six college credits through attendance at a 5-day Institute and on-site consultation by ERIN staff. A coordinated parent program for both special and mainstream children is optional. The teaching adult makes materials and organizes his/her own learning environment to facilitate participation (social-emotional-affective), body awareness and control, visual-perceptual-motor, and language skills. Depending on the age of the child, these are organized into self-help, developmental concept, and academic readiness content areas. Initially, the curriculum approach focuses on general classroom/ home modifications of the physical space and daily time units, learning materials and their organization into learning sequences, the grouping of children, and teacher cuing/monitoring. This is followed by the teaching of specific skills to subgroups and/or individual children by the teacher, parent, or volunteer, with much greater intensity in specialized programs. The child's Individual Education Program is implemented in large and small groups and individually.

Contact Peter and Marian Hainsworth, Co-Directors, ERIN, Inc., P.O. Box 637, Carlisle, MA 01741. (508) 287-0920.

JDRP No. 78-186 **(7/13/78)**
Recertified **(12/84)**
Developmental Funding: None.

Elsmere Project. A basic skills vocational program for the trainable mentally disabled population, ages 5-21.

Description The Elsmere Project addresses Goal 3 of the National Goals for Education by meeting the individual needs of TMH students by providing individualized scheduling of instruction in six essential areas: functional academics, socialization, family life, independent living, prevocation, and vocation. For each area, the curriculum has a double orientation. First, the program emphasizes the acquisition of self-sufficiency to the highest degree possible. The project prepares students to function in the community, to work, travel, shop, enjoy leisure time and relate to others. Second, vocational skills are presented through these learning areas. Thus, skills and attitudes necessary for engaging in work are emphasized in all learning areas. Each student is exposed to a simulated work atmosphere. Students are involved in rudimentary training and work activities such as assembling, packaging and collating. Students participate in a vocational training program which reflects community employment needs. On-the-job training is provided for students in the final stages of the training program. The Glassboro Trainable Assessment Profile (G-TAP), assists the teacher in placing students at the correct functioning level in each of the life skill areas. It is also a useful tool to measure yearly growth and assist the child study team in developing objectives for the Individual Educational Plan (IEP). Because area business leaders are potential employers of TMH citizens, community involvement is an integral part of the project. On-the-job training and student job placement occur through community involvement. Advisory groups and service organizations assist the project by providing information on the skills necessary to prepare students for particular jobs. Parent interest and participation is another component in the success of the Elsmere Project. Parents are provided the background required to perform activities at home that reinforce vocational skills taught at school.

Contact Monika Steinberg, Project Manager, Elsmere Project, Educational Information and Resource Center (EIRC), 606 Delsea Drive, Sewell, NJ 08080. (609) 582-7000, FAX (609) 583-4206.

Developmental Funding: USOE ESEA Titles III and IV-C.

JDRP No. 79-23 (5/17/79)

Modification of Children's Oral Language. A special program for training staff to work with students having language disabilities. Approved by JDRP for language-disabled students, preschool to adult.

Description The Modification of Children's Oral Language program uses the materials and instructional methods of the Monterey Language Program, which combines linguistic theory and behavioral technology. It is universal: appropriate for any individual with a language problem, regardless of the reason for that disability. The curriculum and program design include screening, placement, criterion testing, teaching procedures, branching, and data collection for record keeping and evaluation. With the Monterey Language Program, a teacher can obtain accurate pre- and posttest measures of a student's progress in syntactical expression. The program helps language-deficient individuals acquire new skills in a brief period of time. It is individualized and performance-based. In addition to providing materials, the program provides teachers with an instructional strategy and assists them in becoming proficient in using the materials. Implementation of the program includes training, on-site supervision, refresher conferences, and data monitoring. Aides, parents, or other volunteers may be involved if desired. The language program works with children and adults defined as language-delayed, deaf, hard-of-hearing, mentally retarded, or physically disabled. It serves non-English-speaking, bilingual, or second-language students where appropriate. It is particularly valuable in early childhood education, classes for the educable and trainable mentally retarded, and speech and language centers. It permits language remediation services to be expanded without increasing staff.

Contact George H. Stern, Monterey Learning Systems, P.O. Box 51590, Palo Alto, CA 94303. (415) 969-5450.

Developmental Funding: USOE ESEA Title III.

JDRP No. 73-6 (4/16/73)

Precision Teaching Project. A model designed to remediate and build basic skills (math, reading, and spelling) through setting performance aims, practice sessions, continuous measurement, and data-based decisions. Approved by JDRP for all students (regular and special education), grades K-4.

Description The Precision Teaching Project is comprised of a set of measurement and practice procedures designed to facilitate instructional decisions while at the same time developing strong basic skills. As a measurement tool, Precision Teaching can be used to monitor and make decisions with any teaching technology, methodology, or style. As a practice procedure, Precision Teaching moves students from acquisition, to mastery, to proficiency. One-minute repeated practice sessions build tool skills as well as basic skills. Five steps guide the process: (1) pinpoint a specific academic behavior; (2) select a specific practice sheet that correlates with the current curriculum, set a specific performance standard, and then conduct a series of one-minute practice sessions; (3) score and chart the number of correct and error responses; (4) make data-based curricular decisions; and (5) develop management plans for both individual and group programs.

The costs to the adopter include: (1) Training Manuals, $15 per person, (2) Classroom Implementation Kits, $45 per classroom, (3) Set of Math and Language Arts Practice Sheets (approx. 2000 sheets), $224 per school, and training fee of $750 per day. Total training and implementation costs average $76 per teacher or $4.60 per student. In addition, the adopter is responsible for travel, lodging, and per diem. An adoption commitment can be made by a district, school, or classroom. Adopting units should include building or program administrator, support personnel, and regular and/or special education teachers. Initial training can be completed in one day and is conducted at the adopter site. A follow-up visit is strongly recommended. Awareness materials are available at no cost.

Contact   Ray Beck, Project Director, Precision Teaching Project, P.O. Box 1809, Longmont, CO 80502-1809. (303) 651-2829.

Developmental Funding: USOE ESEA Titles III and IV-C.

JDRP No. 75-25 **(5/6/75)**
Recertified **(5/17/79)**

Regional Program for Preschool Children with Disabilities. Early intervention for disabled children ages 3 to 5. Approved by JDRP for preschool disabled children.

Description This is a comprehensive program of educational services intended to increase the verbal, perceptual, motor, and general cognitive skills of children with disabilities.

Unique features of the program include: The Interactive Teaching Process in which special education teachers, teacher aides and clinical team members provide diagnostic/prescriptive teaching, language intervention and positive reinforcement on a continual basis in the classroom; The Transdisciplinary Team Model through which team members train each other and share roles in assessment, intervention and consultation; Parent Involvement Model, which includes the parent volunteer system, parent group meetings and an individualized approach to parent participation. Replication Training in each or all components is available to any preschool program. Over 450 classroom sites have replicated the Regional Program Model or component of the model. Manuals describing each component are available at cost. One to three days of training are provided based on a needs assessment process with the training site.

Awareness materials are available at no cost. Visitors are welcome at program sites by appointment. Training is conducted at the program site or adopter site (travel, food, and lodging must be paid by adopter or cost-sharing may be negotiated with State Facilitators).

Contact   Carol S. Eagen, Supervisor, Preschool Program, Special Education Department, Putnam-Northern Westchester Board of Cooperative Educational Services, Yorktown Heights, NY 10598. (914) 962-2377.

JDRP No. 81-6 **(6/29/81)**
Recertified **(9/26/85)**

Developmental Funding: USOE BEH, state, and local.

Teaching Research Integrated Preschool (TRIP) Model, The. A model for training staff to work with young children with special needs within typical early childhood settings.

Description The Teaching Research Integrated Preschool (TRIP) Model merges current recommended practice in early childhood special education with developmentally appropriate practices and provides for the individualized instructional goals of children birth to age 6 with special needs. The Model addresses Goal 1 of the National Goals for Education by "ensuring access to high-quality and developmentally appropriate preschool programs that help prepare children for school." Individuals participating in the replication training will acquire knowledge and skills necessary to support children with disabilities within community programs where their typical peers are served. They will acquire the ability to use an environmentally-referenced assessment approach resulting in the selection of functional and environmentally relevant skills for each child. Techniques for incorporating parent participation in all aspects of their child's educational program are taught. Participants will learn how to individualize instructional sequences to the needs of each child and to teach them within naturally occurring group activities in which children with disabilities participate alongside their typically developing peers. Additional components of the model contained in the training include: activity based instruction, data based decision making, collaborative team functioning, and transition planning. Dissemination activities include awareness presentations, brochures and a program video. Replication training is packaged in three, four, and five day modules and is available at the Monmouth, Oregon site. Adopters are responsible for tuition and participant travel expenses. Typical recipients of project services include preschool/day care staff, Head Start staff, early childhood special education supervisors and practitioners including family specialists, and related service personnel.

Contact Joyce Peters, Teaching Research Division, Western Oregon State College, Todd Hall, Monmouth, OR 97361. (503) 838-8812.

Developmental Funding: USOE BEH.

JDRP No. 78-163 **(3/27/78)**
Recertified **(6/86)**

Section 13

Gifted/Talented

* These programs are currently funded by the NDN.

Summary of Program Services for Section 13

Program	Goal*	Page	AWARENESS											TRAINING							
			Dissem. Funds Available		Costs to Potential Adopter			On Site Visitation Available		Materials Available				Staff Available		Costs to Adopter			Certified Trainers Available	Training Time Required
			Other	NDN	Hon	Trav	Per Diem	Home Site	Adopt Site	Free Paper	Video	Film Strip	Other	Home Site	Adopt Site	Hon	Trav	Per Diem	State(s)	Day(s)
SAGE	3	13-3			✓	✓	✓	✓	✓	✓				✓	✓	✓	✓	✓	AK, CO, ID, IL, MS, NJ, NV, NY, OH, OK, OR, SD, TX, UT, VT	1
Success Enrichment, Project (PSE)	3	13-1		✓		✓	✓	✓	✓	✓	✓			✓	✓	✓	✓		CA, GA, ID, KS, KY, MN, MT, NM, NY, OR, SC, TX, UT, WA	2
Success Enrichment/ Art, Project (PSE/Art)	3	13-2	(info. not available)																	

* National Goals for Education—definitions for each goal can be found on pages 5-7.

Success Enrichment, Project (PSE). A program to enrich the language arts of intellectually, academically, and creatively gifted students in grades 4-6.

Audience Approved by JDRP/PEP for gifted and talented students, grades 4-6; field-tested in grades 2-8. This enrichment program in language arts is designed to enrich the education of intellectually and creatively gifted students, as well as students in the regular classroom, special education, Chapter I, multicultural, and "at-risk" students. A curriculum manual that encompasses all phases of the program operation will be provided to each participant.

Description Special enrichment activities are provided for students in grades 2-8 with exceptionally high ability in the areas of language arts. Original students were grouped in enrichment classes of 15 or fewer students per section. Later it was discovered that this can also be accomplished within a regular classroom setting with provisions for flexibility in student outcomes and expectations for varying student ability levels. Project Success Enrichment (PSE) presents educators with a complete, comprehensive curriculum that includes sequential activities—moving students from simple to complex concepts, and instructs teachers in a way that they can make immediate use of the program. Because PSE is very flexible, it can be used at any grade level, with students of all learning styles, abilities, and cultural backgrounds.

Lessons are presented in a hierarchical sequence from skill awareness through skill acquisition, skill mastery, skill application, to skill transfer. At the skill application level, elaboration, originality, divergent thinking, and problem solving are emphasized. Cooperative learning approaches, such as hands-on activities, shared decision making, active participation, and questioning techniques are demonstrated and experienced throughout the program of activities. Self-management and social skills are also stressed, along with a process-oriented approach to the content.

The language arts curriculum includes: (1) Imagery (similes, metaphors, and personification); (2) Vocabulary (descriptive adjectives and work expansion); (3) Sentences (order, types); (4) Literature (Newbery Award winners, literary analysis); and (5) Format (organization, editing, theme). Upon mastery of these topics, learners study in-depth, various types of poetry and short story writing and transfer their literary knowledge to a variety of integrated projects. Both oral and written communication skills are stressed through various teaching strategies. This developmentally sequential language curriculum is embodied in six packets (four to six years of instruction): introductory, short story, poetry, drafting and editing, literary analysis (classics, Newbery Award winners), and projects and evaluation.

Evidence of Effectiveness The portfolio assessment/product evaluation measures the students' growth in language and is evaluated by the comparison of pre and post student samples collected throughout the year and selected by teachers to be rated by a panel of experts (professional writers or artists and/or English, language, or visual arts teachers).

Project Success Enrichment is a statistically proven program in reading, writing, and literary analysis. It requires students to use higher level thinking rather than engaging in a fill-in-the-blanks type of learning. Project Success Enrichment meets National Goal for Education 3 because it assists students in learning to use their minds and further their achievement in the areas of language arts and visual art, so they may be prepared for responsible citizenship, further learning, and productive employment in our modern economy.

Requirements Implementation requirements include: identification of instructors; instructors and principal participate in a two-day Level I inservice; acquisition of curriculum; instruction; possible one- or two-day Level II and Level III follow-up; and posttesting. (These requirements vary depending upon the model program adopted.)

Costs Training expenses involve negotiating an honorarium, which varies from $250-$500 per day, travel, and per diem costs for one trainer. Adopters purchase a training manual and curriculum unit per participant, which ranges from $75-$180, depending upon the resources available.

Services Visitors are welcome at any of our demonstration sites by appointment. Project staff are available for awareness and training sessions, and for follow-up and evaluation services. Project brochures, videotapes, and secondary awareness materials are available upon request.

Contact Carolyn Gaab-Bronson, Project Success Enrichment, Creative Child Concepts, P.O. Box 22447, Seattle, WA 98122-0447. (206) 325-5418.

JDRP No. 83-6 (**3/4/83**)
Recertified (**5/11/89**)

Developmental Funding: ESEA Title III and IV-C.

Success Enrichment/Art, Project (PSE/Art). A program which provides gifted students with an opportunity to go well beyond their gifted and nongifted peers in terms of skill level for three artistic modes: drawing, painting, and claywork.

Audience Approved by PEP for gifted students in grades 4-6; has been field tested in grades 2-8. This enrichment program in visual art is designed to enrich the education of intellectually and creatively gifted students, as well as students in the regular classroom, special education, Chapter I, multicultural, and "at-risk" students. A curriculum manual that encompasses all phases of the program operation will be provided to each participant.

Description Students are grouped for cooperative learning experiences organized into roughly three-hour blocks per week over a seven month period. The curriculum for each program is developmentally sequential, based on learning theory, and integrates the content (academic) and thinking skills by using a specific process approach, which has proven to be very effective. The program emphasizes problem solving, decision making, higher level thinking, and creativity, as well as self-management and social skills.

The art curriculum includes enrichment activities that focus on drawing, painting, and design, claywork and sculpture, and thinking (creative and critical) appropriate for children of all ability levels. The curriculum activities are sequential, use a variety of media, and emphasize: (1) proportion, (2) contour, (3) detail, (4) shape, (5) form, (6) pattern, (7) texture, and (8) use of color. After completing skill awareness and skill acquisition activities, students embark on individual projects.

Project Success Enrichment/Art (PSE/Art) asks students to brainstorm art principles, elements, and techniques, making connections as to their use in drawing, painting, and claywork. The students have an opportunity to work with a variety of media, topics, concepts, and projects, relating art to academics. Students are encouraged to develop creativity, artistic expression, and perceptual skills in an effort to acquire an understanding of how all knowledge is interconnected. The integration of the two programs has become a powerful way to teach, particularly with those students who employ certain learning styles that need experiential, hands-on learning to acquire knowledge and concepts.

PSE/Art has been identified by the National Diffusion Network as meeting National Goal for Education 3 because it assists students in learning to use their minds and further their achievements in the area of visual art, so they may be prepared for responsible citizenship, further learning, and productive employment in our modern economy.

Evidence of Effectiveness Using performance and portfolio assessments of both the process and end products of artwork in any of three media, students involved in the program not only substantially increased their skill by the end of the treatment period, but achieved higher levels of skill than students in another art program. PSE/Art is a statistically proven program in drawing, painting, and claywork. It requires students to use higher level thinking rather than engaging in a fill-in-the-blanks type of learning.

Requirements Classroom and/or resource teachers trained in the use of PSE/Art materials and procedures and use of the program's curriculum, materials, and training manuals.

Costs Start-up costs for the two-day Level I (preservice) training and for the one- or two-day Level II (follow-up) training are based on a $300-$500 per day consulting fee and on purchase of curriculum materials which range from $70-$150 per teacher. Ongoing operational costs vary depending upon the nature of the model as it is implemented. Classroom art supplies are purchased by the school district as needed.

Services Training, consultation, curriculum, materials, and a training manual are available.

Contact Carolyn Bronson, Project Director, Project Success Enrichment/Art, Box 22447, Seattle, WA 98122-0447. (206) 325-5418.

Developmental Funding: USOE ESEA Title III and IV-C.

PEP No. 93-5 **(3/1/93)**

SAGE. A program designed to develop higher level thinking skills and to improve academic achievement by providing a differentiated specialized curriculum for gifted and talented elementary students. Approved for gifted and talented students, grades 1-5.

Description The objectives of the SAGE program are to develop higher order and critical thinking skills and to improve academic achievement by providing a differentiated specialized curriculum for academically/intellectually gifted and talented elementary school students. The regular school curriculum is extended based on a three-fold model incorporating thinking skill development, mini-study units, and independent study. Activities presented in the thinking skills development portion of the curriculum stimulate and challenge students to think and to perform at higher levels of thinking; assist in the development of critical, inductive, deductive, and creative thinking skills; and present specific instruction in areas of information gathering, organizing and using resource materials. Mini-study units, extensions of the basic curriculum, are interdisciplinary in nature, and incorporate thinking skill activities in broad topic areas. The third segment of the SAGE core curriculum is independent study, which allows students to extend and to enrich their knowledge of interest/content areas. A mentorship program, utilizing experts in the areas of student interest, is an outgrowth of independent study.

SAGE develops new themes annually. There is a SAGE Network of adopters who share thematic units as well as curriculum adaptations made for the regular classroom. Thinking skill booklets for the regular classroom teacher are available through the program's supplemental materials component.

The SAGE materials are adaptable to a variety of program designs. Guidelines are provided for schools in the initial program development stages. Schools which already have established a gifted/talented program may use the materials to enhance their current program. The SAGE Tri-Fold Curriculum can be easily implemented in one of three instruction models or a combination of the field-tested models: separate classroom, resource room, consultant teacher. Classroom teachers can be trained to implement SAGE for the academically/intellectually gifted students in the regular classroom.

Contact Effective Teaching Consortium (Etc . . .), P.O. Box 1896, Longmont, CO 80502. (303) 651-1751.

Developmental Funding: ESEA Title IV-C.   JDRP No. 83-43 **(5/27/83)**

Section 14

Special Populations: Adult/Higher/Migrant Education

* These programs are currently funded by the NDN.

Summary of Program Services for Section 14

Program	Goal*	Page	Dissem. Funds Available — NDN	Dissem. Funds Available — Other	AWARENESS — Costs to Potential Adopter — Hon	Trav	Per Diem	On Site Visitation Available — Home Site	Adopt Site	Materials Available — Free Paper	Video	Film Strip	Other	TRAINING — Staff Available — Home Site	Adopt Site	TRAINING — Costs to Adopter — Hon	Trav	Per Diem	Certified Trainers Available — State(s)	Training Time Required — Day(s)
Adult Performance ... (APL) ...	6	14-5			✓	✓	✓		✓	✓					✓	✓	✓	✓	(none)	1-2
BES ... Project	6	14-5			✓	✓	✓	✓	✓	✓				✓		✓	✓	✓	(none)	2
Comprehensive Adult Student ... (CASAS)	6	14-1	✓			✓	✓		✓	✓	✓			✓	✓	✓	✓	✓	CA, CO, CT, IA, ID, IN, KS, KY, MD, MO, NC, OH, OR, WA	2
Early Prevention of School Failure Migrant ...	3	14-6			✓	✓	✓	✓	✓	✓	✓				✓	✓	✓	✓	(none)	2
Learning To Learn (LTL) ...	6	14-6				✓	✓	✓	✓	✓				✓	✓	✓	✓	✓	AL, AR, CT, D.C., FL, GA, HI, MA, MI, MS, NM, NY, PA, VA	1
Migrant Student Record Transfer System (MSRTS)/A Computer Link ... (CLOVER)		14-7	(info. not available)																		
National External Diploma Program (EDP)	6	14-7	✓	✓		✓	✓		✓	✓	✓				✓	✓	✓	✓	CT, MD, NY, VA, WI	3+
National Family Literacy Project (Dissemination Process)	1, 6	14-2	✓		(negotiable)			✓	✓	✓	✓			✓	✓	✓	✓	✓	(none)	3+
New Jersey Youth Corps		14-3			✓	✓	✓	✓	✓	✓	✓			✓	✓	✓	✓	✓	(none)	1-3
Supplemental Instruction (SI): Improving Student Performance and Reducing Attrition	6	14-4	✓		✓	✓	✓	✓	✓	✓	✓			✓	✓	✓	✓	✓	IL, KS, MD, MN, NJ, NY, OR, PA, TN, England, South Africa	3+

* National Goals for Education—definitions for each goal can be found on pages 5-7.

Comprehensive Adult Student Assessment System (CASAS). A program designed to provide comprehensive learner-centered curriculum management assessment, and evaluation systems to education and training programs.

Audience Approved by JDRP for agencies that provide adult basic education, English as a second language, high school completion, and preemployment programs for adults and secondary-level students.

Description Comprehensive Adult Student Assessment System (CASAS) provides learner-centered, competency outcome-based assessment, curriculum management, and evaluation systems to education and training programs in the public and private sector. The system includes more than 80 standardized assessment instruments. The system is used to place learners in programs, diagnose learners' needs, monitor progress, and certify mastery of functional basic skills. CASAS assessment instruments are used to measure functional reading, writing, listening, speaking skills, and higher order thinking skills. All assessment has been validated through field testing. Results are reported as scaled scores ranging from 150 (special learning needs) to 250 (secondary). CASAS scaled scores report learners' literacy levels in employment and adult life skills contexts. This comprehensive system is designed not only to meet the National Goal for Education of improving adult literacy, but to address specific needs of adult learners.

Evidence of Effectiveness Students enrolled in adult and alternative education programs that have implemented key elements of CASAS demonstrate significant learning gains and increased hours of instruction, and achieve increased goal attainment.

Requirements Consultation and training are required for implementation of the system.

Costs The costs for the initial training (approximately 25 people) to an adopter include travel, per diem, a preparation fee of $350, a training fee of $350 per day, and a materials fee per participant. A minimum of two days of training are required for implementation. Implementation costs vary by site.

Services Awareness materials are available at no cost. In addition to initial implementation training and materials, follow-up consultation and additional training is available.

Contact Patricia L. Rickard, Director, 8910 Clairemont Mesa Boulevard, San Diego, CA 92123. (800) 255-1036. E-Mail: prickard@inet.ed.gov

Developmental Funding: California, Section 310 of Federal Adult Basic Education Act.

JDRP No. 84-6 (**3/20/84**)
Recertified (**3/11/93**)

National Family Literacy Project (Dissemination Process). The Project evaluates and validates exemplary family literacy programs and provides to validated programs assistance with awareness, dissemination, and training.

Audience Staff of comprehensive family literacy programs who are seeking evaluation and validation of their programs or of specific components or features of programs.

Description **Background:** The National Family Literacy Project (Dissemination Process) is a service of the National Center for Family Literacy (NCFL) in Louisville, KY. The NCFL is a private, not-for-profit corporation which provides leadership, advocacy, and training for programs providing comprehensive educational and other services to disadvantaged families. The NCFL is the major provider of information, advocacy, and training for the field of family literacy. Family literacy programs offer basic education/literacy training for undereducated parents and preschool education for their young children, as well as parent support and intergenerational activities. Family literacy programs forge the connection between National Goals for Education 1 and 6 by working to improve the skills of preschool children and adults and supporting parents as "first teachers" of their children.

Services: The National Family Literacy Project (Dissemination Process) will identify, select, and validate exemplary practices in family literacy and increase awareness of exemplary models and practices. Programs which serve special populations or have developed particularly efficient or effective processes for service delivery in one or more program components are invited to apply. Services of the Project include: (1) awareness presentations and materials concerning the National Family Literacy Project, (2) assistance for local program staff preparing for the NFLP validation process, (3) feedback for program improvement during all phases of the evaluation process, (4) assistance (for validated model program staff) in developing awareness materials and training for dissemination, and (5) awareness and training for selected models provided by NFLP staff.

Evidence of Effectiveness The Project evaluates the effectiveness of its validation/dissemination activities by: (1) documenting the scope and impact of Project awareness and validation activities, (2) surveying local program staff regarding effectiveness of services, and (3) surveying recipients of training in validated models. The validity of Project processes will also be ensured by the ongoing use of external expert reviewers in the evaluation of programs. Whenever possible, the impact on family literacy program participants will also be assessed by documenting academic and other gains of parents and children, improved parenting skills and parent-child relationships, etc. Substantial gains in these areas have been documented by the NCFL in working with comprehensive family literacy programs. It is expected that programs validated through the National Family Literacy Project will show similar effects.

Requirements For NFLP validation, programs must submit an application which includes a completed self-study and evidence of program effectiveness.

Costs Information about costs is available from the NFLP.

Contact Ronna Spacone, National Family Literacy Project, Waterfront Plaza, Suite 200, 325 West Main Street, Louisville, KY 40202-4251. Phone (502) 584-1133, FAX (502) 584-0172.

Developmental Funding: Foundations, private contributions, and fees. PEP No. 92-17 (**4/7/93**)

New Jersey Youth Corps. A full-time program combining academic instruction with community service, designed to provide dropouts with services not found in traditional adult education programs.

Audience Approved by PEP for dropouts, age 16-25.

Description The New Jersey Youth Corps is a full-time instructional and community service program for school dropouts, with the completion of a high school curriculum and employment as the ultimate goals for each student. Students spend a half day in academic instruction and a half day in community service work. A one-month orientation that includes academic and interest/aptitude assessment is followed by placement in community service work crew projects and continuation in basic skills classes.

The Youth Corps program uses an individualized instructional approach. Instructors diagnose skill areas and design a prescription for remediation in the form of an individual educational plan with career-related goals. Instruction and service interrelate, with new skills and experiences shared between the two components. The curriculum is driven by the General Educational Development Test (GED).

A Corps is typically staffed by basic skills instructor(s), an employability skills instructor, counselor(s), crew leader(s), a job developer, coordinator, and a program director. Staff are full-time and programs operate a minimum of five days per week, 12 months per year. Staff development, monitoring, and evaluation are integrated into the Youth Corps management.

Evidence of Effectiveness Data based on 5,000 participants over a five-year period support the claims that youth who participate in the program are three times more likely to receive a high school diploma than those in traditional programs; five times more likely to be placed in jobs or job training; and likely to complete four times the hours of participants in regular adult programs.

Requirements In addition to the core staff, a site outside the walls of public schools; a site that can develop its own identity is crucial. The learning environment must not replicate an environment that connotes a negative experience for youth. Staff training covering intake procedures, counseling, referral, training, and job placement is required. Also necessary is understanding of the GED testing requirements.

Costs A typical Youth Corps costs about $300,000 per year; an average of $2,000 to $3,000 per participant.

Services Staff training, monitoring for contractual compliance, and evaluation are provided on a regular basis.

Contact **Lynn Keepers, New Jersey Youth Corps, Division of Adult Education, 240 West State Street, Trenton, NJ 08625. (609) 984-5971.**

Developmental Funding: New Jersey State Departments of Education, Community Affairs.

PEP No. 90-10 (**2/9/90**)

Supplemental Instruction (SI): Improving Student Performance and Reducing Attrition.
A program to improve academic performance and retention rates for freshman and sophomore students in high-risk, entry-level college courses.

Audience   Approved by PEP for undergraduate students in high-risk college courses.

Description   Supplemental Instruction (SI): Improving Student Performance and Reducing Attrition is a model of student academic assistance used in higher education that targets high-risk courses rather than high-risk students. SI operates on an outreach rather than a drop-in basis in regularly scheduled, out-of-class study sessions held in proximity to the class. Targeted courses have 30% or higher rate of unsuccessful enrollments (D and F grades, as well as withdrawals). The program is nonremedial and available to all students enrolled in a targeted course.

Campus program directors (SI Supervisors) identify, hire, and train students (SI Leaders) who are deemed content-competent by the faculty member teaching the targeted course. These SI Leaders demonstrate "model student behavior" by actively attending all class sessions, taking notes, and reading all assigned material. These SI Leaders schedule and conduct three or four 50-minute SI sessions per week at times indicated convenient by the majority of the enrolled students. SI integrates learning strategies with course content. Using the course content as a vehicle for learning skills development, SI provides opportunities to discuss the vocabulary of the discipline and complex concepts, organize course material, and practice good questioning in an assessment-free environment. Students who participate in SI earn a higher mean course grade than students who do not participate, including those in a motivational control group (students who desire to attend SI but cannot attend because of schedule conflicts). Differences in performance patterns between SI and non-SI groups are evident regardless of past academic performance on their ethnicity. The rates of unsuccessful enrollment (percent of D and F grades and withdrawals) for SI participants are lower than for nonparticipants. Therefore, rates of unsuccessful enrollment in courses where SI is offered are lower than they were prior to the addition of SI.

Evidence of Effectiveness   **Claim 1:** Students participating in SI within the targeted high risk courses earn higher mean final course grades than students who do not participate in SI. This is still true when differences are analyzed, despite ethnicity and prior academic achievement. **Claim 2:** Despite ethnicity and prior academic achievement, students participating in SI within targeted high risk courses succeed at a higher rate (withdraw at a lower rate and receive a lower percentage of D or F final course grades) than those who do not participate in SI. **Claim 3:** Students participating in SI persist at the institution (reenrolling and graduating) at higher rates than students who do not participate in SI.

Requirements   The SI model is adaptable on a variety of campuses and is compatible with existing academic support programs such as learning or tutoring centers, Student Support Services, and Title III and IV programs. No special equipment is needed for implementation, although some duplication of printed material is helpful. A minimum of one full-time professional staff member is needed to maintain a moderately-sized SI program on campus. Programs targeting a large number of courses may require additional staff.

Costs   Implementation costs vary depending upon the availability of existing staff on the adopting campus who can obtain release time for the operation of this program. The adopting institution bears the cost of a three-day training workshop (approximately $300 per day plus travel expenses) for the SI Supervisor. SI Leaders can be compensated through part-time wage funds, internships or work-study arrangements. An SI Leader spends an average of nine to ten hours per week on a three-credit course and earns approximately $750 per 15-week semester. SI Leaders are usually provided the course text and a means of printed materials duplication.

Services   The Developer/Demonstrator site will furnish complimentary awareness materials to those desiring more information on the model. Awareness conferences and training workshops are regularly scheduled at the Developer/Demonstrator site. A partial waiver of the training fee may be available to institutions committed to adopting the model. Developer/Demonstrator staff and Certified Trainers are available for on-site consultation and training. (The adopting institution covers honoraria and travel expenses.)

Contact   David Arendale, University of Missouri-Kansas City, 5100 Rockhill Road SASS 210, Center for Academic Development, Kansas City, MO 64110-2499. (816) 235-1197, FAX (816) 235-5156. Kim Wilcox. (816) 235-1178. E-Mail: darendale@cctr.umkc.edu

Developmental Funding: University of Missouri-Kansas City.

JDRP No. 81-33 (**12/7/81**)
Recertified (**3/30/92**)

Adult Performance Level (APL) Program.
A competency-based system of education that combines the diagnosis, prescription, teaching, evaluation, and credentialing of life-coping skills.

Description Approved for the general English-speaking population over 18. Adult Performance Level (APL) Program research measured specified minimum competencies an adult must possess to function successfully.

Based on the objectives identified by APL research, a complete curriculum applies reading, writing, speaking, listening, viewing, computation, decision making, and interpersonal relations skills to the content areas of consumer economics, occupational knowledge, health, community resources, and government and law. For example, adults learn how to fill out job application forms, interview for a job, and construct a budget. The curriculum provides the activities and materials needed to teach toward each of the APL life-coping skills objectives.

The APL competency-based high school diploma program offers adults a relevant alternative to the conventional four-year high school program and to the General Educational Development test (GED). Adults can earn a regular high school diploma by demonstrating competencies gained through life skill–oriented adult education programs in combination with those gained through experience. The basic steps to the competency-based diploma are: placement tests, the competency-based curriculum described above (if indicated by scores on placement tests), a series of life-skills activities, and demonstration of an entry-level job skill or postsecondary education skills, or skills in home management/maintenance. (Honorarium plus expenses.)

Contact Elaine Shelton, 2606 Top Cove, Austin, TX 78704. (512) 444-3488.

JDRP No. 75-13 (3/25/75)
Recertified (5/15/79)

Developmental Funding: USOE BOAE.

BES Adult Literacy Project.
A reading program that includes both instructional methods and a curriculum for functionally illiterate adults. Approved by JDRP for functionally illiterate adults in the nonreader or beginning reader category (i.e., those reading below the 4.0 reading level).

Description The BES Adult Literacy Project's instructional methods combine a problem-solving approach with a linguistic analysis of words, sounds, and sentences and a highly structured sequence of oral and written drills. Instruction is provided on an intensive basis over a twenty-week treatment cycle. All instruction is classroom-based and occurs within community centers and churches.

Students participating in the BES Adult Literacy Project have improved their reading skills to a statistically significant degree ($p<.05$) as measured by the Tests of Adult Basic Education (TABE), based upon the results of longitudinal and cross-sectional studies conducted with several cohorts of students.

Staff Development: 12 hours of intensive staff/teacher training is required by a BES teacher/trainer. Curriculum Materials: The BES curriculum is used during training and project implementation. The Curriculum Guide is packaged for dissemination. 10-12 hours of periodic visits are necessary to monitor trainees' development, model teaching methods, and to answer questions on implementation. Project staff is available to provide this ongoing support and technical assistance.

Costs for the program are approximately $183 per student per year initially, but are reduced to $110 per student in subsequent years. For adopters who already employ paraprofessional staff, the costs could be as low as $20 per student. Awareness materials are available at no cost. BES staff are available to conduct workshops and awareness presentations at the project site or elsewhere. Potential adopters are welcome to visit the Project by appointment.

Contact Patricia Medina, BES Adult Literacy Project, 965 Longwood Avenue, Bronx, NY 10459. (212) 991-7310.

Developmental Funding: Out-of-School Basic Skills Improvement Program and Adult Basic Ed. Act, Section 310.

JDRP No. 85-4 (2/26/85)

Educational Programs That Work (1995)

Early Prevention of School Failure Migrant Program (for Spanish- and English-Speaking Children).
A program designed to prevent early school failure in migrant children. Approved by JDRP as an assessment and curriculum planning program for migrant children ages 4-6 in regular or short-term programs.

Description The Early Prevention of School Failure Migrant Program (for Spanish- and English-Speaking Children) is designed to determine the migrant child's strengths and needs. The goal of the program is to reduce the "at risk" factor by assessing needs and strengths and developing an appropriate program for each child. The program provides follow-up activities in kinesthetic, visual, auditory, expressive language, and receptive language. Appropriate program resources and effective teaching materials for large and small group instruction are available. Authentic assessment with a focus on portfolios from early emergent to independent reader and writer is presented.

This program has provided ongoing positive program research and evaluation results from 1974 through 1994. Teacher training workshops and program materials are continually updated. The developmentally sequenced concepts and literature-based curriculum provide children with choices and teachers with a framework for integrating the school curriculum with effective program-developed units, themes, center activities, language experience, and whole language instructional approaches to beginning reading and writing in both small group and total class arrangements. Evaluation of students is conducted with teacher observation and portfolio assessment.

Contact Luceille Werner, National Director, Peotone School District 207U, 114 North Second Street, P.O. Box 956, Peotone, IL 60468. (708) 258-3478 or (800) 933-3478, FAX (708) 258-3484.

Developmental Funding: USOE ESEA Title I (Migrant).

JDRP No. 77-116 **(4/19/77)**
Recertified **(11/84)**

Learning To Learn (LTL): Improving Academic Performance Across the Curriculum.

Description The Learning To Learn (LTL): Improving Academic Performance Across the Curriculum program is the only learning improvement program at the postsecondary level to be approved by JDRP on the basis of both students' **significantly higher grade point** averages and **retention through graduation**. LTL is generally delivered as a 14-week course. The difference it produces in student learning and retention rates is substantial: data show a 20% increase in retention through graduation for four-year college students, a 50% increase in retention for two-year college students. We anticipate that the net effect of the program on a college using this system would be to increase its revenues (through higher student retention rates) and raise its academic standards (by improving students' ability to perform well in academic courses). The LTL system was developed through research in the learning strategies of successful students. Such students: (1) ask questions of new materials, reading or listening for confirmation; (2) break down into smaller units the components of complex tasks and ideas; and (3) devise informal feedback mechanisms to assess their own progress. The LTL system is not a study skills system which loses its impact after students stop using the techniques. Once new LTL behaviors are established, they become part of the learner, integral to his/her thinking process. We think of these methods as comprising a fourth basic skill which facilitates the other three. Studies using statistically equivalent control groups were conducted on two college campuses. The studies showed significantly higher GPAs for students who had participated in the LTL course when effects of course load, sex, race, SAT scores, and previous academic record were removed ($p<.05$). In addition, studies showed significant gains in students' retention through graduation ($p<.001$).

Materials are now available at the **high school and junior high school levels**. Anticipated results are increased **retention through graduation**; improved **grades** in courses across the curriculum; improves scores on **standardized reading and math tests**; improved scores on citywide and statewide **achievement tests**.

Contact Marcia Heiman, Learning To Learn, Inc., Box 38-1351, Cambridge, MA 02238. (617) 492-8477 or (800) 28THINK.

Developmental Funding: Special Services for the Disadvantaged Higher Education Act of 1965, P.L. 89-329.

JDRP No. 83-25 **(6/15/83)**

Migrant Student Record Transfer System (MSRTS)/A Computer Link Offering Variable Educational Records (CLOVER). An education and health system for migrant children, preschool-12. Approved by JDRP as a program for migrant children, preschool through secondary, and teachers, aides, nurses, counselors, and administrators.

Description The Migrant Student Record Transfer System (MSRTS)/A Computer Link Offering Variable Educational Records (CLOVER) is a computerized system with 162 terminals located in 44 states. The system serves 49 states, Puerto Rico, and the District of Columbia. Through the MSRTS/CLOVER the process of receiving, storing and transmitting health and educational information is available to all schools, education and/or health organizations that serve migrant children. Teachers, nurses, aides, administrators, and others have at their disposal educational and critical health data delivered to their state within 24 hours of a child's enrollment. In four days or less, an in-depth record of educational and health data will be received at the state's designated location. This information may direct the adopter in formulating strategies to assist the migrant child in achieving academically. Curricula being taught to migrant children varies according to the established needs of migrant children at various levels. The system's computer is programmed to provide skills-based information in the areas of reading, math, early childhood, and oral language. The health system provides the most updated reporting of health problems to insure continuity of health services by using the International Classification of Diseases (ICD.9.CM) and the physician's *Current Procedural Terminology (CPT), 4th Edition*. Awareness materials are available. Visitors are welcome at program sites by appointment, Monday through Friday 8:00 A.M. through 4:30 P.M. Training is conducted at the program site (adopter paying its own costs). If training is conducted outside the state of Arkansas, costs are to be negotiated. Quarterly workshops are held in February, May, August, and November.

Contact Nolan McMurray, Administrator for Special Services and Technical Advisor, Migrant Student Record Transfer System, Arch Ford Education Building, Capitol Mall, Little Rock, AR 72201. (501) 371-1857.

Developmental Funding: USOE ESEA Title I (Migrant).

JDRP No. 73-19 **(4/5/73)**

National External Diploma Program (EDP). A competency-based alternative high school credentialing program for adults. Approved by JDRP for English-speaking adult students over the age of 18.

Description The American Council on Education sponsers the National External Diploma Program (EDP), an alternative high school credentialing program for adults who have acquired skills through their life experience and who can demonstrate those skills in applied performance tests. EDP provides adults with an assessment and credentialing process that is an alternative to traditional diploma programs such as ACE's own General Education Development (GED). The program provides no instruction. It is an assessment system imbedded in a context of work or homelike simulations. The program has two phases. In the first phase, Diagnostic Assessment, the adult completes six diagnostic instruments which help identify learning deficiencies in basic skill areas. If a deficiency is identified, the adult is given a learning recommendation and is sent into the community to utilize the learning resources available. After the deficiencies have been corrected, the adult enters the second phase, Generalized Assessment. In this phase, the adult must demonstrate 65 generalized competencies in the academic and life skill areas of communication, computation, self-awareness, scientific awareness, occupational preparedness, technological awareness, social awareness, and consumer awareness. The adult must also demonstrate an individualized competency in one of three skill areas: occupational, special, or advanced academic. The assessment system is an open testing system characterized by flexibility in time, pace, and location of testing. It offers adults the opportunity to demonstrate process skills through a variety of documentation forms and to earn a regular high school diploma. Graduates of the program who were surveyed ten months after they received their diplomas reported an increase in continued learning, job promotions and raises, and self-esteem and self-confidence. Training workshop plus center materials and eight program manuals are available (contact the American Council on Education). Equipment required is ordinarily found in an educational setting. Staffing requirements may be met by reassigning existing personnel.

Contact Florence Harvey, Director, National External Diploma Program, The Center for Adult Learning and Educational Credentials, American Council on Education, One Dupont Circle, Suite 250, Washington, D.C. 20036. (202) 939-9475. E-Mail: florence_harvey@ace. nche.edu

Developmental Funding: USOE BOAE.

JDRP No. 79-26 **(5/30/79)**

Educational Programs That Work (1995)

Section 15

Career/Vocational Education

* These programs are currently funded by the NDN.

Summary of Program Services for Section 15

Program	Goal*	Page	Dissem. Funds: NDN	Dissem. Funds: Other	AW Costs: Hon	AW Costs: Trav	AW Costs: Per Diem	On Site: Home Site	On Site: Adopt Site	Materials: Free Paper	Materials: Video	Materials: Film Strip	Materials: Other	Staff: Home Site	Staff: Adopt Site	Train Costs: Hon	Train Costs: Trav	Train Costs: Per Diem	Certified Trainers: State(s)	Training Time: Day(s)
Academy of Finance	3, 6	15-1	✓			✓	✓		✓										CA, DE, FL, MA, MD, NC, NY, OH, TN, WA	2+
Career Awareness Program, Project (Project CAP)	3	15-2			✓	✓	✓		✓	✓	✓			(info. not available)						
Career Education... (CERES)	3	15-3			✓	✓	✓			✓	✓			✓		✓	✓	✓	CA, OR, NM, WI	1
Careerways 2000	3	15-4	✓		✓	✓	✓			✓				✓			✓		(none)	1
Center for Educational Development (CED)/...	3	15-6			✓	✓	✓			✓	✓				✓	✓	✓	✓	(none)	2
Discovery, Project	3	15-6		✓	(negotiable)			✓		✓	✓				✓	(negotiable)				
Tech Prep Program	3	15-5	(info. not available)																CO, KS, KY, OH, TX	1

*AWARENESS: Dissem. Funds Available; Costs to Potential Adopter; On Site Visitation Available; Materials Available. TRAINING: Staff Available; Costs to Adopter; Certified Trainers Available; Training Time Required.

* National Goals for Education—definitions for each goal can be found on pages 5-7.

Academy of Finance. An intensive two-year, academic and work experience program designed to prepare high school students in grades 11-12 for entry-level careers in financial services.

Audience Approved by PEP for students in grades 11-12 from comprehensive high schools who have average or better academic and attendance performances.

Description Academy of Finance is a highly structured academic/work experience program that offers a viable option for students lacking concrete career plans or interests; an avenue for career preparation in financial services; opportunities for women and minorities to gain access to careers in a nontraditional field; and a substantive approach for involving businesses in preparing youth for entry-level jobs. The program supplements the existing curriculum and consists of seven courses that are finance or finance-related plus a college-level finance course, a seven-week paid summer internship at a financial services firm between the student's junior and senior years, and participation in finance-related activities, e.g., annual conference, speakers, and tours. Participation in the Academy of Finance prepares students for productive employment by stressing communication skills, analytic thinking, and workplace basics such as dress, punctuality, and cooperativeness.

Evidence of Effectiveness Evidence from multiple sources support the claims that youth who participate in the program are knowledgeable in finance, economics and its application; are better prepared for employment in entry-level positions than existing entry-level employees; have a higher graduation rate than their respective high schools; and pursue financial services through college and employment. Female and minority students persist in the program and are more likely to go to college and major in financial services than others, as likely to be employed in financial services as others, and to go further in the financial services field than is typical for this group.

Requirements A six-month start-up period for planning and teacher training is recommended. A start-up guide, curriculum materials, and extensive technical assistance, training and support are provided. A school district is required to support continuous teacher training in financial services, e.g., the National Academy Foundation's annual staff development conference, and provide additional professional development activities developed with the local advisory board.

Costs Start-up and ongoing operations are dependent upon **shared** financial and other support from the participating school district and local business sponsors. The first year's **shared** costs for nonpersonnel expenditures are estimated at $26,000, including a $4,000 adoption fee (for curriculum, support materials, newsletters, directory training, and technical assistance in perpetuity), and covers teacher training, materials, special events, three director's conferences, and miscellaneous costs. In addition, the school/business partnership negotiates the sharing of costs for the full-time program director's and administrative support salaries. The district budgets for teachers' salaries; business sponsors budget for paid internships/on-site teacher training; and tuition for the college course is contributed by the local institution of higher education.

Services In addition to training, curriculum, and support materials, a technical assistance team visits new sites during the start-up phase. New sites participate in ongoing training activities, e.g., annual staff development and regional conferences.

Contact   Dr. Christopher Gentile, National Academy Foundation, 235 Park Avenue South, New York, NY 10003. (212) 420-8400.

Developmental Funding: Shearson Lehman/ American Express, Travelers, and local.

PEP No. 91-11 (**3/19/91**)

Educational Programs That Work (1995)

Career Awareness Program, Project (Project CAP). A program for infusing career awareness into the regular curriculum, emphasizing the relationship between careers and basic academic skills.

Audience   Approved by PEP for students in grades K-6.

Description   Project Career Awareness Program (Project CAP) is designed to complement the basic skills curriculum of the school while introducing students to the wide variety of ways in which people work. At the same time, students are able to grow in awareness of themselves in relation to the world of work. Project CAP student materials at each grade level consist of 32 different lessons and learning activity packets. Each learning activity packet contains an academic skill and a career script or story that presents the required tools, tasks, education or training, and economic rewards as well as the concept that work is a way of life. For example, with one packet, fourth grade students learn about the job of a land surveyor and practice a metric measurement skill as part of their math program. The skills range from those in reading and mathematics, to those in science, social studies, and language arts. Packets may be completed in as little as twenty minutes or may be expanded to cover a longer unit of time depending upon the lesson and the individual teacher's plan.

Evidence of Effectiveness   Students participating in the program are significantly more aware of careers than comparable nonparticipating students as measured by a project-developed and validated criterion-referenced test of knowledge of occupations and the training/education required to enter them.

Requirements   Project CAP requires no special staff or facility. Teachers at potential adopting sites are required to attend a four- to six-hour training session and to purchase materials.

Costs   Start-up cost is approximately $130 to cover materials and supplies for a class of 25 students, plus a one-time training expense to cover travel, per diem, and a $200 honorarium.

Services   In addition to training and materials, follow-up consultation is available upon request.

Contact   Lena Sparkman, Coordinator, Project Career Awareness Program, Boston Mountain Educational Cooperative, P. O. Box 13, Greenland, AR 72737. (501) 443-3336.

Developmental Funding: USOE ESEA Title III and local.

PEP No. 78-178R2 (**3/11/93**)

Career Education Responsive to Every Student (CERES). A comprehensive career education program that enhances instructional time and prepares students for employment trends of the future, for grades K-12.

Audience Approved by JDRP for all students grades K-12.

Description Career Education Responsive to Every Student (CERES) is a comprehensive career education infusion program for grades K-12. The program purpose is to provide students with the basic academic and employability skills necessary for competent, productive performance both in school and after leaving school. The program is tailored to the developmental ages of students at the different grade levels. The objectives are that students will: (1) identify and practice responsible work habits, (2) acquire knowledge of diverse occupations (training preparation and job duties), and (3) apply basic skills to career decisions and actions (job-seeking and job-retention).

CERES enhances instructional time and makes education more efficient. CERES prepares students for the employment trend of the future. CERES is easy to use. The materials are self-contained and do not require extensive supplementary resources. They are flexible and may be used by any teacher, with students of various abilities and at various levels, ranging from an individual classroom or school to district-wide use.

CERES includes systematic, institutional management procedures to enhance and strengthen the involvement of local business and community groups.

CERES is a low-cost program to implement. Training costs include training materials ($10 per workshop participant), consultant fee ($600 per day), and presenter travel and per diem expenses. Program implementation (instructional, management, and evaluation) materials are available at cost. CERES materials are appropriate for all students including special education and at-risk youth. Local Educational Agencies should provide release time for training.

Requirements The program's activities are easily transportable since they can be implemented without disrupting existing programs. The program can be adopted by individual teachers, schools, or districts. One day of training is required to get the program started. One day of follow-up inservice is advised.

Services Awareness material is available at no cost. Staff are available for out-of-state awareness, training, and follow-up sessions.

Contact Barbara Baer, Program Co-Director, c/o C.E.R.E.S., 3641 Suite 1B, Mitchell Road, Ceres, CA 95307. (209) 537-5618, (209) 883-0593.

JDRP No. 78-182R 5/25/78 **(4/26/83)**
Recertified **(5/17/89)**

Developmental Funding: USOE Career Education.

Careerways 2000. A decision-making, educational, and career planning project designed to encourage students to explore options without restrictions of stereotyping.

Audience Approved by PEP for students of all abilities in grades 8 through 12.

Description The Careerways 2000 program will help students to be more keenly aware of what they need to be successful in both their academic world today and the work-a-day world tomorrow. The program is designed to focus students' attention on those skills, attitudes, and abilities that will afford them the widest variety of educational opportunities, and career options in the future. The program's newly revised curriculum package features six motivational thirty-minute videocassettes, each focusing on an identified cluster of careers. Accompanying the videocassettes is the *Careerways 2000 Teacher's Guide*, divided into seven instructional units, each containing a number of student activities. Each "Activity" contains a lesson plan, necessary teacher background materials, and student worksheets. The first unit, containing sixteen activities, helps students to focus their thinking on key aspects of the decision-making process. Each of the next six career cluster units includes an overview, highlights of the video program corresponding to that unit, suggested discussion topics, a vocabulary list, a sample list of careers in the field, and an interest survey for students. All seven of the units help students grow in their ability to utilize planning, organizing, and critical-thinking techniques in the decision-making process. The six career cluster areas covered by the program's video cassettes encompass: the Arts, Business and Finance, Industry, the Media, Service, and Science and Technology. Two new chapters have recently been added to the project: *A Student-To-Workforce Academies Model* (including student and mentor handbooks) and *Developing Career Portfolios*.

The video cassettes (available in opened caption) focus on the personal stories of women and men who tell how they identified their goals, used organizing and planning skills in order to meet their educational challenges, and to succeed in their chosen areas of endeavor. These role models are seen "up close" as they perform within their work environments and interact with their fellow workers. As students take an in-depth look at the specific careers being spotlighted, the stories of the role models reinforce and enhance the program's primary goal, which is to help students develop specific strategies for setting and attaining their educational and career objectives.

The program can be implemented as a self-contained career education course of study, or as a unit in a specific subject content area using the *Careerways 2000 Teacher's Guide* as a text. It can also be implemented as a school-wide career education program tracked into appropriate subject content area classrooms related to the career cluster areas under consideration.

Careerways 2000 addresses the National Goals for Education, specifically that students and adults demonstrate competency in challenging subject matter, and are able to compete in the workplace. The program is most appropriate for those audiences seeking emphasis on decision-making and communication skills, gender equity, at risk, and infusion of vocational education and academics (Carl Perkins).

Requirements Implementation will require that the teacher have a $\frac{1}{2}$" VHS videocassette player and a large-screen television set. A one-day teachers' training workshop is recommended.

Costs The Careerways 2000 program curriculum materials are available for $450 per set of six video cassettes and the *Careerways 2000 Teacher's Guide*. Additional copies of the guide and the individual video cassettes may be purchased separately at $75 each.

Services Awareness materials are available at no cost. Program staff are available to attend awareness conferences, or to conduct program training at the site of the requesting agency. (Trainer's per diem and travel costs to be negotiated.)

Contact Jerry McLeroy, Disseminator, Los Angeles U.S.D., 1320 West Third Street, Room 406, Los Angeles, CA 90017. (213) 625-6695 or (213) 625-6682.

Developmental Funding: ESEA, Title IV.

PEP No. 81-31R2 **(3/28/91)**

Tech Prep Program. A program designed to enable secondary students to complete higher-level academic and technical/vocational course sequences.

Audience Secondary students who typically do not enroll in a College Preparatory course of study and do not pursue professional careers or attend four-year universities.

Description Tech Prep was developed collaboratively by representatives of the Richmond County (North Carolina) public schools, the community college, business and industry, and implementation began in 1986. It provides a focused technical education course of study for students planning to attend a two-year community college or technical school. Coursework takes place in Grades 9-14 and emphasizes higher level mathematics, science, and communication skills. The program requires students to maintain grade level competencies throughout K-12 so that they may move into postsecondary studies without remediation. Students are provided formal career guidance activities throughout the K-12 experience to clarify and expand career possibilities. There are seven components needed for the design and implementation of Tech Prep:

(1) Leadership; (2) Staff Development/Realignment; (3) Guidance Redesign (Learner Activities/Materials); (4) Course of Study/Curriculum Development; (5) Articulation of Course Structure (K-14); (6) Evaluation; and (7) Marketing. Tech Prep addresses National Educational Goal 3.

Evidence of Effectiveness Four claims of effectiveness were evaluated. Results showed (1) significant changes in course-taking patterns between high school seniors prior to Tech Prep in 1986 and seniors enrolled in the program in 1992; (2) vocational students mastered academic subjects not previously taken as evidenced by Algebra I and II achievement tests where scores remained stable between 1986 and 1992, although the number of students who participated significantly increased; (3) there is a decrease in the drop-out rate, although the Tech Prep course of study is more rigorous than previous vocational courses of study; and (4) vocational students report attending post-secondary institutions at a higher rate than the State average, although the county is below State average on socioeconomic indicators.

Requirements Strong commitment from the school district, a postsecondary institution, and business and industry is required. Time and resources are needed for each of the Tech Prep components.

Costs Costs will vary depending on staff readiness and availability. Generally, hiring new staff is not necessary. A suggested cost in areas with one community college and one school district is $15,000 for planning activities, staff development and marketing.

Services Services include: (1) On-site visits scheduled monthly; (2) portfolios of materials upon request, and; (3) consultant technical assistance available from several staff persons.

Contact **Myrtle D. Stogner, Director, Richmond County, NC, National Tech Prep Demonstration Site Project, Richmond Community College, P.O. Box 1189, Hamlet, NC 28345. (910) 582-7187, FAX (910) 582-7005.**

Developmental Funding: U.S. ED OVAE, local, state, and private sources.

PEP No. 92-10R2 **(5/1/94)**

Center for Educational Development (CED)/Career Guidance Project. A K-12 infusion model designed to develop knowledge and skills in self-awareness and career exploration. Approved by JDRP for students of all abilities grades 4-12, teachers, administrators, counselors, and community members. This program is also available for and has been used in grades K-3.

Description The Center for Educational Development (CED)/Career Guidance Project is an interdistrict organization that coordinates and delivers a variety of career education services to all county schools. CED has several major components; direct services to students; services to school staffs who need help in planning or implementing career education activities; selection and maintenance of up-to-date career education media and materials for use by all county school staffs; coordination of community resources, such as volunteer aides, speakers, and work experience/exposure sites; conduct parent discussion groups; and a variety of other services, such as career education implementation unit development and services to special education teachers. The approach to career education in Pima County is often referred to as "infusion," that is, the continued demonstration of the relationships between academic subjects and particular occupation or the world of work as a whole. Infusion redirects the focus and intent of school subjects without changing subject content. For example, addition may be taught by totaling prices on restaurant checks in a simulated coffee shop instead of by adding numbers on blank paper. Elementary level activities focus on self-awareness and an introduction to career areas. Activities in grades 7-9 focus on a wider study of careers and use of decision-making skills. Activities at the high school level are aimed at giving students career exploration and uses of academic skills in various careers.

Contact   Don Lawhead, Director, Center for Educational Development, 622 North 7th Avenue, Tucson, AZ 85705. (602) 791-3791, FAX (602) 791-9753.

Developmental Funding: USOE Educational Professions Development Act.   JDRP No. 78-177 (8/10/78)

Discovery, Project. A career exploration and assessment system that provides the participant with "hands-on" work experiences. Approved by JDRP for individuals of all abilities, age 12 and up, including minority groups, disadvantaged and disabled, as well as "typical" populations.

Description Project Discovery was developed to provide students with hands-on work experience. Forty-two programs comprise the Project Discovery system. Students, following detailed instructions, use many of the same tools, equipment and materials as a trained worker in that field.

Students can sample a diversity of work activities to identify likes and dislikes or self-perceived abilities. Students gain an understanding of the basic work requirements and competencies of the occupational/vocational area.

By successfully completing the activities, the student builds self-awareness and self-confidence necessary for career decision-making and vocational training. Project Discovery provides work performance benchmarks that help compare a student's specific knowledge, skills, and abilities to the actual ones required of the occupation. A Guidance and Counseling Component is available to aid in the exploration/assessment interpretation. Designed to be used as self-contained "table top" units, programs are highly portable and contain: Instructor's Notes, Student Instructions (4th-6th grade reading level), Work Performance Benchmarks, supplies and materials, and tools and equipment. Nineteen of the 42 modules are designed with "Special Editions" for special-needs populations, including disabled readers. Modifications of the regular modules were based on field-testing. The resulting Special Editions contain "First Look Books"—specially written and illustrated books (2nd-4th grade level) that introduce and define vocabulary words and concepts, and audio cassettes that read word by word through the activities.

Contact   Timothy W. Hagan, Education Associates, Inc., 8 Crab Orchard Road, P.O. Box Y, Frankfort, KY 40602. (800) 626-2950.

Developmental Funding: USOE BEH, and Career Education.   JDRP No. 78-161 (3/15/78)

Section 16

Approved Programs That Are No Longer Available

The programs listed below were approved by the Joint Dissemination Review Panel (JDRP) or Program Effectiveness Panel (PEP). They have performed exemplary work in improving education, but their availability is now restricted or their services are no longer available.

ACIL
Mesa, AZ
JDRP Approval: 10/4/76
JDRP Number: 74-96

Academically Talented Youth Programs (ATYP), Mathematics
Kalamazoo, MI
JDRP Approval: 6/25/86
JDRP Number: 86-9

Added Dimensions
Lakewood, CO
JDRP Approval: 5/15/75
JDRP Number: 75-46

A.D.V.A.N.C.E.
Salem, NJ
JDRP Approval: 6/15/83
JDRP Number: 83-43

AIRS: Andover's Integrated Reading System
Andover, MA
JDRP Approval: 4/1/85
JDRP Number: 74-25

Akron Follow Through: Project Self (Selected Educational Learning Fundamentals)
Akron, OH
JDRP Approval: 9/12/77
JDRP Number: 77-155

Alphaphonics: Integrated Beginning Reading
San Francisco, CA
JDRP Approval: 2/25/74
JDRP Number: 74-15
(see *KITE* in Section 11)

Alternative Learning Project
Providence, RI
JDRP Approval: 6/6/74
JDRP Number: 74-86

APEC: America's Possible Energy Choices
Rockford, IL
JDRP Approval: 8/18/80
JDRP Number: 80-18

Aprendemos En Dos Idiomas: Title VII Bilingual Program
Corpus Christi, TX
JDRP Approval: 6/27/75
JDRP Number: 75-56

Astra's Magic Math
San Francisco, CA
JDRP Approval: 1/24/84
JDRP Number: 83-54
(see *KITE* in Section 11)

Baptist Hill Kindergarten
Greenville, AL
JDRP Approval: 10/18/74
JDRP Number: 74-102

BASE: Bilingual Alternative for Secondary Education
Miami, FL
JDRP Approval: 4/21/82
JDRP Number: 82-1

BASIC: Basic Adaptable Skills for the Individual Child
Montevideo, MN
JDRP Approval: 9/9/77
JDRP Number: 77-149

BASIC–California Demonstration Program in Reading
San Francisco, CA
JDRP Approval: 3/25/83
JDRP Number: 83-32

BAsic SKills in Reading (BASK)
Manchester, NH
JDRP Approval: 11/84
JDRP Number: 75-68

Boulder Valley Public Schools Follow Through
Boulder, CO
JDRP Approval: 4/22/81
JDRP Number: 77-156b
Recertified: 9/85

Calculator Math
Central Square, NY
JDRP Approval: 3/28/83
JDRP Number: 83-36

California Migrant Teacher Assistant Corps: California Mini-Corps
Oroville, CA
JDRP Approval: 11/17/78
JDRP Number: 78-196

CAM: Demonstration Evaluation Center
Hopkins, MN
JDRP Approval: 3/15/85
JDRP Number: 81-31

Cambridge Follow Through
Cambridge, MN
JDRP Approval: 4/24/82
JDRP Number: 77-156f

CARE: Correlating Art and Reading Essentials
Tallahassee, FL
JDRP Approval: 1/20/82
JDRP Number: 81-49

Career Assessment and Planning
Wyoming, MI
JDRP Approval: 10/14/83
JDRP Number: 83-47

Career Development Programs
Akron, OH
JDRP Approval: 5/25/78
JDRP Number: 78-181

Career Education Resource Center Program
Washington, D.C.
JDRP Approval: 4/22/80
JDRP Number: 80-4

Career Intern Program
Philadelphia, PA
JDRP Approval: 6/1/66
JDRP Number: 77-119

Career Planning Support System (CPSS)
Columbus, OH
JDRP Approval: 5/23/80
JDRP Number: 80-5

Catch-Up
Newport Beach, CA
JDRP Approval: 4/4/73
JDRP Number: 73-34

CATCH-UP–KEEP UP
Tucson, AZ
JDRP Approval: 12/16/74
JDRP Number: 74-120

CDCC: Career Development Center
Coloma, MI
JDRP Approval: 3/16/78
JDRP Number: 78-168

Centralized Correspondence Study: Individualized Home Study
Juneau, AK
JDRP Approval: 5/27/83
JDRP Number: 83-13

C.E.N.T.$. (Creative Economic Notions for Teachers and Students)
Columbia, SC
JDRP Approval: 5/26/82
JDRP Number: 82-30

Chance for Every Child
Warren, MI
JDRP Approval: 7/1/76
JDRP Number: 76-89

CHAPEL HILL Model
Chapel Hill, NC
JDRP Approval: 2/8/83
JDRP Number: 75-73R

CHAPTER I, ECIA PRESCHOOL
Bessemer, AL
JDRP Approval: 4/5/73
JDRP Number: 73-26

Chapter 1 Reading, Grades 2-6
Fort Dodge, IA
JDRP Approval: 4/17/79
JDRP Number: 79-13

Cherokee Follow Through
Cherokee, NC
JDRP Approval: 2/13/81
JDRP Number: 80-50e

CHILD
Geneseo, NY
JDRP Approval: 4/9/73
JDRP Number: 73-23

Child Development Center
Huntington Beach, CA
JDRP Approval: 5/23/79
JDRP Number: 79-21

Child-Parent Centers Program (CPC)
Chicago, IL
JDRP Approval: 4/29/74
JDRP Number: 74-31

Child Study Center (CSC)
St. Petersburg, FL
JDRP Approval: 2/6/74
JDRP Number: 74-116

Classmate 88 Mathematics Computational Skills Program
South Bend, IN
JDRP Approval: 9/9/85
JDRP Number: 85-11

Classroom Intervention
Seattle, WA
JDRP Approval: 11/10/75
JDRP Number: 75-77

Classroom Team Approach
Westminster, CO
JDRP Approval: 12/16/74
JDRP Number: 74-122

Clinch Powell Educational Cooperative
Tazewell, TN
JDRP Approval: 2/25/77
JDRP Number: 77-108

COAST: Cognitively Oriented Approach to Skills Teaching
Chipley, FL
JDRP Approval: 2/4/81
JDRP Number: 77-123c

College Studies for the Gifted (CSG)
Hays, KS
JDRP Approval: 7/2/86
JDRP Number: 86-14

Communication Arts and Science Training (CAST)
Union, NJ
JDRP Approval: 12/5/80
JDRP Number: 80-34

Communication Program
Everett, WA
JDRP Approval: 9/3/75
JDRP Number: 75-64a

Communications Workshop (CWS)
Teaneck, NJ
JDRP Approval: 6/5/78
JDRP Number: 78-191

Community Approach to Year-Round Education (C.A.Y.R.E.)
Aurora, CO
JDRP Approval: 3/15/78
JDRP Number: 78-160

Community School 6 Bronx Follow Through
Bronx, NJ
JDRP Approval: 4/15/81
JDRP Number: 77-102b

Community School 77 Bronx
Bronx, NY
JDRP Approval: 8/24/77
JDRP Number: 77-135

Competency Based Program for Mathematics Mastery (CBPMM)
Pine Bluff, AK
JDRP Approval: 3/8/83
JDRP Number: 83-16

Comprehensive Foundation Studies Program for the High Risk Student
Charleston, SC
JDRP Approval: 7/23/81
JDRP Number: 81-17

Comprehensive Program for Handicapped Preschool Children and Their Families in Rural and Non-Urban Areas
Fargo, ND
JDRP Approval: 11/7/79
JDRP Number: 79-35

Comprehensive Training Program for Infant and Young Cerebral Palsied Children
Wauwatosa, WI
JDRP Approval: 9/3/75
JDRP Number: 75-62

Computerized Pupil Attendance
Russell, KY
JDRP Approval: 5/18/81
JDRP Number: 81-1

Computer Literacy Project
Alma, AR
JDRP Approval: 3/29/83
JDRP Number: 83-38

Computeronics
Tallahassee, FL
JDRP Approval: 12/23/80
JDRP Number: 80-39

Conceptually Oriented Mathematics Program (COMP)
Mesa, AZ
JDRP Approval: 12/6/74
JDRP Number: 74-114

Confluence of Cultures
Alice, TX
JDRP Approval: 6/27/75
JDRP Number: 75-56

CONQUEST
E. St. Louis, IL
JDRP Approval: 2/20/74
JDRP Number: 74-12

Contract Learning for Educable Mentally Retarded Students
Grand Rapids, MI
JDRP Approval: 1/21/75
JDRP Number: 75-11

Corpus Christi Follow Through
Corpus Christi, TX
JDRP Approval: 9/1/77
JDRP Number: 77-140

CRAM: Compensatory Reading and Mathematics Program
Winchester, VA
JDRP Approval: 5/23/79
JDRP Number: 79-16

Cranston's Comprehensive Reading Program (CCRP)
Cranston, RI
JDRP Approval: 6/2/82
JDRP Number: 82-28
Recertified: 5/86

Criterion Reading Instruction Project (CRIP)
Linden, NJ
JDRP Approval: 4/9/73
JDRP Number: 73-32

Cross-Aged Structured Tutoring Program for Math
Boise, ID
JDRP Approval: 3/17/83
JDRP Number: 83-20

Cross-Aged Structured Tutoring Program for Reading
Boise, ID
JDRP Approval: 3/17/83
JDRP Number: 83-20

CUE: Computer Utilization in Education
Central Square, NY
JDRP Approval: 3/28/83
JDRP Number: 83-36

Cupertino Concept: Computer Literacy and Beyond Program
Cupertino, CA
JDRP Approval: 3/30/84
JDRP Number: 83-37R

Curriculum/Modification Through Env. Studies
Jensen Beach, FL
JDRP Approval: 12/18/75
JDRP Number: 75-78

Dale Avenue Early Childhood Education Project
Cape May, NJ
JDRP Approval: 4/16/73
JDRP Number: 73-13

Dayton Direct Instruction Follow Through Project
Dayton, OH
JDRP Approval: 8/24/77
JDRP Number: 77-132
Recertified: 2/85

DEBT
Lubbock, TX
JDRP Approval: 10/21/80
JDRP Number: 80-28

Deficiency Skills Learning Lab
Seneca, SC
JDRP Approval: 2/26/85
JDRP Number: 85-2

DeKalb County Follow Through: A Direct Instructional Model
Smithville, TN
JDRP Approval: 12/29/80
JDRP Number: 80-50a

Des Moines Plan Project
Des Moines, IA
JDRP Approval: 2/11/81
JDRP Number: 80-56

Developing Models for Special Education (DMSE)
Monticello, FL
JDRP Approval: 3/16/79
JDRP Number: 79-6

Developmental Play (DP)
St. Petersburg, FL
JDRP Approval: 12/6/74
JDRP Number: 74-116b

Directory of Representative Work Education Program, 1972-73
Washington, D.C.
JDRP Approval: 6/21/73
JDRP Number: 49

Discovery
Red Oak, IA
JDRP Approval: 3/15/78
JDRP Number: 78-121

Discovery Through Reading
Clarkston, MI
JDRP Approval: 10/23/74
JDRP Number: 74-112

DPI
Long Beach, CA
JDRP Approval: 5/19/82
JDRP Number: 80-20

Duval Consumer Education Curriculum
Jacksonville, FL
JDRP Approval: 4/14/81
JDRP Number: 80-44

Early Childhood Education—All Day Kindergarten
Cincinnati, OH
JDRP Approval: 2/26/74
JDRP Number: 74-16

Early Childhood Preventative Curriculum (ECPC)
Miami, FL
JDRP Approval: 5/23/74
JDRP Number: 74-57

East Las Vegas Follow Through
Las Vegas, NV
JDRP Approval: 2/13/81
JDRP Number: 80-50f
Recertified: 3/85

East St. Louis Follow Through
East St. Louis, IL
JDRP Approval: 9/6/77
JDRP Number: 77-144

ECOLogy: Environmental Career-Oriented Learning
Seattle, WA
JDRP Approval: 12/18/75
JDRP Number: 75-80a

Economic Literacy aka How to Make a Million (HMM)
Bellevue, WA
JDRP Approval: 4/2/85
JDRP Number: 85-6R
(see Save for America in Section 8)

ECOS: Training Institute
Yorktown Heights, NY
JDRP Approval: 5/14/74
JDRP Number: 74-59

Electric Company
Mt. Kisco, NY
JDRP Approval: 4/29/74
JDRP Number: 74-23

Elementary Metric Project
Bismarck, ND
JDRP Approval: 3/16/78
JDRP Number: 78-162

Elmira Follow Through Project
Elmira, NY
JDRP Approval: 4/21/81
JDRP Number: 77-156d

Emerge: The Shop
Dayton, OH
JDRP Approval: 9/22/75
JDRP Number: 75-1

Engineered Classroom Behaviorally Maladjusted
Papillion, NE
JDRP Approval: 6/6/74
JDRP Number: 74-84

Enriching The Curriculum (ETC)
Brookline, MA
JDRP Approval: 3/25/82
JDRP Number: 81-48

Environment and Technology Project
Chicago, IL
JDRP Approval: 6/5/78
JDRP Number: 78-190

Equality
Seattle, WA
JDRP Approval: 5/25/78
JDRP Number: 78-180

ESSP
New Brunswick, NJ
JDRP Approval: 5/14/74
JDRP Number: 74-56

Ethical Issues in Decision Making
White Plains, NY
JDRP Approval: 11/25/80
JDRP Number: 80-31

Every Student Every Day
Morgan City, LA
JDRP Approval: 11/27/78
JDRP Number: 78-198
Recertified: 11/84

Experience Based Career Education (EBCE)
Fond du Lac, WI
JDRP Approval: 9/27/79
JDRP Number: 79-4

Experience Based Career Education (EBCE)–Appalachia Education Laboratory
Charleston, WV
JDRP Approval: 5/7/75
JDRP Number: 75-22

Experience Based Career Education (EBCE)—Far West Laboratory
Berkeley, CA
JDRP Approval: 5/7/75
JDRP Number: 75-22

Experience Based Career Education (EBCE) (NWREL)
Portland, OR
JDRP Approval: 5/7/75
JDRP Number: 75-22

Experience Based Career Education (EBCE) (RBS)
Philadelphia, PA
JDRP Approval: 5/7/75
JDRP Number: 75-22

Expressive Writing in School
Fairfax, CA
JDRP Approval: 2/25/83
JDRP Number: 83-11

Fail Save Continuum of Services for Learning Disabled Students
Albuquerque, NM
JDRP Approval: 9/22/75
JDRP Number: 75-1

FAR (Freshman Attrition Reduction)
Dover, DE
JDRP Approval: 9/11/81
JDRP Number: 81-86

FAST: Functional Analysis Systems Training
Essexville, MI
JDRP Approval: 1/15/75
JDRP Number: 75-4

FASTT, Family and School Teaching Together
Tallahassee, FL
JDRP Approval: 11/19/81
JDRP Number: 81-38

FEED: Facilitative Environment Encouraging Development
Bloomington, IN
JDRP Approval: 7/11/80
JDRP Number: 80-12

First Calculating and Reading Quest
Ogolala, SD
JDRP Approval: 4/4-5/73
JDRP Number: 73-27

FIST: Functional In-Service Training
New Brunswick, NJ
PEP Approval: 7/18/89
PEP Number: 83-35

Flagstaff Remedial Reading Program (Title I)
Flagstaff, AZ
JDRP Approval: 4/5/73
JDRP Number: 73-31

Flippin Follow Through
Flippin, AR
JDRP Approval: 12/29/80
JDRP Number: 80-50d

FLIT: Functional Literacy
Alexandria, VA
JDRP Approval: 3/25/74
JDRP Number: 74-22

Florida Migratory Child Compensatory Program—Language Arts Tutorial Program
Tallahassee, FL
JDRP Approval: 4/9/73
JDRP Number: 73-21

Follow Through Nongraded Learning Model
New York, NY
JDRP Approval: 10/17/80
JDRP Number: 80-27

Follow Through-Portageville Unit
Portageville, MO
JDRP Approval: 4/5/73
JDRP Number: 73-25a

FREESTYLE
Downey, CA
JDRP Approval: 7/11/80
JDRP Number: 80-10

Futureprint
Ontario, CA
JDRP Approval: 6/2/82
JDRP Number: 80-21

GEMS: Goal-based Educational Management System
Sandy, UT
JDRP Approval: 2/16/79
JDRP Number: 79-2

Glassboro Right-To-Read Project
Glassboro, NJ
JDRP Approval: 9/18/74
JDRP Number: 74-93

"GO-Metric": A Supplemental Low-Cost Metric Curriculum
Tulsa, OK
JDRP Approval: 8/10/78
JDRP Number: 78-195

Goldsboro City Follow Through: University of Georgia Model (UGA) - formerly RECEP
Goldsboro, NC
JDRP Approval: 2/2/81
JDRP Number: 80-51e

Good Samaritan
Portland, OR
JDRP Approval: 6/11/81
JDRP Number: 81-12

Have a Healthy Heart (HHH)
Bellevue, WA
JDRP Approval: 12/9/80
JDRP Number: 80-38

Hawaii Basic Skills Remediation Project
Hilo, HI
JDRP Approval: 10/18/74
JDRP Number: 74-108

Hawaii English Program (HEP)
Honolulu, HI
JDRP Approval: 4/29/74
JDRP Number: 74-21

Hawaii Follow Through
Honolulu, HI
JDRP Approval: 4/22/81
JDRP Number: 77-156c

HEAR: Human Educational Awareness Resource
Princeton, NJ
JDRP Approval: 5/31/78
JDRP number: 78-185

HEP/Project ALOHA (Allowing Learners Optimum Human Attainment)
San Jose, CA
JDRP Approval: 4/2-9/74
JDRP Number: 74-28

HIT: High Intensity Tutoring
Highland Park, MI
JDRP Approval: 1/8/74
JDRP Number: 74-9

Home Base
Yakima, WA
JDRP Approval: 1/21/75
JDRP Number: 75-10

Home Start
Waterloo, IA
JDRP Approval: 1/21/75
JDRP Number: 75-9

Houston Bilingual Program
Houston, TX
JDRP Approval: 6/24/75
JDRP Number: 75-52

I-C-E (Instruction-Curriculum-Environment)
Green Bay, WI
JDRP Approval: 5/14/75
JDRP Number: 75-39

IDEA (A Program for Hearing Imparied Infants)
Campbell, CA
JDRP Approval: 5/14/75
JDRP Number: 75-44

Improvement of Basic Reading Skills
Sylacauga, AL
JDRP Approval: 10/18/74
JDRP Number: 74-109

Improving Achievement
Logan, UT
JDRP Approval: 2/25/75
JDRP Number: 75-110

Improving Visual Arts Education
Tucson, AZ
PEP Approval: 8/28/88
PEP Number: 88-16

Indianapolis Follow Through Project
Indianapolis, IN
JDRP Approval: 8/17/77
JDRP Number: 77-120

Individual Education Program in Physical Education (IEP/PE): Physical Education for Handicapped Children
Columbia, SC
JDRP Approval: 12/15/81
JDRP Number: 81-41

Individualized Bilingual Instruction (IBI)
Pasco, WA
JDRP Approval: 4/9/73
JDRP Number: 73-48

Individualized Computer Assisted Remedial Reading Program (I CARE)
Schuykill Haven, PA
JDRP Approval: 5/19/82
JDRP Number: 82-24

Individualized Prescriptive Arithmetic Skills System (IPASS)
Pawtucket, RI
JDRP Approval: 5/27/82
JDRP Number: 82-23
Recertified: 6/5/86

Individual Progress Program (IPP)
Seattle, WA
JDRP Approval: 5/12/82
JDRP Number: 82-15
INSTRUCT
Upper Arlington, OH
JDRP Approval: 5/14/75
JDRP Number: 75-37

Intensive Reading Improvement Program (IRIP)
Chicago, IL
JDRP Approval: 4/29/74
JDRP Number: 74-27

Interactive Curricular Experience
Panama City, FL
JDRP Approval: 4/22/80
JDRP Number: 80-3

IRIT: Intensive Reading Instructional Teams
Hartford, CT
JDRP Approval: 2/20/74
JDRP Number: 74-11

ISCOM
Miami, FL
JDRP Approval: 3/14/83
JDRP Number: 81-19

Jefferson County Adult Reading Program (JCARP)
Frankfort, KY
JDRP Approval: 9/15/82
JDRP Number: 82-19

Kansas City Follow Through Project
Kansas City, MO
JDRP Approval: 8/22/77
JDRP Number: 77-130
Recertified: 8/85

KARE
Erdenheim, PA
JDRP Approval: 5/14/75
JDRP Number: 75-40

Law Education Goals and Learnings (LEGAL)
Miami, FL
JDRP Approval: 8/18/80
JDRP Number: 80-19

Learning Disabilities Early Identification and Intervention
New Orleans, LA
JDRP Approval: 4/19/73
JDRP Number: 80-43

Learning for Life
Boston, MA
JDRP Approval: 12/23/80
JDRP Number: 80-43

Learning to Read by Reading
Jamestown, CA
JDRP Approval: 4/29/74
JDRP Number: 74-37
Recertified: 2-85

Lee County Follow Through: Mathamagenic Activities Program (MAP)
Jonesville, VA
JDRP Approval: 2/2/81
JDRP Number: 81-51d

LEM: Learning Experience Module
Hackensack, NJ
JDRP Approval: 4/9/73
JDRP Number: 73-40

Lincoln County Exemplary Project in Career Education
Hamlin, WV
JDRP Approval: 12/13/73
JDRP Number: 73-2

Living Independence Training
Wheat Ridge, CO
JDRP Approval: 1/24/84
JDRP Number: 84-53

M²C: Math Motivational Centers
Norwalk, CT
JDRP Approval: 3/14/83
JDRP Number: 83-24

Macomb O-3 Regional Project
Macomb, IL
JDRP Approval: 6/17/80
JDRP Number: 80-8

MATCH
Ontario, CA
JDRP Approval: 3/16/78
JDRP Number: 78-167

Math Laboratories for Disadvantaged Students
Honea Path, SC
JDRP Approval: 7/13/76
JDRP Number: 76

Mathematics Achievement Program (MAP)
Chester, PA
JDRP Approval: 7/22/82
JDRP Number: 82-39

Matteson Four-Dimensional Reading Program
Matteson, IL
JDRP Approval: 2/25/77
JDRP Number: 77-109

McCormick Follow Through: University of Georgia Model (UGA)
McCormick, SC
JDRP Approval: 2/2/81
JDRP Number: 80-51c

MECCA: Make Every Child Capable of Achieving
Meriden, CT
JDRP Approval: 3/23/77
JDRP Number: 77-111

Media Now
Red Oak, IA
JDRP Approval: 5/13/75
JDRP Number: 75-34

Medical Insurance: A Procedure for Instituting a Cost-Effective Program
Piscataway, NJ
JDRP Approval: 9/3/80
JDRP Number: 80-14

Merrimack Education Center CAI Project
Chelmsford, MA
JDRP Approval: 6/2/82
JDRP Number: 82-34

Metrics Made Easy
Huntington Beach, CA
JDRP Approval: 7/11/79
JDRP Number: 79-31

Micro-Math
San Francisco, CA
JDRP Approval: 3/17/83
JDRP Number: 83-31

Model Classrooms' Computerized Classroom Management System (CLASS)
Bellevue, WA
JDRP Approval: 3/27/78
JDRP Number: 78-170

Model Learning Disabilities System (MLDS)
University Park, PA
JDRP Approval: 3/23/77
JDRP Number: 77-110

Muscogee Health Project
Columbus, GA
JDRP Approval: 11/19/81
JDRP Number: 81-32

National Migrant Interstate Project
Little Rock, AR
JDRP Approval: 4/9/73
JDRP Number: 73-24

New Adventure in Learning (NAIL)
Tallahassee, FL
JDRP Approval: 5/23/74
JDRP Number: 74-71

New Jersey Writing Project
Monmouth Junction, NJ
JDRP Approval: 5/24/79
JDRP Number: 79-19

Nichols Avenue Follow Through
Washington, D.C.
JDRP Approval: 12/29/80
JDRP Number: 80-50c

NOMAD: Needs and Objectives for Migrant Advancement and Development
Lawrence, MI
JDRP Approval: 4/9/73
JDRP Number: 73-21a

Northern Cheyenne Follow Through
Lame Deer, MT
JDRP Approval: 9/9/77
JDRP Number: 77-151

Northwest Special Education (NWSE)
Columbus, ND
JDRP Approval: 1/15/75
JDRP Number: 75-7

Oakland Follow Through
Oakland, CA
JDRP Approval: 9/9/77
JDRP Number: 77-150

Occupational and Career Development
Marietta, GA
JDRP Approval: 1/18/74
JDRP Number: 74-7

Occupational Versatility (O.V.)
Bellingham, WA
JDRP Approval: 4/17/73
JDRP Number: 73-12

Opening the Doors
Princeton, NJ
JDRP Approval: 12/9/80
JDRP Number: 80-36

PA: Project Advocate—Northwestern Illinois Association
DeKalb, IL
JDRP Approval: 7/23/75
JDRP Number: 75-61

Packets to Assist Literacy
Chipley, FL
JDRP Approval: 12/18/81
JDRP Number: 81-43

PAL: Public Advancing In Learning
Denver, CO
JDRP Approval: 4/4-5/73
JDRP Number: 73-33

Parent-Child Early Education Program (Saturday School)
Florissant, MO
JDRP Approval: 5/23/74
JDRP Number: 74-47

Parents Readiness Education Project (PREP)
Redford, MI
JDRP Approval: 5/9/74
JDRP Number: 74-51

PECP
Vienna, WV
JDRP Approval: 9/26/79
JDRP Number: 79-37

PEGASUS: Personalized Educational Growth and Achivement with Selective Utilization of Staff
Princeton, IL
JDRP Approval: (info. not available)
JDRP Number: 1

PEGASUS-PACE
Tuscaloosa, AL
JDRP Approval: 4/29/82
JDRP Number: 82-16

PEOPEL: Physical Education Opportunity Program for Exceptional-Handicapped Learners
Phoenix, AZ
JDRP Approval: 3/28/79
JDRP Number: 79-10

Peoria 0-3 Project
Peoria, IL
JDRP Approval: 2/15/79
JDRP Number: 79-1

Philadelphia Follow Through (BARC)
Philadelphia, PA
JDRP Approval: 9/1/77
JDRP Number: 77-143

Pickens County Follow Through
Jasper, GA
JDRP Approval: 2/2/81
JDRP Number: 80-51b

Pierce County Vocational/Special Education Cooperative
Tacoma, WA
PEP Approval: 3/2/88
PEP Number: 88-05

Pilot Project for Articulatory Disordered Children
Burlington, IA
JDRP Approval: 12/6/74
JDRP Number: 74-117

Plattsburgh Follow Through
Plattsburgh, NY
JDRP Approval: 2/4/81
JDRP Number: 77-154b

Pocatello Follow Through (MAP)
Pocatello, ID
JDRP Approval: 2/2/81
JDRP Number: 80-51a

Posen-Robbins Career Awareness Series In Early Childhood
Chicago, IL
JDRP Approval: 10/14/83
JDRP Number: 83-49

Positive Alternatives to Student Suspensions (PASS)
Clearwater, FL
JDRP Approval: 12/6/74
JDRP Number: 74-116a

Pre-Algebra Development Centers
Chicago, IL
JDRP Approval: 5/13/75
JDRP Number: 75-33

Pre-Kindergarten Prescriptive Teaching Program for Learning Disabled Children
Fargo, ND
JDRP Approval: 2/25/75
JDRP Number: 75-12

PRIDE
Yeadon, PA
JDRP Approval: 9/12/79
JDRP Number: 79-20

PRIOR
Fort Collins, CO
JDRP Approval: 5/30/79
JDRP Number: 79-24

Program for Children with Down Syndrome and Other Developmental Delays
Seattle, WA
JDRP Approval: 9/3/75
JDRP Number: 75-64b

Program for Early Education of Children with Handicaps
Wichita Falls, TX
JDRP Approval: 7/10/79
JDRP Number: 79-30

Programmed Tutorial Reading (PTR)
Farmington, UT
JDRP Approval: 3/18/74
JDRP Number: 74-17

Project 50/50
North Oxford, MA
JDRP Approval: 3/26/84
JDRP Number: 84-13

Project for the Severely Handicapped Child
Miami, FL
JDRP Approval: 12/4/79
JDRP Number: 79-29

Project Management Basic Principles and Techniques
Pine Hill, NJ
JDRP Approval: 5/14/75
JDRP Number: 75-44

Proviso Reading Model
Maywood, IL
JDRP Approval: 6/17/80
JDRP Number: 80-9

Psychomotor Learnings for Academic Yields (PLAY)
Bristol, VA
JDRP Approval: 4/22/80
JDRP Number: 79-38

Public School 33 Manhattan Follow Through
New York, NY
JDRP Approval: 2/4/81
JDRP Number: 80-48

Public School 92 Manhattan Follow Through
New York, NY
JDRP Approval: 2/4/81
JDRP Number: 77-123b

Public Schools of Choice: High School in the Community (HSC)
New Haven, CT
JDRP Approval: 5/15/75
JDRP Number: 75-45

Pupil Transportation: A Procedure for Co-operative Purchase of Special Education Services
Piscataway, NJ
JDRP Approval: 9/3/80
JDRP Number: 80-15

R-3: Readiness, Relevancy and Reinforcement
San Jose, CA
JDRP Approval: 2/20/74
JDRP Number: 74-13

RAM: Reading and Micro-Management
Bakersfield, CA
JDRP Approval: 3/29/83
JDRP Number: 83-39

Randolph County Follow Through
Elkins, WV
JDRP Approval: 3/2/81
JDRP Number: 81-149b

READ
Pittsburgh, PA
JDRP Approval: 4/29/74
JDRP Number: 74-30

Reading Achievement Program (RAP)
Chester, PA
JDRP Approval: 10/21/81
JDRP Number: 81-28

Reading and Content-area Resource Center (ReCaRe)
West St. Paul, MN
JDRP Approval: 2/25/83
JDRP Number: 82-22R

Reading Education Accountability Design: Secondary (READ:S)
Coeur d'Alene, ID
JDRP Approval: 2/25/83
JDRP Number: 83-4
(see *Literacy Links* in Section 10)

Reading/English Rotation Project
Thomson, GA
JDRP Approval: 4/5/73
JDRP Number: 73-45

Reading Improvement
Burgaw, NC
JDRP Approval: 10/18/74
JDRP Number: 74-103

Reading Improvement by Teaching Effectively (R.I.T.E.)
Phoenixville, PA
JDRP Approval: 9/9/85
JDRP Number: 85-12

Reading Improvement Program—Secondary Schools Reading Laboratory
Parkerburg, WV
JDRP Approval: 7/1/76
JDRP Number: 76-84

Reading-Individualized Remedial Laboratories/Math
Albany, GA
JDRP Approval: 10/18/74
JDRP Number: 74-107

Read-Write
Summit, NJ
JDRP Approval: 11/25/80
JDRP Number: 80-30
Recertified: 1/30/86

REAL
Lebanon, NH
JDRP Approval: 9/12/77
JDRP Number: 77-154

Re-Ed School of Kentucky
Louisville, KY
JDRP Approval: 4/9/73
JDRP Number: 73-39

Research Exchange for Computerized Individualized Programs of Education (RECIPE)
Sarasota, FL
JDRP Approval: 3/4/83
JDRP Number: 83-10

Richmond Follow Through
Richmond, VA
JDRP Approval: (info. not available)
JDRP Number: 77-146

Right To Read: Wilson Jr. High School
San Diego, CA
JDRP Approval: 3/25/74
JDRP Number: 74-21

RIPPS
Portsmouth, RI
JDRP Approval: 12/16/74
JDRP Number: 74-124

Rose F. Kennedy Center
Bronx, NY
JDRP Approval: 3/25/82
JDRP Number: 82-3

San Diego City Schools Follow Through
San Diego, CA
JDRP Approval: 2/13/81
JDRP Number: 81-50g
Recertified: 6/85

San Jose Nutrition Education Project (SJNEP)–Nutrition Through Science
San Jose, CA
JDRP Approval: 2/17/82
JDRP Number: 82-3
Recertified: 9/85

SCAT
Kissimmee, FL
JDRP Approval: 12/23/80
JDRP Number: 80-45

School Volunteer Development Project
Miami, FL
JDRP Approval: 12/18/75
JDRP Number: 75-79

SCORE
South San Francisco, CA
JDRP Approval: 12/22/80
JDRP Number: 80-42

SDR: Systems Directed Reading
Richardson, TX
JDRP Approval: 6/6/74
JDRP Number: 74-83

SEAPORT: Student Education Assuring Positive Organized Reading Techniques
Newport, RI
JDRP Approval: 4/9/73
JDRP Number: 73-29

Secondary Credit Exchange Program
Sunnyside, WA
JDRP Approval: 4/17/77
JDRP Number: 77-113

Senior Elective Program
Rumsson, New Jersey
JDRP Approval: 9/18/74
JDRP Number: 74-91

Sequential Physical Education Reform: The M-5 Project
Marion, NC
JDRP Approval: 5/13/78
JDRP Number: 78-172

SHARE Project
Tucson, AZ
JDRP Approval: 5/12/75
JDRP Number: 75-31

SIGMA: System for Individually Guiding Mastery Attainment
San Diego, CA
JDRP Approval: 5/8/79
JDRP Number: 79-17

Simu-School
Dallas, TX
JDRP Approval: 6/6/74
JDRP Number: 74-77

Slice of Life
Sunnyvale, CA
JDRP Approval: 10/21/83
JDRP Number: 83-46

SMART (Success in Mathematics Through A Rural Reading Technique)
Daytona Beach, FL
JDRP Approval: 12/6/74
JDRP Number: 74-90

South Douglas County Early Childhood Education Project
Myrtle Creek, OR
JDRP Approval: 4/29/75
JDRP Number: 75-113

Special Education Preschool Program
Minneapolis, MN
JDRP Approval: 9/3/75
JDRP Number: 75-65

St. John Valley Bilingual Education Program
Madawaska, ME
JDRP Approval: 6/24/75
JDRP Number: 75-54

St. Paul Open School
St. Paul, MN
JDRP Approval: 6/6/74
JDRP Number: 74-85

Strategies In Early Childhood Education
Oshkosh, WI
JDRP Approval: 5/29/74
JDRP Number: 74-75

STAY: School To Aid Youth
Moore, OK
JDRP Approval: 4/9/73
JDRP Number: 73-43

Success
Kingston, WA
JDRP Approval: 5/7/75
JDRP Number: 75-28

Success Environment
Atlanta, GA
JDRP Approval: 4/5/73
JDRP Number: 73-5

Success for the SLD Child
Wayne, NE
JDRP Approval: 4/9/73
JDRP Number: 73-14

Systematic Instructional Management Strategies (SIMS)
Minneapolis, MN
JDRP Approval: 5/15/79
JDRP Number: 79-18

Talent Development
Miami, FL
JDRP Approval: 9/22/75
JDRP Number: 75-70

Team Oriented Corrective Reading (TOCR)
Wichita, KA
JDRP Approval: 4/5/73
JDRP Number: 73-28

Title I Remedial Reading Program
Fort Lauderdale, FL
JDRP Approval: 8/21/74
JDRP Number: 74-89

Topeka Outdoor-Environmental Education
    Project
Topeka, KS
JDRP Approval: 5/6/75
JDRP Number: 75-15

Training for Turnabout Volunteers
Miami, FL
JDRP Approval: 6/2/81
JDRP Number: 81-11

Trenton Follow Through
Trenton, NJ
JDRP Approval: 8/26/77
JDRP Number: 77-139

Tulare Follow Through
Tulare, CA
JDRP Approval: 8/19/77
JDRP Number: 77-127

TV Reading and Communication
South Salem, NY
JDRP Approval: 4/29/82
JDRP Number: 82-16

UCLA Allied Health Professions Publication
Los Angeles, CA
JDRP Approval: 12/13/73
JDRP Number: 73-1

Understand
Arlington, MA
JDRP Approval: 12/16/74
JDRP Number: 74-121

Upstairs School
Portland, OR
JDRP Approval: 4/5/73
JDRP Number: 73-30

Urban Arts Program
Minneapolis, MN
JDRP Approval: 5/7/75
JDRP Number: 75-27

U-SAIL: Utah System Approach to
    Individualized Learning
Salt Lake City, UT
JDRP Approval: 10/4/76
JDRP Number: 76-95
Recertified: 9/84

Uvalde Follow Through
Uvalde, TX
JDRP Approval: 2/13/81
JDRP Number: 81-50i

Vermont Children's Special Services Project
Montpelier, VT
JDRP Approval: 5/18/83
JDRP Number: 83-50

Waterloo
Waterloo, IA
JDRP Approval: 9/6/77
JDRP Number: 77-148

Waukegan Effective Schools Approach
Waukegan, IL
JDRP Approval: 8/19/77
JDRP Number: 77-126

Wayne Career Education Program
Wayne, NJ
JDRP Approval: 10/21/83
JDRP Number: 83-48

Weeksville School/Bank Street College Follow
    Through
Brooklyn, NY
JDRP Approval: 9/12/77
JDRP Number: 77-156

Weslaco Reading/Language Arts
Weslaco, TX
JDRP Approval: 5/17/83
JDRP Number: 83-2

West Hills Follow Through
New Haven, CT
JDRP Approval: 4/24/81
JDRP Number: 77-156g

Williamsburg County Follow Through
Kingstree, SC
JDRP Approval: 12/19/80
JDRP Number: 80-50b

WWAS: Women in World Area Studies
St. Louis Park, MN
JDRP Approval: 12/22/80
JDRP Number: 80-40

Zoo Opportunities Outreach (ZOO)
Burlington, NC
JDRP Approval: 9/17/81
JDRP Number: 81-18

Section 17

Indices

* These programs are currently funded by the NDN.

Index I
Exemplary Programs
by State

COLORADO

CONNECTICUT

DISTRICT OF COLUMBIA

FLORIDA

GEORGIA

HAWAII

IDAHO

ILLINOIS

INDIANA

MINNESOTA

Family Oriented Structured Preschool Activity (FOSPA) ("Seton Hall" Program) *(St. Cloud)* **11-12**

Focus Dissemination Project *(South St. Paul)* **3-7**

Reading Power in the Content Areas (RP) *(Minneapolis)* **4-11**

Religion In Human Culture (RIHC) *(Minneapolis)* **8-13**

Study Skills Across the Curriculum *(West St. Paul)* **10-14**

MISSISSIPPI

Gulfport Follow Through: University of Georgia Model (UGA) *(Gulfport)* **10-16**

Leflore County (Mississippi) Follow Through Project *(Greenwood)* **10-18**

MISSOURI

DeLaSalle Model *(Kansas City)* **3-3**

Diagnostic Prescriptive Arithmetic (DPA) *(Louisiana)* **6-13**

Parents As Teachers *(St. Louis)* **11-8**

Starwalk *(Kansas City)* **7-23**

Supplemental Instruction (SI): Improving Student Performance and Reducing Attrition *(Kansas City)* **14-4**

Webster Groves Even Start Program *(Rock Hill)* **11-10**

Writers Project, The *(Florissant)* **4-14**

MONTANA

CReating Independence through Student-owned Strategies (Project CRISS) *(Kalispell)* **10-5**

Diagnostic Prescriptive Arithmetic (DPA) *(Helena)* **6-13**

Physical Management *(Billings)* **9-12**

NEBRASKA

Administrative Cooperative in Education *(Columbus)* **2-6**

NEW HAMPSHIRE

FISH BANKS, LTD. *(Durham)* **7-4**

Image-Making Within the Writing Process *(Durham)* **4-5**

NEW JERSEY

CLIMB Plus *(Middlesex)* **10-2**

Elsmere Project *(Sewell)* **12-12**

Individualized Language Arts: Diagnosis, Prescription, and Evaluation *(North Bergen)* **5-7**

Institute for Creative Education (ICE) *(Sewell)* **10-17**

Institute for Political and Legal Education (IPLE) *(Sewell)* **8-11**

NEW YORK

NORTH CAROLINA

OHIO

OKLAHOMA

OREGON

PENNSYLVANIA

RHODE ISLAND

TENNESSEE

TEXAS

WISCONSIN

WEST VIRGINIA

Index II
ERIC Descriptors

To help readers locate NDN programs for a given content or problem area, selected ERIC descriptors have been assigned to all active programs described in the catalogue. To make this index easy to use, only basic program features and special target audiences have been included.

ADMINISTRATION

Comprehensive Adult Student Assessment System (CASAS) **14-1**

Outcomes-Driven Developmental Model (ODDM) **2-3**

Program for School Improvement, The (PSI) **2-4**

Resident Supervisory Support for Teachers (RSST) **2-6**

Sharing Successful Programs **2-7**

See also
Financial Services
Program Administration
School Districts

ADULT EDUCATION

Adult Performance Level (APL) Program **14-5**

All Children Totally InVolved in Exercising (ACTIVE) **12-10**

BES Adult Literacy Project **14-5**

Comprehensive Adult Student Assessment System (CASAS) **14-1**

Learning To Learn (LTL): Improving Academic Performance Across the Curriculum **14-6**

Modification of Children's Oral Language **12-12**

National External Diploma Program (EDP) **14-7**

National Family Literacy Project (Dissemination Process) **14-2**

ALTERNATIVES

See
Nontraditional Education

ANTHROPOLOGY

Stones and Bones: A laboratory approach to the study of biology, modern science, and anthropology **7-24**

ARITHMETIC

Calculator Assisted Mathematics for Everyday Living (CAMEL) **6-13**

Comprehensive School Mathematics Program (CSMP) **6-2**

Diagnostic Prescriptive Arithmetic (DPA) **6-13**

First Level Mathematics (Kindermath) **6-5**

Flint Follow Through: The School Effectiveness Model **4-15**

Success Understanding Mathematics (SUM) **6-12**

Systematic Teaching And Measuring Mathematics (STAMM) **6-14**

Systems Approach to Individualized Instruction (SAII) **10-19**

ART

High/Scope Preschool Curriculum **11-5**

Kindergarten Integrated Thematic Experiences (KITE) **11-6**

Learning To Read Through the Arts Program **4-8**

Success Enrichment, Project (PSE) **13-1**

Success Enrichment/Art, Project (PSE/Art) **13-2**

AURALLY HANDICAPPED

See
> *Hearing Impairments*

AUTISM

Developmental Therapy Model **12-11**

Teaching Research Integrated Preschool (TRIP) Model, The **12-14**

BASIC SKILLS

BES Adult Literacy Project **14-5**

Career Awareness Program, Project (Project CAP) **15-2**

Career Education Responsive to Every Student (CERES) **15-3**

Increase Maximal Performance by Activating Critical Thinking (IMPACT) **10-8**

Student Team Learning (STL) **10-18**

See also
> *Arithmetic*
> *Communication Skills*
> *Language Arts*
> *Mathematics*
> *Reading*
> *Remedial Mathematics*
> *Remedial Reading*
> *Writing*

BEHAVIOR PROBLEMS

Curriculum for Meeting Modern Problems (The New Model Me—2nd Edition) **9-10**

Diversified Educational Experiences Program (DEEP) **3-6**

Inservice (Promoting Positive Attitudes Toward Learning) **1-7**

Learncycle: Responsive Teaching **1-7**

Responding to Individual Differences in Education (Project RIDE) **1-5**

Social Decision Making and Problem Solving **9-5**

Systematic Screening for Behavior Disorders (SSBD) **12-8**

BILINGUAL EDUCATION

Early Prevention of School Failure Migrant Program (for Spanish- and English-Speaking Children) **14-6**

First Level Mathematics (Kindermath) **6-5**

Hinsdale Central Foreign Language Program, The **5-4**

Kindergarten Integrated Thematic Experiences (KITE) **11-6**

Modification of Children's Oral Language **12-12**

P.I.A.G.E.T. (Promoting Intellectual Adaptation Given Experiential Transforming), Project **11-9**

CAREER EDUCATION

Academy of Finance **15-1**

Career Awareness Program, Project (Project CAP) **15-2**

Career Education Responsive to Every Student (CERES) **15-3**

Careerways 2000 **15-4**

Center for Educational Development (CED)/Career Guidance Project **15-6**

City-As-School (CAS) **3-1**

COoperative Federation For Educational Experiences (COFFEE) **3-6**

Discovery, Project **15-6**

CEREBRAL PALSY

Multi-Agency Project for Pre-Schoolers (MAPPS) **12-5**

Teaching Research Integrated Preschool (TRIP) Model, The **12-14**

CIVICS

Choices for the 21st Century **8-1**

Kids Voting USA **8-4**

See also
> *Legal Education*

CLASS ORGANIZATION

Classroom Organization and Management Program (COMP) 2-1

Computers Helping Instruction and Learning Development (Project CHILD) 10-4

Diversified Educational Experiences Program (DEEP) 3-6

Program for School Improvement, The (PSI) 2-4

COMMUNICATION SKILLS

Cognitively Oriented Pre-Primary Experience (COPE) 11-11

Developmental Therapy Model 12-11

Focus Dissemination Project 3-7

High/Scope Preschool Curriculum 11-5

Kenosha Model: Academic Improvement through Language Experience 5-7

Teaching Activities for Language Knowledge (TALK) 5-6

Teenage Health Teaching Modules (THTM) 9-8

TV Reading S.T.A.R. (Scripts, Taping, Acting, Reading) 4-17

See also
Language Arts

COMMUNITY

See
School Community Programs

COMPETENCY-BASED EDUCATION

Adult Performance Level (APL) Program 14-5

Early Recognition Intervention Network (ERIN) 12-11

Exemplary Center for Reading Instruction (ECRI) 4-4

Flint Follow Through: The School Effectiveness Model 4-15

Inservice (Promoting Positive Attitudes Toward Learning) 1-7

Literacy Links 10-10

Modification of Children's Oral Language 12-12

More Effective Schools/Teaching Project 2-2

National External Diploma Project (EDP) 14-7

Systematic Teaching And Measuring Mathematics (STAMM) 6-14

COMPOSITION

See
Writing

COMPUTER ASSISTED INSTRUCTION (CAI)

Computer Education for Language Learning (CELL) 4-2

Computers Helping Instruction and Learning Development (Project CHILD) 10-4

First Level Mathematics (Kindermath) 6-5

Individualized Prescriptive Management System for Underachievers in Reading (IPIMS) Reading Center 4-16

Physics—Teach To Learn 7-14

QUILL: Writing with Computers 4-16

Save For America 8-9

Systematic Teaching And Measuring Mathematics (STAMM) 6-14

Title I Mathematics Computer Assisted Instruction (CAI) 6-15

Utilizing Computers In Teaching Secondary Mathematics (UCTSM) 6-16

COMPUTER LITERACY

Comprehensive Adult Student Assessment System (CASAS) 14-1

Computer Assisted Diagnostic Prescriptive Program (CADPP) in Reading and Mathematics 10-3

Individualized Prescriptive Management System for Underachievers in Reading (IPIMS) Reading Center 4-16

Systematic Teaching And Measuring Mathematics (STAMM) 6-14

MAINSTREAMING

MASS MEDIA

MATHEMATICS

MEDIA

MENTAL RETARDATION

PEER TEACHING

Healthy For Life (HFL) **9-3**

Student Team Learning (STL) **10-18**

PERCEPTUAL DEVELOPMENT

Cognitively Oriented Pre-Primary Experience (COPE) **11-11**

Perception+ **11-13**

PERFORMANCE-BASED EDUCATION

See

Competency-Based Education

PHYSICAL DISABILITIES

All Children Totally InVolved in Exercising (ACTIVE) **12-10**

Early Recognition Intervention Network (ERIN) **12-11**

Every Child A Winner with Physical Education (ECAW) **9-2**

Modification of Children's Oral Language **12-12**

PHYSICAL EDUCATION

Achievement-Based Curriculum (ABC) - Project I Can **12-10**

All Children Totally InVolved in Exercising (ACTIVE) **12-10**

Athletic Health Care System **9-1**

Every Child A Winner with Physical Education (ECAW) **9-2**

Physical Management **9-12**

See also

Movement Education

PRESCHOOL EDUCATION

Cognitively Oriented Pre-Primary Experience (COPE) **11-11**

Early Prevention of School Failure (EPSF) **11-11**

Early Prevention of School Failure Migrant Program (for Spanish- and English-Speaking Children) **14-6**

Early Recognition Intervention Network (ERIN) **12-11**

Family Oriented Structured Preschool Activity (FOSPA) ("Seton Hall" Program) **11-12**

High/Scope Preschool Curriculum **11-5**

Modification of Children's Oral Language **12-12**

Mother-Child Home Program (MCHP) of the Verbal Interaction Project, Inc. **11-12**

Multi-Agency Project for Pre-Schoolers (MAPPS) **12-5**

National Family Literacy Project (Dissemination Process) **14-2**

Perception+ **11-13**

Programming for Early Education of CHildren with Disabilities (PEECH) **12-6**

Regional Program for Preschool Children with Disabilities **12-13**

PRESERVICE TEACHER EDUCATION

Active Teaching and Learning (ATaL) **1-1**

Resident Supervisory Support for Teachers (RSST) **2-6**

PROBLEM SOLVING

Adventure, Project **10-16**

Comprehensive School Mathematics Program (CSMP) **6-2**

Critical Analysis and Thinking Skills (CATS) **10-6**

Decision-Making Math (DMM) **6-3**

Institute for Creative Education (ICE) **10-17**

Interdependent Learning Model (ILM) **10-17**

Mathematics Achievement Program through Problem Solving (MAPS) **6-7**

ME-ME Drug & Alcohol Prevention Education Program **9-11**

Ombudsman **9-11**

SAGE **13-3**

Science-Technology-Society: Preparing For Tomorrow's World (PFTW) **7-23**

Social Decision Making and Problem Solving **9-5**

SCREENING TESTS

SELF-CARE SKILLS

SOCIAL STUDIES

See also
Humanities
Legal Education

SPECIAL EDUCATION

SPEECH DISABILITIES

WORK EXPERIENCE PROGRAMS

WRITING

Index III
Exemplary Programs:
Alphabetical

D

E

F

G

H

I

J

K

L

M

N

O

P

Q

R

S

T

U

V

W

Y

TO ORDER additional copies of *Educational Programs That Work (EPTW),* please mail this order form or phone toll free with credit card orders. Purchase orders are also accepted (via FAX or mail).

O R D E R   F O R M

Billing Address

_____

_____

_____

_____

Phone _____

Shipping Address   Same as billing address? ☐

_____

_____

_____

_____

Phone _____

CODE #	DESCRIPTION	PRICE	QTY.	COST
6PB21	Single Copy	$ 14.95		
6PB21	1-4 Case Lots*	$180.00		
6PB21	5-10 Case Lots*	$165.00		
6PB21	11+ Case Lots*	$150.00		
—	Sopris West Catalog of Programs (1994-1995)	FREE		
* 30 copies per case \ ** 10% of cost, $3.50 minimum		Shipping/Handling**		
		TOTAL COST OF THIS ORDER		

Method of Payment

○ VISA   ○ MasterCard   ○ Check/Money Order   ○ Purchase Order No. _____
  (Make payable to: Sopris West.)   *(A copy of P.O. MUST be enclosed.)*

☐☐☐☐☐☐☐☐☐☐☐☐☐☐☐☐

(Credit Card Number)

Credit Card Expiration Date   ☐☐ / ☐☐
                MONTH   YEAR

_____

(Please print name of cardholder.)

_____

(Cardholder please sign here.)

3 EASY WAYS TO ORDER

—— **1** ——

Mail Order Form:
Sopris West, 1140 Boston Avenue, P.O. Box 1809, Longmont, CO 80502-1809

—— **2** ——

Call Toll Free:
1-800-547-6747

—— **3** ——

FAX:
1-303-776-5934